QUEEN SALOME

QUEEN SALOME

*Jerusalem's Warrior Monarch
of the First Century B.C.E.*

Kenneth Atkinson

*To Rosemary:
Thanks for helping to
make this book possible.*

Kenneth Atk—

McFarland & Company, Inc., Publishers

Jefferson, North Carolina, and London

LIBRARY OF CONGRESS CATALOGUING-IN-PUBLICATION DATA

Atkinson, Kenneth, 1960–
    Queen Salome : Jerusalem's warrior monarch of the first
century B.C.E. / Kenneth Atkinson.
        p.   cm.
    Includes bibliographical references and index.

    ISBN 978-0-7864-7002-0
    softcover : acid free paper ∞

    1. Salome Alexandra, 139–67 B.C.   2. Jews — Kings and
rulers — Biography.   3. Palestine — Biography.   I. Title.
DS121.8.A5A85 2012   933'.04092 — dc23   [B]   2012013098

BRITISH LIBRARY CATALOGUING DATA ARE AVAILABLE

Front cover: Fanciful portrait of Queen Salome Alexandra from
Guillaume Roville's 1553 book of iconography (Wikimedia
Commons); background © 2012 Shutterstock

Manufactured in the United States of America

McFarland & Company, Inc., Publishers
   Box 611, Jefferson, North Carolina 28640
   www.mcfarlandpub.com

To my brothers,
Kevin Atkinson
and
Ronald Atkinson

Acknowledgments

I thank Hershel Shanks of the Biblical Archaeology Society (http://www.biblicalarchaeology.org/) for allowing me to excerpt portions of my article, "The Salome No One Knows: Long-time Ruler of a Prosperous and Peaceful Judea Mentioned in Dead Sea Scrolls," that appeared in *Biblical Archaeology Review* 34 (2008) 60–65, 72. Selected portions of this article appear mainly in chapters one and four. I am grateful to Lauri Donahue (http://themaccabeequeen.com/) for providing me with a copy of her 2003 play, "Alexandra of Judea" (http://www.bakersplays.com).

The following graciously provided images for this book:

Alexander sarcophagus (A.D. Riddle/BiblePlaces.com)

Dead Sea Scrolls, Habakkuk commentary (Library of Congress, LC-matpc 13013/www.LifeintheHolyLand.com)

Queen Shlomzion St (Daniel Frese/BiblePlaces.com)

Samaria Hellenistic city tower (David Bivin/ www.LifeintheHolyLand.com)

Queen Salome Alexandra, courtesy of Wikimedia Commons (http://commons.wikimedia.org)

All other images have been provided by Todd Bolen (Todd Bolen/BiblePlaces.com)

Table of Contents

Abbreviations, Nomenclature, and Markings

Abbreviations of ancient texts generally conform to *The SBL Handbook of Style: for Ancient Near Eastern, Biblical, and Early Christian Studies*, edited by Patrick H. Alexander, John F. Kutsko, James D. Ernest, Shirley A. Decker-Lucke, and David L. Petersen, and published by Hendrickson in 1999. Major abbreviations frequently cited, and terms of importance, are describe below for the benefit of the reader. References to the Palestinian Talmud are cited according to the numbering of *The Talmud of the Land of Israel: A Preliminary Translation and Explanation*, Jacob Neusner, et al., editors and translators, published by University of Chicago Press in 1982–1993. Unless specified, the word *Talmud* refers to the Babylonian version.

Abbreviations of Major Ancient Books

Ag. Ap. — Josephus, *Against Apion*
Ant. — Josephus, *Antiquities*
Life — Josephus, *Life of Josephus*
War — Josephus, *Jewish (Judean) War*
Contempl. Life — Philo, *On the Contemplative Life*
Fug. — Philo, *On Flight and Finding*
Good Person — Philo, *That Every Good Person is Free*
Spec. — Philo, *On the Special Laws*

Common Terms

B.C.E./C.E. — (Before the Common Era) and C.E. (Common Era) are the preferred scholarly designations for B.C. and A.D.

Judea — A land the Bible also calls Israel and Judah. The Romans later named it Palestine. It includes today's Israel and Palestine, and during some of its existence portions of modern Jordan, Lebanon, and Syria.

Judean — A resident of Judea. Usually a Jewish person.

Mishnah (m.) — A second century C.E. religious text that preserves many ancient traditions from Salome Alexandra's time.

Talmud: Babylonian (b.) — An eclectic compendium of legal materials and other narrative writings compiled in Babylon around 500 C.E. and revised for a few centuries afterwards.

Talmud: Palestinian (p.) — An eclectic compendium of legal materials and other narrative writings compiled in Tiberius, Israel, slightly before the Babylonian Talmud.

Tanak — An acronym formed from the first letters of the Hebrew names for the traditional three divisions of the Bible (Old Testament): *Torah* (Law); *Nevi'im* (prophets); and *Kethuvim* (writings). The vowels are added to facilitate pronunciation.

Nomenclature and Markings

[Salome Alexandra] — Bracketed word(s) restored from missing section of a document.

(Salome Alexandra) — Explanatory material added to clarity meaning.

[...] — Portion of text missing.

Special Notes Pertaining to the Dead Sea Scrolls (Adapted from SBL Handbook of Style, 76)

There is considerable diversity in the way that the Dead Sea Scrolls are numbered. The first seven scrolls discovered were given names. The most prominent of these discussed in this book are the *Rule of the Community* and *The Damascus Document*. These texts are sometimes cited by their numerical designation. All scrolls without names begin with a number indicating which of the eleven caves it was discovered, followed by "Q" to designate the site of Khirbet Qumran.

When a manuscript is fairly complete it is cited by column and line number as follows:

1QS III, 12 — Cave 1, Qumran, *Rule of the Community* (*Serek Hayahad* in Hebrew), column 3, line 12.

Most Dead Sea Scrolls survive only in fragments, only some of which can be pieced together. When there are several fragments, they are numbered separately as follows:

1Q27 1 II, 25 — Cave 1, Qumran, document number 27, fragment 1, column 2, line 25.

Fortunately, the majority of the Dead Sea Scrolls discussed in this book have names.

Preface

I should tell you here the story of Octavia, wife of Mark Antony and sister of Augustus; that of Porcia, Cato's daughter and wife of Brutus; that of Caia Caecilia, wife of Tarquinius Priscus; that of Cornelia, Scipio's daughter; and of countless others who are very celebrated: and not only of our own, but of barbarian nations; as that of [Salome] Alexandra, wife of Alexander [Jannaeus] king of the Jews, who,—after her husband's death when she saw the people kindled with fury and already up in arms to slay the two children that he had left her, in revenge for the cruel and grievous bondage in which the father had always kept them,—so acted that she soon appeased their just wrath, and by her prudence straightway won over for her children those minds which the father, by countless injuries during many years, had made very hostile to his offspring.—Baldessar Castiglione (1478–1529 C.E.), *The Book of the Courtier,* 1528

In 76 B.C.E. Alexander Jannaeus (ca. 125/127–76 B.C.E.), king of Judea (modern Israel), was fighting an unpopular war against the Nabatean Arabs of present-day Jordan. His legion was struggling to capture the fortified citadel of Ragaba. As his army was poised to make their final assault, the unexpected occurred—Alexander Jannaeus died. His army, deep in enemy territory, faced two new threats: one was external while the other potentially came from within its ranks. To the north, tribes in Syria appeared ready to take advantage of the absence of the imperial forces to invade Judea.[1] At home, the king's political, military, and religious enemies were preparing to wage civil war to seize his capital of Jerusalem. Then, into this world of turmoil and crisis arose a woman largely erased from history—Queen Salome Alexandra.

A Forgotten Queen

Salome Alexandra (ca. 141 B.C.E.–67 B.C.E.) is virtually unknown today. She is an ancient example of what we would call an outlier—an exceptional person whose accomplishments are so extraordinary that they appear to defy

1

explanation.[2] Salome Alexandra was so unique that historians — both ancient and modern — have largely ignored her, rather than try to explain the perplexing circumstances that brought her to power. She was one of the ancient world's greatest monarchs. Archaeologists have uncovered her vast palace in the oasis of Jericho. European Jews told stories about her bravery as late as the sixteenth century C.E.[3] The writers of the Talmud[4] describe her reign as a golden age.

Salome Alexandra lived at a pivotal time in the ancient Near East — the period of Jewish independence. Her family had fought a long, but successful, war to create the Judean state. Her life almost coincided with its existence. She was likely born the year after her people had won their freedom from their Syrian overlords; she died less than four years before the Romans destroyed her nation. She knew all its kings; she even appointed one of them. Before she reached adulthood, she witnessed countless wars, state sponsored atrocities — even crucifixion — assassinations, matricide, and cannibalism. Murderous clergy, corrupt politicians, disease, death, famine, and violence against women were commonplace during her lifetime. Her nation was seldom at peace; its existence was always precarious; and the neighboring powers were constantly trying to conquer it. Yet, Salome Alexandra somehow defied the odds and survived the many perils of her day to become Judea's sole monarch, military leader, and custodian of its religion when she was sixty-four years old. She was effectively the last independent ruler of her nation until her present-day descendants fought a war for independence in 1948 to create the State of Israel.

Such success at a rather advanced age clearly takes ambition, drive, and talent. Salome Alexandra certainly possessed all these qualities in abundance. But it also requires a unique combination of circumstances to come to fruition. All outliers are the products of their time. This is true of Salome Alexandra. There was a short period of history during which a woman could have ruled Judea. Salome Alexandra was not only born during this unique epoch, but at the most opportune time: the beginning of Judean independence. If she had been born a few years earlier or later, it is doubtful that she would have achieved anything important. In the decades before her birth her people were locked in a desperate struggle for their survival, and were powerless to determine their own fate. There were no opportunities for a female to excel at anything outside the home. The same is true if she had been born later. The Romans conquered her nation four years after her death. It took over two thousand years for her homeland to regain its independence.

Salome Alexandra owed almost everything to the timing of her birth. She not only grew up in a free nation, but she enjoyed advantages afforded to few. She had the right parents: she was born into Judea's most elite family, the Maccabees, whose deeds Jews still celebrate at the festival of Hanukkah. (Her descendants were later named the Hasmoneans after their ancestor Hasmon.) She cultivated friendships with the most powerful pagan queens of antiquity: the Cleopatras of Egypt and Syria. These women not only helped her nation, but their successful rule in their homelands convinced the Judeans to look to their own women for political and military leadership.

Salome Alexandra was an exceptional person to have taken advantage of her unique opportunities: when given the chance to become her nation's ruler, she rose to the occasion and transformed the age in which she lived for the better of her subjects. Kings submitted to her will; foreign rulers helped her stay in power. She brought Jews and pagans together to create a truly unique period of history that the rabbis considered a Golden Age. This book not only tells the amazing story of Salome Alexandra's life, but the remarkable tale of this forgotten period when women ruled the Middle East.

A Question Unanswered

I have always been interested in the past. As this book will show, it is often full of surprises. Although I did not realize it during the early stages of my research, my varied background provided me with many of the skills and ideas that proved essential in writing about one of history's most unusual, but neglected, periods. My years working in factories in the Detroit area made me appreciate the toils of the common person, whose stories are seldom preserved in the historical record, but whose labor has shaped all historical periods. Four years of active duty in the U.S. Army — three stationed in West Berlin surrounded by the infamous Berlin Wall — acquainted me first-hand with the rigors of military life, and the struggles of those living in dictatorial regimes. My military assignment further increased my interest in the past, and gave me ample time to travel to the great historical sites and museums throughout Europe and the Middle East. These opportunities, coupled with much independent study, further stimulated by a craving to learn more about Hebrew, Greek, and Roman antiquity, compelled me to embark on a great adventure to experience Salome Alexandra's world first-hand.

After my discharge from the Army — honorable I am proud to say — I spent two and a half years as a full-time traveler, backpacking throughout the Middle East and Europe. I also lived for a time at Kibbutz Kfar Hanassi, north of the Sea of Galilee, in the land that Salome Alexandra ruled, where I was exposed to the rigors of agricultural life.

After gaining basic experience in archaeology, I was fortunate to earn

Gamla from the east. The Jewish town of Gamla dates to the Hellenistic and Roman eras. Josephus fortified the site and witnessed the future Roman Emperors Vespasian and Titus destroy the city and kill most of its inhabitants in 67 C.E. The city derives its name from the Aramaic word for camel, given to the town because of its distinctive shape (Todd Bolen/BiblePlaces.com).

positions as a supervisor on several excavations in Israel. Most important of these was the site of Gamla, a village built during Salome Alexandra's lifetime.[5] The historian Josephus (37–95/6 C.E.) watched the Romans besiege and destroy it in 67 C.E.: he even fortified it to withstand an attack. Josephus immortalized its downfall in his famed book, *The Jewish War*. Digging up arrowheads, catapult stones, and other detritus of war, I was able to literally touch relics of the past used to murder countless innocent civilians. This experience gave me a greater appreciation of the horrors of siege warfare, a terror that Salome Alexandra likely experienced first-hand as a young child.

In addition to digging up the past from Salome Alexandra's lifetime, I literally walked many of the roads the characters in this book traversed. I lived much like the common folk of her day, sleeping in dangerous, crowded, squalid lodgings. I also spent several months in a tent surrounded by land mines; slept on the decks of ships while keeping a watchful eye out for bandits; and lodged for a summer in a Jerusalem church beneath a staircase like Harry Potter. On several occasions I was stranded and forced to seek shelter in parks, bus stations, train depots, and the forest. Having endured many dangers from people (even a stoning), animals (including wild boars), and the elements on

Gamla catapult balls in Qatzrin Museum. Archaeologists have uncovered approximately 2,000 ballista stones from Gamla. These stones were thrown into the city during battle by the ancient Roman ballista, a catapult that flung heavy stone balls over city walls during sieges. These items are located in the Qatzrin Museum, Israel (Todd Bolen/BiblePlaces.com).

both land and sea during my travels, I have come to appreciate the achievements of those who lived in the past, for whom such perils were not unusual occurrences but commonplace events.

My life experiences greatly enriched my academic work when I returned to the university to pursue graduate education in biblical studies, antiquity, and world religions. Although I could not have known it at the time, my graduate education occurred at an opportune moment for a future biographer of Salome Alexandra. The Dead Sea Scrolls were released to the public in 1991 while I was a student. I was fortunate to study under one of the newly appointed translators of these documents. The excitement of reading photographs of then unpublished Hebrew and Aramaic texts in class led me to pur-

sue the period of the Dead Sea Scrolls, and to continue with doctoral studies
to understand their historical background.

It was in my early days of reading about the Dead Sea Scrolls that I first
encountered the name Salome Alexandra. She is mentioned twice in these
ancient texts. I had never heard of her before. My efforts to find out more
about her were unsuccessful because most academic books and reference works
simply gloss over her nine-year reign: scholars typically consider it of little
importance. None of my professors could tell me why the community of the
Dead Sea Scrolls was apparently obsessed with her. These documents not only
mention her by name, but they also contain several precise historical allusions
to her. But no one could answer what is perhaps the most important, and
perplexing, question of all: How did Salome Alexandra become the ruler of
a sexist society when she had two grown sons?

I originally planned to write this book about the women of the ancient
Middle East, especially those mentioned in the Dead Sea Scrolls. This was
not the book I wanted to produce, but the only one I was convinced it was
possible to complete. I could find hardly anything about Salome Alexandra:
nobody had ever tried to write her biography. The ancient Jewish historian
Josephus, whose books provide our sole extant account of her life, documents
the last nine years of her life. With so little information available, I thought
it was impossible to write an entire book about her. But as I continued to
research her life, I kept returning to the nagging question from my early graduate school days: How did Salome Alexandra became her nation's sole ruler,
lead troops in battle, and change her country's religion?

As I struggled to write the first biography of Salome Alexandra, I came
upon a novel way to proceed that had thus far eluded me. I realized it is possible to document her entire life and times, but not through the traditional
tools of academia. Salome Alexandra's story almost requires the creativity of
a novelist. Historians, however, do not have the luxury of making up anything,
not even the weather.[6] After almost giving up my quest to write her biography,
the solution came to me in an unexpected flash of insight — birthdays!

Subjects in antiquity celebrated the birthdays, and lamented the deaths,
of their rulers. Josephus fortunately provides us with the exact year when
Salome Alexandra died, as well as her age. He furnishes the same information
for most of Judea's rulers, including her family. I realized this information
was the solution I needed to fill in the missing years of her life. I began by
making a chronological chart listing all the known dates of births and deaths
of the important people of the period from Judea's independence to its 63
B.C.E. destruction by the one-time ally of Julius Caesar (ca. 100–44 B.C.E.),
the Roman General Pompey the Great (106–48 B.C.E.). I then combed through
all the ancient historical works of this time to see what took place for each

year of Salome Alexandra's life. I then asked myself where she likely was when these events occurred, and how they shaped her personality. This gave me the basic outline of a book, and a new direction in which to proceed.

Writing this book has been an exciting journey of discovery into a strange, violent, unusual, but familiar world. My quest to document Salome Alexandra's life and times, however, has been difficult. Writing can be laborious, slow, and at times sheer agony. Fortunately, the travails of putting pen to paper and searching through dusty forgotten tomes in libraries have often been interspersed with moments of immense joy. My efforts have led to the accidental discovery of documents that have never been used to reconstruct Salome Alexandra's reign. Many were surprisingly written long after her death, and come from such varied locations and times as Ptolemaic Egypt of the Greeks, Babylon of the rabbis, Constantinople of the Byzantine Christians, and writings of the Italian Renaissance. That so many people from such diverse locales and times mention Salome Alexandra is a testament to her importance, and shows that she was not always a forgotten queen.

This book reconstructs a remarkable period of history when women ruled men in the Middle East, a society never known for its gender inclusiveness. But it is also an amazing story of success; the tale of a woman who changed the times in which she lived. It is a testament to the power of the individual: the formative force that continues to shape history.

Like all tales, Salome Alexandra's story has its heroes and its villains: sin is unfortunately prevalent in every age. Women are usually the saints of this book rather than its sinners. Salome Alexandra fortunately emerges from the stories of the male historians of the past as a decent person: even her critics praise her piety and her goodwill. She is a rare example of a politician who used her office to benefit the lives of all her subjects. Her influence did not merely extend to the political sphere, but the religious as well. She convinced her fellow Jews that it was possible to adapt their ancient faith to their rapidly changing times without diluting its core values. If not for Salome Alexandra, both Judaism and Christianity would have developed differently. She literally shaped our world.

In Gratitude

Success is always a group effort. I have many people to thank, all of whom have somehow contributed to the writing of this book. First and foremost is the graduate college of the University of Northern Iowa (Cedar Falls) for granting me a professional development leave during the fall of 2005 to research and write portions of this book and several related academic studies. It is a pleasure to work at such a fine public institution whose administration is dedicated to the teaching of scholarship. My colleagues in the department of history at the University of Northern Iowa have provided me with a warm and nurturing environment in which to work, and have encouraged me in my academic endeavors. Next I must thank Janet V. Crisler of the Crisler Biblical Institute (now the Crisler Library of Ephesos, Turkey) for inviting me to share my interest in Salome Alexandra and women in the Dead Sea Scrolls with the public at a wonderful conference in the beautiful city of Pebble Beach, California, in 2001. It was the enthusiasm of the attendees at this event, and their desire to learn more about Salome Alexandra and other warrior queens of antiquity, that convinced me to write this book. Both Janet, and Crisler board chair, Linda R. Cain, further encouraged me to pursue this research during a delightful trip to Turkey in the summer of 2002. Through the diligent efforts of the staff of the access services department of the University of Northern Iowa's Rod Library, especially Rosemary Meany and Linda Berneking, I have been able to obtain numerous obscure books and articles in several languages that were necessary to complete this biography. Librarians are the unsung heroes of scholarship: without them professors would have little to teach, and virtually nothing to write about.

My wife, Laura Praglin, has willingly allowed me to share my life with Salome Alexandra for several years, and tolerated my obsession with the past. My mother, Carol Lambert, has always encouraged my work, and for many years put up with a wayward son who spent far too much time living like a vagabond in far-flung places visiting obscure ruins.

Sources and Translations

This book, although written for a popular audience, is based on ancient texts written in several obscure languages. Unless indicated, all translations are my own from the critical editions listed in the bibliography under "primary texts." I have aimed for translations that communicate the meaning of the ancient authors, believing that most readers are not interested in arcane academic debates, but simply want to learn about Salome Alexandra and her fascinating world. For this reason I have avoided esoteric academic debates and extensive reference notes. Readers interested in the basis for my arguments will find citations to all the primary sources and major secondary works on the topic. I plan to write an academic tome on this period that will contain a detailed scholarly apparatus replete with footnotes to obscure monographs and scholarly debates. I hope this book not only introduces readers to this fascinating woman, but also gives them some insight into the academic process, and how researchers reconstruct our lost past.

A Forgotten Queen, a Forgotten World

The Untold Story of Salome Alexandra

> The brief stories of Abigail, the Shunnamite, the wise woman of Tekoah, and the Prophetess Huldah, reveal that woman held a high position during a period of advanced civilization. Queen Esther, the daughters of the Levites who sang in the temple, Susannah and Judith, the wise and pious Queen Salome Alexandra, and the many great women of the Talmud, like Beruriah and Yaltha, all testify to the lofty position woman had in ancient Jewish society.— Isaac M. Wise (1819–1900 C.E.), "Women as Members of Congregations," 1876

When people hear the name Salome, they immediately think of the infamous dancing girl of the Gospels. Herod Antipas — the man Jesus denounced as a "fox"— had married his brother's wife, Herodias. When John the Baptist denounced this illicit union, Herod Antipas cast him into prison. It was Herodias's daughter, Salome, who danced before Herod at his drunken birthday gala. Her performance so pleased Herod that he promised her anything she wished: up to half his kingdom. At her mother's urging, Salome asked for the head of Herod's most famous prisoner on a platter. Fearful of breaking his word before his guests, Herod granted Salome's request and ordered John the Baptist beheaded.[1]

In antiquity there was a considerably more famous Salome who was revered for centuries. She was so admired that generations of mothers, Herodias apparently among them, named their daughters Salome in her honor. This Salome was the only woman to govern Judea as its sole ruler. She is even mentioned in the Dead Sea Scrolls: the lone woman, and one of only eighteen people, named in the scrolls.[2] She presided over a number of religious reforms that shaped the Judaism of Jesus' day as well as our own. During a time of chaos, men chose her to lead their nation and fight their battles. Yet, this remarkable woman has been largely erased from history. Her name is Queen Salome Alexandra. This is her first biography.

A Time of Confusion, a Time Like Our Own

Salome Alexandra's world was a time of uncertainty and confusion. It had been this way since the conquests of the Macedonian general Alexander the Great (356–323 B.C.E.), who brought Greek civilization, foreign ways, and new religions to the Middle East. Alexander spread Greek civilization throughout the territories he conquered. As a result, many people in Salome Alexandra's homeland of Judea had adopted Greek culture, a phenomenon known as Hellenism, whose chief hallmark is not only cultural but also religious tolerance. For many pious Jews, Hellenism constituted nothing less than a threat to Judaism's very survival, since God had commanded, "You shall have no other gods before me."[3]

In 167 B.C.E., Antiochus (IV) Epiphanies (ca. 215–163 B.C.E.), the Hel-

The "Alexander Sarcophagus," a late 4th century B.C.E. marble sarcophagus from Sidon in Lebanon. Constructed for a nobleman or a local king, it is considered a masterpiece of Hellenistic art. Its carvings, which bear traces of their original paint, depict Alexander the Great fighting the Persians. It is located in the Istanbul Archaeology Museum, Turkey (A.D. Riddle/BiblePlaces.com).

lenistic Greek king of the Seleucid Empire (modern Syria) and heir to a portion of Alexander the Great's empire, in effect declared war against Judaism. Forsaking the tolerance that had come to define Hellenism, Antiochus banned circumcision, Sabbath observance, dietary laws, and temple sacrifices. In reaction, a Jewish priest named Mattathias ignited a resistance movement to expel the Syrians and create an independent Jewish state. His son Judas — nicknamed Maccabee ("the Hammer") for his military prowess — eventually recaptured Jerusalem and rededicated the temple. After his death, his brothers Jonathan and Simon continued their family's struggle for independence. Each became not only Judea's secular ruler, but also its high priest. They and their descendants became known as the Hasmoneans, a name that refers to Mattathias's great-grandfather, Hasmon. These were Salome Alexandra's illustrious ancestors, whose deeds are still recounted at the Jewish festival of Hanukkah.[4]

Salome Alexandra belonged to this widely hated family who claimed to oppose Hellenism, but who actually embraced it with a greater zeal than their foes. Just before her birth, they succeeded in creating the first independent Jewish state in over four hundred years. She was likely born a year after it was founded; she almost lived to see its destruction (the Romans conquered it less than four years after her death). Later generations considered her Judea's greatest monarch, and the only legitimate female occupant of its throne.

Salome Alexandra's reign was unprecedented. During her time in power, she altered her nation's religion, controlled the Jerusalem temple, helped change her country's legal system to increase women's rights, and led troops in battle. Men praised her leadership and her piety. She ended an unpopular war, curtailed religious strife, reformed the economy, and presided over the greatest period of peace and prosperity in her nation's history. Later generations looked back on her reign as a golden age. She was one of history's greatest rulers, and the last legitimate monarch of an independent Judean state until 1948.[5] Yet few know her name or the remarkable story of her life.

A Reluctant Chronicler

Most of what we know of this turbulent period comes from the first-century C.E. Jewish historian Josephus (37–ca. 100 C.E.), a contemporary of New Testament figures like Paul and Jesus' brother James. But as regards our heroine Salome Alexandra, Josephus is often uncharacteristically brief, omitting important details and even providing contradictory accounts in his two great works, *The Antiquities of the Jews* and *The Jewish War* (about the great Jewish revolt against Rome in 66–70 C.E., during which Josephus betrayed his own people and defected to the Romans). His account of her life in his

Antiquities, which is longer than his earlier *War*, consists of approximately seven-and-a-half pages of printed text. (Josephus devotes nearly the same amount of space to the less than one-year reign of her brother-in-law, the Hasmonean monarch, Judah Aristobulus.[6]) It only covers her nine year reign and ends with her death. Although he is not particularly sympathetic to Salome Alexandra (unlike the later rabbis of the Talmud), even he had to acknowledge her remarkable achievements.

Josephus had little interest in documenting Salome Alexandra's reign. He wrote his books in Greek for pagans to explain Judaism's practices and history, and to show that the Judeans had a heritage as illustrious as the Greeks and the Romans. But he had to document her time in power because he was a proud member of her family, the Hasmoneans. When he later wrote his autobiography, he began it with this declaration of his noble lineage:

> My ancestry is not without significance, having originated from priests long ago.... I have a share of royal ancestry from my mother because the children of the Hasmoneans, of whom she was a descendant, for a very long time served as high priests and exercised the kingship of our nation [*Life* 1].

Many Judeans were not impressed with his pedigree, which he cites in part to buttress his credibility as an historian. One, his opponent, the Jewish historian Justus of Tiberius, wrote a book challenging Josephus's version of his time as a general during the war against Rome. But Josephus won the battle of words; he managed to suppress Justus's writings by gaining the patronage of the Roman Emperor, and Rome's elite.

Josephus's historical books would fail the modern test of academic impartiality, being anything but fair and balanced. He deliberately shapes — in many instances distorts — his accounts of the Hasmonean period in light of his life experiences and beliefs.[7] Denounced as a traitor and a liar for his account of his military command during the Jewish war against Rome, Josephus tried to redeem his reputation by emphasizing his loyalty to his new country and his literary patrons. He urges all conquered races to submit to Roman rule because he is convinced God wills it.

Josephus was very interested in political power, both good and bad. Like other classical writers, he believes that women who usurp political authority are a threat to the social order. God, he emphasizes, now favors the Roman Empire: to oppose it is to defy the Almighty. He is convinced that Salome Alexandra and her female relations took power through conspiracies, which he is reluctant to disclose in full. In each story, Josephus portrays these women as devious; they all have an insatiable lust for power.[8] He singles out Salome Alexandra's reign as a disaster, and blames her for the loss of Jewish independence.

In our quest to reconstruct Salome Alexandra's life and times, we must seek to disentangle Josephus's opinions from historical fact. We cannot do so without first unraveling complex motivations that led him to compose histories of his homeland. A former enemy of the Roman Empire, Josephus wrote his books in its capital as a privileged citizen, and counted the Flavian Emperors Vespasian (reigned 69–79 C.E.) and Titus (reigned 79–81 C.E.) as his patrons; he even affixed their name to his and became known in Rome as Flavius Josephus. It is, unfortunately, impossible to tell Salome Alexandra's story without relying on his books. In the absence of other sources, at times the historian has no choice but to repeat his accounts almost verbatim. But there are problems with his books.

Using Josephus's works to write a biography requires imagination coupled with the skills of a detective. It is necessary at times to penetrate Josephus's mind and learn how he worked in order to disentangle the historical Salome Alexandra from his fictional portrayal of her. Fortunately, we can often accomplish this because Josephus is a sloppy historian. Since his native language was Aramaic, and his Greek was rather poor by the literary standards of the time, he frequently copied lengthy paragraphs from his Greek sources verbatim, interspersed with his own commentary and historical reconstructions. Scholars can tell that Josephus is reproducing an earlier text because his Greek is often inferior to the passages he copies. In some instances we can identify the books he used. A few, such as the *Letter of Aristeas* (an apocryphal account of the Bible's translation into Greek) and I Maccabees (a history of Salome Alexandra's ancestors), are still extant. But the majority of these works are lost.

Josephus's two books that document Salome Alexandra's life, the *War* and the *Antiquities,* are very different. He tells us he used literary assistants when he wrote the *War* to improve his Greek style. The result is a rather polished book that provides a fairly reliable account of the Hasmonean period, including Salome Alexandra's time in office. It portrays her as a pious and strong-willed ruler who presided over an unprecedented period of peace and prosperity. When he later wrote his *Antiquities,* he had a more ambitious agenda. Instead of documenting Jewish political history from the Hasmonean period until his own time, Josephus set out to chronicle his faith from the creation of the world until the outbreak of the great Jewish war against Rome in 66 C.E. Salome Alexandra plays less of a role in this book; he greatly diminishes her participation in important affairs and conceals many of her accomplishments.

Josephus faced a major problem when he set out to write his *Antiquities*—Rome's literary and political climate had changed. Many of his contemporaries had been exiled, or sentenced to death, for supposedly undermining Roman values, or criticizing the Emperor. In his *War* Josephus was free to describe Rome's aggressive intentions to conquer Judea. However, when he wrote his *Antiquities,* it was dangerous to publicly criticize the Roman Emperor. Consequently, he had no choice but to present the Romans more favorably. He blamed the Jews for the Roman conquest of 63 B.C.E. and the demise of Judean independence: if he had not done so, he could have been charged with treason. Josephus also needed a scapegoat, which he found in Salome Alexandra. In his *Antiquities* he makes the improbable claim that she was responsible for the Hasmonean state's destruction that took place four years after her death.[9]

Josephus's *Antiquities* is not a literary masterpiece. When he wrote it, he did not have assistants to help him with his Greek style. He often copies lengthy passages from his sources verbatim, instead of writing his own narrative, as a way of masking his poor Greek. Like his contemporaries, he seldom cites his sources (the reference note had not been created). For his account of the Hasmonean period he often used the lost histories of Nicolaus of Damascus. Unfortunately, Nicolaus did not like the Hasmoneans. He was a friend, counselor, and court historian of the Jewish king Herod the Great (ca. 74–4 B.C.E.). Infamous for his attempt to kill the infant Jesus, Herod also removed Salome Alexandra's sons from power and established a pro–Roman dynasty of Jewish rulers that lasted for over a century. Nicolaus despised the Hasmoneans because their descendants, especially Salome Alexandra's granddaughters, had opposed his patron. When we read negative sections about Salome Alexandra in Josephus's *Antiquities,* they are often from Nicolaus's book.

Josephus fortunately supplements Nicolaus's historical writings with a book written by a member of a Jewish religious movement known as the Pharisees. This chronicle generally portrays Salome Alexandra favorably. Because it was likely written much earlier than Nicolaus's book, and since it often agrees with Josephus's earlier *War,* we can assume it contains more accurate depictions of Salome Alexandra. Josephus also used now lost pagan histories written by Strabo, Timagenes, and others in his *Antiquities,* which often preserve very reliable information about the Hasmoneans.[10]

Josephus did not like women. He was not interested in documenting their achievements. He has preserved so little about Salome Alexandra — just mere fragments — that no one has used his *War* and *Antiquities* to write her biography. But he does tell us much about her turbulent world, and her violent family, the Hasmoneans. His books show that it was a dangerous time to be alive. Salome Alexandria lived in a violent age in which the most unimaginable cruelties were commonplace. She witnessed wars, countless murders, crucifixions, matricide, suicides, religious-inspired violence, state-sponsored torture, and siblings kill one another in their pursuit of power. Incest, cannibalism, infanticide, and wartime atrocities were not unusual occurrences in her world. Salome Alexandra managed to defy the odds to become the only Judean female to rule her country, lead its men in battle, alter its religion, and preside over its greatest period of peace and prosperity. She shaped the faith from which contemporary Judaism, Christianity, and Islam emerged.

Salome Alexandra lived during a time when many rulers thought they were gods; their subjects willingly obeyed their divine command to kill their foes. But Salome Alexandra's family was forbidden from claiming divine status. They used religion to convince their subjects to carry out their ill intentions; they promised them eternal life in heaven in exchange for committing evil deeds. Salome Alexandra witnessed the birth of religious strife and sectarianism. Faith and politics merged during her lifetime, and brought untold suffering to her people. Her family essentially created religious martyrdom, a phenomenon that plagues our world today. They used it as a political tool to rally the masses to their cause. Only when she ruled did her nation see peace. Yet the tale of how she changed the times in which she lived, and helped shape our world, remains one of antiquity's great untold stories.

This book assembles for the first time in over two thousand years all the extant evidence about Salome Alexandra. It examines such varied writings as ancient scraps of paper discovered in the Judean desert to obscure Jewish historical books and neglected Christian chronicles. Recent archaeological and textual discoveries, such as the Dead Sea Scrolls, continue to reveal new information about her. These documents show that there were other pious female religious leaders in her day, whose achievements have yet to be documented in full. These include the mysterious women of the Dead Sea Scrolls and the dancing Jewish female philosophers of Egypt. We will meet them in our story because they shed much light on Salome Alexandra's life and times.

Signs of Character

The men who wrote the history books chronicling the Hasmonean period chose not to document the lives of women because they were convinced that individuals, not social movements, shape history. Character, they believed, is the key to understanding historical events since human nature is unchanging. They regarded history as an indispensable tool for understanding the present. Men, the ancients were convinced, are the force that shapes and maintains society, and molds character. Persuaded that Aristotle's dictum "actions are signs of character" is true, ancient writers and readers looked to the behavior of men in the past to predict how similar persons would act in the present. Because most ancient historians did not believe women had the capacity to rule, they tended to present females as weak and incapable of holding power: they were not considered fit role models.[11]

Josephus shared the views of his pagan contemporaries and believed that history explained character. His books are largely biographies of individuals that explore their virtues and faults. He intended them to serve as moral examples. For this reason, his books are full of speeches and dialogues that illustrate morality. He and his contemporary historians fabricated these addresses to give their readers insight into the character of their subjects, and the temper of their times. But there is a problem with their accounts: the ancient world was sexist. Men — Jewish and pagan alike — preferred not to record the deeds of the remarkable women of the past, lest females of their day seek to imitate them. This is particularly true of Josephus. He has preserved so little about our queen that we are uncertain whether Salome Alexandra was her actual name.

1

The Silent Women of Judea
Recovering Salome Alexandra's Name

A silent woman is a gift from the Lord.—*Ben Sira*, 26:14

Women in the ancient world were occasionally seen, seldom heard, and rarely mentioned in the written record. Despite her affluence and fame, we know little about Salome Alexandra. Her only surviving chronicler, Josephus, preferred to document the deeds of men; he did not even record the names of his wives or female relations in his autobiography. It is unlikely that he would have written anything about Salome Alexandra if she had not been Judea's monarch. He so believed the scriptural adage, "A silent woman is a gift from the Lord," that he preferred, whenever possible, not to write anything about women. As noted above, he recorded so little about our queen that we are uncertain whether Salome Alexandra was her actual name.

Uncovering Her Name

Names were very important in Salome Alexandra's Judea; they were chosen with great care. Either parent could select a baby's name. It was customary to name a son after his father, and a daughter after her mother. Most Judeans had a single name. To avoid confusion, men customarily added the name of their father, or their place of birth, to their own. But the situation was different for women. They were usually identified by the name of their protector, typically their father.[1]

Salome Alexandra is one of the few women whose names have been preserved in the historical record of ancient Judea. Unlike men such as "David son of Jesse" or "Jesus of Nazareth," she was not known by the name of her father or her place of birth. She was called Salome Alexandra. Her name—

lacking any reference to a guardian — signifies her independence from men. Yet, the name by which she has been known for over two thousand years may not be her actual name.

Salome Alexandra's name is unusual. It is bilingual. Salome is Hebrew, or possibly Aramaic (it is often difficult to distinguish between the two), while Alexandra is Greek. Her two names not only tell us something about her family, but about her life and times as well. In the wake of Alexander the Great's conquests, Greek became the *lingua franca* of the ancient world. Aristocratic Jews, such as the historian Josephus and presumably Salome Alexandra's parents, knew Hebrew, Aramaic, and Greek. But it was not Greek that the common Judeans spoke in the marketplaces of Jerusalem, or in the countless hamlets that dotted the countryside, but the languages of the Bible (Old Testament) — Hebrew and Aramaic. The latter had largely replaced the former long before Salome Alexandra's birth, although some Jews, such as the famed Essenes (the likely authors of the Dead Sea Scrolls), preferred Hebrew.

The majority of Judeans avoided Greek names. All the Jewish sages of antiquity, with only two exceptions, bore Hebrew or Aramaic names. Nearly all the approximately nine hundred Dead Sea Scrolls — many of which were written during Salome Alexandra's reign — are in Hebrew; a large number are in Aramaic; relatively few, mainly translations of the Bible, are in Greek. Because religious Jews avoided all things Greek, Salome Alexandra's Hellenistic name, Alexandra, is rather unusual for a woman in first century B.C.E. Judea.

Salome Alexandra's Greek and Hebrew names identify her as a woman rooted in two often irreconcilable cultural and religious spheres: polytheistic Hellenism and monotheistic Judaism. Her parents undoubtedly had chosen her two names to proclaim their allegiance to the new cosmopolitan Hellenistic world order, as well as to show they still followed the traditions of their ancestors. They had undoubtedly been influenced by the new practice among Judea's elite of courting the Greeks. At first zealous opponents of Hellenism, Salome Alexandra's ancestors had become its chief proponents. After they had taken the high priesthood, they quickly adopted Greek ways.

The first Hasmoneans (Mattathias, Judas, Jonathan, and Simon) did not have Greek names. Beginning with Salome Alexandra's father-in-law, John, commonly known by his Greek name Hyrcanus, the Hasmoneans customarily had Greek names (Aristobulus, Antigonus, and Alexander). This practice was apparently not confined to men; Salome Alexandra's sister-in-law and granddaughters were named Alexandra. All the Hasmonean rulers with Greek names were immensely unpopular, except for Salome Alexandra. After her death her Hebrew name, Salome, became the second most popular female name.[2]

Ordinary Judeans, for whom religion dominated virtually every facet of life, despised Salome Alexandra's family because they had embraced Hellenism.

Bet Guvrin Tomb of the Sidonian. Used from the 3rd to the 1st centuries B.C.E., this tomb likely housed an official of the Sidonian (from Sidon in Lebanon) and Greek communities and his family. The tomb contains niches for the bodies and is elaborately decorated with a variety of Hellenistic mythological images and animals. It shows the spread of Hellenism throughout Salome Alexandra's homeland (Todd Bolen/BiblePlaces.com).

Many of her subjects did not consider her family truly Jewish, even though some of her relatives were high priests, since they viewed Hellenism and Judaism as incompatible. The irony was that many pagans never regarded the Hasmoneans as Greek, despite their overt embracement of their culture.

Because the Hasmoneans were never completely accepted as members of either Jewish or pagan society, it is not surprising that we know little about Salome Alexandra. She was not only a woman living in a sexist, male-dominated culture, but she was also a member of a widely despised family of rulers and high priests who often put their political self-interests before God. Her ancestors had chosen to cast their lot with Hellenism without considering the potential consequences their decision posed for the Jewish faith, and the future of the Judean state. Given Salome Alexandra's background, it is quite astonishing that later Jews considered her the most pious of the Hasmoneans.

Josephus refers to our queen only by her Greek name, Alexandra. It is the only known Greek Hasmonean female name.[3] But Josephus certainly knew her Hebrew name since he had access to very ancient sources from her time. He was proud of his Hasmonean lineage and would have been acquainted with much family lore, including the names of all his ancestors, both Hebrew and Greek. If he used her Greek name to imply that she was a devoted Hellenist, he failed miserably since her piety and faithfulness to Jewish teachings is evident throughout his books.

The rabbis always referred to Salome Alexandra by her Semitic name, Salome. They apparently did so to obscure her family's association with Hellenism. Unfortunately, by the time they wrote their accounts the correct pronunciation of her name had become garbled through centuries of transmission. They call her Shel-Zion, Shalmonin, Shalmza, Shlamto, and similar names. One esteemed historian of ancient Judaism has remarked on this confusion that Salome Alexandra is "a queen whose name no one can get straight."[4] After two thousand years of uncertainty, we now know her actual name.

A Name Recovered

Salome Alexandra is mentioned twice in a collection of ancient manuscripts known as the Dead Sea Scrolls. Scholars believe that an extremely devout group of Jews known as the Essenes, who had rejected Salome Alexandra's family as their rulers and high priests, wrote and collected these precious documents.[5] Unlike the majority of Jews, the Essenes were convinced that Salome Alexandra's family was ritually impure and refused to worship with them in the temple. Some retreated to the wilderness of the Dead Sea where they built the world's earliest known monastery at a place called Qumran. The Essenes closely watched her and her family from their desert retreat. They did so because they believed that her reign marked the imminent arrival of the messiah, whom they expected to cleanse the temple and remove her family from power.

When the Romans destroyed Qumran during the great Jewish War against Rome of Josephus's day, the Essenes hid their precious scrolls, including those mentioning our queen, in nearby caves. They hoped to retrieve them after God's messiah exterminated the Romans in the final battle between good and evil. But divine help was not forthcoming; the Romans killed the Essenes and destroyed their settlement. Their priceless texts remained forgotten for over two thousand years until a shepherd accidentally found them in 1947.

The name Dead Sea Scrolls is a misnomer since few of these documents are scrolls — most are scraps! They are perhaps the world's largest jigsaw puzzle. The problem is that most of the pieces are missing. Scholars have nevertheless devised several ingenious techniques to help them reconstruct these incomplete texts. They first separate the fragments based on the material upon which they are written: Papyrus reeds or animal skins. Then the texts are sorted by their handwriting (scholars have become quite adept at recognizing the penmanship of individual scribes). Sometimes experts are lucky and discover fragments that fit together. Unfortunately, few can be connected since their edges have rotted. Working with the scrolls requires much patience, and is often an exercise in creativity rather than science. We frequently have no way of knowing whether pieces with identical handwriting belonged to the same text since scribes copied many scrolls.

After decades of meticulous effort, scholars have determined that the Dead Sea Scrolls include the partial remains of over nine hundred different compositions. The biblical texts are the most important since they are the world's oldest copies of the Old Testament in the original Hebrew and Aramaic. The Dead Sea Scrolls even include fragments of the Greek translation of the Old Testament, which shows that Hellenism had penetrated Judea's most remote and conservative religious settlement. The remaining texts in this collection include biblical commentaries, debates over ritual purity, calendars, prayers, hymns, and historical writings pertaining to the foundation of the Essene sect and its early leader — the mysterious Teacher of Righteousness. But it is what these texts lack that is most perplexing of all — names. Although the Dead Sea Scrolls include the remains of over nine hundred documents, they only mention eighteen people by name! All are men with one exception — Salome Alexandra.

The Dead Sea Scrolls reveal that Shelamzion was Salome Alexandra's actual name. Because these texts were written during her lifetime, or shortly thereafter, there is no doubt this was her given name. This finding confirms a rather remarkable prediction made in 1899 by the French scholar Charles Clermont-Ganneau, who proposed that Shelamzion is her Semitic name. He came to this conclusion after finding two ossuaries (stone burial boxes for bones) containing the remains of two women named Shelamzion, both of whom may have been named after our queen.[6]

In 1990 archaeologists discovered a burial complex in Jerusalem that provides additional information about Salome Alexandra's name. It contains the remains of two Jewish families who had migrated to Jerusalem from Syria, including two sisters. The ossuaries containing the remains of these women include their Greek and Hebrew names: clear evidence their parents were Hellenized Jews. One ossuary has the Hebrew name "Shelamzion" caved on its side, which its engraver translated into Greek as "Selampsin." Josephus and a Jewish marriage contract discovered near the site of the Dead Sea Scrolls transliterate this Semitic name into Greek in almost the same manner. Ossuaries from other caves, however, write out this name into Greek as either "Selamsios" or "Selamseion," showing that it was pronounced several ways.[7]

The ossuary containing the remains of Shelamzion's sister illustrates the problem scholars face in determining how ancient Semitic names were pronounced. Hebrew and Aramaic did not print vowels in antiquity (they also use the same alphabet). Consequently, Semitic names can be vocalized several ways. Shelamzion's sister spelled her name with the consonants "sh," "l," "w," and "m." They are translated on her ossuary into Greek as "Salome" (the letter "w" can also represent the vowel "o"), which shows this is how she pronounced her name. These consonants are often vocalized as "shalom," meaning "peace." Other texts and inscriptions append "Zion," which is the ancient name of Jerusalem. If Shelamzion is Hebrew, then her full name should be translated as "the peace of Zion." If Aramaic, it likely means "the perfection of Zion."[8]

The extant literary and archaeological evidence shows that the name Shelamzion was pronounced several different ways in antiquity and that the "Zion" suffix was sometimes omitted. The name Shelamzion is apparently the longer form of the name Salome. Selampsin, and likely Selamsios and Selamseion, are apparently nicknames, or shorter versions, of Shelamzion. Shelamzion, and its variant Salome, became the second most popular female name after Salome Alexandra's reign (only Mary was more common). For countless generations mothers, presumably with the permission of their husbands, chose to name their daughters after Judea's only legitimate female Hasmonean ruler. Because a large percentage of Judean women were named after our queen, many likely spelled or pronounced it different ways to distinguish themselves from the countless other women with whom they shared the same name.[9]

Shelamzion Alexandra was undoubtedly our queen's actual name. But we cannot rule out that she may have pronounced it as Salome. Because she is commonly known as Salome Alexandra, I will use this name. I doubt she would object since this is the first book to tell the complete story of her remarkable life.

Voices of the Dead

We can occasionally supplement Josephus's writings with another source to uncover new evidence about Salome Alexandra's life and times — archaeology. Skeletons provide much information about the lives of her contemporaries. Damaged vertebrae, broken bones, and signs of arthritis, for example, indicate excessive wear and tear on the body. Illnesses and discomforts we take for granted were deadly in her time. Something as simple as an abscessed tooth was a potentially life-threatening affliction. This is because infection frequently spread throughout the bloodstream and slowly ate away the jawbone: there was no antibiotic or medicine to alleviate the pain. Ancient skeletons often exhibit signs of debilitating illnesses and injuries. They reveal that Salome Alexandra's world was one of immense suffering. This was especially true of the poor.

When archaeologists uncover the skeleton of an ancient Judean, they can usually determine whether the person was rich or poor simply based on the way it was buried. Judeans, like people of all ages, were interred according to their social status. The rich were placed in elaborately decorated mausoleums that proclaimed their wealth. They often adorned their tombs with inscriptions to ensure that future generations would remember them. Tourists to Jerusalem can still marvel at several mausoleums from Salome Alexandra's lifetime such as the so-called Tomb of Absalom or Zechariah's Tomb, both of which are adjacent to the Jerusalem temple. These monumental edifices provide us with a glimpse into the lives of Judea's rich and powerful, who could afford to build impressive monuments that have managed to survive the count-

Monumental Hellenistic and Roman tombs at the base of the Mount of Olives in the Kidron Valley adjacent to the Jerusalem Temple. The left tomb is traditionally attributed to David's son Absalom while the right is associated with the burial site of the biblical prophet Zechariah. The pyramid atop the latter tomb is similar to those that once adorned the burial monuments of Salome Alexandra's ancestors, the Maccabees (Todd Bolen/BiblePlaces.com).

less wars since their construction. Consequently, we have many tombs and bones of affluent Judeans to help us understand how they lived and died.

The situation is very different for the poor. Ignored in life and death, archaeologists seldom find any physical trace of their existence. This is because most were buried in crude shallow holes, with only a heap of stones to mark their graves. There are no inscriptions to record their names or their occupations. Their graves are so plain, and often unrecognizable, that they are usually discovered by accident, typically by bulldozers. Once uncovered, they are immediately reburied in anonymous mass pits, and forgotten, unless they need to be removed again to make way for new construction.[10]

Salome Alexandra was certainly interred inside a magnificent tomb that would have contained an inscription bearing her two names — Shelamzion Alexandra. Rich and poor alike would have visited it long after her death. Unfortunately, we do not know where it was located or anything about its appearance. Because her husband's mausoleum was in Jerusalem — she likely chose its design and selected its location — she too was undoubtedly buried there, and not in the Hasmonean ancestral plot in Modi'in (modern Israel) where most of ancestors were laid to rest. Although no trace of Salome Alexandra's sepulcher survives, we can use the description of the monumental tomb her ancestor Simon constructed to help us imagine what it must have looked like.

The anonymous author of 1 Maccabees (a book that describes how Salome Alexandra's ancestors created the Judean State) preserves the following detailed description of the tomb Simon constructed to honor his family:

> Simon built a monument over the tomb of his father and his brothers; he elevated it so high so that it could be seen by everyone. It was constructed with polished stone at the front and back. He also made seven pyramids, side by side, for his father and mother and four brothers. He decorated each with an elaborate arrangement, and put tall columns around them. He placed suits of armor for a permanent memorial on the columns, and next to the suits of armor he carved ships, which could be seen by everyone who sailed the sea [1 Macc. 13:27–29].

Modeled after the Mausoleum of Halicarnassus (modern Turkey) — one of the seven wonders of the ancient world — the pyramids that once adorned this great edifice show the extent to which Salome Alexandra's ancestors had abandoned traditional Jewish customs in their effort to become more like the Greeks. Simon's monument did not highlight his family's position as Judea's high priests, or commemorate their fight against the pagan Seleucid kings of Syria to preserve the Jewish faith. Rather, he built it to glorify war: past, present, and future. The ships and armor that lined its facade bore witness to his family's dream of transforming their fledgling Judean state into a Hellenistic empire that dominated land and sea. It was a monument that extolled Hellenism.

Simon's tomb still evoked wonder in Josephus's day, two hundred years after its construction. But when he visited it, the magnificent suits of armor and the sculptures of the ships had vanished. Pious Jews of his time, living under Roman occupation, apparently had come to regard them as idolatrous and despised symbols of Judea's decline and destroyed them. Perhaps in their frenzy to erase Hellenism's legacy, they also desecrated the tombs of the Hasmoneans, and possibly Salome Alexandra's final resting place as well.[11]

Salome Alexandra's two names show that she lived in a schizophrenic world when Jews and Gentiles alike struggled to balance the competing forces of change and tradition. Unfortunately, Jewish monotheism and Hellenistic polytheism could never live in harmony alongside one another. Choices had to be made. Salome Alexandra grew up in a violent world of divided loyalties. It is to this distant time and its many problems that we now turn in our quest to uncover the forces that shaped her early years.

2

A World of Divided Loyalties
Hellenism, Judaism, or Both?

What has Athens to do with Jerusalem?— Tertullian (ca. 160–220 C.E.), *De praescriptione Adversus haereticorum*, 7.9

The story of Salome Alexandra's life is a tale of two clashing civilizations — monotheistic Judaism and polytheistic Hellenism. She lived in an age when Jews killed in the name of God, confident their good intentions would outweigh their evil deeds. Many charged their enemies on the battlefield with suicidal ferocity, certain that God would bestow upon them the crown of martyrdom — eternal life in paradise. Two thousand years after Salome Alexandra's death people still murder one another in her homeland, and elsewhere, in the name of her God. Martyrdom is Hellenism's evil offspring.

Salome Alexandra lived in a country torn apart by profound social unrest, multiculturalism, economic uncertainty, gender disparity, war, and religious strife. Her people increasingly found themselves enmeshed in a contentious debate over such seemingly modern issues as immigration, the erosion of traditional values, and the connection — that is, whether there should be any — between religion and politics. These issues proved divisive and often led to violence. The debate over whether Hellenism and monotheism were compatible was never settled during her lifetime. It was still raging centuries later when the Christian writer Tertullian asked, "What has Athens to do with Jerusalem?"

Dual Loyalties: The Problems of Hellenism

Tertullian's famous question touches at the central issue that plagued Jewish society in Salome Alexandra's Judea, namely whether pagan Greek philosophy and its system of morality was compatible with Jewish Scripture. For Tertullian, and many Jews, the answer was a resounding No! Philosophy is the product of demons; Scripture is the fruit of divine wisdom. Yet, like the Jews of Salome Alexandra's day, the Christian apologists increasingly came under Hellenism's influence.

The Jews were supposedly among the first groups to have been exposed to Hellenism. Some allegedly had served as mercenaries in Alexander the Great's army.[1] The Greeks who had settled in Judea and the territories he had conquered throughout the Middle East identified themselves as citizens of the new Hellenistic states, such as Ptolemaic Egypt or Seleucid Syria. They quickly adopted the local religions and cultures. But assimilation was impossible for the Jews: God had banned them from worshipping the gods of their neighbors, or embracing foreign ways. The Lord had commanded them to live apart from the surrounding nations as God's chosen people. Then Hellenism changed everything when it forced the Jews of Salome Alexandra's homeland to choose assimilation or resistance.

Hellenism survived the death of its dynamic proponent, Alexander the Great. But his generals did not share his charisma: none commanded the respect and loyalty of his army. They fought countless wars to carve out their own kingdoms from his once vast and united empire. Although they lacked his magnetism, they managed to create successful Hellenistic states largely because the Persian king Darius (the man whom Alexander the Great had defeated) had ruled over his diverse lands as an absolute despot. Because Darius had removed any potential threat to his authority, his abrupt death left a leadership vacuum that Alexander the Great's generals filled through Hellenism. They granted local priests and officials some measure of cultural and political autonomy to ease the trauma that afflicts all conquered nations. By embracing cultural and religious diversity, Alexander's successors pacified their new subjects, and gained acceptance as the region's monarchs. But the Jews were different: They were the only people of the ancient Near East unwilling to accept Hellenism's foreign gods and pagan institutions. Their only viable option to maintain their traditional religion and lifestyle was to create their own state, free from foreign influences.

Salome Alexandra's family, the famed Hasmoneans, ignited a revolution to create an independent Jewish nation, and restore Judaism to its pristine condition before Hellenism had contaminated it. They were ironically not innovators, as many continue to view them, but followers. They astutely observed the temper of their time, namely the growing Jewish discontent towards Greek rule and the imposition of foreign faiths, and acted accordingly to unite their people, and attain secular and sacerdotal powers. Salome Alexandra's ancestors promised the Judeans a theocracy free from the taint of

Hellenism. Using faith as a call to arms, they urged their countrymen to fight a holy war against the Hellenists. Ironically, the nation they created was to a great extent forged from, and modeled after, the Greek society they supposedly opposed. Salome Alexandra's family became Judea's Hellenized high priests, and later its despots and kings.

A Faith Compromised

Hellenism threatened Judaism's survival because it brought Jews into close contact with people the Bible deemed impure. Ancient Judaism was a religion dominated by purity: it made a distinction between impurity and sin. There were numerous ways for a person to become ritually impure, such as through contact with an unclean animal, a corpse, mold, and contaminated utensils. Even diseases, especially skin disorders, made a person ritually impure. Sexual immorality, murder, and idolatry were among the most common types of moral pollution in ancient Judaism. It did not matter whether an individual became impure through some deliberate violation of God's laws or by accident since the result was the same — alienation from God. Only religious rituals conducted by Judaism's all-male priesthood could remove the stain of ritual or moral impurity and restore a person's previous standing before God as a pure member of the covenant community. Hellenism made this spiritual restoration and cleansing difficult when it introduced foreign ways to Salome Alexandra's homeland of Judea, and a lifestyle the Bible denounced as impure.

Salome Alexandra and her fellow Jews believed the divine laws regarding ritual purity were a blessing, not a curse. They were meant to maintain their connection with God. For this reason, the Judeans of her day were obsessed with purity. They believed that their temple in Jerusalem was the visible sign of God's presence with the Jewish community, and the only place where they could remove the taint of their ritual and moral impurity. Its destruction a century after Salome Alexandra's death left Judaism in a crisis. The rabbis largely blamed Hellenism for this catastrophe because it had transformed Judea from an isolated and religiously conservative province into a multicultural society in which many Jews, including the priests, were corrupt. They believed that Hellenism had caused men to purchase the high priesthood — Judaism's most sacred office — for money.[2] Hellenism was clearly here to stay not merely because its religion or culture was better, but because it had already taken hold of, and completely transformed, Judea's financial system.

Economics has been perhaps the major catalyst of religious reform throughout history. This is also true of Hellenism, which brought transnational commerce, new forms of land tenure, and a rather efficient system of taxation to Judea. Salome Alexandra's homeland was no longer an idyllic provincial territory where people eked out a meager existence off the land in isolation from their neighbors. Its future was now inextricably connected with the fates of the newly emerging Hellenistic states, especially those in Egypt and Syria.

In the early days after Alexander the Great's death, Judea became a little Egypt. Greeks who resided in Hellenistic centers such as the great Egyptian city of Alexandria administered it.[3] The Greek commercial and administrative apparatus quickly took hold as taxation was farmed out to Jews with a rudimentary knowledge of Greek. Once Hellenism had altered Judea's economic system, it merely needed the backing of the country's intellectuals to make its foothold permanent and dominate Judean society and religion. The Greeks found their greatest champion among the most unlikely of all Judeans — the priests.

The priests were the crème de la crème of Judean society. They were men chosen by God to maintain the Jerusalem temple and conduct the rites necessary to remove the taint of ritual and moral impurity. For centuries the high priests, in the absence of a king, had served as Judea's de facto rulers. A passage from the anonymous first century B.C.E. writer known as pseudo–Hecataeus (he was erroneously identified as the famed fourth-third B.C.E. pagan philosopher and historian Hecataeus of Abdera) provides us with a glimpse of how the Greeks viewed the high priests of Salome Alexandra's day:

> He [Moses] chose men of the greatest elegance and best qualified to lead the nation, and appointed them priests; and he ordained that they should devote themselves with the temple and the honors and the sacrifices offered to their God. These same men he appointed to be judges of all major disputes, and entrusted to them the protection of the laws and customs. This is why the Jews never have a king, and their leadership is regularly vested in whichever priest is considered superior to his colleagues in wisdom and virtue. They call this man the high priest, and believe that he acts as a messenger to them of God's commandments. It is he, they say, who in their assemblies and other gatherings announces what God has ordained, and the Jews are so submissive in such matters that they immediately fall to the ground and pay homage to the high priest whenever he expounds God's commandments to them [*On the Jews* quoted in Diodorus, *Library of History,* 40.3, 5–6].

Because the Jews of Salome Alexandra's time believed the priests were their spiritual bridge between their community and God, the Hellenists devoted great effort to win them over to their cause. But Judea turned out to be the only place in antiquity where Hellenism failed to produce a truly multicultural society that celebrated religious diversity. It only brought war and irreparably fractured Judaism.

Because the high priest controlled the Jerusalem temple, and determined the way Judaism was practiced, his adoption of Greek culture affected all Jews. Looking back at this tumultuous time with two thousand years of hindsight, it should not be surprising that so many Judeans found Hellenism too enticing to resist. It permeated virtually every aspect of life: language, religion, commerce, war, architecture, dress, government, literature, and philosophy. By Salome Alexandra's day, Hellenism and Judaism could no longer be separated. Her ancestors had merely waged a war to supplant one form of Hellenistic Judaism for another.

A Time of Religious Confusion

Hellenism upset the traditional status quo by exposing ordinary Judeans to foreign religions. For the first time in history, Jews were faced with a perplexing choice of new and often exotic faiths. Egyptian gods such as Isis, Osiris, Apis, Horus, Anubis, and others, quickly spread throughout the Middle East and Europe. Some of these newly imported religions, such as the religion of the Great Mother Cybele — a fertility deity of the Phrygians — incited terror and fear. Her ecstatic faith included orgiastic rites that sometimes culminated in self-castration!

While the more sordid Hellenistic faiths receive a disproportionate share of attention in ancient and modern literature, most were rather tame. Few demanded mutilation; the Greeks abhorred it! Many Hellenistic religions were similar to contemporary mega churches; they were as much social clubs as houses of worship. Pagans found these new faiths attractive because they fulfilled one of humanity's most central longings — the desire for companionship. Members of these religions often held meals to honor their chosen deity, which were frequently accompanied by excessive libations. These exotic beliefs, in keeping with Hellenism's focus on the individual and its teachings of personal salvation, demanded loyalty to a religious leader and fellow members of the cult. Initiates of some of these Hellenistic religions underwent clandestine ceremonies, during which they pledged never to reveal the secrets of their faith. Scholars collectively refer to them as "mystery religions" since their adherents took all knowledge of their secret rites with them to the grave.

Judea was not the only ancient society to have debated the pernicious influence of Greek religions. The Roman Republic at this time was obsessed with Hellenistic culture and the mystery religions. The cult of the Bacchanalia proved to be one of the most enduring and problematic of these foreign faiths. Its devotees worshiped Bacchus (a.k.a. Dionysus), the patron god of wine. In its early days when it was a predominately female religion, it inspired dread and curiosity among men. The women of the Bacchanalia, it was said, devoured live animals during their clandestine nocturnal assemblies. They supposedly held common meals during which they adopted the vices of men, including abusive sexual acts.

The Roman historian Livy (59 B.C.E.–17 C.E.) recounts the fear that the Bacchanalia incited in Rome in the time of Salome Alexandra's sons. Men had co-opted it and sexual immorality had become a dominant feature of its meetings — a practice that undoubtedly enticed many of both genders to undergo its secret initiations. Because women still officiated as its priests, the Bacchanalia, despite the increased participation of men, still aroused suspicion. Earlier, in 186 B.C.E., the Roman Senate unsuccessfully attempted to curtail the activities of this supposedly insidious cult, largely because it treated women as equals. It placed limitations on the number of females allowed to attend its meetings, and closely monitored its activities. However, murals in private homes, as well as reliefs depicted on sarcophagi, show that, despite the government's best efforts to hasten its demise, the Bacchanalia remained popular for centuries.[4]

The cult of Dionysus illustrates the allure of the Hellenistic religions for the Jews of Salome Alexandra's Judea. Dionysius was popular throughout the Middle East. Public celebrations and religious processions were held in his honor, during which women dressed in ceremonial costumes. The famed Roman general Mark Antony even came under the sway of this exotic faith during his trysts with the infamous Egyptian queen Cleopatra VII (69–30 B.C.E.). He identified himself with the god Dionysius while she proclaimed herself the reincarnation of the goddess Isis. Some Jews became captivated by this foreign cult and even celebrated a feast in honor of Dionysus; a few tried to erect a shrine to him in the Jerusalem temple. The Egyptian Pharaoh Ptolemy (IV) Philopator (222–205 B.C.E.) apparently tried to merge this religion with Judaism when he branded Jews with the emblem of Dionysus. The Syrian tyrant Antiochus (IV) Epiphanes (175–164 B.C.E.) apparently did the same, and ordered Jews to wear ivy wreaths and walk in processions to Dionysus. Although scholars debate the historical reliability of these tales, these stories show that many pagans in antiquity thought that Judaism and the cult of Dionysus were somehow connected. Over time, some Jews even adopted this belief and saw no problem worshipping both Dionysius and the God of the Bible.[5]

Pagans in the Hellenistic world were not only bound to one another by religion, but also by their citizenship in the *polis* (plural *poleis*), the city. It was the center of Greek religious and civic life. Alexander the Great had built many *poleis* throughout the Middle East; they became cultural outposts of Hellenism. Citizenship in a *polis* was not based merely on tribal affiliation, but on a pledge of allegiance to the Hellenistic city-state. Although the farmers and merchants who comprised the bulk of Judea's population lived in the countryside, they were immediately affected by the growth of these new Hellenistic centers. They had no choice but to interact with other cultures and faiths in these metropolises, which quickly became the primary market for their goods. Consequently, the city became the new battleground in the war between polytheism and monotheism.

No Judean city was more important than Jerusalem — the site of God's holy temple. All Jews tried to visit it whenever possible. Now, with Hellenism's ascendancy, pilgrims to the sacred city rubbed elbows with Greeks and other pagans. Jerusalem was rapidly becoming a cosmopolitan city where many faiths and cultures lived in tension alongside one another. It was inevitable that any move by the Jewish Hellenists to transform Jerusalem into a *polis* would bring civil war to Judea.

The conflict between the traditionalists, who resisted any change to their ancestral Jewish practices, and the Hellenists, who wanted to modernize Judean religion and culture, erupted in the most unlikely of places — the gymnasium (plural gymnasia). No city was deemed Hellenized unless it had at least one. An amalgam of a health club and a university, the ancient gymnasia included athletic facilities for such pursuits as running and wrestling, and libraries for intellectual stimulation. Within its halls citizens debated the merits of the latest philosophical fads, attended civic assemblies to decide matters of public policy, and conducted business. Beginning at the age of fourteen, boys began a curriculum in their local gymnasium that included the art of fighting, especially the use of the javelin and archery, to prepare them for political or military leadership. In theory, all citizens — regardless of their ethnic or geographical origin — were considered Hellenized if they received a gymnasium education and mastered the Greek language. The Greeks considered all others, regardless of their beliefs and cultural practices, barbarians. The Hasmoneans fared worse than other ruling families since many pagans did not deem Judea a lawful state, but an illegitimate "robber" nation.[6]

Many Greeks regarded the Jews as xenophobic because they refused to embrace Greek customs, particularly the gymnasia. Jews considered it a pagan institution since images of Greek gods, typically Hermes, lined its facade and members exercised in the nude. Those Jews who were willing to overlook these more unsavory aspects of Hellenistic life still faced a problem. The Greeks prized the human form; they abhorred bodily mutilation. But God commanded all Jewish males to be circumcised as infants to mark them as the Chosen People. However, a few found a way to overcome this seemingly insurmountable physical impediment and become physically indistinguishable from the Greeks.

In their desperate quest to become Hellenized, some Jews took a step that is simply unimaginable, if not downright shocking. They underwent a painful and life-threatening operation to remove all physical trace of their circumcision. There were actually surgeons skilled in this procedure. They used various methods to accomplish this seemingly impossible task. The most common entailed cutting or piercing the foreskin's remnant, stretching it over the head of the circumcised penis, and fastening it with twine, a ring, or a pin to facilitate the growth of new skin.[7] Unfortunately, Jews who resorted to this rather drastic and extremely uncomfortable measure — there was no anesthesia to mask the pain or antibiotics to prevent infection — were often considered neither fully Greek nor completely Jewish, but cultural misfits in two worlds.

Not all Jews believed that Judaism and Hellenism were so incompatible that one had to resort to such a drastic measure as reverse circumcision to become part of Greek society. A glimpse at the wide variety of Jewish literature popular in Salome Alexandra's day shows that a number of highly educated Jews had embraced Hellenism, yet remained loyal to the central tenants of their faith. The anonymous Jewish author dubbed Ezekiel the Tragedian (second century B.C.E.) wrote a play about Moses that imitated the style of the Greek playwrights. The Jewish scholars Demetrius (third century B.C.E.) and Eupolemus (second century B.C.E.), moreover, produced historical works about Jews that are reminiscent of Hellenistic literature. In their quest to outdo the Hellenists, some Jews made the rather implausible argument that the Greeks had borrowed their philosophy from the Jewish Scriptures.

Hellenism and Scripture

It is impossible imagine a time when the Bible did not exist. The Jewish Scriptures, known to Christians as the Old Testament and to Jews as the Tanak, are the product of Hellenism.

During the third and second centuries B.C.E., the savants of Alexandria's great library in Egypt worked tirelessly to preserve the cultural heritage of Western civilization. The librarians of Alexandria knew that their priceless literary treasures were literally disintegrating on their shelves. But there were too many for them to copy on a regular basis since reproducing a book by hand took considerable time and expense. Choices had to be made. To make certain the most important texts were transcribed on a regular basis, the librarians of Alexandria created the concept of the classic. They compiled lists of works they believed should be preserved for future generations. Their selections were controversial. Successive generations of scholars periodically revised them to reflect changing times and waning interests. Some, such as Pindar, Aeschylus, and Sophocles, are still read while others, like Anacreon, Stesichorus, and Ibycus, are largely lost and forgotten.[8]

We take the Bible for granted today. But it was still a revolutionary innovation in Salome Alexandra's day. Her Bible was not a book, but a collection of miscellaneous scrolls whose contents were still the subject of intense debate. Everyone in her day had a different version of it.[9] Because of this textual diversity, Scripture alone could not bring unity to her faith. Rather, the high priest largely determined what constituted normative Judaism. When Salome Alexandra took the throne and chose the high priest, she became one of her country's leading interpreters of God's word.

Of the many places were Jews lived, none embraced Hellenism with greater zeal than those who resided in Egypt. Over time they became completely Hellenized and lost their ability to read the Jewish Scriptures in the original Hebrew and Aramaic; they only spoke Greek. Because Judaism, unlike the faiths of Hellenism, is a religion of the book, this linguistic deficiency created an immense theological problem. Ironically, Hellenism rescued the Jews when it offered a way to preserve their written heritage. In the process, the Greeks of Egypt forever changed the way we read the Bible.

According to the apocryphal *Letter of Aristeas*— a text likely written around 250 B.C.E.— the Jewish community of Egypt produced the first translation of the Bible. The pagan monarch Ptolemy (II) Philadelphus (282–46 B.C.E.) was the patron of this immense enterprise. He invited Jewish sages from Jerusalem to bring copies of their scared texts to Egypt and translate them into Greek. The project took place in the famed port city of Alexandria, which was home to both the Pharos lighthouse (one of the seven wonders of the ancient world) and the greatest library in history. For many Jews and pagans, the placement of a Greek copy of the Jewish scriptures in this famed institution was tantamount to placing Hellenism's imprimatur on the Bible.

The translation of the Jewish scriptures from Hebrew and Aramaic into Greek is known as the Septuagint, which means seventy. This rather unusual name refers to the legend that seventy (or, according to some traditions, seventy-two) Jewish scholars translated it. The Septuagint was so popular that it was even used in Salome Alexandra's Judea. Nevertheless, most Judeans, because they spoke Hebrew and Aramaic, tenaciously clung to their original texts. But Egyptian Jews preferred to read the Bible in Greek translation, which they regarded as authoritative as the original. The writers of the New Testament, which was also written in Greek, followed their example and used the Septuagint; they rarely cite the Hebrew and Aramaic original. Contemporary Orthodox churches still read, and translate from, the Septuagint, making it the oldest translation of the Bible in continuous use. But most contemporary Jews and Christians prefer to follow the example of the Jews of Hellenistic Egypt and read their Scripture in languages other than the original. Bible translation is Hellenism's legacy.[10]

God as "She"

Educated Jews of Salome Alexandra's day did not have to read the Septuagint to encounter Hellenism. They had many competing forms of Judaism from which to choose. Ironically, all had adopted selected aspects of Greek culture to confront Hellenism's turmoil. Although most overlap with one another, for the sake of simplicity, we will divide them into three categories: Apocalyptic, Wisdom, and Mystery.

Jews who wanted to maintain the traditional Jewish belief in God's providence found solace in apocalyptic writings. This type of Jewish literature taught that Judea's current political situation was part of God's mysterious plan. Apocalyptic texts purport to contain hidden divine revelation that is typically imparted through an angelic intermediary. Most include detailed descriptions of God's final judgment of humanity and destruction of the wicked. Many of these writings, such as the first century B.C.E. work known as 1 Enoch — a book quoted in the New Testament Epistle of Jude and included in the canon of the Ethiopian Christian church — recount the heavenly journeys of humans who had supposedly glimpsed God's celestial throne. The book of 1 Enoch was immensely popular in Salome Alexandra's day; the Dead Sea Scrolls include several fragmentary copies of it. Many Jews found it comforting because it emphasizes that God has set limits to Hellenism's advance.[11]

Wisdom literature is an ancient genre whose roots extend back to Pharonic Egypt. The Jewish Bible is full of Egyptian influences, especially in the Book of Proverbs. The famed author Ben Sira moved from Jerusalem to Egypt to establish his own wisdom school. A devout Torah observant Jew, his book, which is named after him, is permeated with Hellenistic thought. It is included among the writings known as the "Apocrypha": a miscellaneous group of texts that did not make it into the Old Testament, but which several branches of Christianity consider sacred.

Ben Sira uses imagery that appears pagan. The biblical concept of wisdom is one prominent example. In Hebrew — a language that inflects for gender — wisdom is a feminine noun. (The Hebrew word for Law, "Torah," is also feminine.) Ben Sira personifies wisdom as a female intermediary between God and humanity. This rather unusual teaching, although largely indebted to Hellenistic thought, has a scriptural basis. Chapter eight of the biblical Book of Proverbs personifies God as a woman in the marketplace selling wisdom.

Many Jews viewed this figure, commonly known as Lady Wisdom, as God's consort through whom the universe had come into existence. This teaching profoundly affected nascent Christianity, which used this doctrine in the prologue to the Gospel of John to portray Jesus as the incarnation of divine wisdom. Whenever Christians read this Gospel passage in worship, they unknowingly praise God through the language of Hellenism.[12]

Because the biblical authors often describe God in feminine terms, it should not be surprising that some Jews during the Hellenistic period viewed the goddesses Isis as an incarnation of their God. Ben Sira even uses language reminiscent of the Isis legends; a clear demonstration of Hellenism's impact on his life and thought. This should not be shocking since the worship of Isis spread from Egypt throughout the Middle East, including the leading cities of Judea, in the wake of Alexander the Great's conquests. Archaeologists have even uncovered fragments of a relief depicting Isis outside the Jerusalem temple, suggesting that some Jews apparently believed her religion was compatible with Judaism.[13]

Judaism never developed mystery religions like the Bacchanalia. But it did produce an extensive body of esoteric writings reminiscent of them. The Pseudo-Orphic Fragments (ca. late third early second century B.C.E.)—a collection of Jewish poems pseudonymously attributed to the poet and musician Orpheus (he supposedly could charm animals)—merge pagan images and Jewish Scripture to portray monotheism as a divine mystery. Its author claimed that salvation depends on the acquisition of correct wisdom, the repudiation of idolatry, and the recognition of God's revelation. The famed Egyptian Jewish sage Philo (ca. 20 B.C.E.–ca. 50 C.E.) even wrote an entire book about a Jewish community in Egypt in which men and women lived as monks and participated in feasts that he described as similar to "the Bacchic rites." His accounts of their meals, and his allusions to this mystery religion, show that his Jewish audience was conversant with the practices and teachings of some of Hellenism's more esoteric faiths.[14]

A Liberating Curriculum

The arrival of Hellenistic faiths in the Middle East was accompanied by a heightened awareness of the need for education. The famed Cleopatra VII — the woman who captivated the likes of Julius Caesar and Mark Antony — was among the most erudite females of her time; she was fluent in the languages of the Ethiopians, the Troglodytes, the Hebrews, the Arabians, the Syrians, the Medes, and apparently the Parthians.[15] While few men or women attainted her linguistic proficiency, there is evidence that many Hellenistic females were educated.

The basic Hellenistic scholastic curriculum was the same for boys and girls, and included reading, writing, music, and sometimes painting. Boys received additional instruction in gymnastics while girls learned dance. Although educational opportunities for women greatly expanded during the Hellenistic period, few girls were literate. Nevertheless, these women have left an abundance of evidence in the literary and archaeological record. We have numerous Egyptian contracts in which the primary signatory is a female, which suggests that their husbands were illiterate. Terracotta figurines and tombstone reliefs from Alexandria, moreover, often portray females writing. These fragments from the past suggest that female literacy, at least among the elite, was fairly common.

Some erudite Hellenistic women were renowned for their intellectual abilities. The grammarian Hestiaea (ca. 250 B.C.E.), for example, wrote a treatise on the historicity of the Trojan War while Diophila (ca. 300 B.C.E.) penned an important work on astronomy. Other women were famous for their poetic skills. Anyte of Tegea (early third century B.C.E.) is a prominent example. She is the first epigrammatist to project a distinct literary persona. Her poems are full of images of women, children, and landscapes; she even wrote tender epitaphs for deceased animals. The poet Erinna (ca. fourth century B.C.E.), known as "a maiden bee" because her poetry was said to be a sweet as honey, wrote a poem called "The Distaff" that deals with female adolescence, dolls, and young wives. Nossis (ca. 300 B.C.E.), from the southern Italian port of Locri, produced an extensive body of women-centered poetry, some of which is slightly homoerotic. Hellenistic women even dabbled in matters that many today would deem unsavory, such as the production of sex manuals.[16]

Greek philosophy is traditionally regarded as the realm of such male luminaries as Plato, Socrates, and Aristotle. But few today are aware that Hellenistic women were among its most ardent practitioners. The school of philosophy known as Neopythagoreanism (second century B.C.E.–second century C.E.), which is based on the writings of the Greek philosopher and polymath Pythagoras (ca. 570 B.C.E.–ca. 495 B.C.E.), is our sole extant body of Greek prose literature written by females in the pre–Christian era. Perictione (fifth century B.C.E.), who was named after the famed philosopher Plato's (428/7–348/7 B.C.E.) mother, was among its most famous members. She wrote, "Let a woman not think that noble birth and wealth and coming from a great city and having the honor and love of celebrated and regal men are necessities."[17] Many pagan and Jewish women attended academic institutions in Alexandra, while others participated in philosophical movements such as Epicureanism, Cynicism, and Platonism. Unfortunately, the contributions of these great female writers are largely ignored in the Liberal Arts core curriculum that forms the basis of most contemporary university instruction in the West.

Salome Alexandra did not have to read the works of these great female writers to be influenced by their teachings. She knew, and undoubtedly met, many articulate and highly literate women from the royal families of Egypt and Syria. During the Hellenistic period, several Hasmonean females were highly educated and achieved political power. Salome Alexandra's granddaughter, Alexandra, was an extremely literate woman and a gifted politician. She wrote letters to the famous Cleopatra (VII) denouncing the Jewish king Herod the Great. Assuming her skills were not unique, many women from prominent Jewish families, like their pagan contemporaries, were likely literate during the Hellenistic period.

Salome Alexandra was fortunate to have lived during a unique era when women, for the first time in Judean history, were allowed to assume positions of leadership. In the nearby Roman Republic, which was rapidly expanding its influence throughout her homeland, the age of the so-called "new woman" was dawning. These females dared to compete with males in the political and sexual realms; some even pursued illicit affairs with younger men simply for pleasure. Latin poets actually promoted this inversion of traditional gender roles and depicted women as dominant and men as subservient. According to Salome Alexandra's contemporary, the Roman writer Varro, women increasingly asserted themselves in public by defying social conventions. They offended many when they refused to lie down at meals, which was the custom in antiquity.[18] Greek culture greatly helped to erode, but not entirely eliminate, gender inequality. By the time Salome Alexandra assumed Judea's throne, even the Jews had come to believe that it was no longer inappropriate for a competent female to govern men. If not for Hellenism, Salome Alexandra would never have ruled her people.

It was ironically the men of the Hasmonean family who were in the forefront of the revolution to expand the rights of Judean women. They increasingly looked to the neighboring Hellenistic kingdoms of Egypt and Syria for guidance, where women were exerting their independence. In these countries, shortly before Salome Alexandra's birth, women began to rule over men: some males even worshipped them. Egyptian and Syrian women even saved Salome Alexandra's husband from his enemies and preserved the Hasmonean dynasty for her to rule. Because Salome Alexandra knew several of these Egyptian and Syrian queens, we should not underestimate their impact on her reign and her country.

While amazing warrior queens were ruling the Middle East, Salome Alexandra's ancestors were beginning to forge a new nation. The tale of their lives is quite violent and tragic. Although they may appear quite primitive by our contemporary standards, the men of Salome Alexandra's family were very modern in one respect — they chose a woman as their political and military leader.

3

A Family of Warrior-Priests
The Hasmoneans

War is the care and the business of men. — Aristophanes (ca. 446–386 B.C.E.),
Lysistrata, 520

Of all the kings to have ruled the Seleucid Empire, none was worse for the Jews than Antiochus (IV) Epiphanes. In 167 B.C.E., he effectively declared war against Judaism. Salome Alexandra's ancestors successfully fought this madman to save the Jews from annihilation. But their astonishing victory did not bring peace to Judea, or purify Judaism of its pagan accretions. Her family created a new aristocracy of Hellenistic warrior-priests who lusted for absolute power.[1]

A Land Divided, a People United?

Salome Alexandra's Judea was a land of remarkable geographical diversity that made it difficult to rule, and nearly impossible to unite its many peoples. It extended 160 miles in length, from the Anti-Lebanon Mountains in the north to the Dead Sea in the south. Mt. Hermon, approximately 9,230 feet in elevation, is her country's highest point while the Dead Sea, at 1,083 feet below sea level, is its lowest spot. At various times in its history, her nation extended an additional 118 miles south to the Red Sea. Despite these impressive geographical dimensions, Salome Alexandra's Judea was quite narrow. From its eastern border, the Jordan River, to the Mediterranean Sea was a mere 50 miles. Despite its relatively small size, Judea contains some of the greatest topographical and climatic variation on earth. In winter it is possible to ski atop Mt. Hermon and surf in the Red Sea the same day; the driving time between the two is a mere six hours.[2]

39

Life has always been difficult in Salome Alexandra's homeland. Farmers had a hard time growing crops there because of its lack of rainfall; some areas of the country are still largely uninhabitable. Potable water was always difficult to find, both for the countless Greek armies that traversed Judea in their quest to conquer it and for its inhabitants. The one hundred mile coastal section from the northern port of Haifa to the city of Gaza (modern Gaza Strip), near the Egyptian border, contains only thirty-five water sources. Because ancient armies and merchants generally traveled fifteen miles per day, few of these wells would have been accessible for each leg of their journey along this route.[3] Because most inland roads did not possess enough water sources for large numbers of men and animals, Judea was a difficult country to traverse. Countless men, women, and children perished along its byways for lack of water.

Judea is fortunate to have a large body of fresh water, the Sea of Galilee, in its northern region. The Jordan River connects this great lake with the Dead Sea, some forty miles to the south. Unfortunately, the Jordan River cannot be used for agricultural or commercial purposes because it sits in a deep ravine. Its torrential currents and many bends make navigation impossible. Because the Sea of Galilee too is in a deep depression, farmers in antiq-

Caesarea Philippi sacred area. Located at the base of Mt. Hermon, Caesarea Philippi is the location of a large cave that was the site of pagan worship during the Hellenistic era. The spring that emerged from the cave in antiquity was one of the sources of the Jordan River. The ruins of the Temple of Pan contain niches carved into the walls of the cliff that once contained images of the Greek nature deity Pan (Todd Bolen/BiblePlaces.com).

uity could not use it for irrigation. The harsh realities of this barren and desolate region clearly call into question the Bible's claim this is the Promised Land.

It is difficult to find accurate descriptions of Salome Alexandra's country since ancient Jewish writers tended to exaggerate it size and fertility. Josephus portrays it as a veritable paradise:

> Now concerning the country of Samaria, it is located between Judea and Galilee ... and is entirely the same nature as Judea; for both countries consist of hills and valleys, and are especially suitable for agriculture, and are very fruitful. They are thickly wooded, and are full of autumnal fruit, both that which grows wild, and that which is the effect of cultivation. They are not watered by many rivers, but primarily by rainwater, of which they have no want. As for those rivers that they have, all their waters are very sweet. Because of the regions's excellent grass, their cattle produce more milk than other places; and, what is a certain sign of its prosperity is that it is full of people [*War* 3.48–50].

Despite some well-watered areas, Salome Alexandra's country was no Garden of Eden. Much of it was barren and geographically isolated. But Jews were not interested in this tiny speck of land because of its agricultural potential. It was their spiritual homeland; it was the site of their temple; and it was the place where their high priests resided. But most important of all, God had a special presence, and longstanding relationship, with the Jews of this land.

The area of Samaria, to Judea's north, is, as Josephus notes, a hot, barren, and hilly region. Salome Alexandra's father-in-law annexed it during her childhood; few Jews lived there. It is named after a group that had intermarried with the pagan population that settled in the region following the Assyrian conquest of the eighth century B.C.E. Over time, its inhabitants, the Samaritans, separated from Judaism and developed a distinctive religion. They produced their own version of the Bible, containing only the five books of Moses, to further separate them from their Judean kin.

According to Josephus, Alexander the Great had given the Samaritans permission to build their own temple. Two inscriptions on the Greek island of Delos (250–175 B.C.E. and 150–50 B.C.E.) bear witness to its fame.[4] When Salome Alexandra was about thirty, around the time she gave birth to her first son, her father-in-law destroyed this shrine and annexed Samaria.

Idumea, to Judea's south, is a dry and barren region with rolling hills suitable for olives, fruit, and grazing. A semi-nomadic pagan group known as the Idumeans lived there. Although their origin and ethnicity continues to elude scholars, they had some degree of kinship with the Jews. They practiced circumcision and regarded Abraham, whose burial site at Hebron was under their control, as their ancestor. Salome Alexandra's father-in-law annexed Idumea when she was in her early thirties and forced its population to convert to Judaism. She and her husband later appointed an Idumean named Antipas to high political office. The Romans later chose his grandson, known to history as Herod the Great (ca. 73/74 B.C.E.–4 B.C.E.), as Judea's king in place of her children. His reign witnessed much bloodshed, and a monumental building campaign whose achievements, such as the Western Wall of the Jerusalem temple and the great port of Caesarea, are still visible today. But Herod is best known for his failed attempt to kill another potential rival to his throne — the infant Jesus.[5]

Of all the regions that made up Salome Alexandra's Judea, none was more fertile and populous than the Galilee to Samaria's north. Later home to Jesus of Nazareth and most of his twelve apostles, it contains the region's only large body of fresh water, the Sea of Galilee. Although Josephus is prone to exaggeration when it comes to his homeland, we one again turn to him for a description of this area:

> Concerning the Galilees, which are two, one called the Upper Galilee and the other called the Lower Galilee ... their soil is rich and fertile, and full of all kinds of plants, so much so that its fruitfulness invites even the laziest to farm them; accordingly, it is all cultivated by its inhabitants, and no part of it lies idle. Moreover, the cities are close together, and the many villages are full of people. Because of the richness of their soil, the smallest of them contain above fifteen thousand inhabitants [*War* 3.35, 41–3].

The Galilee was more bountiful than Judea or Samaria. Its abundant rainfall allowed its farmers to grow a wide variety of crops, especially olives, grapes, and grains. It was also known for its ethnic diversity and conflict. Dubbed "Galilee of the Gentiles" by the biblical prophet Isaiah, it was the site of many wars. The author of the New Testament Book of Revelation chose the Galilean city of Megiddo as the site of the final eschatological conflict between God and Satan — the so-called battle of Armageddon ("Armageddon" is the Greek transliteration of the Hebrew phrase "hill of Megiddo").[6] The Galilee will play an important role in our story since Salome Alexandra and her husband lived there for a short time.

Salome Alexandra's homeland was known throughout the Middle East and southern Europe for its agricultural products. Many of Judea's crops, fish, and goods were shipped throughout the Hellenistic, and later Roman, world. But transporting these products was quite difficult. Ships in antiquity were the best and most efficient way to travel. A dealer in Judea's lucrative olive oil industry could transport two to three thousand five-gallon jars, weighing nearly one hundred pounds each, over vast distances in a single ship. But to do the same on land required countless donkeys or oxcarts to carry them.

Unfortunately, goods and armies had to adopt the latter means of transport in Judea since there were no navigable rivers connecting it with the coast. Most travelers, merchants, and legions had to cross Judea's harsh, hot, and desolate terrain by foot. Water was always a problem; shade was a necessity; and danger was always present. Roads were difficult to use: many were crude, uneven, and worn dirt paths; and bandits potentially lurked around every rock or corner. In an age before the credit card, travelers had to carry their money and valuables with them, which made any journey perilous.

Locating provisions was perhaps the greatest danger Salome Alexandra's people faced when they moved throughout her kingdom. Travelers had to carry water and food with them lest they run out of supplies before reaching a settlement. Most people went on foot because animals were expensive: the poor could not afford them and the rich needed to carry many supplies to feed them along the way. Trained soldiers marching through Judea's desert would have needed at least nine quarts of water each day, and at least three pounds of food. Because these were difficult to procure in many areas, armies had to carry large quantities of food and water on their backs. A trained military force marching eight hours per day under Judea's desert sun, carrying fifty-pound packs, would have suffered hardships we can scarcely imagine. Civilians would have fared worse. Yet, all Judeans had to traverse this harsh terrain to worship in Jerusalem for the three great pilgrimage festivals — God commanded it![7]

During Salome Alexandra's lifetime the Hasmoneans not only annexed Samaria, Idumea, and Galilee, but portions of the lands beyond the Jordan River: Gaulanitis, Batanea, Auranitis, Trachonites, and Peraea (all in portions of modern Syria and Jordan). These territories included many pagans. Her husband unsuccessfully attempted to expand the Hasmonean state northwards when he attacked the port of Tyre (modern Lebanon), and the lands of the Nabatean Arabs (modern Jordan) to the east of the Jordan River. These unsuccessful campaigns led to untold loss of life and brought an influx of foreigners to Judea. Relationships between the Jews and the peoples of these regions were always tense. Although Salome Alexandra ended hostilities between the Jews and the Arabs when she took power, violence among these groups continues to plague the lands she once ruled.

Sandwiched Between Hellenism

The Judea of Salome Alexandra's childhood was a very different country than the vast land she would one day govern. It was a small and insignificant nation. None of its neighbors would have paid any attention to it if not for its unique geographical position. Judea was sandwiched between the two great Hellenistic powers of the Middle East: Ptolemaic Egypt and Seleucid Syria. Both considered Judea their rightful possession.

Alexander the Great's generals, Ptolemy (367–282 B.C.E.), Seleucus (ca. 358–281 B.C.E.), and their successors, fought five major wars for Judea. Ptolemy and his descendants controlled it for well over a century. During their tenure as its occupiers, the Ptolemies accelerated its pace of Hellenization. Buildings and fortifications of this time exhibit the hallmarks of foreign influence while imported Greek wine jars bear witness to the new culinary tastes of Jerusalem's elites, who quickly adopted the Hellenistic lifestyles of their conquerors. Judea's political situation changed when the Seleucids annexed her homeland. But the Egyptians never gave up their dream of recapturing it. They tried unsuccessfully several times to take it back, and nearly succeeded when Salome Alexandra's husband became king.

Hellenism not only brought foreign masters to Judea, but a new language as well. Greek was the official tongue of the Hellenistic world. By the time the Syrians wrested Judea from the Ptolemies (195 B.C.E.), it had become the primary language of Judea's administration and commerce. A Greek inscription from the Jezreel Valley in the Galilee shows the extent to which Greek dominated trade. It records six official letters between local officials and the Seleucid king Antiochus (IV) Epiphanes. Even the Essenes of Qumran — the likely authors of the famous Dead Sea Scrolls — used Greek, which shows that this ultra-conservative religious community did not consider this language objectionable. By the time of Salome Alexandra's birth, Hellenism had penetrated virtually all aspects of Judean society. She was likely fluent in Greek as well as the biblical languages of Hebrew and Aramaic. Although she was thoroughly Hellenized, she remained zealously loyal to her ancestral faith.[8]

Scholars continue to debate the extent to which Hellenism had penetrated Judean society in Salome Alexandra's day. Although few common Judeans spoke Greek fluently, or attended public readings of Homer or the great pagan Hellenistic authors, they were nevertheless greatly influenced by Hellenism. The Jewish priests — the likely consumers of the fine wine imported from the Greek island of Rhodes, whose jars archaeologists have discovered in Jerusalem — made certain that even poor Judeans came into contact with Greek culture when they transformed the high priesthood into a Hellenistic institution.[9] Whenever Jews went to Jerusalem to worship in the temple, they had to jostle through its narrow streets with pagans to reach the sanctuary. Once there, these simple pilgrims had to present their offerings to priests whose embracement of Hellenistic culture many believed defiled God's holy place.

The stories of the ordinary Judeans of Salome Alexandra's time, and their opinions of Jerusalem's priests, are irretrievably lost. The discovery of a few simple and crudely executed tombstones in poor Greek suggests that some tried to imitate the Hellenists.[10] But this book is not the story of these common Jews: it is about a woman from Judea's most elite Hellenized family. It is about the affluent and the powerful: rulers, high priests, and kings. For this reason, her story is the tale of two worlds — Hellenism and Judaism.

Religion for Sale

No one in Salome Alexandra's Judea faced a more difficult task balancing the competing forces of Hellenism and Judaism than the high priest. This was especially true in the early days of Greek rule. As the holder of this sacred office during the period of Egyptian suzerainty, Onias III (?–175 B.C.E.) was Judea's sacerdotal head and its chief political authority. However, he not only acted in the interests of the Jews, but the Egyptians as well. He tried to present Hellenism in a Jewish guise by allowing his people to retain their distinctive religious and cultural identity, while acknowledging the authority of the Greeks. Onias also oversaw the Egyptian monarch's share of the money that was deposited in the Jerusalem temple (shrines in antiquity served a banks). When the Syrians expelled the Ptolemies from Judea, he had to make a decision whether to maintain his allegiance to his former patrons, or seek accommodation with Judea's new masters. Time was not on his side; he had to act quickly; a rash decision could prove fatal.

God did not grant Onias the gift of prophecy. Despite the near certainty that Egypt would not regain its former holdings for the foreseeable future, he remained loyal to the Ptolemies. Yet, despite his mistaken political calculation, the situation likely would have turned out in his favor, if not for his brother Jason.

Jason, unlike his sibling, was not loyal to the Egyptians. He decided to cast his lot with Judea's new overlords. His name illustrates the extent to which Hellenism had taken hold of Judean society by this time. He is the first Judean leader to take a Greek name. His birth name is Jesus; it is typically translated in English as Joshua. In 175 B.C.E. he shocked his people when he purchased the high priesthood from the new Syrian monarch, Antiochus (IV) Epiphanes, for two hundred and forty talents.

Jason (175–172 B.C.E.) immediately sought to appease his Seleucid overlords by accelerating Judea's transformation into a Hellenistic fiefdom. He offered Antiochus an additional one hundred and fifty talents in exchange for the right to establish a gymnasium in Jerusalem. It became so popular that some priests neglected their duties at the sacrificial altar in order to watch its

Tomb of the Jewish high priest Jason (175–72 B.C.E.) in Jerusalem, seen from the south. Egyptian-style pyramid tombs became common in the Hellenistic period. This sepulcher shows the extent to which the Jewish high priests had abandoned traditional customs in their effort to become more like the Greeks (Todd Bolen/ BiblePlaces.com).

athletic contests. Because the high priest and the temple priests controlled Judaism and presided over the offerings, their adoption of Hellenism affected all Judeans. Jerusalem was now a Hellenistic *polis*; Judaism was now a Hellenistic religion.

Although many Judeans considered Jason a usurper, they grudgingly accepted him as their spiritual leader since he had the biblically mandated pedigree to hold the high priesthood. But what would happen, many wondered, if an unqualified person should purchase this sacred office? Unfortunately, the Judeans did not have to wait long for this nightmarish scenario to become a reality.

In 172 B.C.E., an ardent Hellenist named Menelaus bought the high priesthood (172–162 B.C.E.) from the Seleucids. Unlike Jason, he did not possess the proper pedigree to hold this sacred office. His investiture created a crisis for all Judeans. The Bible commands Jews to worship in the Jerusalem temple; to assemble there for the three great pilgrimage festivals; and to send their contributions there for its upkeep.[11] Because the high priest was necessary for the observance of the Jewish holidays, and for the temple to operate, rejecting him was tantamount to disobeying God. For this reason, most Judeans believed they had no choice but to accept this illegitimate high priest as their spiritual leader in order to follow God's laws.

Onias and Jason refused to pledge allegiance to Menelaus. Now, three claimants vied for recognition as Judea's rightful high priest. All had vast legions of loyal followers willing to fight to restore their candidate to his former office. Given this tense situation, civil war was inevitable.

Menelaus was willing to do anything to retain power, even violate God's commandment not to murder. He convinced Antiochus's chief official, Andronicus, to assassinate Onias. The anonymous author of the biblical Book of Daniel considered his murder a major turning point in history and warned, "After sixty-two weeks, an anointed one (=Onias) shall be cut off and shall have nothing, and the troops of the prince who is to come shall destroy the city and the temple."[12] The author believed Antiochus (IV) Epiphanes fulfilled this prophecy when he declared war against Judaism and desecrated the temple.

Jason acerbated an already tense situation when he gathered a thousand discontented men, attacked Jerusalem, and drove Menelaus from the city. Antiochus Epiphanes's retaliation was swift and brutal. He sent his envoy Apollonius to quell the dissent. Apollonius captured Jerusalem by stealth, razed its walls, and built a Seleucid fortress in the city known as the Akra. By this time the Jewish community had become so divided that some Hellenized Jews chose to support the Seleucid occupation and took up residence in the Akra. The Seleucids restored Menelaus to his position as high priest, but appointed a Phrygian (modern Turkey) named Philip as the city's political leader. Judea was now a province of the Seleucid Empire and Menelaus was merely a minor religious functionary.

Antiochus Epiphanes realized that the Jewish high priest had long served as Judea's religious and political leader. As looked further into the history of this sacred office, he noticed many similarities between Judaism and the cult of the Bacchanalia. He was not the first to see this relationship: rumors circulated at the time that the Jews worshipped an ass — a figure often used to represent Dionysus — in their temple.[13] Antiochus Epiphanes was convinced Judaism was an insidious faith that posed a direct threat to his empire's security. He was determined to eradicate it.

In 167 B.C.E. Antiochus Epiphanes effectively outlawed Judaism. He ordered that sacrifices to the god Zeus be conducted regularly in the Jerusalem temple. According to the book of 2 Maccabees:

> The temple was filled with wickedness and shouts by the Gentiles, who consorted with prostitutes and had intercourse with women within the sacred

precincts, and also brought in things for sacrifice that were unfit. The altar was covered with abominable offerings that were forbidden by [Jewish] law. People could neither keep the Sabbath, nor observe the festivals of their ancestors, or even acknowledge that they were Jews [2 Macc. 6:4–6].

Antiochus Epiphanes forced Jews to march in a procession wearing wreaths of ivy in honor of Dionysus, and ordered anyone who practiced circumcision or observed the Sabbath to be executed. Without a miracle, there would be no Judea or Judaism.

The Might of "The Hammer"

Judea's salvation came from the most unlikely locale, an obscure village named Modi'in. Salome Alexandra's ancestor Mattathias lived there. His loathing for the Seleucids exceeded Menelaus's love of Hellenism. One day a Seleucid official and his retinue arrived in Modi'in to enforce Antiochus Epiphanes's edict that all Jews make a public offering to the pagan gods. They brought an altar with them for the occasion. The situation was tense; no one knew what to do; defiance of the king's order meant certain death and destruction to the village.

When a Jew decided to comply with the Syrian edict and worship the pagan gods, Mattathias accompanied him to the altar. But he was not there to sacrifice, but to murder. The anonymous author of 1 Maccabees describes the scene in vivid detail:

When Mattathias saw it, he burned with zeal and his heart was stirred. He became overcome with zealous anger; he ran and murdered him on the altar. At the same time he killed the king's officer who was forcing them to sacrifice, and he destroyed the altar. Thus he acted zealously for the Law ... Mattathias shouted in a loud voice: "Let every one who is zealous for the Law and obeys the covenant join me!" Then he and his sons fled to the hills and left behind all their possessions in the city. Many who were seeking righteousness and justice abandoned their possessions and went down to the desert to live with them [1 Macc. 2:24–29].

Mattathias led the first war fought in defense of monotheism. It unfortunately would not be the last waged in the name of God on Judean soil.

Mattathias and his five sons did not hesitate to bend Jewish law when it suited their needs. They came up with a new weapon to motivate the masses — martyrdom. To rally sacrificial victims to his cause, Mattathias offered immortality. Salome Alexandra's ancestors largely created the theological concept of bodily resurrection: a belief that subsequently became a central tenant of the Christian faith. The Hellenistic emphasis on the individual helped facilitate its incorporation into Judaism. Resurrection first appears in the Bible in the Book of Daniel; a work that alludes to Mattathias and his sons. With this new doctrine as a recruiting tool, Mattathias created an army more vicious than any force the Seleucids could muster. Jews now charged the Syrians on the battlefield with unprecedented ferocity, confident if they died they would receive an eternal reward in paradise for their religious zeal.[14]

Salome Alexandra grew up hearing tales of her amazing Hasmonean forebears: Mattathias and his sons John, Simon (high priest 142–134 B.C.E.), Judas, Eleazar, and Jonathan (high priest 152–142 B.C.E.). These men had challenged the might of the Seleucid Empire to save her faith and create an independent Jewish nation. Her story is also the tragic saga of this powerful and dysfunctional family. Salome Alexandra's life almost spanned the entire duration of the Hasmonean state. She was born shortly after Simon created it; she knew all of its rulers, kings, and high priests. It reached its zenith during her reign. The Romans conquered it less than four years after her death. She was undoubtedly its greatest ruler. Her life is remarkable by any measure, yet she receives scant attention in the historical record. In order to understand how she defied the odds to rule Judea, lead men in battle, and alter her nation's religion, we must begin with the day her father received the sad news that his wife had given birth to a girl.

4

Seeking Judea's Missing Women
Uncovering Salome Alexandra's Lost Years

It is a disgrace to be the father of an undisciplined son, but the birth of a daughter is a loss.—*Ben Sira*, 22:3

The birth of a child brought great joy to family and friends alike in Salome Alexandra's Judea, as long as it was not a girl. Her misogynist society only valued boys. Like everything else in her homeland, sexism was rooted in Scripture: "The birth of a daughter is a loss." The Lord never granted women full equality: God banned them from the priesthood. For these, and many other reasons, Salome Alexandra's father would have regretted the news that his wife had given birth to a girl. But if God had told him that his daughter would become Judea's greatest ruler, he undoubtedly would have rejoiced at the news of her birth.

A Tainted Birth

God has always been sexist. Female prophets and role models are rare in Scripture: there is no evidence that a woman wrote any book of the Bible. Men have always served as the primary transmitters of God's revelation, as well as its principal interpreters. Given the prevalent sexism in antiquity, it is not surprising that the men who produced the Jewish Bible (the same is true of Christian Scripture) canonized books that are largely biased against women, and which attribute their inferior status to God's divine plan. Ancient Judaism was largely a man's religion: women were its most impure practitioners.

Many contemporary readers of Scripture fail to understand that ritual defilement and sin were not synonymous in ancient Judaism. There were many ways for a person to contract ritual uncleanness without committing any moral transgression. The accidental mixing of certain foods, such as meat or milk, rendered a person ritually impure. Contact with blood was among the most common, and feared, mechanisms through which ritual impurity was spread to others. It was sacred to God:

> Be certain that you do not eat the blood; for the blood is the soul, and you shall not eat the soul with the meat. Do not eat it; you shall pour it out on the land like water. Do not eat it, so that all may go well with you and your children after you, because you do what is right in the sight of the Lord. [Deut. 12:23–25].

Because childbirth and menstruation result in the excretion of blood, all mature females were ritually impure for a significant portion of each month.

The joy normally associated with the birth of an infant was quickly stifled for a mother since her newborn's blood made her ritually impure. She had to undergo an immediate period of isolation, lest she contaminate others. The gender of her child determined the length of her ritual defilement. If she bore a boy, she was unclean for seven days. A thirty-three day period of "blood purification" then followed, during which she was not allowed to enter the temple or touch any holy object. But if she bore a girl, her periods of defilement and "blood purification" were doubled.[1] At the completion of this divinely mandated isolation period, the new mother had to go to the temple to have a male priest remove her impurity so she could once again worship alongside men.

No Time to Grow Up

Salome Alexandra lived in a world full of children: it must have been very noisy. It was a difficult time for young and old alike, especially mothers. Raising infants was exhausting and arduous since, in an age before reliable methods of birth control, families were quite large. Frequent wars, infectious diseases, and routine illnesses, for which there were no viable treatments before the invention of antibiotics, ensured that many infants never reached adulthood. Historical records from ancient Judea indicate that whenever a two-year drought occurred, famine quickly followed since families had to eat the seeds needed for next year's planting.[2] In Salome Alexandra's world joy, sadness, misery, birth, and death were constant companions.

Life in the ancient world was particularly hard for married women. They were entrusted with the primary care of the young, the management of the household, and the preparation of food: all arduous tasks that took up most of the day in the pre-modern era. This toil started quite early. The extant literary evidence suggests that most Jewish women married in their late teens or early twenties. Jewish women in Babylon often wed earlier, in their early or mid-teens, to husbands who were close to twenty years of age. Judean men, in contrast, tended to delay matrimony until around the age of thirty.

The custom of early betrothal greatly complicated the lives Judean women since it prolonged their childbearing years. Young brides could anticipate twenty-nine years of fertility, between the ages of fifteen to forty-four. During this time a wife could expect to give birth to five or six children. The early Ptolemaic Greek poet Posidippus (310–240 B.C.E.) wrote poignant epigrams (short, clever, statements) about women he knew in Egypt that help us to understand the consequence of early marriage. In one of his epigrams he praises an eighty-year-old woman who lived to see the grandchild of her great-granddaughter. This could have been possible only if she, and each of her female descendants in succession, married by the age of fifteen. Unfortunately, few women in antiquity witnessed the birth of so many of their descendants. Childbirth was a major killer before the advent of modern medicine, which meant that a newly married woman could look forward to attending the funerals of several of her children, grandchildren, and female relations.[3]

Gamla house with grindstone. This kitchen from a house located in the Hellenistic ruins of Gamla is identical to those in which Salome Alexandra's female contemporaries would have spent much of their lives. The heavy grindstone made of a large basalt stone is located atop a flat stone counter. Grain was placed in the opening on the stone's top, and the women of the family moved the stone back and forth with a wooden handle (not preserved) to grind grain for baking (Todd Bolen/BiblePlaces.com).

Women in antiquity were aware of the harsh reality that sons were more important than daughters. Nevertheless, all infants shared one great injustice — a short childhood. Until the end of the Middle Ages the young were regarded as miniature adults; their lives were full of turmoil and uncertainty.[4] Children born in Salome Alexandra's day knew they had to grow up rather quickly. They were expected to toil alongside their parents in the field, or work in some cottage industry to help their family eek out a meager living.

Child labor was divided by gender in the ancient world. Boys worked alongside their fathers, typically in the fields or in various types of manual labor. Girls spent the bulk of their time at home under the care of their mothers learning the so-called feminine crafts: cooking, weaving, basket making, and childcare. The young of both genders were expected to help pick crops during the harvest. But unlike boys, girls had very little freedom; they could not move about the village unaccompanied by a male guardian. Because children were an invaluable source of labor, few families could afford the time or expense to provide them with an education. The young learned quite early that life is harsh, and often short.

We know nothing about Salome Alexandra's childhood. But her social status allows us to make a few educated conjectures about her early years. She certainly never harvested crops or toiled in some cottage industry to help her family survive. She undoubtedly experienced the joys that we associate with modern childhood, namely time to play, learn, and grow up. She likely had servants to perform the most rudimentary chores: her lifestyle would have been regarded as privileged in any age. Unlike most Judean boys and girls, she had the luxury of an education; likely a private tutor hired by her parents. But she did share one thing in common with her less fortunate peers — she was expected to marry quite young. Until she wed, despite her privileged upbringing, she faced many dangers unique to her sex.

The Price of Chastity

The period between childhood and marriage was the most dangerous time in a young girl's life. It was fraught with great anxiety for her entire family, especially her father. The sage Ben Sira opines on this matter:

> A daughter keeps her father awake, and the anxiety she causes takes away his sleep — in her youth, lest she not marry, and having married, lest she be hated, in virginity, lest she be defiled and she become pregnant while in her father's house, with a husband, lest she be unfaithful, and having married, lest she be infertile. Constantly watch over a headstrong daughter, lest she make you a laughingstock to enemies, the talk of the city and the object of gossip, and she

shame you before a multitude. Do not let her parade her beauty before any man, or spend time with women. For a moth comes out of clothes, and from a woman comes woman's wickedness [Sir. 42:9–13]

Ben Sira's misogynistic comments are rooted in the harsh reality of marriage in Salome Alexandra's homeland. It was not an institution based on love — it was an economic transaction.

A young girl's potential worth as a bride was not calculated according to her beauty or her personality, even though suitors preferred females with these attributes, but solely by her sexual status. In the marital marketplace no commodity was more prized than virginity. During the Hellenistic period, Judean fathers adopted a variety of measures to ensure their daughters remained chaste until marriage. The first century C.E. Jewish scholar Philo tells us that homes in Alexandria, Egypt, were designed to keep women confined to dark, rear, and interior rooms. Seldom permitted to enjoy fresh air, or the open expanse of the patio, young Egyptian girls had to remain content to peer out their windows to catch a glimpse of the outside world. Yet, Ben Sira warned fathers that even windows could be a temptation: he suggested they deny their daughters the luxury of an unobstructed view. When outdoors, a Jewish girl had to cover her head, typically with a kerchief, a hairnet, or a cloth band, to hide her features. Salome Alexandra lived in a world in which women were rarely seen or heard — because men preferred it that way.[5]

There was an ironic element to the ancient custom of female seclusion. Fathers not only confined their daughters for their own protection, but also because they feared their seductive powers. Once again we turn to the sage Ben Sira to help us understand this rather peculiar, and disturbing, belief. He warned fathers that young girls possess a voracious sexual appetite: "She will sit in front of every fence post and open her quiver to every arrow" (Sir. 26:12). This rather sexist remark is not entirely his creation. Rather, it had rather ancient roots that went back the beginning of the Bible.

The Book of Genesis contains a story that is seldom read in public. It is about angelic beings, the "sons of God," who were unable to resist the charms of earthly women. They left their heavenly abode to have sex with them. Their illicit assignation produced offspring so monstrous that God destroyed them, along with all humanity, in the great flood: only the righteous Noah and his family were allowed to survive.[6] Because even angels were unable to control their sexual urges, Judean fathers went to great lengths to protect the virginity of their daughters from the lustful advances of earthly men. They preferred early marriage since it significantly reduced the time they were responsible for the care and protection of their daughters.

Most Judean girls were betrothed and wed when they were quite young. Josephus mentions that the daughters of the first century C.E. Jewish king

Agrippa were married when they were sixteen, ten, and six years of age. This was the second union for Agrippa's eldest daughter, who likely wed for the first time when she was only thirteen. Evidence from Egypt suggests that girls there typically married later, around twelve, to slightly older spouses.

Girls were under great pressure to become engaged quite young since failure to marry was tantamount to death. An Egyptian inscription laments the passing of a twenty-two-year-old Jewish woman who died while betrothed, "ripe for marriage like a rose in a garden nurtured by fresh rain." Unmarried and without children, this girl essentially ceased to exist since their was no one to carry on her name. To avoid such a tragic fate, nearly all of Salome Alexandra's female contemporaries — rich and poor alike — were typically wed, and mothers, before they reached our modern age of legal consent.[7]

Many today consider child marriage appalling. It was common in antiquity, but only for women. Men were typically much older than their brides. Philo, one of the more sophisticated representatives of his faith, remarked that men should marry between twenty-eight and twenty-five years of age. His contemporary Josephus apparently subscribed to this opinion and did not take a wife until he was about thirty. The extant historical information from ancient Judea and Jewish communities elsewhere in the Hellenistic world suggests that he was not unusual: thirty was the customary age of marriage for Jewish males. (In Roman society women typically married in their mid-teens to men who were often ten years older.)[8] While a young girl, Salome Alexandra's father would have been expected to betroth her to a considerably older man. Like other females her age, she would have had little, if any, role in the selection of her spouse.

The Price of Marriage

A girl was fortunate if she grew to love the man her father chose to be her husband. A fragment from a Dead Sea Scroll of Salome Alexandra's day illustrates the extent to which Judean females were merely chattel. It offers the following rather unsettling interpretation of the biblical laws regarding betrothal:

> If a [father betroths his daughter to a man], he must tell him all her defects. Why should he bring upon himself the judgment [of the curse that Moses said], "Cursed be the one who misdirects a blind person in his path" [4Q271 3 lines 8–9 interpreting Deut. 27:18].

What makes this passage particularly appalling is that it occurs in a lengthy section dealing with honesty in business: it treats women as mere property.[9]

A father who fails to disclose his daughter's defects to a potential suitor could, according to this text, be accused of fraud!

Philo's advice to a man who wishes to marry shows how little control Judean women had over their lives in Salome Alexandra's day:

> If, you should find the affections of your heart and soul centered on a young girl, go to her parents if they are living, and if not, to her brothers or other males who have custody of her, and disclose to them your desires towards her, as a free man should, ask for her hand in marriage and beg that you may not be found unworthy of her. For none of those who have custody of the young girl would be stupid enough to oppose your earnest request, especially, if upon examination, he finds that your feelings are not false or superficial, but genuine and firmly established [Philo, *Spec.* 3.67–68].

The girl is never allowed to speak: her opinion does not matter. Men haggled over brides just like they bartered in the market for sheep, cattle, and fruit!

We do not know if Salome Alexandra's future husband, Alexander Jannaeus, asked her father for her hand in marriage. Since he was the son of Judea's high priest and ruler, John Hyrcanus, we can assume that he too had little choice in the selection of his wife. John Hyrcanus in all likelihood chose Salome Alexandra for his son: her father likely had little to say in the matter.

Under normal circumstances Alexander Jannaeus would have paid Salome Alexandra's father a bride price (*mohar*), which was a sum of money given to the bride's parents to finalize the marriage contract. However, traditional Judean betrothal customs had undergone considerable change during the first century B.C.E. The bride-price was apparently no longer exchanged at the time of betrothal. Instead, an agreed upon sum that was to be paid to the young girl in the event of divorce or the death of her husband was specified in a document known as the *ketubbah*. Not surprisingly, the young girl's sexual status determined her monetary value. Egyptian Jewish marriage contracts dating back to the fifth century B.C.E. show that the *mohar* for a virgin was double that of widow or divorcée. Because the Talmud, although written nearly a millennia later, reflects this ancient practice, virgins were presumably valued at the same price during Salome Alexandra's lifetime.[10]

It was customary for a father to sweeten the *ketubbah*, and make his daughter a more desirable bride, by specifying the dowry in advance: money, goods, or property that she brought into the marriage and which technically belonged to her. Wealthy families offered great sums befitting their social status to make their daughters attractive for affluent and important suitors. But the dowry was often a great burden for the less fortunate. Philo urged the rich to help the poor provide their daughters with an ample dowry. The Judeans considered it so important that no circumstance, even death, prevented it from being given to the bride. If a father died before his daughter's wedding, the dowry was taken from his estate. Love, however, seldom factored into these financial arrangements since the couple often did not know one another. If a bride died before her wedding, the groom was exempt from mourning her passing. If he was a priest, he was not even allowed to defile himself by attending her funeral.[11]

A father was not the only person concerned for a bride's welfare: the groom had an interest in protecting his investment. He was expected to provide his wife with the traditional necessities of life: food, clothing, and shelter. Of the three, clothing was the only item that was discretionary: no society would have allowed a man to starve his wife or deny her shelter. Because garments in antiquity were loosely draped over the body, they were extremely durable and nearly impossible to outgrow. Many Judean women wore clothes that had been passed down through several generations; they seldom acquired the materials to make new garments. Because dye was a luxury of the rich, most women in Salome Alexandra's day would have looked quite drab. But as a princess, she would not have had to worry about such frugalities. She undoubtedly had access to fineries that were beyond the imagination of ordinary Judean women: elaborate dresses, the best food and medical care, and the comforts of a luxurious palace. But none of this would have mattered if she lost her most prized possession before her marriage — her virginity.

The Bible is quite harsh and unforgiving regarding premarital sex, but only for girls. It did not matter whether the relationship was consensual or not. According to the divine laws that God had given to Moses,

> if a man seduces a virgin who is not betrothed, and has sex with her, he shall pay her the bride price [*mohar*] and marry her. If her father refuses to give her to him, he must still pay him the customary bride price for virgins [Exod. 22:16–17].

This law merely regards the girl as a piece of damaged property; she has no say regarding her own body. Her partner, or violator, as long as he pays restitution, faces no further repercussions.

The biblical commandment allowing a father to marry his daughter to her seducer — a man who may have been her rapist! — is clearly unjust by modern standards. But it did not matter whether the young girl had lost her virginity through consensual sex or through force, since the consequence was the same — she would have had a difficult time finding a spouse. Judean men wanted virgin brides. The father of an unmarried non-virgin was legally bound to disclose her sexual status to any potential suitor in advance of betrothal or marriage. Failure to do so could potentially damage not only his reputation but also his family's, since a deceived husband could lodge a virginity suit. The biblical Book of Deuteronomy required the accused bride to undergo the following public humiliation should a suitor claim martial fraud:

> The father and mother of the girl shall take the proof of her virginity and bring it to the elders at the city gate. There the father of the girl shall say to the elders, I gave my daughter to this man in marriage, but he has come to hate her, and now he says terrible words against her, claiming: "I did not find your daughter a virgin." But here is the proof of my daughter's virginity! And they shall spread out the sheet before the elders of the city. Then the city elders shall take the man and reprimand him, besides fining him one hundred silver shekels, which they shall give to the girl's father, because the man slandered a virgin in Israel. Moreover, she shall remain his wife, and he may not divorce her as long as he lives. But if the accusation is true, and there is no evidence that the girl is a virgin, they shall bring the girl to the door of her father's house and there the men of the city shall stone her to death, because she committed a crime against Israel by prostituting in her father's house. By this means shall you purge the evil from your midst [Deut. 22:15–21].

Salome Alexandra had no reason to fear such allegations. As the future daughter-in-law of Judea's high priest, she would have been protected from any sexual violation. But for ordinary unattached girls, rape remained a constant threat. This is one of the many worries that led Ben Sira to write that the birth of a daughter was an occasion for great sorrow.

The New Testament provides some additional evidence about the precarious status of betrothed Judean girls. According to the Gospels of Matthew and Luke, Jesus' mother Mary became pregnant while betrothed to a man named Joseph. At first unaware of his wife's divine state (Christians believe her pregnancy was due to the immaculate conception), Joseph wrestled with two rather unsettling options. He could follow biblical law and expose her as an adulteress. If Josephus had chosen this course of action, Mary could have been stoned to death since her pregnancy provided obvious proof of her sexual transgression.[12] But few adulterous men would have been executed in ancient Judea since none, if charged, would have confessed to an illegal sexual act. A girl's testimony against her violator, moreover, would have been discounted since it was impossible to prove male paternity in antiquity: only a man's word counted. Joseph literally had the power to determine whether Mary would live or die.

Joseph's decision to acknowledge paternity had legal consequences: he could not change his mind and claim Jesus was not his son. A child born during betrothal was considered legitimate if the father accepted it as his offspring. If Joseph had not recognized Mary's child as his son, the community would have considered Jesus a *mamzer* ("bastard"). The Jewish Hellenistic composition known as the *Wisdom of Solomon*, which was likely written in Alexandria, Egypt, during Salome Alexandra's lifetime, shows how many Jews regarded children of questionable paternity:

> The children of adulterers will not reach maturity, and the offspring of an

unlawful sexual union will perish. Even if they live long they will be of no account, and they will not be held in honor when they become old. If they die young, they will have no hope or comfort on judgment day. For the end of an unrighteous generation is terrible [Wis. 3:16–19].

The Bible is clear that any child born out of marriage is illegitimate and permanently defiled: "No *mamzer* shall be admitted into the congregation of the Lord; none of his descendants, even in the tenth generation, shall be admitted into the congregation of the Lord."[13]

Sexual mores were changing rapidly in Salome Alexandra's day. Her society was becoming more liberal and biblical customs were often ignored. Because hormones were no different in the first century B.C.E. than today, it should not be surprising to find occasional references in ancient literature to premarital sex. There is some evidence that attitudes varied according to geographical location. Later written tradition tells us that the Galileans considered the Judeans promiscuous because they allowed the couple to spend an hour together before they entered the bridal chamber on their wedding day. As a result of their supposedly lax oversight of young girls, the Galileans could not be certain of a Judean bride's virginity before her marriage ceremony.[14]

We can be certain that Salome Alexandra's virginity was never called into question because the priests were obsessed with the ritual purity of their bloodlines. Everyone watched them closely to make certain they only entered into lawful unions. Josephus tells us that priestly lineages were even kept in the public registry for verification.[15] The marriage of a high priest was the most important of all. Philo writes on this matter:

> The high priest must not propose marriage to a mere virgin, but a virgin daughter of a priest descended from a family of priests, so that both bride and bridegroom belong to a single house and in a sense have the same blood ... but ordinary priests are allowed to marry the daughters of non-priests [*Spec.* 1.110–11].

Since there could be no doubt about the legitimacy of the high priest's male offspring, all Judeans were concerned with the martial practices of the clergy. Because Salome Alexandra's husband and two sons served as high priests, she was clearly a virgin at the time of her marriage.

A Royal Wedding for All

Marriage was so important in Salome Alexandra's Judea that even ordinary peasants were treated like royalty when they wed. Brides were adorned with beautiful apparel, and veiled, while grooms wore a crown. The wedding pageant was not merely part of the festivities, but it had legal ramifications.

It served as a public declaration by two families that a lawful marriage between their children had taken place. The entire community would have recognized any infant born nine months later as legitimate: the husband would have needed considerable proof to claim otherwise.

If the story of the marriage in Cana preserved in the Gospel of John describes customs that were practiced in Salome Alexandra's day, then weddings were among the few public occasions when women mixed freely with men. In some instances they lasted for seven days, and ended when the couple entered a special chamber. Rabbinic literature mentions that the bride went into this room first. According to some sources, a married woman prepared the wedding bed and helped the bride undress. Classical writings suggest that the groom arrived shortly thereafter and, after reciting a short prayer, consummated the marriage while the festivities continued outside. Later Jewish literature mentions the presence of two specially appointed friends who examined the couple before and after intercourse to verify that the marriage had been consummated. They also kept the evidence of the bride's virginity, the bloodstained sheet, to prevent the groom from destroying it and lodging a false virginity suit.[16]

By Salome Alexandra's day, Jews had largely abandoned the biblical custom of retaining the bloodstained sheet for future exhibition in case of a virginity suit. Josephus, Philo, and the Dead Sea Scrolls do not mention this ancient practice. Jews, perhaps under the influence of Hellenism, may have grown rather uncomfortable with this archaic rite. But there is some evidence that a physical examination of the bride took place before the wedding to determine her virginity, which shows that despite any advances in women's rights that had taken place in Salome Alexandra's Judea, a woman's word was worthless.[17]

An Unusual Union?

The Hellenistic kings of the Middle East were obsessed with their bloodlines. They devised some rather unique, and by modern standards unpleasant, customs to keep them absolutely pure. To the East of Judea, the Ptolemies adopted the ancient Egyptian custom of brother-sister marriage — traditionally taboo in Greek society — to preserve the purity of their royal bloodline. Although Greeks, they also practiced the Egyptian religion and portrayed themselves as incarnations of the Egyptian gods. Because marriage between a deity and a mere mortal would have contaminated their lineage, they had no choice but to marry their siblings to keep divinity, power, and wealth within their family.

To the north of Judea, the Seleucid kings of Syria found another way to maintain the purity of their royal bloodline. Although they never embraced brother-sister marriage, they sanctioned unions that were perhaps even more shocking to our modern sensibilities. The founder of the dynasty, Seleucus I Nicator (305–281 B.C.E.), married his son to his current wife, Stratonice, who had already borne him a daughter. Many subsequent Seleucid rulers married their sister-in-laws or cousins.[18]

The Hasmoneans restricted marriage for the same reason as their Egyptian and Seleucid counterparts. But they faced many obstacles in their quest to safeguard the purity of their royal bloodline. The Bible condemns sibling marriage as incest. Scripture also bans marriage to a mother or stepmother. But the Hasmoneans were rather clever and, after much reflection, they discovered an apparent loophole in God's divine laws that permitted them, like their Hellenistic neighbors, to keep marriage, power, and wealth within their family. God never prohibited marriage with a cousin, an uncle, or a niece. Josephus mentions two marriages between Hasmonean cousins: both were Salome Alexandra's sons. Because her family served as high priests and engaged in cousin marriage, the Judeans must have considered this practice acceptable.[19]

Because marriages between cousins within priestly families was apparently common in Judea, Salome Alexandra's father must have been descended from a long line of Hasmonean priests. Since Josephus was both a priest and a proud descendant of the Hasmoneans, he was likely her ancestor. Because he considers her a legitimate member of this family, she was clearly a Hasmonean by birth, and not through marriage.

Salome Alexandra undoubtedly belonged to an ancient family of Hasmonean priests. Although the priests were Judea's nobility, not all priests were equal. According to the Bible, King David had divided them into twenty-four families that were descended from the sons of Moses's brother Aaron: Eleazar and Ithamar. The Hasmoneans belonged to the priestly line of Joiarib; it was the first of the twenty-four priestly families that served in the temple on a rotation system. Although in theory all were equal, Josephus tells us that Joiarib was considered the elite (he was biased since he claimed descent from this family).

John Hyrcanus, as Judea's high priest and ruler, could have chosen daughters from any of the twenty-four priestly families to wed his sons. Given the Hasmonean propensity to keep marriage within the family, he undoubtedly selected women from Joiarib. Salome Alexandra's family likely belonged to the priestly line of Joiarib and served in the temple alongside their relatives. Prior to the Maccabean rebellion, her parents likely lived in the ancient Hasmonean seat of Modi'in. By the time she was born, the Hasmoneans had taken up residence in Jerusalem, which was certainly the place of her birth.

Salome Alexandra's marriage to Alexander Jannaeus, through whom she acquired the throne, was a September/May match. If the dates Josephus gives are correct, she was twenty-nine years old at the time and he was between fourteen and sixteen. The math is not easy, but it is there if you look carefully: Salome Alexandra, who ruled for nine years, died at seventy-three, which would make her sixty-four years old when she ascended the throne in 76 B.C.E. Her husband, Alexander Jannaeus, reigned for twenty-seven years (103–76 B.C.E.), which would make her thirty-seven years old in 103 B.C.E. when he became king. He was either forty-nine or fifty-one when he died (his age at the time of his death is uncertain due to variants in the manuscripts). Alexander Jannaeus was either twenty-four or twenty-two when Judah Aristobulus's widow, Salina Alexandra, placed him on the throne. The result: a bride of twenty-nine and a groom of somewhere between fourteen and sixteen.[20]

It is highly unlikely that a young man of fourteen or sixteen would have chosen a twenty-nine-year-old woman as his wife. The marriage of Salome Alexandra and Alexander Jannaeus was almost surely arranged by their parents, which was the custom of the time. It was clearly an unhappy union. But most scholars believe it was not her first tragic marriage. Most assume that she was a widow, and was forced to wed her brother-in-law in accordance with the biblical rules of levirate marriage.[21]

The name *levirate marriage* comes from the Latin (long the dominant ecclesiastical language of the Western Church) word *levir*, which is a translation of the Hebrew word for brother-in-law (*yabam*). According to the Bible:

> When brothers live together, and one of them dies without a son, the dead man's wife shall not be allowed to marry a stranger. Her husband's brother must marry her and have sex with her to perform a brother-in-law's duty to her. Her first-born son from this marriage will continue the name of her dead husband, so his name will not be blotted out from Israel [Deut. 25:5–6].

Levirate marriage treats the widow as mere property, whose primary purpose is to breed a male heir to inherit her late husband's estate. But this seemingly cruel institution was intended as a mechanism to help her survive. In a world that prized only virgin brides, a widow would have had a difficult time finding a spouse. Levirate marriage guaranteed her a protector from her late husband's family, and the opportunity to produce children to care for her in her old age. It may be a cruel institution, but many in Salome Alexandra's Judea were convinced that the possible alternatives for an unattached female were worse — abandonment, slavery, or prostitution.

A widow had no choice when it came to levirate marriage. She was required to have sexual relations with her brother-in-law to produce a son.

But he had the option of refusing to marry her. There were, however, some rather severe consequences should he choose to do so. Scripture allowed her to spit in his face and remove his sandal: both signs of disrespect. This is one of the few instances in the Bible where a woman is allowed to condemn a man in public. But she is not granted any additional rights. The man is the focus of this humiliating ritual; he is cursed for failing to live up to his societal responsibilities, and produce a male heir to carry on his late brother's name. She is left to fend for herself.

By the Hellenistic period many Jews apparently had come to view levirate marriage as an archaic and sexist institution. They apparently found it problematic since it contradicts the biblical laws of incest forbidding marriage to a sister-in-law. Josephus found it so troubling that he used a rather sexist argument to justify it: he regards the widow as her brother-in-law's sexual chattel. He claims levirate marriage was intended to keep property and inheritance within the family. No surviving text tells us what women thought of this institution.[22]

There are four reasons why Salome Alexandra could not have contracted a levirate marriage. First, no ancient writer mentions such a union: there is absolutely no evidence that she married her husband's brother, Judah Aristobulus. Second, marriage to a widow, a divorced woman, or a prostitute disqualified a man from serving as high priest. Because Salome Alexandra's husband, Alexander Jannaeus, was high priest, she could not have been a widow when she married him: if she had, he would have been ineligible to hold this sacred office. Third, Josephus always refers to Hyrcanus (II) as the son of Salome Alexandra and Alexander Jannaeus. If she had entered into a levirate marriage, Hyrcanus (II) would have been the legal son of Judah Aristobulus and Salome Alexandra. Fourth, Josephus tells us that Judah Aristobulus was married to Salina Alexandra. If Josephus did not claim that Salina and Salome were the same person, neither should we. For these reasons, we can say with confidence that Salome Alexandra was a virgin when she married Alexander Jannaeus.[23]

Salome Alexandra was married to her husband for approximately thirty-five years. She was twenty-nine when she wed him; she was sixty-four when he died. We have no idea what their relationship was like, but it clearly grew acrimonious over time. He displayed few of the attributes one expects of a high priest: he consorted with concubines and murdered many of his religious opponents. We do not know whether Salome Alexandra ever fell out of love with him, assuming she had any feelings of devotion towards him at all. Even if she hated him, it would have been difficult for her to terminate their union.

We know little about divorce in ancient Judea. Although the Egyptian Jewish community at Elephantine Island allowed women unilateral divorce, there is no evidence it was permitted in Salome Alexandra's Judea. Josephus writes that two women from the Herodian family terminated their marriages, but he denounces these dissolutions as contrary to Jewish law: they were apparently the exception rather than the rule.[24] Given the economic status of most Judean females, it is safe to say that divorce was seldom, if ever, a viable option. A poor woman could not have afforded to leave her spouse; and a rich woman, with rare exceptions, would not have been allowed to disgrace her family by initiating a separation. Under no circumstances can we imagine the wife of a high priest seeking to terminate her marriage. Only Alexander Jannaeus's death could have released Salome Alexandra from her vows. Unfortunately, their marriage lasted for over three decades.

The Lost Women of Judea

Scholars face an insurmountable obstacle in attempting to reconstruct the lives of the married women of Salome Alexandra's time — there is little evidence they existed! The names of 267 Judean women from the period between 330 B.C.E.–200 C.E. have been preserved in the historical and archaeological record. For this same span, we know the names of approximately 2,300 males. These figures are startling for what they reveal: if factual, they indicate that women made up only 11.3 percent of Judean society. But this figure cannot be correct since demographic studies show that females generally comprise 50 percent of any population: a society with less than this number of women would be facing rapid extinction.[25] This low number is attributable to sexism. The names of Judean females were seldom preserved in the written record, or etched in stone. This makes Salome Alexandra even more unique for her time since she was known by her name alone: her family has been erased from the historical record.

Archaeologists have uncovered some surprising information about life among Judea's elite that helps us to understand the dangers of Salome Alexandra's world. In 1960 construction workers accidentally discovered a burial cave in the Jerusalem suburb of Giv'at Hamivtar. It was full of burial boxes known as ossuaries: a clear indication this tomb belonged to one of Judea's elite families. One of the ossuaries in this tomb bears the name of a young Judean male named Yehochanan. When archaeologists opened it, they found a 4½-inch nail protruding from his right heel bone — he had been crucified! After an agonizing and prolonged death (crucifixion was intended to be slow and often lasted for days) the Romans had trouble removing the bent nail that held his foot to the upright beam of his cross. They had no choice but to leave it embedded in his ankle. It is our only extant evidence of crucifixion.

There are several explanations to account for the absence of any other physical remains of crucifixion from the archaeological record. Nailing a body to a cross took time and required much iron, which was a valuable commodity in antiquity. The Romans preferred to tie their victims to the horizontal beam of the cross for reasons of cost and efficiency; they crucified as many as 6,000 at a time. Crucifixion without any nails would have left little, if any, physical trace on the bones. Nailing was merely done to increase pain and suffering. In order to make crucifixion more humiliating, and to amuse themselves, Roman soldiers sometimes nailed victims to crosses in different positions. But even nailing would be difficult to detect since rain and moisture usually degrade skeletal remains. As for the nails of these victims, there is rather revolting reason for their absence from the archaeological record: people wore them as amulets to harness their supposed healing powers.[26]

Public crucifixion is a horror we cannot imagine in our so-called civilized world. But this was not true in Salome Alexandra's Judea. Yehochanan's burial reveals that even the affluent were not immune from violence. Salome Alexandra knew the horror of this type of execution firsthand: her husband in a fit of anger crucified 800 Judeans in a single day! Even women were crucified in her homeland.[27]

A look at Yehochanan's family reveals some shocking facts about the precarious lives of women in Salome Alexandra's homeland. Archaeologists found the remains of eleven males, twelve females, and twelve children in his family's tomb. Two, a sixteen-year-old man and a twenty-four-year-old woman, appear to have been burned to death. Another female perished from a mace blow. One child died from an arrow wound to the back of its head, while three others perished from malnutrition. Despite their elite status, approximately 14 percent of the individuals in this tomb were murdered![28]

In 1990 archaeologists discovered another burial cave in Jerusalem containing the remains of the former high priest Caiaphas — the man who participated in Jesus' trial! Several ossuaries in his sepulcher contain the names of women, including a Salome and a Miriam. Caiaphas presumably named this Salome, likely his daughter, after our queen. As the offspring of a high priest, she would have led a life of affluence like Salome Alexandra.

We would not expect to find evidence of violent death in Caiaphas's family since he was the high priest. Nevertheless, the mortality figures of his relations are shocking. Of the sixty-three individuals interred in his tomb, 40 percent died before their fifth birthday. Nearly 63 percent never reached puberty.[29] Because Caiaphas and his family presumably had access to better diet and medical care than most Judeans, these figures are rather startling. They counter the traditional belief that higher social status should be expressed in the archaeological record through lower mortality rates. This tomb shows that even priestly families like Salome Alexandra's led precarious lives that few of us can comprehend.

The Remembered Queen

Salome Alexandra is largely forgotten today. But this was not true in antiquity. Generations of mothers after her death named their daughters Salome to honor the woman who had once ruled men. The archaeological evidence suggests that she lived in a cruel world in which even rich women were not immune from violence. Yet, she managed to defy the odds, survive numerous wars — both civil and foreign — and other untold dangers to become her nation's sole monarch at the rather advanced age of sixty-four. These are remarkable feats for a woman of any era.

To understand the many impediments Salome Alexandra had to overcome before she became Judea's monarch, we must recount the life of the man who shaped the times in which she and her husband lived — her father-in-law, John Hyrcanus. His legacy cast a dark shadow over her entire life. He was a cruel, violent, and heartless man who brought untold suffering to his people. He became immensely unpopular when he changed Judea's religion. When Salome Alexandra took power, she immediately undid all his reforms to bring about an unparalleled period of peace and prosperity. Yet, Josephus was convinced that John Hyrcanus, not Salome Alexandra, had presided over Judea's Golden Age — a time of miracles.

5

John Hyrcanus
The Prophet?

John [Hyrcanus] lived the remainder of his life very happily, and ruled the government in a most extraordinary manner for thirty-three years. He died, leaving five sons. He was truly a blessed man.... He possessed the three most desirable things in the world: the rule of the nation, the high priesthood, and the gift of prophecy. — Josephus, *War* 1.68.

High priest; politician; warrior; and the last Hasmonean to have fought the Seleucids in Mattathias's war of independence to create a Jewish state — John Hyrcanus was all these and much more. He was a prophet; he performed miracles. Salome Alexandra was seven years old when he became Judea's high priest and political leader; she was thirty-six when he died. Although she lived nearly half her life under his rule, and married his son, Josephus tells us nothing about their relationship. In his *Antiquities* he implies they never met. Yet, no other person shaped her life more than John Hyrcanus. Because we cannot tell her story without telling his, we must examine the tumultuous life of the man Josephus considered "blessed" by God to see how he shaped her world.[1]

An Unexpected Heir

Salome Alexandra and John Hyrcanus had one thing in common: they both had two names. One is Hebrew; the other is Greek. His Hebrew name is Yehohanan, which means "God has been gracious." It is sometimes translated as Jonathan, but most frequently as John. Many of his subjects, however, called him Hyrcanus: a Greek name of unknown derivation that some ancient writers believed referred to his conquest of the Hyrcanian (modern Iran) people.[2]

John Hyrcanus is Josephus's hero. He apparently named his first-born son after him.[3] Josephus fancied himself a priest, a general, and a prophet like John Hyrcanus. There is no doubt these men held the first two offices, but whether either was a prophet must remain a matter of faith since history cannot prove the miraculous. Although Josephus emphasizes the similarities between himself and his idol, there were some profound differences. Josephus's religious, political, and military accomplishments were minimal. He never became high priest, head of state, or led troops to a great military victory like John Hyrcanus. Josephus, moreover, was a man shaped by his times while John Hyrcanus changed his nation as he saw fit. But the greatest difference between the two is that Josephus helped destroy Judea while John Hyrcanus played an instrumental role in creating the Hasmonean State.

When we read Josephus's accounts of the Hasmonean period, we must keep in mind that his admiration of John Hyrcanus causes him to overlook many of his hero's flaws and mistakes. Josephus depicts him as a charismatic man with the ability to inspire greatness in others. He claims God blesses him more than any Hasmonean ruler, and preserves him through countless adversities and misfortunes. Yet, despite all his accolades, Josephus knows that his hero is a deeply flawed man. John Hyrcanus is violent, heartless, impious, and often showed little regard for his people or his family. Josephus, despite his efforts to praise him, believes his hero made the greatest mistake in Hasmonean history when he bequeathed his kingdom to his spouse.

John Hyrcanus's wife is one of the greatest personalities of the Hellenistic period. Yet, Josephus tells us nothing about her — not even her name. This omission should not be surprising since he never mentions the names of his own wives in his autobiography. When describing the remarkable story of John Hyrcanus's life, we must remember that he did not rule alone, but that his spouse undoubtedly played a major role in his administration, and should be given some credit for his successes. Unfortunately, we know nothing about how she lived, just the tragic story of how she died. But she was not the first prominent woman to have dominated Hasmonean men. John Hyrcanus's formidable mother clearly molded his character, and led him to believe that the interests of the Judean state would best be served by entrusting it to his wife. We do not know her name; we only know how she died.

The Warrior-Priest

John Hyrcanus was one of Simon's four sons. If the author of 1 Maccabees lists them according to their ages, then he was the second in order of birth.[4] His elder brother, Judas, was likely named after John Hyrcanus's famous uncle and freedom fighter, the legendary "Hammer." Simon apparently named his third son, Mattathias, after his father, whose defiance of the Seleucid edict banning Judaism ignited the Maccabean rebellion. Although John Hyrcanus was born into Judea's most distinguished family, he was not supposed to succeed his father as high priest and political leader: positions first held by his uncle Jonathan. Simon was apparently grooming Judas to assume these roles, but his plan did not come to fruition. John Hyrcanus's improbable rise to power is among the most extraordinary and sordid tales in the remarkable history of the Hasmonean family.

Simon was the last surviving son of Mattathias when he became Judea's high priest and political leader. But he was an accidental ruler; he earned these positions simply by outliving his siblings. For reasons unknown, his father, Mattathias, had chosen Simon's younger brother, Judas, to lead his movement. Simon was apparently known more for his discerning intellect than his military prowess. According to one undoubtedly apocryphal tale, Mattathias said to his sons, "Here is your brother Simon who, I know, is wise in counsel; always listen to him; he shall be your father."[5] After Judas's death, Jonathan led his family's movement. He exceeded all expectations by becoming the first of Mattathias's children to assume the high priesthood. When the Seleucid monarch Trypho assassinated him, Simon assumed his brother's offices.

Salome Alexandra was likely born in 141 B.C.E., just one year after Simon became Judea's high priest and political leader. Although many likely thought he would not amount to much, he accomplished the impossible — he broke free from the Seleucids and created the Hasmonean State. Salome Alexandra grew up during this celebrated era when one of the original Maccabees ruled Judea. It was a glorious time of hope; and then things quickly took a turn for the worse. After achieving unprecedented greatness, Simon sunk to a new low. He adopted all the vices, but few of the virtues, of his pagan neighbors. Hellenism destroyed him.

In his latter years Simon became a mere shadow of the great man who had led the Judeans in their successful fight for freedom. When the Seleucids violated their treaty and invaded Judea, Simon's people expected him to protect them. Now too old in years and too weak in spirit, he passed the mantel of leadership to his sons, John Hyrcanus and Judas, telling them:

> My brothers and I and my father's house have fought the wars of Israel from our youth until this day, and things have prospered because of our deeds: we have saved Israel on many occasions. But I am now old, but you thankfully are mature enough. Take my place and my brother's; go out, and fight for our nation, and may the help from heaven be with you [1 Macc. 16:2–3].

John Hyrcanus saved the day, and turned the tide of battle in Judea's favor by leading the first recorded Hasmonean cavalry charge. Now that there was peace, Simon decided to make a tour of his territories, accompanied by two of his sons, Judas and Mattathias. We do not know why John Hyrcanus did not go along. His absence proved fortuitous; it saved the Hasmonean dynasty from certain extinction.

The accounts of Simon's trip indicate that it was not undertaken merely for matters of state. Rather, it was an opportunity for him and his two sons to burden his hosts with the obligation of throwing elaborate parties for the royal entourage. Josephus and 1 Maccabees portray it as a rather unflattering moment in the history of the Hasmonean dynasty. They agree that Simon had become a debauched Hellenistic monarch. The feasts held in his honor were more typical of the Greek symposia (male drinking parties) than the traditional Judean fare; they culminated in bouts of excessive drinking. Alcohol nearly ended the Judean state.

According to the extant accounts, Simon decided to visit his son-in-law Ptolemy at the fortress of Dok, along the Jordan River. He literally walked into a trap. Ptolemy was secretly in league with the Seleucids. He waited until his royal guests were inebriated and assassinated them. Simon's rather unbecoming death marks the end of an era; there were no sons of Mattathias to lead the nascent Judean State.

It is here where the details become unclear. Josephus and 1 Maccabees agree that John Hyrcanus was not there that fateful night and that Ptolemy sent assassins to Gazara (modern Israel) to kill him. The author of 1 Maccabees insists that Ptolemy murdered Simon and his sons, but says nothing about his spouse. But Josephus claims that Ptolemy took Simon's wife and sons captive. Faced with such irreconcilable accounts, it is difficult to determine which to believe. As is often the case, the truth is likely somewhere in the middle. Josephus likely copied this story from the lost history of Nicolaus of Damascus, who loved telling tales of Hasmonean misfortune. The most likely scenario is that Ptolemy killed Simon and all his sons, except John Hyrcanus. He only took Simon's wife captive. By keeping Simon's sons alive, Nicolaus diminishes the heroism of John Hyrcanus's mother: Nicolaus implies that she would not have been so courageous if her children had not been present.

John Hyrcanus eluded Ptolemy's assassins and reached the safety of Jerusalem. Once there, he quickly underwent the public consecration ceremony to become Judea's high priest. After amassing a sizable army, he set out for Dok. What happened next is among the most tragic stories in Judean history.

Dok was nearly impregnable. Situated high above the lush oasis of Jericho, it was well outside the range of the artillery of the time. Today, it is reached by a rather precipitous climb up narrow and twisting steps (it is the site of a Greek Orthodox monastery marking the spot where, according to later Christian tradition, Satan tempted Jesus). Its inaccessibility did not matter

Jericho Docus Byzantine church (aerial view from east). Located above the city of Jericho, atop the traditional mountain where Satan tempted Jesus, the Hasmonean Fortress of Dok guarded the roads that passed through the oasis of Jericho. Here, Salome Alexandra's father-in-law, the high priest John Hyrcanus, besieged Ptolemy to rescue his mother. The ruins of a later Byzantine Christian church sit atop the Hasmonean fortress (Todd Bolen/BiblePlaces.com).

to John Hyrcanus; he was determined to do anything to rescue his mother. Ruins of siege works there dating to this time bear physical witness to his determination to capture it.[6] But Dok proved impenetrable. In desperation, he ordered his men to scale its steep cliffs. Ptolemy tortured his mother atop Dok's walls to halt their advance. Her tragic end is a story worth telling in full, not only for the insight that it sheds on the women of the Hasmonean family, but also for what it tells us about Salome Alexandra's future father-in-law.

A Mother Like no Other

According to the version of Dok's siege Josephus chose to preserve, John Hyrcanus became panic-stricken when he saw Ptolemy's henchmen torturing his mother and brothers. But she is the central character of his account: John Hyrcanus's siblings, despite Josephus's assertion to the contrary, were certainly dead. Nevertheless, Josephus's account of this blockade is remarkable. Because it is unlikely that he would have fabricated such a tale of female heroism — especially one that portrays John Hyrcanus unfavorably — we can be certain that the basic details of Josephus's account are trustworthy.

Josephus's description of John Hyrcanus's mother's defiance of Ptolemy is among the most moving passages in his books:

> His mother was neither unshaken by the torture she received nor the death threats. She stretched out her hands and begged her son not to be moved by her injuries to spare such an impious man; to her, death at Ptolemy's hands would be better than a long life, as long as he avenged the wrongs that he had done to their family [*War* 1.58].

John Hyrcanus's mother did not merely appeal to her belief in life after death to encourage him to avenge his father's death. Rather, she alluded to a famous incident that had taken place during the Seleucid monarch Antiochus (IV) Epiphanes's persecution as a call to martyrdom.

During the darkest hours of the Maccabean rebellion, when it appeared the Judeans would never win their independence, the Seleucids arrested an unnamed mother and her seven sons for practicing Judaism. To convince her to renounce her faith, Antiochus Epiphanes ordered her children tortured and killed before her eyes. She watched helplessly as the Syrians cut out each of her sons' tongues, scalped their heads, and amputated their hands and feet before casting them into a hot cauldron. Instead of yielding to her oppressors' demands to forsake her religion,

> she encouraged each of them in their ancestral language. Filled with a noble spirit, she reinforced her women's reasoning with a man's courage and said to them, "I do not know how you came into being in my womb. It was not I who gave you life and breath, nor I who set in order the substance of which each of you is composed. The creator of the world, who shaped humanity and ordained everything, will in his mercy give life and breath back to you again, because you love his laws more than you love yourself" [2 Macc. 7:21–23].

After watching her children suffer and perish, this unnamed mother voluntarily went to her death, confident that God would right this injustice, if not in the this lifetime, then in the next. But John Hyrcanus did not act in such a glorious manner; he abandoned his mother to a slow and horrible death. The reason for his callous act — religion.

"For Six Years You May Sow Your Land"

According to the Bible, every "seventh year" is a time of physical and spiritual renewal when debts were cancelled and slaves were set free. Known as the Sabbatical Year, it was not merely a time of remission from labor, but a period of rest for the land as well:

> For six years you may sow your land and harvest its yield; but the seventh year you shall let it rest and lie fallow, so that the poor among your people may eat; and what they leave behind the wild animals may eat [Exod. 23:10–11].

The Sabbatical Year was a symbolic return to Eden and a time of spiritual reflection. Hired workers and immigrants were free to harvest anything that grew naturally. The Judeans were supposed to trust God to provide for their needs. But the biblical idea of the Sabbatical Year did not always correspond to reality in Salome Alexandra's Judea. With no manna forthcoming, her people had no recourse but to plant their crops; the land was sometimes not allowed to return to its pristine state; debts were often not forgiven; and slaves frequently toiled with no release in sight.

If all Judeans had observed the biblical proscription to the letter, and refrained from planting crops during the Sabbatical Year, massive famine would have ensued and the economy would have collapsed (modern Jews and Christians ignore this biblical precept for these reasons). Because a large number of Jews did observe it, the government was forced to fund a stimulus package to alleviate famine and curtail economic distress.[7]

Josephus tells his readers that the Sabbatical Year was like the Sabbath: God prohibited fighting during both.[8] As high priest, John Hyrcanus would have been expected to observe God's laws to the letter. Because the Sabbatical Year arrived while he was trying to rescue his mother, he had no choice but to end his siege and leave her in God's hands. Or did he?

There is a problem with Josephus's account of John Hyrcanus's behavior — the Bible does not ban fighting during the Sabbatical Year. In the early years of Mattathias's rebellion, the Seleucids killed Jews who had refused to fight on the Sabbath. Mattathias quickly realized this religious prohibition put the Judeans at a great military disadvantage. He therefore ordered his men to wage war on the Sabbath. His decree proved decisive in defeating the Seleucids, and creating the Judean state. Because the Hasmoneans by this time had long fought their enemies on the Sabbath, there was no need for John Hyrcanus to curtail his siege. His subsequent actions call into question Josephus's entire story. Shortly after he abandoned his mother, he took up arms to defend himself against a Seleucid invasion even though it was still the Sabbatical Year.

John Hyrcanus had a practical reason for allowing his mother to die a slow and cruel death. While he was besieging Ptolemy, he received word that the Seleucid monarch Antiochus Sidetes (reigned 138–29 B.C.E.) was preparing to invade Judea. The speed and timing of this assault are not coincidental.

Josephus suggests that Ptolemy had acted in league with the Seleucids: they likely promised him territory and a title in exchange for murdering the Hasmonean royal family.

Now facing a war on two fronts, John Hyrcanus decided his best option was to abandon his mother and defend Jerusalem. His abrupt departure left Ptolemy free to do as he wished. Ptolemy killed John Hyrcanus's mother and fled to the Hellenistic metropolis of Philadelphia, east of the Jordan River (modern Jordan). There, he sought and received sanctuary from a local despot named Zeno. John Hyrcanus never avenged his mother's death; if he had, Josephus would have certainly told us so.

Salome Alexandra was six years old at this time. Her future husband, Alexander Jannaeus, would not be born for another eight or ten years. Although we cannot say with certainty that she was in Jerusalem with John Hyrcanus, it is unlikely that her family would have been elsewhere. Jerusalem was Judea's largest fortified city; the capital of the Hasmonean State; the site of Judaism's most sacred shrine; and the home of the high priests. If not already residing there, Salome Alexandra's family certainly would have sought sanctuary with their relatives in Jerusalem at this time. Likely trapped inside the city during the Seleucid siege, the young Salome Alexandra undoubtedly witnessed countless horrors, only a few of which Josephus describes. Those he records are quite disturbing to read, even though they took place over two thousand years ago. What makes them particularly appalling is that the worst were not committed by the enemy, but by her future father-in-law.

The Wrath of the "Pious"

Nothing in the ancient world was more feared than siege warfare; it often lasted for years. Josephus knew this first-hand; the Romans had besieged him in the Galilean city of Jotapata for forty-seven days.[9] Women, children, and the elderly, as Josephus notes, fared worst in this type of combat since food was often restricted to fighting men. The disease and famine that inevitably accompanied most sieges forced people to follow their baser instincts to survive. This was true of Antiochus Sidetes's siege; it quickly compelled Judea's elite to abandon all semblance of civilization. But no one trapped in Jerusalem acted worse than John Hyrcanus. He did something so atrocious, and presumably well-known to his readers, that Josephus could not omit it from his narrative.

Antiochus Sidetes surrounded Jerusalem with a deep ditch and seven military camps. He then built one hundred mobile siege towers, each three stories in height. The sound of these weapons' massive beams pounding the city's walls must have been horrifying and incessant; battering rams were often used day and night. We can scarcely imagine how the young Salome Alexandra felt witnessing death first-hand. The trauma she experienced at this time may explain her later reluctance to engage in gratuitous violence when she became Judea's ruler: she always sought novel ways to make peace with her nation's longstanding enemies that avoided bloodshed.

Antiochus Sidetes had the advantage since siege warfare almost always favors the assailant rather than the besieged. Able to bring in fresh supplies and additional men, only an outbreak of disease, or the unexpected arrival of an opposing force, could curtail his assault. Knowing that his adversary would eventually breach Jerusalem's walls, John Hyrcanus adopted a rather audacious strategy to thwart the Syrian assault. He sent raiding parties outside the city to attack the Seleucid siege engines. His men inflicted great causalities on their unsuspecting foes, and damaged their implements of war. Soon afterwards, a downpour alleviated Jerusalem's water shortage. Many Judeans, and likely some Seleucids, must have considered this temporary reversal of fortune nothing less than a miracle. But it proved short-lived; the siege continued. With no relief forthcoming, and hope quickly fading in the city, John Hyrcanus decided to do something many of his people considered unforgivable.

In a desperate bid to extend Jerusalem's rapidly dwindling supplies, John Hyrcanus expelled all noncombatants. His edict presumably did not include the families of the rich and powerful, or the military. Despite this callous act, Josephus tries to exonerate his hero by focusing on Antiochus Sidetes's equally coldhearted response:

> Antiochus [Sidetes] prevented those who had been expelled from the city to pass through his camp, and, trapped between the two lines, they were starving [*Ant.* 13.241].

John Hyrcanus's plan had backfired. Now the sound of the battering rams was muffled by the desperate pleas of Jerusalem's citizens caught between two warring forces, each determined to kill the other.

A Time for Celebration?

The Festival of Tabernacles, also known by its Hebrew name "Sukkoth" (booths), is, along with the Festival of Unleavened Bread and the Festival of Weeks, one of the three religious holidays the Bible requires all Jews to observe in Jerusalem. Josephus calls it "very sacred, holiest, and most important" of the three.[10] Children like Salome Alexandra looked forward to its celebration because it involved the ancient equivalent of family camping. The Bible commands Jews to construct and reside in simple reed huts (*sukkoth*) for seven

Sukkot priestly blessing panorama. Also known as the Festival of Booths or Tabernacles, the agricultural holiday of Sukkot remains one of the most popular
Jewish celebrations. It originally commemorated the end of the autumn harvest
and the beginning of planting, and later became associated with the Jerusalem
Temple and Salome Alexandra's family (Todd Bolen/BiblePlaces.com).

days to remind them of the shelters their ancestors had lived in during the
Exodus when Moses led the Jews out of Egyptian slavery. Celebrants also
carry the lulav — a bundle of palm, willow, and myrtle branches — and a
lemon-like fruit called an *etrog* to symbolize God's sovereignty over creation.[11]

Tabernacles was of great political importance to the Hasmoneans. It is
the only biblical holiday connected with the Jerusalem temple. When King
David's son Solomon, the wisest man in the Bible, built this sanctuary, his
dedication ceremony coincided with the beginning of Tabernacles. Centuries
later, under the leadership of Nehemiah and Ezra, the Jews were allowed to
return to Jerusalem from their captivity in Babylon. Facing many dangers,
they persisted and rebuilt the temple, reinstated the sacrifices, and celebrated
Tabernacles for the first time in nearly seventy years. On this occasion the
prophet Zechariah delivered a rather ominous sermon predicting war and
drought if the Jewish community ever failed to observe this holiday.

The Festival of Tabernacles was particularly important to the Hasmoneans because of its connection with the Jerusalem temple. According to
the author of 1 Maccabees, after the Jews had expelled the Seleucids from
Jerusalem, Judas the "Hammer" established an eight-day holiday to celebrate
the cleansing of the temple. According to the book of 2 Maccabees, the Jews
celebrated this new festival, known as Hanukkah, "with rejoicing in the manner of Tabernacles." After Judas's brother, Jonathan, was consecrated as the
first Hasmonean high priest during Tabernacles, this holiday effectively became
a yearly celebration of his family.[12]

The arrival of Tabernacles presented John Hyrcanus with a great dilemma. If he failed to observe it, his subjects would likely view the Seleucid siege of Jerusalem as the fulfillment of Zechariah's prophecy of doom and give up all hope. But to celebrate such a joyous festival while Jews he had expelled from the city were literally screaming and dying just outside the city's walls was unconscionable. His subjects agreed. They defied his order, opened the gates, and let the refugees inside. Facing a potential coup, John Hyrcanus had no recourse but to seek a diplomatic solution to retain his position as Judea's political leader and high priest.

According to Josephus, John Hyrcanus sent envoys to Antiochus Sidetes requesting a seven-day truce to celebrate Tabernacles. Sidetes not only agreed, but he gave the Jews bulls and vessels of gold and silver filled with spices for their celebration.[13] The two immediately began negotiations to end the siege. Antiochus Sidetes asked for the port city of Joppa, the return of towns Simon had supposedly annexed from Seleucia, and the placement of a Syrian garrison in Jerusalem. John Hyrcanus refused to accept the latter condition since his father had expelled these Seleucid soldiers from the city. In lieu of this request, he offered three hundred hostages and five hundred talents. Antiochus Sidetes accepted, but demanded the demolition of Jerusalem's walls, a military alliance, and the payment of tribute. John Hyrcanus agreed; however, he was short of cash. To meet his financial obligation, he committed a sacrilege by plundering King David's tomb. He found so much wealth inside its vaults that he had enough left over to hire a mercenary army.

In a later section of his *Antiquities*, Josephus preserves several Roman senatorial decrees that he likely copied from actual documents. One of these, which mentions an "Antiochus," apparently dates to this time and offers another explanation for the end of the siege. It claims that John Hyrcanus had sent a delegation to Rome to renew his late uncle Judas's treaty. The Roman Senate recognized Judean sovereignty, but refused to commit troops to help the Hasmoneans fight the Seleucids. John Hyrcanus nevertheless scored a diplomatic coup, and likely saved Judea, when the Senate gave his emissaries money from the public treasury for their return, along with a decree guaranteeing their safety. It was nothing less than a public declaration that the Romans would not tolerate the Seleucid annexation of Judea.

The Romans left Antiochus Sidetes no choice but to abandon his dream of conquering Salome Alexandra's homeland. But he had a problem: he needed a way to save face, and not appear weak. The fortuitous arrival of a religious holiday gave him a way out of his predicament. Religious tolerance was a hallmark of Hellenism; the Greeks had always respected the gods of the peoples they had conquered. By showing amnesty towards his adversary, and furnishing the sacrifices and accouterments necessary to celebrate Tabernacles,

Antiochus Sidetes could portray himself as a merciful monarch who respected all faiths, while avoiding a confrontation with Rome. His plan worked. Even Josephus ironically acknowledges that Antiochus Sidetes, not John Hyrcanus, subsequently became known as "the Pious."[14]

A Reluctant Ally

In 130/129 B.C.E., just over five years after Antiochus Sidetes's siege of Jerusalem, John Hyrcanus accompanied his former nemesis on a military campaign to Parthia. Salome Alexandra was eleven or twelve at the time — old enough to realize the magnitude of this unprecedented event. It was a dangerous venture because the Parthians were among the fiercest warriors in the antiquity. Their vast empire stretched from Seleucia's eastern border to the Persian Gulf (modern Iran) and beyond. Given its vast size and population, it was virtually impossible for the Seleucids to subdue Parthia; the mighty Roman Empire never conquered it. Nevertheless, Antiochus Sidetes had good reason to attack the Parthians — they were holding his brother captive.

Storage jars, cooking vessels, and bowls such as these would have been found in all homes in Salome Alexandra's Judea. The jars held grain, oil, water, and other foodstuffs. Such jars would have also held provisions for soldiers (Todd Bolen/BiblePlaces.com).

The ostensible goal of Antiochus Sidetes's expedition was to restore Seleucid honor by winning the release of its former king, his brother Demetrius III (king ca. 97/6–87 B.C.E.). Ten years earlier, Demetrius had invaded Parthia in a foolish bid to emulate Alexander the Great's conquests. The campaign ended in disaster and the Parthians took him prisoner. Antiochus Sidetes's plan to free his sibling was as dangerous as it was reckless. He had to penetrate far into Parthian territory, locate his brother, and fight his way back to Syria. He needed John Hyrcanus's legions to accomplish this impossible mission.

The Jews were among the fiercest warriors in the ancient world. Many countries employed Jewish soldiers, including the Ptolemies and the Seleucids. Alexander the Great recognized their military skills and incorporated Jewish troops into his army. Jewish soldiers later saved Julius Caesar during the Roman civil wars.[15] Given their long and distinguished military history, Antiochus Sides apparently believed that John Hyrcanus's legions were necessary to defeat the Parthians.

Josephus tells us nothing about John Hyrcanus's preparations for this expedition. But he could only have gathered the needed troops through mass conscription and the hiring of additional mercenaries. Both measures would have been extremely unpopular; they would have required a considerable increase in taxation. But there was a problem: Antiochus Sidetes was overconfident and ill-prepared. John Hyrcanus must have realized this, and feared he would die in a distant land fighting a futile cause that was not his own.

If the Roman historian Justin's account of this expedition is even partially factual, it had virtually no chance of success. (Justin's book is an abbreviated version, with his own additions, of the lost history of the first century C.E. Celtic [modern France] Roman historian Pompeius Trogus.) Justin's description of Antiochus Sidetes's baggage train makes it sound like he was planning a vacation rather than an invasion:

> There was as much provision in it for luxurious living as for fighting a war; 80,000 men-at-arms were attended by 300,000 camp followers, most of whom were cooks, bakers, and actors. There was so much silver and gold that even the common soldiers used nails of gold in the soles of their leather boots, and walked atop the substance people so love that they fight over it with the sword. Even their cooking pots were made of silver. It was as though they were marching to a banquet rather than to a battle [Justin, *History*, 38.10.2–4].

If Justin's description sounds rather implausible, what happened next is even more remarkable.

Josephus was so worried his readers would doubt the veracity of his account that he took the unusual step of identifying his source: a book by the esteemed historian Nicolas of Damascus. According to Nicolaus, the fortuitous arrival of a religious holiday once again saved John Hyrcanus from a catastrophe. This time it was the agricultural festival known as Pentecost (*Shavu'o*t in Hebrew), which was also known as the Festival of Weeks. Josephus writes:

> After defeating Indates, the Parthian general, and setting up a victory monument at the Lycus River, Antiochus (Sidetes) stayed there two days at the request of the Jew (John) Hyrcanus because of a festival of his ancestors during which Jews are forbidden to travel. Nor does he (Nicolas of Damascus) speak falsely in saying this; for the Festival of Pentecost had come round, following the Sabbath, and we are not permitted to travel either on the Sabbath or on a festival [*Ant.* 13.251–2].

As we have already noted, Josephus's statement is false. No such biblical prohibition existed. But did Antiochus Sidetes know this?

The Jewish liturgical calendar is punctuated with frequent religious observances. Given the length of ancient military campaigns, which were often prolonged due to the slow rate of travel by foot and horse, it was inevitable that a major holiday would take place during Antiochus Sidetes's expedition. John Hyrcanus merely took advantage of Pentecost's fortuitous arrival to devise a stratagem to save his life, and spare his army.

Pagans were just as punctilious observers of religious rituals as the Jews. Their priests consulted the entrails of sacrificial animals before their armies went into battle. If the omens were not deemed propitious, campaigns were often halted. Given their superstitious nature, and their fear of offending any deity, Antiochus Sidetes's pagan soldiers would have been reluctant to undertake military action if John Hyrcanus — the high priest of all Jews — claimed that fighting during Pentecost would bring his god's wrath upon their expedition. Antiochus Sidetes, "the Pious," had no choice but to temporarily halt his expedition.

While Antiochus Sidetes and his legions waited for the Jews to complete their celebration, the Parthians took advantage of this unexpected delay in battle to amass additional forces. The tension must have been unbearable for Antiochus Sidetes. With the enemy nearby, he had to leave John Hyrcanus and the Hasmonean legions behind: he presumably ordered them to catch up with the expedition after Pentecost. Although Josephus does not provide a full account of what happened next, he implies that John Hyrcanus and his men simply packed up their bags and returned home, confident that Antiochus Sidetes and the Seleucid army would come to an untimely end.

Now stuck in hostile terrain, and with winter approaching, Antiochus Sidetes had to seek out friendly villages for help. The Parthians, having been informed of the precarious state of his army, made a surprise attack. The Seleucid troops fled in panic. Antiochus Sidetes died fighting the Parthian general Arsaces VII (a.k.a. Pharaates II; 171–128 B.C.E.) without the aid of his valued Jewish legions. When his soldiers brought his body home in a silver casket, the Seleucids mourned the passing of their once great empire.

Syria never recovered from this disaster. Antiochus Sidetes's brother Demetrius eventually made his way home. Although he regained his throne, he failed to unite his people. After his untimely death six claimants fought one another for the next twelve years until a remarkable group of women filled Seleucia's leadership vacuum. One, Cleopatra Selene (ca. 135–ca. 9 B.C.E.), helped Salome Alexandra's husband expand the Hasmonean State. After her death, Syria became a province of the Roman Republic. And all this happened because John Hyrcanus refused to fight during a religious holiday!

There is one problem with Josephus's account of Antiochus Sidetes's Parthian campaign—he does not mention it in his *War*. In this book, he claims that John Hyrcanus undertook an extensive series of military expeditions, including an invasion of Syria, while Antiochus Sidetes was alive. He also writes that John Hyrcanus crossed the Jordan River to besiege the city of Medaba (modern Jordan) for six months, and then captured Samaria, located between Syria and Judea: However, in his *Antiquities*, Josephus insists that Salome Alexandra's husband captured Medaba.[16] Which of his irreconcilable accounts are we to believe? Fortunately, archaeology provides the answer.

Sieges leave telltale marks in the archaeological record. Burned cities, smashed pots, and coins provide valuable dating evidence that scholars can compare with the written record. When we look at the dates of the destruction levels at the sites John Hyrcanus conquered, they reveal that neither of Josephus's books is correct. All the extant physical evidence shows that the cities he conquered were actually destroyed in 112/111 B.C.E., which is nearly eighteen years after Antiochus Sidetes died in Parthia.[17] By this time, the Seleucid Empire had fragmented into several weak states that posed no threat to Judea. Archaeology shows that John Hyrcanus waited nearly two decades after Antiochus Sidetes's death before he ventured outside Judea. He was a cautious and timid ruler. Josephus clearly tried to obscure this fact in both his books.

The medieval chronicle *Josippon* (a Hebrew book likely written sometime in the tenth century C.E. that was erroneously attributed to Josephus) preserves another account Antiochus Sidetes's Parthian expedition. It agrees with Josephus that the Seleucids halted their expedition so the Jews could celebrate a religious holiday. But one version of *Josippon* includes material likely taken from an ancient pagan source, which suggests that John Hyrcanus was a traitor. It claims he colluded with the Parthian monarch Phraates (II) to betray Antiochus Sidetes. Phraates purportedly told John Hyrcanus that the Greeks were their common enemy since they had defiled the Jewish temple and ransacked the Parthian Empire. He convinced John Hyrcanus to betray the Seleucids.

John Hyrcanus agreed to Phraates's offer and led the Seleucids into a trap. In exchange for his cooperation, the Parthians curtailed their activities eastward, and avoided Hasmonean territory. If Josippon's account is true, then Pentecost was merely a ruse; John Hyrcanus used it as a pretext to avoid fighting. It also explains how the Parthians knew the whereabouts of the Seleucid army, and why John Hyrcanus's valued legions mysteriously disappeared before the final battle. John Hyrcanus lied to Antiochus Sidetes: he never planned to help him defeat the Parthians.

John Hyrcanus was safe. However, he was reluctant to expand his kingdom eastward. The Parthians could potentially consider him a threat if he encroached on their land. He also had to consider the possibility that the Seleucids could rebuild their empire and seek revenge. For this reason, he feared campaigning in any of their territories or near their borders until he was certain the Syrian kings were no threat. This is why he waited eighteen years after the death of Antiochus Sidetes before venturing outside Judea. Later Jewish tradition may provide confirmation for this historical reconstruction. The Talmud recounts a visit of a Parthian delegation to Jerusalem during the reign of Salome Alexandra's husband, which provides evidence that John Hyrcanus had made a treaty with them that was still effect decades later.[18]

The Bad Samaritans?

The year 111 B.C.E. was a time of great carnage and immense joy. Salome Alexander was a newlywed. She was twenty-nine years old; her husband, Alexander Jannaeus, was either sixteen or fourteen. She was likely pregnant with their first child, Hyrcanus (II); he was likely born the next year. But any joy she and her spouse felt at the prospect of starting a family was tempered by thoughts of war. After nearly two decades of inactivity, John Hyrcanus chose this year to destroy another religion just beyond his border in Samaria.

Josephus includes a love story in his *Antiquities* that supposedly took place during the time of Alexander the Great that helps us understand John Hyrcanus's treatment of the Samaritans. According to this tale, Manasseh, the brother of the Jewish high priest Jaddus, had fallen in love with a Samaritan woman named Nikaso, the daughter of the Samaritan governor Sanballat. When the two married, Manasseh's family rejected their daughter-in-law because of her Samaritan bloodline. Judea's elders threatened to expel Manasseh from the temple unless he divorced Nikaso. Manasseh chose love over his sacred office, left the priesthood, and moved to Samaria. Sanballat promised to build him a temple atop Mount Gerizim in Samaria.[19]

Mt. Gerizim (left) and Mt. Ebal (right) with the modern city of Shechem in the foreground, seen from the east. In the Hellenistic period the Samaritans built a temple atop Mt. Gerizim and appointed their own priests to officiate over its offerings. The Hasmoneans refused to tolerate the existence of this shrine and destroyed it (Todd Bolen/BiblePlaces.com).

It does not matter whether Josephus's story is true since fiction can motivate people to kill just as easily as fact. He merely records a tale that was widely circulated in Salome Alexandra's day; she undoubtedly heard it countless times. Because most Judeans, apparently Josephus among them, believed it was true, it helps us understand why John Hyrcanus hated the Samaritans.

During the Hellenistic period the Samaritans produced their own version of the Bible that contains only the five books of Moses. In the Samaritan Scripture, God commands the Jews to build their temple atop Mt. Gerizim in Samaria and not in Jerusalem. Josephus mentions that many Judean priests moved to Samaria and served in Manasseh's shrine. For John Hyrcanus, two high priests claiming to speak on behalf of the same God in adjacent territories in rival temples was an intolerable situation. He set out to remedy this state of affairs by abolishing the Samaritan religion.

John Hyrcanus was ruthless in his treatment of the Samaritans. According to Josephus, he sent his sons Antigonus and Judah Aristobulus to besiege their capital city, known as Samaria. In desperation, its beleaguered citizens called on the Seleucid king Antiochus Cyzicenus for help. Josephus includes the following apocryphal story that apparently circulated in Salome Alexandra's time to show that God sanctioned this campaign:

> On the very day on which his sons fought with [Antiochus] Cyzicenus, [John] Hyrcanus, who was alone in the temple, burning incense as high priest, heard the divine voice saying that his sons had just defeated Antiochus [Cyzicenus]. And coming out of the temple he told this news to the entire multitude, and it actually happened [*Ant.* 13.282–3].

Josephus also writes that whenever John Hyrcanus presented offerings in the temple, the sacred stones on his high priest's robe glowed.[20] After his death, these stones remained dim and Judea's high priests no longer heard the divine voice. God, Josephus was convinced, hated the Samaritans and loved John Hyrcanus.

John Hyrcanus next invaded the land of the Idumeans to Judea's south. They also had a religious connection with the Judeans. Both claimed Esau, brother of the biblical patriarch Jacob, as their ancestor. John Hyrcanus

Tower ruins of the Hellenistic city of Samaria, capital of the Samaritans. John Hyrcanus's sons, Judah Aristobulus and Antigonus, destroyed the city along with the nearby Samaritan Temple (David Bivin/www.LifeintheHolyLand.com).

allowed them to retain their land provided they accept circumcision and follow Jewish law. Fortunately, this decree was not as harsh, or painful, as it sounds since the Idumeans already practiced circumcision.[21]

The Rise of Religious Sectarianism

John Hyrcanus's reign witnessed the birth of a new phenomenon that would quickly divide Salome Alexandra's world — religious sectarianism. During the Hasmonean period Judaism splintered into three movements that competed with one another to win the souls of ordinary Judeans. Each was convinced that God was on its side. Of the three, the Pharisees and the Sadducees were the most prominent. The third, the Essenes, eschewed politics, rejected mainstream society, and refused to worship in the temple. Josephus, who for a short time in his rather remarkable youth joined all three, describes the basic differences between them as follows:

> As for the Pharisees, they say that only certain events are the work of fate, but not all; concerning some events, it depends upon ourselves whether they shall take place or not. The sect of the Essenes, however, declares that fate is mistress of all things, and that nothing happens to a person unless it is in accordance with her decree. But the Sadducees do not believe in fate, they insist there is no such thing, and that human actions are not achieved in accordance with her decree, but that we possess the power to determine our own actions, so that we ourselves are responsible for our own well being, and we suffer misfortune through our own stupidity [*Ant.* 13.172–3].

The Pharisees and the Sadducees are best known from their appearances in the New Testament Gospels. (The Bible makes no mention of the Essenes.) Jesus often clashed with the Pharisees, and at times denounced them as "hypocrites" and "a brood of vipers."[22] The New Testament Book of Acts, however, offers a slightly less polemical account of the Pharisees and the Sadducees that provides some additional information about their religious beliefs. According to its author, traditionally identified as the physician Luke, "The Sadducees say that there is no resurrection, or angels, or spirit; but the Pharisees accept all three."[23] Because Jesus and the early Christians believed in resurrection, they viewed the Pharisees as their greatest rivals. For this reason, the Gospels and the Book of Acts cannot always be trusted to present a fair and balanced portrayal of the Pharisees. Although many today despise them, the Pharisees were not all bad — Salome Alexandra was one of them!

The Pharisees were popular in Salome Alexandra's day and Jesus' time because they believed in something known as the Oral Law. According to Josephus:

> The Pharisees had passed on to the people certain regulations handed down by former generations that were not written in the laws of Moses. The Sadducees reject this teaching: they maintain that only those regulations should be considered valid which were actually written down [in Scripture], and that we are not to observe laws handed down by our forefathers [*Ant.* 13.297].

The Oral Law was immensely popular. The Hasmonean high priests were originally Pharisees and observed it. This abruptly changed when a man named Eleazar falsely claimed that John Hyrcanus was a bastard and therefore unqualified to serve as high priest.[24]

Josephus is certainly correct that Eleazar's accusation was baseless since it was later made against Salome Alexandra's husband.[25] Nevertheless, slander, even when clearly false, can irreversibly damage a person's reputation. According to Josephus, John Hyrcanus demanded Eleazar be punished for his scandalous remark. When the Pharisees rejected his request, an opportunistic Sadducee named Jonathan urged him to outlaw them. In a fit of rage, John Hyrcanus renounced his allegiance to the Pharisees. The Hasmoneans were now Sadducees, that is, except for Salome Alexandra: she remained a committed Pharisee her entire life.

The End of an Era

John Hyrcanus died after ruling Judea for thirty-one years. Josephus chose not to record the details of his hero's death, or describe the turmoil that undoubtedly followed his defection from the Pharisees. Since there is no evidence that he perished on the field of battle — Josephus surely would have told us if he had — he presumably died at home of an illness, or simply succumbed to the effects of old age. Josephus suggests that his death marked a significant change in Hasmonean tradition. He was not buried in his family's ancestral home in Modi'in with the other Maccabean freedom fighters, but in Jerusalem. In his *War*, Josephus writes that John Hyrcanus's tomb was still a prominent landmark on the eve of the great Jewish revolt against Rome that erupted in 66 C.E.[26] It dominated Jerusalem's landscape, and served as a perpetual reminder that this was the city and the temple of the Hasmoneans.

For Josephus, John Hyrcanus, not Salome Alexandra, had presided over Judea's Golden Age. With his passing, God no longer performed mighty deeds; the high priests no longer had direct access to God; the sacred stones on the high priest's robe no longer glowed; and the divine voice was forever silent. But Josephus believed that his hero had made a terrible mistake when he named his wife as his successor. It was an act that changed the course of history in ways John Hyrcanus could not have foreseen.

6

A Judean Woman Who Did Not Know Her Place

Salina Alexandra

A craving for illegitimate rule is a terrible thing and, in the majority of cases, to acquire it demands cruelty. Rarely is it attained by chance; usually it is necessary to employ deceit or violence.—Boccaccio (1313–1375 C.E.), "Athaliah, Queen of Jerusalem," in *De mulieribus claris,* 51.11

The women of the Hasmonean family were not the first females to have ruled a Jewish state. There was one other; she governed seven centuries before Salome Alexandra's birth. We know her name because the authors of the Bible did not want her to be forgotten. The story of her life is a sordid tale of murder, deception, and political intrigue. Josephus's readers knew it quite well; he includes her tragic tale in his *Antiquities.* She was a woman who did not heed the Italian Renaissance writer Boccaccio's warning against the illicit acquisition of power; she had "a craving for illegitimate rule." Her name is Athaliah.

A Nation Divided

Athaliah (reign ca. 842/41–837/35 B.C.E.) lived in a divided country.[1] Two centuries before her birth, ten of the twelve tribes, the descendants of the biblical patriarch Jacob's dozen sons, had broken away from their kin to form the northern kingdom of Israel, which was located in the regions of Samaria and Galilee. The Bible considers it an illegitimate nation because its monarchs were not descendants of King David. Its priests angered God when they built pagan temples in violation of the biblical commandment that sacrifice could only take place in Jerusalem. Despite the efforts of prophets such as Elijah and Elisha to enforce strict monotheism there, polytheism was rampant. In 721 B.C.E. God allowed the Assyrians to destroy it and deport much of its population. They never returned; they are often called the ten lost tribes of Israel. Athaliah was from the northern kingdom; her father was its king.

The biblical writers were reluctant to tell us much about Athaliah, except for her name and tragic death. The few details they provide are confusing. It is uncertain whether she was the daughter of King Omri or his son Ahab. In all probability, Ahab was her brother and Omri, Israel's ruler, was her father. But what is not in dispute is that she is among the most infamous persons in the Bible.

Athaliah's life abruptly changed when her father proposed an alliance with his enemy Jehoshaphat (reign ca. 873/72–848/47 B.C.E.), monarch of the small southern kingdom known as Judah, to end their longstanding military conflict. At that time, Judah was a tiny nation centered around Jerusalem: it included only a small portion of what would eventually become Salome Alexandra's Judea. Jehoshaphat needed to make peace with its northern neighbor to survive. Athaliah was the property to be exchanged for a treaty between the two warring nations. Her father sent her to Jerusalem to marry Judah's crown prince, Jehoram.

Athaliah's husband was a violent man. When he became king he executed his six younger brothers and other potential rivals. He was an inept ruler; his army once deserted him in battle. During his ill-fated reign, the surrounding nation's refused to send him their required tribute. The biblical authors believed God punished him with a painful inflammation of the abdomen. He died when his bowels fell out.

Athaliah and Jehoram had a son named Ahaziah (reign ca. 841/40 B.C.E.). He became king after his father's death. She was given the title Queen Mother; an honored and powerful position in ancient society. If not in name, she was in reality Judah's sovereign. She exerted great influence over matters of state; she may have accompanied the armies of the northern and southern kingdoms during their joint campaign against the Arameans. Judah prospered during Ahaziah's reign. Then chaos unexpectedly engulfed both countries. When Ahaziah traveled to the northern kingdom to visit its ailing monarch, Joram, an Israelite general named Jehu murdered both rulers, and proclaimed himself Israel's king.

Athaliah took advantage of the resulting pandemonium and seized power in the southern kingdom. She ordered the assassination of all surviving males of David's line, and introduced the cult of Baal in the Jerusalem temple. She ruled as Judah's sole monarch for six years. But she was unaware that she had failed to murder all of King David's descendants. One of her grandsons, Joash (a.k.a. Jehoash; reign ca. 837/35–800/796 B.C.E.), survived. A woman had saved him from her purge. The Bible wanted us to know her name — Jehosheba.

Jehosheba was Joash's aunt. She presumably arranged for the young boy to live with his great uncle, the high priest Jehoiada. The biblical author does not make it clear whether Joash knew his true identity. Jehoiada likely trained him to become a priest. When Joash reached his seventh birthday, Jehoiada felt the time was right to reveal publicly the boy's royal bloodline, and restore the Davidic monarchy. He sent messengers throughout the country to summon the priests and tribal heads to a clandestine meeting. According to Josephus's retelling of this biblical story, Jehoiada stood the young Joash before them and said, "This is your king from the house that God had prophesied would reign as king forever."

Josephus embellishes the biblical narrative of Jehoiada's coup to portray Athaliah as an emotional cripple.[2] He writes that when she "saw the boy standing on the platform and wearing the royal crown, she tore her garments and demanded death for the conspirators." Everyone ignored her command. Jehoiada ordered her execution, but pleaded, "Let her not be killed in the house of the Lord." An enraged mob took her outside the temple and murdered her at the gate of the king's mules. A crowd destroyed her temple of Baal and killed its priests. According to the biblical author, "all the people of the land rejoiced" when they heard of Athaliah's death

Generations of writers have appealed to Athaliah's tragic life to warn of the potential dangers of a female monarch. The French dramatist Jean Racine's (1639–99 C.E.) 1691 tragedy, Athaliah (Athaliei), greatly exaggerates her cruelty. He includes an imaginary scene in which God torments her in a dream; like Josephus and the biblical authors, he enjoys recounting her downfall. The Florentine author Giovanni Boccaccio (1313–1375 C.E.) was inspired by his mentor Petrarch's De viris illustribus (Lives of Famous Men) to write a similar study devoted to biographies of important women. His book, De mulieribus claris (Famous Women), is the first modern work devoted exclusively to the supposed weaker sex. Boccaccio also takes a few liberties in recounting Athaliah's story. He portrays her as a "savage woman." But Salome Alexandra — recognized in her day as Judea's only legitimate female ruler and its greatest monarch — is notably absent from his book.

A Successor Like No Other

The biblical writers clearly hated Athaliah because of her gender. But there is no scriptural basis for their rebuke. The Bible is surprisingly silent regarding female rule; God never said only men could govern. The author of the third century C.E. *Sifre Deuteronomy* (a commentary on the biblical Book of Deuteronomy) saw a need to close this divine loophole and added to the biblical verse, "You will set a king over you," the words "a king, not a queen."[3]

John Hyrcanus knew Athaliah's story quite well. But he was confident that his wife's gender did not disqualify her from secular rule. By appointing his spouse as his political successor, he had taken an important step toward legitimizing the Hasmonean dynasty. During the time of the Bible, David's descendants had ruled as kings while the high priests. The latter were unrelated to the monarch and presided over the temple. All this changed when the Babylonians removed the last Davidic monarch, Zedekiah (reign 597–587/86 B.C.E.), from power in 587/6 B.C.E. Judea became a theocracy (a religious state) and the high priests functioned as its political and spiritual leaders. But it was understood that this was a temporary arrangement: when the Davidic messiah arrived, he would restore kingship to Judea. The Hasmoneans violated this longstanding status quo when they united political and secular rule. John Hyrcanus apparently tried to restore the biblical separation of powers by naming his wife as his political successor. Josephus thought this was the greatest blunder in Judean history.

John Hyrcanus could appoint his spouse as Judea's monarch, but not as its high priest since God decreed that only men could become priests. Although Josephus does not tell us John Hyrcanus's choice for this sacred office, he implies that he wanted Salome Alexandra's husband to assume this position. But two of John Hyrcanus's sons, Judah Aristobulus and Antigonus, were unwilling to accept his decision. They used the period between their father's public declaration to restore the biblical separation between sacerdotal and secular powers and his death to prepare a coup. They did not merely seek to overthrow their mother, but to transform Judea into a Hellenistic state ruled by a king. According to Josephus:

> After their father's death the eldest son [Judah] Aristobulus changed the government into a kingdom, which he judged the best form. He was the first [Hasmonean] to put a crown on his head [*Ant.* 13.301].

Josephus's carefully crafted prose is quite revealing. He does not say that the Judeans crowned Judah Aristobulus king, but that he "put a crown on his head."[4] Whatever unrecorded evil deeds he may have committed during this time pale in comparison with his first act as Judea's monarch.

According to Josephus, after he proclaimed himself king, Judah Aristobulus gave his brother Antigonus honors equal to his own. He then imprisoned his remaining siblings, including Salome Alexandra's husband, and did something so horrendous, and presumably well known, that Josephus could not omit it from his account:

> He imprisoned his mother, who had disputed the royal power with him — for [John] Hyrcanus had given her supreme authority — and he was so cruel that he allowed her to die of starvation in prison [*Ant.* 13.302].

Josephus's terse statement that Judah Aristobulus's mother had "disputed the royal power with him" suggests that she did not give up her position as "mistress of the realm" without a fight. During John Hyrcanus's period of physical decline, she must have assumed political power; Salome Alexandra's husband likely served as high priest. Unfortunately, we will never know the full story of her short reign since Josephus only tells us how she died. We do not even know her name.

Salome Alexandra's Uneasy Year

At this terrible juncture in his tragic account of the Hasmonean family, Josephus introduces his readers to one of the most important characters in our story — Salome Alexandra's husband, Alexander Jannaeus. He was twenty-one or twenty-three at this time; she was thirty-six. While he languished in prison for the entirety of Judah Aristobulus's reign, she remained in Jerusalem with their children. It was a tense time; her future was uncertain. She likely feared that Judah Aristobulus and Antigonus would execute her spouse and two sons since they were potential rivals for power. But before the year ended, her situation unexpectedly changed: Judah Aristobulus was dead and her husband was Judea's king and high priest. To understand how this unexpected event came about, we must examine a rather mysterious, and largely overlooked, passage in Josephus's book in which he attributes this unexpected change in the royal succession to John Hyrcanus's gift of prophecy.

Josephus inserts the following apocryphal story in his account of the reign of Salome Alexandra's husband:

> Of all his sons [John] Hyrcanus loved best the two elder ones, Antigonus and Aristobulus; and once when God had appeared to him in a dream, he asked him which of his sons was destined to become his successor. And when God showed him the face of Alexander [Jannaeus], he was grieved that this one should be the heir of all his possessions, and so he let him be brought up in the Galilee from his birth [*Ant.* 13.322].

Josephus's story creates a major chronological problem. Alexander Jannaeus had been married to Salome Alexandra for seven years before John Hyrcanus's death. If Josephus is correct, then John Hyrcanus never met Alexander Jannaeus. Moreover, even if John Hyrcanus knew Salome Alexandra, according to Josephus, he could not have had any contact with her after her marriage to Alexander Jannaeus. However, Josephus places Salome Alexandra and her spouse in Jerusalem at the time of John Hyrcanus's death. This suggests that she and Alexander Jannaeus had arrived, or possibly moved there, while John Hyrcanus was alive. If Salome Alexandra and her new spouse lived in the Galilee for a short time, they certainly knew John Hyrcanus. But where did the royal couple live and why did John Hyrcanus send them away from Jerusalem?

Josephus provides us with a detailed description of the Galilee that can help us answer these questions:

> Galilee, with its two divisions known as Upper and Lower Galilee, is surrounded by Phoenicia and Syria.... On the south the country is bordered by Samaria and the territory of Scythopolis up to the waters of the [River] Jordan; on the east by the [Gentile] territory of Hippos, Gadara, and Gaulanitis ... on the north Tyre and the country of the Tyrians. The Lower Galilee extends in length from Tiberius [on the Sea of Galilee] to Chabulon, which is not far from Ptolemais on the [Mediterranean] coast.... The two Galilees have always resisted hostile invasions, for the inhabitants are from infancy trained for war.... The land is so rich in soil and pasturage and has such a large number of fruit trees, that even the laziest are tempted to devote themselves entirely to the pursuit of agriculture [*War* 3.35–42].

As Josephus notes, the Galilee was full of many large cities. But pagans inhabited most of them in John Hyrcanus's time: there were so many that the prophet Isaiah dubbed the region "Galilee of the Gentiles."[5] John Hyrcanus would not have sent his son to live among pagans, especially while he was fighting them. For this reason, we can exclude the Upper Galilee, particularly its eastern section, from consideration, since few Jews lived there.

Salome Alexandra and Alexander Jannaeus must have resided somewhere in the Lower Galilee. This region later became the cradle of Christianity. But the Galilean capital of Tiberius, and the many Jewish towns Jesus visited, were not yet built, or were still under pagan control. This leaves the western portion as the most likely place where she and her husband resided. The problem is that the great pagan city of Ptolemais, one of the most strategic ports in the Middle East, was located there. Although it may seem like an improbable place, John Hyrcanus likely sent his son and daughter-in-law to live there.

At this time the territory surrounding Ptolemais included a small Jewish population that traced its origin to the time of the Bible. The Hasmoneans had struggled to annex this territory to their kingdom. Simon had fought the Seleucids in this region. His campaign forced some of its Jewish inhabitants to seek refuge in Judea. Later, when John Hyrcanus conquered Samaria, he sent his sons Judah Aristobulus and Antigonus to campaign northwards, deep into the Lower Galilee, just south of Mount Carmel along the Mediterranean coast. The two apparently fought there to connect this small Jewish region with their newly-won territories in Samaria. When Salome Alexandra's husband became king, he used patriotism to unite his people. He sought to increase his popular support by waging a war to free this ancient Jewish community from Gentile control and thereby become known as a defender of his faith.[6]

Although we cannot conclusively say that Alexander Jannaeus and Salome Alexandra resided in the Lower Galilee, it remains the only likely place. No other Galilean territory was under direct Hasmonean control at this time. There is one additional piece of evidence to support this thesis. It comes from the Dead Sea Scrolls. To understand this valuable clue, we must delve briefly into the arcane field of linguistics.

Aramaic was the dominant language in Salome Alexandra's Judea. Because most of the Bible is written in Hebrew, some conservative Jews, such as the writers of the Dead Sea Scrolls, preferred Hebrew to Aramaic. The scrolls and other texts reveal that several sounds had disappeared from spoken Hebrew by the Roman period before Jesus' birth. One prominent example is the letter "h." It was originally pronounced "ch," but gradually changed to a softer sound analogous to the English sound "ha." Linguists trace this development to Phoenicia, located in modern Lebanon, whose inhabitants spoke a similar Semitic language. In the second century B.C.E. Phoenician groups such as the Itureans migrated to the northern Galilee from modern Lebanon and influenced its regional dialect. The Hasmoneans unwittingly accelerated this linguistic change when they conquered the region.

Dead Sea Scroll commentary on the biblical book of Habakkuk. This scroll, known as a pesher, recounts events of Salome Alexandra's lifetime and ends with the 63 B.C.E. Roman destruction of her homeland (Library of Congress, LC-matpc-13013/www.LifeintheHolyLand.com).

The Galilean dialect appears in Judea in a Dead Sea Scroll known as the *Habakkuk Pesher* (it contains allusions to Salome Alexandra and her husband). The best explanation to account for this northern dialect in a southern Judean text is that Alexander Jannaeus spoke with a Galilean accent. Some of his subjects, the author of the *Habakkuk Pesher* included, likely imitated his pronunciation. (In the New Testament, Peter's northern accent betrayed him as a Galilean.)[7]

There is a problem with Josephus's claim that Alexander Jannaeus never met his father. He insists that John Hyrcanus sent him to live in the Galilee at the time of his birth, which was in 125 or 127 B.C.E. But John Hyrcanus did not capture the Galilee until nearly two decades later, in 108 B.C.E., when Alexander Jannaeus was between seventeen and nineteen years old. By that time, Alexander Jannaeus and Salome Alexandra had been married for three years. Both clearly knew John Hyrcanus; he certainly arranged their marriage; and they must have returned to Jerusalem before his death. The couple likely lived in the Galilee for three years, between the time of John Hyrcanus's conquest of the region and Judah Aristobulus's inauguration. Salome Alexandra's eldest son, Hyrcanus (II), would have been nearly three years old at the time. This means that he too lived in the Galilee; he may have been born there. John Hyrcanus likely knew his grandson as well as his son and daughter-in-law. We do not know when Salome Alexandra's youngest child, Aristobulus (II), was born since Josephus never tells us his age. However, we cannot rule out that he was born in the Galilee.

Salome Alexandra and her husband lived in the Galilee for a relatively short amount of time. But how do we account for the evidence of the Dead Sea Scrolls, which suggest that Alexander Jannaeus carried the linguistic marks of his Galilean sojourn for the remainder of his life?

It is highly unlikely that Alexander Jannaeus acquired a Galilean accent during such a short span of time. In all probability, he faked it for political reasons, just as modern politicians often mimic the regional accents of their constituents to curry their favor, and win their votes. Alexander Jannaeus likely feigned a northern accent to show that he was no political insider, but a champion of the Galilean Jews. There is no evidence that Salome Alexandra spoke with a northern accent. Given her strong-willed disposition, and her frequent confrontations with her husband during their marriage, it is highly unlikely that she imitated his contrived dialect.

Josephus likely invented his strange tale of John Hyrcanus's dream to conceal a rather unpleasant fact: Judah Aristobulus's coup was directed against his mother and Salome Alexandra's husband. John Hyrcanus appointed his wife as Judea's secular ruler, and Alexander Jannaeus as its high priest, before his death. If his plan had been successful, Judea would have become a Hellenistic state like Syria and Egypt, where women ruled over men.

John Hyrcanus moved Alexander Jannaeus to the Galilee for his own safety. Alexander Jannaeus's brothers likely wanted to murder him when they learned of their father's passing. During his time in the north, Alexander Jannaeus likely studied Scripture and learned the sacred rituals of his faith from this ancient Jewish community that had survived amidst pagans since the time of the Bible. John Hyrcanus and his wife likely thought they could handle matters in Jerusalem until it was safe for him to return.

This reconstruction offers the most reasonable explanation for John Hyrcanus's rather unusual choice of an older bride for his rather young and immature son. He and his wife apparently selected Salome Alexandra because of her maturity. John Hyrcanus likely hoped she could groom Alexander Jannaeus for his future role as high priest, and help him become accustomed to working alongside a dominant woman. He was certainly forced to marry her since no young man would have wanted such an elderly bride. But she would have been the perfect choice for this apparently shy and timid young man. She had already become familiar with the intrigues of the Hasmonean court and knew the teachings of the Sadducees and the Pharisees. She was the perfect tutor for a potential king in training. But she must have been a formidable, strong-willed, and independent woman to have remained single in a world in which females, especially royals, were expected to marry quite young.

John Hyrcanus's choice of Salome Alexandra as his daughter-in-law is also surprising for another reason — her religious affiliation. She was a committed Pharisee. There is evidence that many influential women like her supported this religious faction.[8] The Pharisees apparently welcomed their patronage since they had lost political power after John Hyrcanus had become a Sadducee. It is possible that John Hyrcanus thought that a union between one of his sons and a devout Pharisee would increase his family's political and religious support, and help his son retain power after his death. This was a real concern, for the Pharisees later waged war to overthrow Salome Alexandra's husband. As we will see, John Hyrcanus made an excellent choice: even Josephus acknowledges that the Judeans praised Salome Alexandra's piety, and her devotion to the Pharisees.

Salome Alexandra and Alexander Jannaeus presumably returned to Jerusalem immediately after John Hyrcanus's death. Things unfortunately did not turn out for them as planned: Alexander Jannaeus's mother met a cruel death and he ended up in prison. It is very possible that Alexander Jannaeus's mother had tried to imprison Judah Aristobulus and Antigonus to prevent them from usurping power. This would explain their horrible treatment of her. Because Josephus acknowledges that she did not relinquish her position as Judea's sovereign, they must have removed her by force. Men recognized her as Judea's lawful ruler: some of her husband's supporters undoubtedly met their deaths trying to place her on Judea's throne. But some of her partisans did not give up their fight to fulfill John Hyrcanus's dream. They soon found a new champion in Judah Aristobulus's wife — Salina Alexandra.

A Troubled Queen

Wife of king Judah Aristobulus; the potential mother of the next Hasmonean monarch; and the daughter-in-law of the murdered successor to the throne, Salina Alexandra was all these and more. Although she played one of the most important roles in Hasmonean history, we know virtually nothing about her. But a close reading of Josephus's accounts suggests that she was a formidable woman who literally changed the course of Hasmonean history. But until now, the true story of the role she played in shaping her nation has never been told.

Josephus does not tell us Salina Alexandra's name in his *War*. In a cryptic passage, he merely states that after Judah Aristobulus's death, "The woman released his brothers raising Alexander (Jannaeus) to kingship."[9] However, in his *Antiquities* Josephus makes a rare departure from his custom of using Greek names for the Hasmoneans to identify this mysterious woman, and reveal her Hebrew name:

> After the death of Aristobulus his wife Salina, called by the Greeks Alexandra, released his brothers — for Aristobulus had imprisoned them, as we have said before — and appointed Jannaeus, also known as Alexander, king [*Ant* 13.320].

Josephus undoubtedly copied this passage from some ancient history of the Hasmonean family. Unfortunately, he only quotes what is likely the first line of the chapter about Salina Alexandra, which likely contained much lost information about her.[10] His short excerpt from this book is important because it portrays her and Alexander Jannaeus as equals: The two are leaders in their own right and are known by their names alone. It provides indirect evidence that a complete account of her life once existed, which Josephus and his successors chose to ignore.

We can make a few plausible assumptions about Salina Alexandra's life based on what we have learned about Salome Alexandra's youth. Since the Hasmoneans preferred to keep power within their family, Salina Alexandra was likely related to her husband; she was possibly his cousin. Because Judah Aristobulus was John Hyrcanus's eldest son, Salina Alexandra presumably married him, in accordance with prevailing custom, when she was quite young. Salome Alexandra was likely much older since she wed late in life. The two women likely knew one another from childhood since the Hasmonean family was a rather close-knit group.

The Egyptian Jewish scholar Philo (ca. 20 B.C.E.–ca. 50 C.E.) provides some insight concerning the gender norms of Salome Alexandra's time that may help us to understand how the Judeans viewed her and Salina Alexandra. He reflects the prevailing belief that women were either masculine or feminine: the former bore sons while the latter produced daughters.[11] Salome Alexandra demonstrated her masculinity by giving birth to two future kings and high priests. Salina Alexandra was apparently barren, and therefore worse than feminine since there is no indication she had any children. Because there was apparently no heir to the throne, Antigonus was the only available candidate since his brothers — Salome Alexandra's husband included — were in prison. However, most Judeans hated Judah Aristobulus and Antigonus for murdering their mother. Many Judeans must have looked to Salome Alexandra's husband as the rightful successor. But it was doubtful he would survive his captivity. Only Salome Alexandra and her sister-in-law could free him. But only if they could eliminate Judah Aristobulus and Antigonus.

Loved by Pagans

Salina Alexandra dominates much of Josephus's account of Judah Aristobulus's reign. She is assertive; she commands men; and she is the most powerful member of the royal family. Unfortunately, he tells us little about her or her husband, except for his final days in power. His obituary, however, provides a few valuable clues concerning his character. Josephus writes that Judah Aristobulus was known by the nickname Philhellene (lover of Hellenism), a clear indication of his commitment to Greek culture.[12] He also mentions that pagan historians regarded him as a kind, modest, and great king. Having achieved such renown in less than a year, he abruptly becomes ill and dies. What caused his sudden demise?

Josephus opens his account of Judah Aristobulus's tragic life with an incident that took place in 104 B.C.E. during the Festival of Tabernacles. Let us permit Josephus to relate what happened:

> On one occasion when Antigonus had returned from a victorious campaign, as the season of the festival during which the tabernacles are erected to God was near, [Judah] Aristobulus fell ill, and Antigonus, arrayed in great splendor and accompanied by his heavily-armed soldiers, went up to the temple to celebrate the festival and to pray for his brother's recovery. [*Ant.* 13.304].

According to Josephus, "evil men" had devised a plan to take advantage of this incident to undermine the harmonious relationship between the two brothers. They informed Judah Aristobulus that Antigonus was in the temple preparing to seize power. Who are these "evil men"? We can be certain of one thing — they were not all men.

Because this was the first Festival of Tabernacles celebrated by a Hasmonean king, the Judeans would have viewed Judah Aristobulus's absence as a portent of bad things to come. Zechariah, after all, had predicted terrible consequences should the Judeans not observe this festival. Also, because the outward appearance of masculinity was paramount for kings to retain power, many Judeans would have viewed Judah Aristobulus's inability to fight his battles, and preside over a religious ceremony, as a sign of his physical and mental weakness.

Josephus provides an important clue about Judah Aristobulus's precarious physical condition that helps us to understand the tragic events of his short reign. He mentions that Antigonus had just returned from a successful campaign. Josephus records one military expedition during Judah Aristobulus's time in power; it was against the Itureans to the north of the Sea of Galilee. According to Josephus, he gave them the option of circumcision or exile. They presumably chose the latter, which may explain why pagan historians of the time praised him so highly. Unlike other conquerors of the period, he had apparently annexed territory with little or no bloodshed.[13]

If the conquest of Iturea was a great victory for Judah Aristobulus, it was a devastating loss for his brother. By ordering the abrupt end of this campaign, Judah Aristobulus had prevented him from winning a great victory in his own name. He also had apparently chosen someone else to serve as high priest during the Festival of Tabernacles. Antigonus had good reason to be angry and suspicious of his brother.

At this point in his narrative Josephus introduces his readers to the true architect of Judah Aristobulus's demise — Salina Alexandra. Earlier, he refers to the plotters responsible for ending his reign as "evil men." In the Greek language in which Josephus wrote his books, the masculine plural can refer to men or both sexes. In such instances, which are common in this language, translators must use context as a guide to determine an author's intended meaning. But in this case Josephus's meaning is clear since Salina Alexandra dominates his narrative. She orchestrates the plot to bring down the first Hasmonean king. She is the leader of Josephus's so-called "evil men."

According to Josephus, Judah Aristobulus refused to believe the reports that Antigonus was preparing a coup. Over time, his courtiers changed his mind. Now convinced that his throne was in danger, he ordered his brother to appear before him unarmed as a test of his fealty. Salina Alexandra, privy to all that went on in the royal fortress, intercepted the courier. According to Josephus, the queen [Salina Alexandra] and the men who were plotting with her against Antigonus persuaded the messenger to say the opposite, namely that his brother, (the king), had heard that he had made himself a suit of armor for war, and he wanted him to wear it when he appeared, in order that he might see it [*Ant.* 13.308–9].

The fourth century C.E. Latin translation of Josephus, which was wrongly attributed to the ancient historian Hegesippus (his name is likely a corruption of Josephus), provides a slightly longer account of this incident. It states that Salina Alexandra not only changed the message, but that her husband was so ill and inattentive that he never read it.[14] She was in charge of all official correspondence: She was Judea's actual ruler.

Josephus provides a valuable clue about Judah Aristobulus's psychological state when he informs his readers that he was staying in the Baris fortress rather than the splendid Hasmonean palace. He must have taken refuge there for his protection: he was clearly hiding from his brother and political enemies. Ill and completely isolated from his surroundings, he had to rely on trustworthy supporters to keep him informed of events outside. As one of the few persons with unfettered access to him at this time, Salina Alexandra was in the ideal position to engineer his downfall. She used the temple incident to drive her husband mad.

Antigonus literally walked into Salina Alexandra's trap. Josephus tells us that her husband — or, more likely, Salina Alexandra writing in his name — had given his soldiers standing orders to execute Antigonus if he appeared in the Baris bearing weapons. When he arrived armed, the guards executed him. According to Josephus, when Judah Aristobulus heard the news,

> he was immediately seized by remorse for the murder of his brother, and this was followed by illness; he lost his mind because of his guilty deed; he was overcome with pain in his intestines, and he vomited blood [*Ant.* 13.314].

He died shortly afterwards. But there is likely more to the story.

Josephus records a rather strange tale in his *Antiquities* in which he attributes Judah Aristobulus's untimely death to fate, and not to Salina Alexandra's cunning.

According to Josephus, an Essene elder named Judah had predicted the day and location of Antigonus's death. But when Antigonus was spotted in the temple on his way to the Baris on the predicted day of his death, Judah realized that his prognostication was wrong. He had told everyone that Antigonus would die at Strato's Tower before sunset (it was nearly sixty-five miles from Jerusalem). Judah urged his disciples to kill him in accordance with the scriptural edict that false prophets must be executed since there was no way Antigonus could reach Strato's Tower that day. Before the sentence could be carried out, the crowd learned that Antigonus had been assassinated in an underground passage in the Baris that was nicknamed Strato's Tower.[15]

Josephus includes this story to show that Antigonus would have died that day regardless of Salina Alexandra's actions. Nevertheless, despite his effort to diminish her role, he acknowledges that fate chose her to lead men in a plot to execute a Hasmonean king — an event that even Judah the Essene had not foreseen.

A "Fool" for a Husband?

Judah Aristobulus's precipitous physical and mental decline is suspicious and completely unexpected. Josephus relates that a rather unfortunate accident occurred shortly before his death:

> One of the servants who waited on him was carrying his blood away and he slipped and spilled it — by a divine power, I believe — on the very spot where the stains made by the blood of the murdered Antigonus were visible [*Ant.* 13.314].

After being informed of this accident, Judah Aristobulus became inconsolable. He cried out that God is punishing him for the murder of his brother and dies.

A modern criminologist would certainly consider this death suspicious. A robust young man suddenly becomes ill, paranoid, and then suffers vomiting and intense abdominal pain before literally dropping dead. Today, we would immediately test the corpse for signs of poisoning. In the absence of any physical remains, we must use a combination of conjecture and inference to determine the most likely suspect. In any period the burden of suspicion would fall upon his wife.

Josephus inserts a few subtle clues throughout his story that imply Salina Alexandra murdered her spouse. They are only visible to readers well versed with the sordid life of Judea's greatest king, David. Like Judah Aristobulus, David had a powerful spouse; her name was Abigail. The circumstances of how they met and became husband and wife are rather suspicious, and shed some valuable light on Judah Aristobulus's mysterious death.

Abigail's story begins during the reign of Judea's first monarch, a man named Saul (reign ca. 1079/47–1007 B.C.E.). David came to his attention after he had killed the Philistine giant Goliath. He served Saul as a loyal vassal; his military reputation quickly eclipsed his master's. Saul was prone to bouts of madness; David played the harp to relieve his suffering. When Saul became convinced that David was conspiring with his son Jonathan to seize power, he tried to murder him. Jonathan helped him flee to the Judean desert to escape his father's wrath.

David gathered a large body of discontented men and lived with them in the desert as a fugitive. They survived by demanding protection money from the local gentry in exchange for guarding their flocks. On one occasion, a wealthy man named Nabal refused to compensate David's men for their unsolicited services. Viewing this as an affront to his honor, David vowed to kill him. Before he could act, Nabal's wife, Abigail, intercepted him and apologized for her husband's conduct. She implored him to spare his life, saying, "My Lord, do not take seriously this ill-natured fellow, Nabal; for as his name is, so is he; Fool is his name, and folly is with him."[16] David accepted her apology and gifts, and promised not to harm her husband, his servants, or his property. It was God, David concluded, who had sent the wise Abigail to prevent him from committing murder.

The biblical writer is rather sparse with details; he expects his readers to carefully probe each word of this story for hidden clues. He states that Abigail returned home to find her husband intoxicated and feasting like a king. The next morning she told him what had taken place. Then, Nabal's "heart died within him; he became like a stone."[17] He died ten days later. Did Abigail poison her foolish husband?

The biblical narrator has inserted a rather obvious clue that points towards Abigail as Nabal's murderer. It escapes the notice of modern readers who know this story only in translation. Nabal is the Hebrew word for fool! This was certainly not his actual name. Rather, the biblical author calls him a fool to highlight his churlish demeanor, and his gullibility in failing to recognize the danger that his wife posed.[18] David married Abigail shortly after Nabal's death. There is no mention that she, or anyone, mourned her late husband's passing.

Although Josephus does not explicitly state that Salina Alexandra poisoned her husband, his overt allusion to this biblical story suggests he thought she did. There is no mention in his account that Salina Alexandra mourned her husband. Furthermore, Josephus provides another clue that something was amiss in the Hasmonean household, which supports our reconstruction of events when he writes about Judah Antigonus's reign:

> Now his death clearly proves that there is nothing more powerful than envy and slander, and nothing more easily disrupts goodwill and the ties of nature than these influences [*Ant.* 13.310].

The Greek phrase "ties of nature" refers to the basic order of things, including the gender differences between men and women. Josephus, by using this phrase, implicitly acknowledges that a woman brought down the first Hasmonean king. Later, he attributes the demise of the Judean state to Salome Alexandra's deeds. Like her sister-in-law, she supposedly had disrupted the "ties of nature" by acting like a man.

The End of an Era

Salina Alexandra murdered the first Hasmonean monarch. But this was not her most noteworthy feat. Josephus admits that what she did next was unprecedented: she relinquished the throne and appointed Salome Alexandra's husband as Judea's next king and high priest! Because it is more difficult to give up power than acquire it, Salina Alexandra was truly one of history's greatest rulers, although her reign was among its shortest.

Salina Alexandra was actually Judea's third legitimate female monarch; John Hyrcanus's wife was its first; and Salome Alexandra was its second. With no children to succeed her, Salina Alexandra handed the throne to Salome Alexandra's husband, confident that he would bow to her wishes. But her nation's future rested not with the men of the Hasmonean dynasty, but with a new group of rulers with unprecedented powers — the warrior queens of Syria and Egypt. It is to these remarkable, but largely forgotten women, that we now turn in our tale to see how they shaped Salome Alexandra's world, and our own.

7

Warrior Queens to the North
Cleopatra Thea and Her Descendants

> Being a commoner, she became queen and preserved her dignity until her death, without recourse to the persuasive charms of a courtesan, but employing self-control, courteous dignity, and virtue, she deserves to be remembered with honor. And, in addition, having given birth to four sons, she loved them up to her death, and showed toward all of them an unsurpassable goodwill and affection, although she outlived her husband for a considerable time. — Tribute to Apollonis of Cyzicus, Queen of Pergamum (241–197 B.C.E.) in Polybius (ca. 220–118 B.C.E.), *Histories*, 22.20.2–4

When people hear the name Cleopatra, they immediately think of the dazzling beauty who mesmerized the greatest Romans of her day — Julius Caesar and Mark Antony. Celebrated by Shakespeare and Hollywood for her wiles, her physical attributes, and her powers of seduction, she is one of history's most infamous women. But her contemporaries did not focus on her appearance, her sexuality, or her charms. They extolled her political savvy, her vast erudition, and her considerable linguistic skills. Few are aware she was the last of a long line of distinguished female rulers of Syria and Egypt to have borne the name Cleopatra.

The subject of this chapter is the most important of the several Cleopatras to have ruled Syria. She had a more tumultuous and dramatic life than the legendary Cleopatra (VII) known to everyone today. She embodied many of Queen Apollonis's virtues the Greek historian Polybius so elegantly extols, and a considerable number of vices as well. Wife of four successive Seleucid kings, mother of at least four sons (all became kings) and two daughters, she became her nation's first female monarch. She helped shape the world in which we live by saving Salome Alexandra's Judea. Her name is Cleopatra Thea.[1]

The Offspring of the "Syrian"

Cleopatra Thea (ca. 164–21 B.C.E.) was born into a family whose women were destined to rule the Hellenistic Middle East. Her famed grandmother, Cleopatra I (ca. 204–176 B.C.E.), was the daughter of the Seleucid monarch Antiochus (III) and Queen Laodice (III) of Pontus. Her name, Cleopatra, is Greek and means "having a glorious father" or "renowned in her ancestry." With royal blood from two families coursing through her veins, the Syrian, as she was known in antiquity, became a conqueror of nations like Alexander the Great.[2] But she did not subdue them by force, but through her offspring. Nearly all her female descendants became queens; several ruled Egypt and Syria.

The Syrian's life abruptly changed when her father decided to make peace with his enemy, the Egyptian king Ptolemy (IV) Philopator (ca. 244–204 B.C.E.). Because of their mutual mistrust, they decided to ratify their agreement with a royal marriage. They agreed to exchange the Syrian for peace. Her father sent her to Egypt to marry a complete stranger, the crown prince Ptolemy (V) Epiphanes (ca. 210–180 B.C.E.). She was ten years old at the time; her intended spouse was about fifteen or sixteen. Their wedding took place in 193/44 B.C.E. at the city of Raphia, near Judea's southern border. A generation later, a disagreement erupted over the terms of their union. The citizens of Alexandria, Egypt, maintained that her dowry included southern Syria and much of Judea. Others claimed that the tax revenues of Judea and Samaria were supposed to be divided between bride and groom. This dispute was a contributing factor that led to the great war between the Seleucids and the Ptolemies on Judean soil that erupted shortly after Salome Alexandra's husband became king.[3]

The Syrian and her husband had two sons and one daughter. They gave their children traditional family names. They boys were both named Ptolemy. Historians call the elder Ptolemy VI (ca. 186–45 B.C.E.) and the younger Ptolemy VIII (ca. 184/3–116 B.C.E.); but in antiquity, the former was known as Philometor and the latter as Physcon. They named the girl Cleopatra after her mother; scholars refer to her as Cleopatra II (ca. 185/4–115 B.C.E.). Nearly all subsequent males of the Ptolemaic household bore the name Ptolemy while most daughters were named Cleopatra. Upon her husband's death in 180 B.C.E., the Syrian ruled as regent for her eldest son, Philopator. In reality, she was Egypt's sovereign since the royal inscriptions place her name before his.[4]

Cleopatra Thea was the Syrian's granddaughter. She came from a remarkable family of formidable women. Her mother, Cleopatra II, and her sister, Cleopatra III (ca. 160/55–101 B.C.E.), also ruled Egypt; both were passionate supporters of the Jews. Like her grandmother, Cleopatra Thea was traded for peace, and forced to spend the remainder of her days living in a foreign land.

Cleopatra Thea's father, Philometor, hated his brother, Physcon. At this time Physcon was king of the small insignificant kingdom of Cyrene (modern Libya) in North Africa. Not content to rule a desert realm, he was determined to wrest power from his elder brother. As a goodwill overture, Philometor offered him Cleopatra Thea's hand in marriage. Physcon agreed, made peace with his sibling, and waited impatiently for the impending nuptials. But Philometor had no intention of marrying her to his brother. When Cleopatra Thea was fourteen or fifteen, he betrothed her to Alexander Balas (reigned 150–46 B.C.E.), the new ruler of Syria. This union was problematic since her intended spouse was actually a pretender to the Seleucid throne. He claimed he was the son of Antiochus (IV) Epiphanes — the man Salome Alexandra's ancestors had fought to create an independent Judean state. Despite his clearly bogus pedigree, Balas managed to seize power and make an alliance with the Roman Senate. Cleopatra Thea's father believed that a treaty with this new, inexperienced, yet powerful new king was in his best interest.

Cleopatra Thea and Balas married at the Syrian port of Ptolemais approximately twenty years before Salome Alexandra's birth.[5] As a young girl, Salome Alexandra certainly heard stories of this grand occasion from members of her family. Her ancestor Jonathan had attended as Balas's honored guest: he sat on the royal dais between the groom and the bride's father. He gave the royal couple lavish gifts of gold. But he was not there merely to celebrate Cleopatra Thea's marriage. This ceremony was also an official declaration that the Hasmoneans were now allies of the Seleucid Empire. Jonathan could not have known it, but all subsequent Judean rulers would have to contend with Cleopatra Thea's offspring and her female relations.

Alexander Balas had good reason to use his wedding to court the Hasmoneans. Because he was a new monarch with an uncertain future, he thought the powerful Jewish legions could help him retain the throne should civil war erupt in Syria. In exchange for Hasmonean support, he allowed Jonathan to anoint himself the first Hasmonean high priest. The ceremony took place in 153/2 B.C.E. during the Festival of Tabernacles. Alexander Balas sent Jonathan a purple cloak — the color of royalty in antiquity — and a crown as tokens of his new office. He also numbered him among the prestigious order of the king's "friends." Unfortunately, events were taking place in Asia Minor (modern Turkey) that would threaten this new alliance.

Turmoil in Seleucia

Balas was an inept ruler. He allowed his mistresses and court sycophants to govern in his stead.[6] Cleopatra Thea's father kept a close eye on him; Balas's court minister Ammonius may have been a Ptolemaic spy. It must have been a terrible time for Cleopatra Thea. She and her father quickly grew to mistrust her husband. But there was a more dangerous person who hated him. He was a man who would change Cleopatra Thea's life. His name is Demetrius II (reigned 239–229 B.C.E.). He was the eldest son of its previous monarch, Demetrius (I). Aware of the growing discontent in Seleucia, he decided the time was right to stage a coup, and remove Cleopatra Thea's husband from power.

Demetrius was about fourteen years old when he decided to overthrow Balas. After hiring a skilled corps of mercenaries, he traveled to the strategic city of Antioch (modern Turkey) to seize power. Many towns, including some of Judea's adversaries, joined his cause. Only Jonathan and the Jews remained loyal to Balas.

The civil war between Balas and Demetrius immediately spread to Judea. Jonathan and his army fought Balas's opponents near Azotus, along the Judean coast. The battle was quite horrendous and marked a significant turn in Hasmonean fortunes. After winning the initial engagement, Jonathan chased the survivors into the temple of Dagon, where they sought protection under the time-honored and sacrosanct law of sanctuary. He refused to accept their pleas for clemency and burned them alive. As a reward for this atrocity, Alexander Balas gave him a golden clasp — a great honor and a public sign of the king's respect — and the nearby city of Ekron (modern Israel) and surrounding territories.

The Jews had saved Alexander Balas's kingdom. Unfortunately, fortune quickly turned against them when Cleopatra Thea's father unexpectedly arrived in Judea, fearful of his son-in-law's weakness, and Jonathan's growing power. Philometor surprised everyone when he announced that he had come to support Demetrius. Jonathan had no choice but to abandon his Seleucid patron and accompany the Egyptian army to Syria. During their trip, Philometor placed garrisons in many of Jonathan's towns — the first step towards the Egyptian annexation of Judea.[7]

When Philometor arrived in Ptolemais, he immediately annulled Cleopatra Thea's marriage and, as one historian has bluntly described it, handed her to Demetrius "as if she were a piece of furniture."[8] The twenty-year-old Thea now found herself married to a fourteen-year-old prince who was about to set out with her father to kill her former spouse!

Philometor and Demetrius met Balas in battle at Antioch. During the engagement, a Syrian war elephant startled Philometor's horse. Balas's men threw him to the ground and fatally wounded him. However, Philometor clung to life for five days. Before he died, his men brought him Balas's severed head.

A Tragic Marriage

Cleopatra Thea's second husband, Demetrius, was a tragic figure. His youth and political inexperience hampered his ability to reign effectively over Seleucia's vast empire. But her new marriage was good for the Jews. Demetrius had no choice but to make peace with the Hasmoneans to save his kingdom. He summoned Jonathan to Ptolemais to reconfirm his former honors, including his right to hold the high priesthood, and gave him a partial remission of taxes and a portion of Samaria. In exchange, Jonathan agreed to leave the Seleucid garrison in Jerusalem and remain a Syrian ally. In the meanwhile, Seleucia began to fall apart. Foreign mercenaries revolted, looted, and murdered as they pleased. The youthful Demetrius was rapidly loosing control of his realm. In desperation, he called on his new Jewish ally for help.

Jonathan sent 3,000 of his troops to Antioch. They killed 100,000 and carted off much plunder. Confident that his kingdom was now secure, and perhaps to assuage his people's anger at Jonathan for his earlier atrocity in the temple of Dagon, Demetrius broke his treaty with the Hasmoneans. He then sought revenge against his internal political foes. His purge forced many Syrians to flee the country. Facing an uncertain future, they looked to Cleopatra Thea's infant son as their savior.

The renewal of the Seleucid civil wars disrupted the lives of all Syrians, especially Cleopatra Thea. Balas's former general, Diodotus, kidnapped her young son, Antiochus (reigned 145/4–40 B.C.E.), during the fighting. He gave him the lofty title Antiochus Theos Epiphanes ("God Manifest") Dionysus and proclaimed him king. Diodotus used the boy's popularity to amass an army. He captured Antioch and forced Cleopatra Thea's husband to flee.

Jonathan was confident that Demetrius would soon be deposed. He decided to turn against him and champion the cause of Cleopatra Thea's young son. In exchange for Jewish support, the young Antiochus — in reality Diodotus acting on his behalf— gave the Hasmoneans unprecedented honors. The author of 1 Maccabees preserves a letter written on behalf of the boy king conferring upon Jonathan the high priesthood, additional grants of land, and the title "King's Friend." Diodotus also sent Jonathan lavish gifts and allowed him to dress in purple, the traditional color of monarchs. He also gave Jonathan's brother, Simon, the title of governor from the Ladder of Tyre (modern Lebanon) to the border of Egypt. In exchange, Jonathan and Simon fought successful battles in Galilee, Lebanon, and Damascus (modern Syria) to make Cleopatra Thea's son king in place of her husband.

Emboldened by his new honors, Jonathan increasingly began to act like a monarch of an independent nation. He sent delegations to Rome and Sparta (modern Greece) to establish diplomatic relations. As Jonathan continued to increase the size of his military, Diodotus began to worry more about the Jews than Demetrius. He decided to act before Jonathan could declare independence, and possibly make an alliance with Seleucia's enemies. Diodotus used his considerable powers of persuasion to convince Jonathan to accompany him to Ptolemais with a small body of men. It was a trap. Diodotus took him prisoner and demanded an exorbitant ransom. Although Simon tried to win his brother's release, Diodotus murdered him.

About this time Cleopatra Thea received word that her son, Antiochus, had developed some internal ailment — purportedly a kidney stone — that required immediate surgery. He died during the operation. Many Syrians believed that Diodotus had bribed the physicians to make certain he did not survive the procedure. Diodotus immediately proclaimed himself Antiochus's successor, and took the rather pretentious title Tryphon ("the magnificent").

The Magnificent

Tryphon was a commoner who, through a combination of his charismatic personality and sheer luck, had managed to become ruler of a portion of the Seleucid Empire. But he failed to recognize that he owed his popularity to the young Antiochus. Many Syrians were convinced he had murdered Cleopatra Thea's son. Because the boy had been so popular, many of Tryphon's allies abandoned him, and pledged their fealty to Cleopatra Thea and her new spouse.

Tryphon was desperate. He decided to curry the favor of the Roman Republic by sending the Senate a large golden statue of the goddess Victory as a bribe. Instead of recognizing him as Seleucia's king, the senators etched the name of Cleopatra Thea's son on its base: a clear declaration they considered Tryphon a usurper and a murderer.[9]

The assassination of Cleopatra Thea's son ironically led to the creation of the Hasmonean state. Demetrius realized he needed the Jews to defeat Tryphon. In order to secure their support, he promised them anything they wished. He recognized Simon as the second Hasmonean high priest, pardoned him for helping Tryphon, and gave the Jews exemption from all past and future taxes and tributes, and the right to build new fortifications in Judea. According to the author of 1 Maccabees,

> the yoke of the Gentiles was removed from Israel ... and the people began to write in their documents and contracts, "In the first year of Simon the great high priest and commander and leader of the Jews" [1 Macc. 13:41–2].

This year, 143/2 B.C.E., marks the birth of the Hasmonean state. Salome Alexandra was likely born the following year. She was among the first royal children to grow up in a free and independent Judea: she almost lived to see its destruction in 63 B.C.E., less than four years after her death.

Simon began a brutal campaign to expand his new country. He conquered the pagan town of Gazara (modern Israel), removed its population, and resettled it with Jews.[10] This city was important because it dominated a strategic pass through the mountains that connected Jerusalem with the port of Joppa (modern Israel). He also expelled the Seleucid garrison in Jerusalem, which had been a longstanding source of contention between the Judeans and the Syrians. The author of 1 Maccabees portrays this time as an idyllic period of peace and prosperity when "all the people sat under their own vines and fig trees, and there was no one to make them afraid."[11] These were the best of times for the Jews. But for Cleopatra Thea this was the worst year of her life. Her twenty-year-old husband decided to risk his nation's future in a foolish bid to conquer Parthia.

Danger from the East

The Parthian Empire was an Iranian civilization that ruled much of the Middle East and Asia for nearly four hundred years (ca. 247 B.C.E.–220 C.E.). At its height, it encompassed the modern countries of Iran, Iraq, Georgia, eastern Turkey, Turkmenistan, Afghanistan, Tajikistan, Pakistan, Kuwait, and most of the Persian Gulf states. At this time its king, Mithridates the Great (134–63 B.C.E.), had virtually unlimited capital and inexhaustible legions. He believed he could take advantage of Seleucia's strife and annex a portion of its territory.

In 141 B.C.E. Mithridates moved his forces west and conquered Babylon. He then dealt the Syrians a severe psychological blow when he captured the city of Seleucia-on-the-Tigris, the original capital of the Seleucid Empire. When Greek refugees fleeing Mithridates's advance arrived in Syria, Demetrius realized he had to act to quickly to prevent an invasion of his homeland. He abandoned his hunt for Tryphon and, in 140 B.C.E., declared war against Parthia.

Cleopatra Thea had apparently grown accustomed to her spouse during these turbulent years. She and Demetrius had three children: a daughter, Laodice, and two sons, Seleucus (V) and Antiochus (VIII). Before departing for Parthia, Demetrius sent Cleopatra Thea to the coastal town of Seleucia-in-Pieria for her safety. Although none of the historical accounts tells us anything about Cleopatra Thea's activities at this time, it is unlikely that Demetrius would have entrusted the powers of state to anyone other than her. Although she did not bear the title, she was in reality Seleucia's first queen regnant.

Demetrius's campaign began quite well. The region's Greek population welcomed him as their savior. He won a series of engagements against Mithridates's generals. But just when he was on the verge of a decisive victory, tragedy struck his expedition. The Parthians captured him. They exiled him to Media (modern Iran), deep within their empire.[12]

We know little about the turmoil that took place in Seleucia in the wake of Demetrius's defeat, except for one rather unusual incident. According to the historian Strabo, a general of Demetrius named Sarpedon made an unsuccessful effort to wrest the city of Ptolemais from Tryhon. After their victory, Tryphon's soldiers were marching along the shore in celebration when a tsunami engulfed them:

> A wave from the sea, like the rising tide of the ocean, submerged the fugitives; and some were carried off into the sea and destroyed, while others were left dead in the hollow places; and then, after this wave, the ebb tide uncovered the shore again and revealed the bodies of men lying among dead fish [Strabo, *Geography*, 16.2.26].[13]

Despite this seemingly divine portent, Tryphon managed to retain this vital port, which the Persians had formerly used as a base to invade Egypt.

Demetrius had a younger brother named Antiochus (VII) Euergetes (reigned 138–29 B.C.E.). He is commonly known as Sidetes after the town of Side in Pamphylia, in modern Turkey, where he had spent much of his youth living in exile. When he heard of his brother's capture, he became determined to return home and take power. But Tryphon controlled the coast, and prevented him from landing in Seleucia. Then Sidetes's fortunes unexpectedly changed when Cleopatra Thea made a momentous and unprecedented decision — she proposed marriage to him and offered him Seleucia's crown.[14]

In late 137, or perhaps early 138 B.C.E., Cleopatra Thea, for the third time in her life, married a Seleucid king. She was likely twenty-seven; her new husband was twenty-one. Their union proved quite popular; many of Tryphon's soldiers even pledged their allegiance to her and her new spouse.

Cleopatra Thea's husband was determined to kill Tryphon. He chased him throughout Syria. The first century C.E. Roman writer Frontinus, in his compendium of military stratagems, claims that Tryphon once escaped by throwing money on the road, which his pursuers stopped to pick up.[15] Antiochus Sidetes eventually tracked him down in the eastern region of Apamea (modern Syria), near the place of his birth. Cornered, and with no possibility of escape, Tryphon committed suicide. His death ended the latest round of Seleucid civil wars. Unfortunately, troubling times were ahead for Salome Alexandra's people — Sidetes decided to annex Judea.

Savior of the Jews?

Josephus tells us nothing about Cleopatra Thea at this time. We have already recounted her husband Sidetes's role in executing Simon; his aborted siege of John Hyrcanus in Jerusalem; how he invaded Parthia to win his brother's release; how John Hyrcanus thwarted his expedition through an elaborate ruse; and how he died in battle. But threats of Roman reprisals may not have been the only factor that led him to curtail his siege of Jerusalem, and make peace with the Hasmoneans. Another person may have played an instrumental role in saving Salome Alexandra's homeland — his wife.

There is considerable circumstantial evidence that Cleopatra Thea ended her husband's siege of Jerusalem. She came from a pro–Jewish family. Her mother (Cleopatra II) and sister (Cleopatra III) were ardent supporters of the Jews: both had Jewish generals in their armies and the Jews fought for them during Egypt's civil wars. Because the women of the Ptolemaic dynasty had a longstanding tradition of supporting the Jews, Cleopatra Thea likely favored them. Cleopatra Thea apparently convinced Sidetes to abandon his plan to annex the Hasmonean State and grant the Jews the same protections they enjoyed in Egypt.[16]

It is possible that Cleopatra Thea met our queen. She died in 121/20 B.C.E. when Salome Alexandra was either nineteen or twenty years old. Salome Alexandra may have accompanied her father-in-law, John Hyrcanus, during some state visit to meet Cleopatra Thea. Relations between this powerful pagan queen and the Hasmonean State were apparently quite cordial. Having prospered during her reign, the Jews would have been quite troubled to hear of her new and unforeseen predicament. A man now threatened the stability of the entire Middle East; his arrival was literally the shock of Cleopatra Thea's life.

An Ill-Fated Return

While Cleopatra Thea and her third husband were fighting Tryphon, her former spouse, Demetrius, had resigned himself to his captivity. He began to wear eastern clothing; he grew the traditional long Parthian beard; and he married king Mithridates's daughter, Rhodogune. They had at least two children. But his efforts to assimilate failed: he longed for home, and his former wife. He tried to escape twice. His situation looked hopeless. Then an old acquaintance paid him an unexpected visit.

Demetrius had a friend. His name was Callimander. He vowed to rescue his king from captivity. Unfortunately, the extant account of Demetrius's confinement recount only the most rudimentary elements of Callimander's epic journey, during which he undoubtedly experienced many harrowing adventures. Disguised as a Parthian, he paid some Arabs to guide him through the desert to Babylon. From there, he traversed the length and breadth of the Parthian Empire alone and undetected. He somehow located Demetrius in distant region of Media. The two escaped, but were quickly caught. Mithridates was so enthralled at Callimander's tale that he rewarded him handsomely for his loyalty to his former master. But Demetrius was not so lucky; Mithridates gave him a royal rebuke, sent him back to his wife, and further restricted his movement. Callimander chose to live in exile with Demetrius.

When Demetrius's Parthian wife gave birth to another child, his captors gave him some additional freedom of movement. But they had underestimated the abilities of the ever-resourceful Callimander. He and Demetrius escaped again. This time they almost succeeded; they were captured near the Seleucid frontier. Mithridates mocked Demetrius by sending him some golden dice to pass away his time.

Demetrius's situation changed suddenly when Phraates, Parthia's new monarch, received word that Sidetes had invaded his territory. Phraates released Demetrius, hoping that he would start a civil war in Seleucia to remove his sibling from power; however, Sidetes died in battle. Phraates tried to recapture Demetrius, but it was too late. Demetrius made it to Syria, presumably accompanied by his loyal friend Callimander.

Few historical figures have experienced as many tragedies as Cleopatra Thea. Her first marriage ended in divorce; the Parthians took her second spouse captive; her third husband died in battle; and her son Antiochus had been murdered. Demetrius, moreover, had compounded her grief by taking two of their children, Seleucus and Laodice, with him on his Parthian expedition; both were captured. Seleucus remained a prisoner in Parthia; his subsequent fate is unknown. Phraates married Cleopatra Thea's daughter, Laodice. She presumably bore him children; she too disappears from the historical record.[17] Still grieving over their loss, Cleopatra Thea faced the shock of her life when Demetrius unexpectedly appeared at her doorstep dressed as a Parthian demanding his former positions as Seleucia's king and her spouse!

Demetrius's Parthian confinement had crippled him psychologically. In the absence of any contemporary reports of his mental state we must look to other evidence to reconstruct his mindset. Fortunately, he minted coins during his two reigns that allow us to chart his precipitous physical and psychological decline. In contrast to the robust youthful king on the face of his earlier currency, his later coins depict him in Parthian garb with long hair and a lengthy beard.[18] He looks tired, worn out, and indecisive. His subsequent behavior suggests the years of captivity had taken a great toll on his psyche.

Cleopatra Thea found herself in the unenviable position of having to reconcile with Demetrius after a twelve-year absence. For the fourth time, she married a Seleucid king.[19] But her second union with Demetrius was very different from her first: she wed a widely hated man. Many Syrians had perished in Demetrius's Parthian debacle: a large number still languished in captivity, including two of Cleopatra Thea's children, with no hope of release. There was no rejoicing in Seleucia at the return of its former monarch. Cleopatra Thea realized that her husband could never retain power. She was convinced he had to be removed if the Seleucid Empire was to survive. She decided to dispose of him.

The historian Appian claims that Cleopatra Thea was driven by jealousy. She supposedly hated Demetrius because he had married a Persian noble during his captivity.[20] But she had better reasons to eliminate him than mere infidelity. Now thirty-eight years of age, she was confident of her abilities and a proven leader. Many Syrians believed she was the only suitable candidate for the throne. If there was any doubt about Demetrius's instability to rule, his first act as king made it clear to his subjects that immediate steps needed to be taken to remove him from power. He announced his intention to invade Egypt, overthrow Cleopatra Thea's family, and become its Pharaoh.

The Madness of King Demetrius

At this time Cleopatra Thea's stepfather, Ptolemy Physcon, was married to her mother, Cleopatra (II). Their union came apart when he took his stepdaughter, Cleopatra (III), as his second wife (she was Cleopatra Thea's sister). Although polygamy was common in Egypt, marriage between a king, his wife, and his stepdaughter was unprecedented. (We will recount this sordid episode in the next chapter.) Unsuccessful in her effort to remove her husband and daughter from power, Cleopatra (II) went to Cleopatra Thea for help. She quickly realized that she could easily manipulate Demetrius. She promised to make him Egypt's king if he eliminated her lecherous husband and traitorous daughter.

Demetrius naively accepted his mother-in-law's offer even though it was clear to everyone that she would never give up power, especially to her unstable son-in-law. But her plan was doomed from the start; Physcon received advanced warning. He blocked Demetrius at Pelusium, Egypt's traditional border. Unable to move forward, and reluctant to return home in disgrace, he was uncertain what to do. Meanwhile, revolts against his rule erupted throughout Seleucia. He had to rush home to save his kingdom. The Judeans had no choice but to remain idle, and watch Seleucid troops march through their country.

Physcon decided to take advantage of Seleucia's turmoil by replacing

Cleopatra Thea's husband. He chose an obscure son of an Egyptian merchant named Alexander (reigned 128–23 B.C.E.). To make him a more suitable candidate, Physcon created a fictitious royal genealogy; he claimed that Alexander was Cleopatra Thea's adopted son from her first marriage.[21] Her subjects did not believe this improbable story. They contemptuously referred to the puppet-king Alexander as Zabinas ("the bought one").

Cleopatra Thea realized that her position as Syria's queen was precarious. The pretender Zabinas threatened to take control of her country. At this time, she was ruling part of Seleucia from the strategic port city of Ptolemais while her husband was fighting Zabinus. After Demetrius lost a battle and fled to her for safety, she decided to abandon him and take power in her own name.

With no safe haven left, Demetrius fled to the nearby island kingdom of Tyre (modern Lebanon) to seek sanctuary in its temple of Heracles Melkart. The city's governor arrested him while his ship was in the harbor and executed him. Many Syrians were convinced Cleopatra Thea had arranged his murder.[22]

Now a mature woman of thirty-nine, Cleopatra Thea was, for the first time in her life, master of her own destiny. No longer content to be handed from one man to another, she vowed to determine her own future. In 126/5 B.C.E. she took the unprecedented act of assuming power without a man at her side. She minted silver coins with her portrait alone: a public proclamation that she was Seleucia's sovereign. Her attire is surprisingly plain for a queen. There is no jewelry to indicate her office; a simple veil covers her corn rolls and crown. The reverse depicts a cornucopia along with the inscription "Queen Cleopatra Thea Euteria" (Queen Cleopatra, Goddess of Plenty). She looks much older and she appears more determined than her earlier depiction alongside Balas. After decades of living with incompetent men, it was a bold proclamation to her subjects that she was on her own.

A Mother Betrayed

Cleopatra Thea enjoyed widespread support as Seleucia's first queen regnant. But some of her subjects felt uncomfortable having a strong-willed female monarch. Perhaps they would have welcomed her as their sole ruler under better circumstances. But civil war was looming once again. Zabinas was still trying to take control of the entire Seleucid Empire. Cleopatra Thea likely realized that her subjects needed a strong male presence on the throne. After four marriages, she refused to wed again. She decided the best course of action was to appoint a co-ruler. She named Antiochus (VIII), her sixteen-year-old son by Demetrius, her co-regent.

Crowned Antiochus Epiphanes Philometor Callinicus ("Manifest, mother loving, and illustrious in victory"), many of his subjects called him Grypus ("hook-nose") because of his distinctive proboscis. Although he was purportedly quite ugly, he looked very much like his mother (both bore the family's prominent nose). Cleopatra Thea issued coins to celebrate their joint rule, and to show her subjects that it was not a partnership of equals. Grypus (reigned 126/5–96 B.C.E.) appears in her shadow: her portrait literally obscures his. The two hated one another. But they decided to temporarily put aside their mutual mistrust when they received word that Zabinas had proclaimed himself king in Antioch and threatened to take control of the entire country.

In meantime Cleopatra (II) had reconciled with her brother-husband (Ptolemy Physcon) and daughter (Cleopatra III). The three once again ruled Egypt as triple monarchs. Cleopatra Thea realized that she needed to mend her relationship with her Egyptian kin so that they would no longer support Zabinas. Ironically, she decided that the best course of action was to propose a royal union. She arranged for her niece, Cleopatra Tryphaena (ca. 95–ca. 51 B.C.E.), to leave Egypt and marry her son.

Tryphaena was the daughter of Cleopatra Thea's sister, Cleopatra (III). She was about sixteen or seventeen years old when she wed the young hooknose. As part of the agreement, Cleopatra Thea received Egyptian military aide to help eliminate Zabinas. Zabinas was so desperate for funds to continue his fight against her that he melted a statue of the goddess Victory from the temple of Jupiter in Antioch to sell its valuable metal.[23] His subjects expelled him from the city for this sacrilege. Grypus poisoned him.

Zabinus's death did not bring Cleopatra Thea peace. She quickly discovered that she faced an even greater enemy — her son. Grypus believed his marriage to an Egyptian princess ensured good relations with the Ptolemies for the foreseeable future, and gave him the right to govern Seleucia alone. Mother and daughter began to conspire against one another. The historian Justin, who recounts Cleopatra Thea's downfall with great delight, attributes her demise to her insatiable "lust for power." According to his account, when Grypus returned exhausted from a hunt she offered him a cup of wine. Suspicious at this uncharacteristic display of maternal affection, he correctly surmised that the beverage contained poison and forced her to drink it. She died shortly afterwards. In the words of Justin, "The queen was beaten by a crime that recoiled on its author, and died by the poison which she had prepared for another."[24]

A Tarnished Reputation

The chroniclers of history have not been kind to Cleopatra Thea. They portray her as a villain for supposedly trying to assassinate her son: they ignore her many achievements. Married to four successive kings, she held power for nearly forty-two years in various capacities. During this lengthy span of time, she survived countless wars, political intrigues, the deaths of all her spouses, the loss of a son and daughter to the Parthians, and much more. Yet, throughout these terrible circumstances she managed to hold her nation together by acting as its de facto monarch when her husbands were fighting their endless wars of conquest. When Demetrius returned from captivity, many Syrians preferred to have her as their ruler, confident she was a better candidate than any male, even her sons. She could not have accomplished anything without the support of Syria's political establishment, its military, and its citizens. She was clearly a popular and well-loved queen.

Historians must use the biased accounts of male chroniclers to reconstruct Cleopatra Thea's final days. Fortunately, the surviving annals of her time provide enough information to offer a likely scenario of how she died. Although the historians exonerate Grypus, it is very likely that he — an amateur toxicologist and the author of several poems about poisonous herbs — fabricated his mother's assassination attempt to conceal his evil deed.[25] According to Justin, Grypus not only forced Zabinas to drink poison, but he also attempted to poison his half-brother, Antiochus Cyzicenus, as well. Grypus had the means, the motivation, and the pharmaceutical acumen to mix a toxic brew for his mother. Grypus certainly poisoned Cleopatra Thea.

Cleopatra Thea was a woman of considerable intellectual abilities and political savvy. Yet, she is virtually unknown today. But she was not the only powerful Seleucid queen; her siblings were equally formidable rulers. Without these women it is unlikely the famed Cleopatra (VII) would have challenged the might of the Roman Empire. These lesser-known Cleopatras of Egypt changed the course of modern history by saving the Hasmonean dynasty. If not for their involvement in Judea's affairs, there never would have been a Queen Salome Alexandra. It is to these remarkable Egyptian women that we now turn in our quest to understand Salome Alexandra and her world.

8

Warrior Queens of Egypt
Cleopatra II and Cleopatra III

She richly deserved her infamous death — she had driven her own mother from her marriage bed, made two daughters husbandless by marrying them to their brothers in turn, she exiled one son and then made war against him, and treacherously plotted the death of another son after robbing him of his throne. — Epitaph for Cleopatra III (ca. 160/55–101 B.C.E.), Justin, *History*, 39.4.6

She committed murder, adultery, and incest to satisfy her insatiable lust for power. Her people worshipped her as the living incarnation of the goddess Isis. A devout pagan, she loved the Jews; several synagogues were dedicated to her and her family.[1] Salome Alexandra owed her throne to this woman; she literally saved the Hasmonean dynasty and the city of Jerusalem. If not for this pagan queen, contemporary Judaism, and likely Christianity, would have developed differently. The granddaughter of the Syrian (Cleopatra I) and the daughter of the formidable protector of the Jews (Cleopatra II), she has been called "the most domineering of the Macedonian-Hellenistic queens."[2] Although few today have heard of this woman, everyone in antiquity, Jew and Gentile alike, knew her name — Cleopatra (III).

A Noble Lineage

Cleopatra III (ca. 160/55–101 B.C.E.) belonged to the second generation of powerful Hellenistic Egyptian queens. Her grandmother, the Syrian, and her grandfather, Ptolemy (V) Epiphanes, had three children: Ptolemy (VI), Ptolemy (VIII), and Cleopatra (II). Upon her husband's death in 180 B.C.E., the Syrian became the first Hellenistic female to hold power, although ostensibly as regent for her eldest son. However, her name appears before his in the royal inscriptions: a clear and unambiguous proclamation that she was the senior partner in this fictional co-regency.[3]

The Syrian must have been a rather impressive woman. She continued to influence Egypt's political affairs long after her death. Her eldest son and heir, Ptolemy (VI), was only eight or nine years old at the time of her passing. Before her death, she appointed a palace eunuch, Eulaios, and a Syrian salve, Lennaios, to govern on his behalf until he came of age. The willingness of her subjects to tolerate this unusual state of affairs suggests that she had prepared them for this caretaker government, whose purpose was apparently to ensure that her son would marry his sister.

Incest was customary among Egypt's royals; the Greeks abhorred it. The Syrian's great-great grandfather, Ptolemy (II), became the first of Egypt's Hellenistic rulers to adopt this foreign practice when, in 217 B.C.E., he married his elder sister, Arisone (II). She was a rather formidable woman; she fought alongside her husband at the battle of Raphia. Although no historian tells us why the young Ptolemy (VI) chose to revive this practice three decades later, it is perhaps not reading too much into the ancient narratives to see the Syrian's hand at work. She apparently realized her son needed a strong female presence, and arranged for him to marry his sister. He was apparently quite appreciative of his mother's guidance and added the title Philometor ("Mother Loving") to his name.[4]

Preserved for Posterity?

We can learn more about the Syrian's influence over her descendants by looking at her and her family's surviving portraits. She is depicted on the front of a coin and her son Philometor is on the reverse. The two bear the prominent nose of the Syrian's father, King Antiochus (III) the Great.[5] Because there are no certain coin images of her daughter, Cleopatra (II), or her granddaughter, Cleopatra (III), it is difficult to tell them apart. The two are often confused with the Syrian (I) since all preferred to wear their hair in long ringlets like the goddess Isis. However, a translucent alabaster-like marble head with traces of paint, acquired in 1977 by Vassar College, has been tentatively identified as Cleopatra (II). Its hair — two large coiled locks with horizontal striations surrounding the face — is reminiscent of statues of the goddess Isis, the patron deity of the Ptolemaic queens. This woman bears the family's characteristic long straight nose and prominent eyes. If it is a depiction of Cleopatra (II), then it reveals something rather remarkable about her family that may explain why it is so difficult to distinguish her from her female relations: she, her brother Philometor, and likely their daughter Cleopatra (III) looked alike. Many must have viewed them as the Syrian's incarnations.[6]

Because Jews at this time viewed images as a violation of the second commandment, we have no pictures of Salome Alexandra or her Judean contemporaries. But there is a depiction of another Salome that gives us an idea of Salome Alexandra's likely appearance. Because her family intermarried with the Hasmoneans, this woman may have shared many of our queen's physical features. It belongs to the wife of Aristobulus, great-grandson of Herod the Great, who ruled the small Syrian kingdom of Chalcis (57–92 C.E.). Although few have heard of him, many know the story of his spouse: Christians revile her to this day; she is the evil woman of Oscar Wilde's 1896 play *Salome*. She is the infamous dancing girl of the Gospels who, at her mother's urging, asked for the head of John the Baptist on a platter.

Aristobulus's coins depict him on the front and Salome on the reverse. She wears a headband and an erring, but no crown or other jewelry befitting her royal status. She was about forty years old when this coin was minted, which is the same age as Salome Alexandra when her husband became king. But there may be another, more shocking, depiction of this infamous Salome. A second-century C.E. marble panel from the Roman city of Petra in Jordan likely portrays her holding John the Baptist's head.[7] This Salome must have been a rather powerful woman to appear on a coin at a time when Jews were reluctant to make images of their rulers.

Aristobulus's wife was almost certainly named after Salome Alexandra. But here is where the similarity ends: the two had virtually nothing in common. It is unfortunate that whenever most people hear the name Salome, they immediately think of the woman who helped murder John the Baptist, and not her remarkable predecessor, Salome Alexandra.

The Syrian's Dysfunctional Children

The marriage of Cleopatra (II) and Philometor appears to have been a happy union. They had at least four children: Cleopatra (III), Cleopatra Thea, Ptolemy Eupator, and another son named Ptolemy.[8] Everything appeared to be going well for the young couple until their younger brother's demonic character emerged. He not only tormented them, but Egypt's Jews as well.

The Syrian's youngest son was among the most unusual rulers in history. His official name is Ptolemy (VIII) Euergetes (II) Tryphon. He was also called "Ptolemy the younger" to distinguish him from his elder brother, Philometor. Some of his detractors preferred to call him Kakergetes ("the malefactor"), which was apparently intended to mock his name Euergetes ("the benefactor"). But a large number of his subjects, and many ancient historians, called him

Physcon ("Potbelly") because of his considerable girth.[9] We will follow their lead and refer to him by this sobriquet.

If the ancient descriptions of Physcon's appearance contain even a modicum of truth, he was truly deserving of his unflattering moniker. The Stoic philosopher Panaetius, who met Physcon as part of a Roman delegation, provides us with the following account of his rather unusual demeanor:

> Owing to his luxury he was grotesquely obese, and his belly was so large that no one could put their arms around him; he wore a tunic that reached down to his feet, with sleeves that extended to his wrists, and he never by chance walked outside except on this occasion [Panaetius as quoted by Athenaeus, *The Deipnosophists*, 12.73].[10]

During this meeting Scipio, the delegation's leader, whispered to Panaetius, "The Alexandrians have already received some benefit from our visit. Thanks to us they have finally seen their king walking."[11] But the historian Justin's description of Physcon's appearance is the most revolting of all:

> He was as comical a person as he was a cruel one to his fellow-citizens. He had an ugly face, and was short in stature; and he had a bloated stomach more like an animal's than a man's. The repulsiveness of his appearance was heightened by his dress, which was exceedingly fine-spun to the point of transparency, just as if he had some motive for exhibiting what a decent man should have made every effort to conceal (Justin, *History*, 38.8.9–10].

Physcon's grotesque appearance, and his apparent lack of taste in clothing, caused many to overlook his considerable intellectual gifts. He was a brilliant philologist, the author of a critical study of Homer, and the writer of 24 books of *Hypomnemata* (a compendium on topics as diverse as the animals of Libya, the birds in the Alexandrian zoo, and the mistresses of Pharaoh Ptolemy II).[12]

Sometime between October 5 and November 12, 170 B.C.E., Cleopatra and her two brothers became co-rulers. Never before had three persons, let alone siblings, governed Egypt together. Documents from this time refer to all three as Pharaohs, and a relief depicts them alongside one another presenting offerings to eight of Egypt's gods and goddesses. This triple monarchy was so unusual that it even caught the attention of the author of the biblical Book of Daniel, who predicted its demise. However, the third century C.E. Christian writer Prophery was unwilling to acknowledge that the Bible recognizes the legitimacy of a female monarch. In his commentary on Daniel, he identifies these "three kings" as Philometor, Physcon, but substitutes the Armenian ruler Artaxias—a man who had nothing to do with Egypt or Judea—for Cleopatra.[13]

It did not take a biblical prophet to foresee that the triple monarchy was doomed to fail. The animosity between Cleopatra's two brothers was exacerbated by their vastly different temperaments. Philometor was a kind and submissive man who was popular with his people. Physcon was violent, hot tempered, and determined to wrest power from his siblings at any cost. The two hated one another. Cleopatra, although close to her eldest brother, apparently got along with both of her siblings.

Cleopatra and Philometor underestimated their brother's deviousness and popularity with the masses. In late 164 B.C.E., Physcon had gathered enough support to expel his sibling from Egypt. She remained in Alexandria and became his co-ruler. Philometor traveled to Italy to court the favor of the Romans in a bid to regain power and expel his brother. A master political strategist, he engaged in some rather unusual theatrics to persuade the Roman Senate back his claim to Egypt's throne. Instead of accompanying the royal entourage that greeted him in the port of Ostia to Rome, he insisted on walking there like a commoner. Once in the capital, he took up residence in a hovel with an artist friend. His plan worked; the Senate made amends for this breach of diplomatic protocol by honoring him as a visiting king.

While Philometor was in Rome courting the Senate's favor, Cleopatra worked behind the scenes to help him return. The two carried on an extensive correspondence; she kept him informed of Physcon's actions, especially his growing unpopularity. The Roman Senate decided to intervene when they heard the Alexandrians had risen up against him. They sent a delegation to Egypt to urge the three siblings to reconcile. After considerable negotiations, the Syrian's offspring reached an accord: they agreed to divide the Ptolemaic Empire. Philometor and Cleopatra would rule Egypt and Cyprus while Physcon would govern the North African region of Cyrenaica. The three issued a general decree of amnesty pardoning certain crimes that had been committed before August 17, 163 B.C.E. Its publication brought peace to Egypt and made the triple monarchy's restoration official.[14]

A stone inscription discovered near the Acropolis in Athens, Greece, sheds some light on Cleopatra's fame at this time. It lists the victors in the equestrian competitions at the Panathenaic Games; a quadrennial sporting event held in conjunction with a religious festival to honor the goddess Athena's birthday. Cleopatra is listed among the victors for the 162 B.C.E. competitions. But she was not the only member of her family to have sponsored a team; her brother-husband Philometor also won an event. Both apparently entered horses, jockeys, and chariots in these games to proclaim their restoration as joint monarchs the preceding year. Her win at this prestigious sports competition — commemorated in stone for posterity — proclaimed to all her victories in the traditionally male-dominated arenas of sport and politics.[15]

While Cleopatra and Philometor were winning international acclaim in the realm of sport, their brother was plotting against them. The Roman-brokered treaty was domed to fail since it made Physcon king of a wasteland. He was determined to wrest power from his siblings at any cost. Physcon tried to invade the island nation of Cyprus, which he planned to use as a base for attacking Egypt. His expedition failed: he returned to North Africa in disgrace.

Physcon's future looked uncertain. After thwarting an attempt on his life, which many believed his brother had ordered, he decided to adopt a new strategy to increase his power. It was so unusual and unexpected that it forced the Roman Senate to reassess its Egyptian policy — he bequeathed his kingdom to the Roman Republic.

Physcon was a shrewd political strategist. He knew the Romans would eagerly accept his offer since they had fought for centuries to control North Africa. But he placed two stipulations in his will. First, he must die childless. Second, the Romans must agree to defend him against all his enemies, which included his brother Philometor. The Roman Senate agreed to his conditions, ratified his will, and deposited copies of it in Rome and the shrine of Apollo in the North African city of Cyrene. Physcon was Rome's new ally. But his stratagem to win the Senate's favor proved unnecessary. He soon became Egypt's ruler after his brother died fighting Cleopatra Thea's husband, Alexander Balas.

Philometor's unexpected death left Physcon free to seize Egypt's throne without any threat of Roman interference. Because most of Philometor's army was still in Syria, there was little Cleopatra could do to stop him. Her situation looked hopeless; Alexandria was defenseless. Then the son of the last legitimate Jewish high priest came to her rescue.

Salvation from the Jews

Onias (IV) was Egypt's most important Jew. He was the leader of its Jewish community and a loyal supporter of Cleopatra (II). He had his own army and legions of loyal followers scattered throughout the country. But it was not his military might or his influence at the court that made him so powerful. Egypt's Jews pledged their allegiance to him because he was the son of the last lawful high priest, Onias III (?–175 B.C.E.).

An unlawful claimant to the high priesthood had murdered Onias (III). His son, Onias (IV), had remained in Judea throughout the entire Maccabean rebellion, and witnessed Judas the "Hammer" capture and rededicate the Temple in 164 B.C.E. He apparently expected Salome Alexandra's ancestors to name him high priest in place of his deceased father. When they usurped this

Ruins of the Jewish city of Tell el-Yehudiyeh in Egypt established by Onias IV, seen from the north. Archaeologists continue to search for the Jewish temple he built near this site (Todd Bolen/BiblePlaces.com).

sacred office, Onias (IV) left Judea with a loyal band of followers for Egypt. Cleopatra and Philometor welcomed them. According to Josephus, he made a rather unusual request of the royal couple. He asked for permission to build a Jewish temple in the Egyptian town of Leontopolis. It was a rather unusual locale for a Jewish shrine since it sat amidst a ruined temple to the Egyptian cat goddess Bastet, and the buried remains of thousands of mummified felines.

We know little about this unorthodox temple whose location continues to elude archaeologists. Josephus tells us it was smaller and less elaborate than Jerusalem's temple; it purportedly resembled a tower. Despite its unusual history and location, many Jews recognized it as a legitimate shrine. The rabbis later ruled that offerings made there were acceptable to God, but its priests were ineligible to serve in the Jerusalem temple.[16] There may be an explanation for this rather surprising concession. According to Josephus, the biblical prophet Isaiah had predicted its construction:

> In that day five cities in the land of Egypt will speak the language of Canaan and swear allegiance to the Lord of Hosts; one will be called the City of Destruction. In that day there will be an altar to the Lord in the middle of the Land of Egypt, and a pillar to the Lord near its border [Isa. 19:18–19].

The Greek translator of this biblical book attempted to make Onias's temple more legitimate by changing "City of Destruction" to "City of Righteousness."

When we read the remarkable story of Salome Alexandra and her family, we must remember that while her husband and sons presided over the sacrifices in Jerusalem's temple, another group of Jewish priests were performing many of the same rituals, and celebrating the Jewish holidays, in Egypt. But unlike the Hasmoneans, these men were descendants of the last rightful occupant of Judaism's most sacred office. Salome Alexandra's family was unable to destroy this rival shrine because Egypt's rulers protected it. The Hasmoneans must have occasionally lost sleep, fearful that Onias and his followers would return to Judea, accompanied by Egypt's vast army, to seek their rightful place as its high priests. This nightmarish scenario almost became a reality when, during the reign of Salome Alexandra's husband, the sons of Onias (IV) appeared in Judea in command of Egyptian troops.

No previous ruler had treated the Jews better than Cleopatra (II) and Philometor. If we are to seek a likely reason for their devotion to Judaism, we should perhaps look no further than their mother. As an exile herself, the Syrian likely identified with the Jews who, like the Greeks, were a cultural minority in Egypt. Although we may never know the exact reasons that led Cleopatra (II) and her late husband to grant Onias (IV) land for his temple, she and her daughter benefited greatly from this alliance: the Jews became the protectors of the Ptolemaic queens.

Onias (IV) went to Alexandria with his Jewish legions to defend Cleopatra. Unable to repulse them, Physcon retailed against Alexandria's innocent Jewish community until a woman stopped him. Josephus's account of his atrocity is so shocking that it is worth quoting in full:

> Ptolemy Physcon, though not daring to face the army of Onias [IV], had arrested all the Jews in the city with their wives and children, and placed them, naked and in chains, to be trampled to death by elephants, the beasts being actually made drunk for the purpose. However, the outcome was the reverse of his intention. The elephants did not harm the Jews, but rushed at Physcon's friends, and killed a large number of them. Afterwards Ptolemy [Physcon] saw a terrible apparition, which forbade him to injure these people. When his favorite concubine, whom some call Ithaca and others Eirene, begged him not to commit such a great atrocity, he yielded to her and repented of what he had already done and was about to do. The Judeans living in Alexandria celebrate this day as a festival, rightly, since God visibly delivered them [*Ag. Ap.* 2.53–55].

The Jews were not the only group to have felt Physcon's wrath. He purged Alexandria of many Greek intellectuals, including the famed Aristarchos of Samothrake (ca. 217–145 B.C.E.), director of the Museum library. Then hostilities ceased when Cleopatra and Physcon agreed to marry and become coregents.

An Unhappy Union

Cleopatra (II) undoubtedly recalled the events of late 144 or early 143 B.C.E. with great joy; it was perhaps the happiest year of her life. She gave birth to a son while her husband, Physcon, underwent the traditional coronation ceremony in the ancient city of Memphis. Because the Egyptians viewed this coincidence as an auspicious event, the couple named their child Ptolemy Memphites after this city. She was now immensely popular since her subjects regarded her, Physcon, and Ptolemy Memphites as a divine triad of father, son, and sister-wife/mother.[17] Cleopatra was both goddess and mother of a god.

Cleopatra undoubtedly regarded February 18, 142 B.C.E., as the worst day of her life. But Physcon and his subjects believed it was a particularly auspicious day because two divine births had taken place. The first was the Apis Bull, Egypt's most sacred animal. The Greek traveler Herodotus (widely regarded as the founder of history) provides the following information about this divine creature that he picked up during his travels throughout Egypt:

> The Apis, or Epaphus, is the calf born from a cow, which is never afterwards
> allowed to conceive another. The Egyptians claim that a flash of light
> descends upon the cow from heaven, and causes her to give birth to the Apis.
> The calf which is called the Apis has distinctive markings: a white square on
> its forehead, an image of an eagle on its back, double the number of hairs on
> its tail, and the mark of a beetle on its tongue [Herodotus, *Histories* 3.28].

The Egyptians worshipped the Apis Bull as a living manifestation of the god Ptah (the Greeks believed this bull was the son of their supreme deity Zeus). It lived in a shrine in Memphis under the dotting care of special clergy. When it died, the priests embalmed its body and interred it in a royal tomb alongside its predecessors, and began a search for its next incarnation.

The other divine birth to have occurred on February 18, 142 B.C.E., was a royal heir. Designated by scholars as Ptolemy (IX) Soter (II), he was given the title "distinguished in his birth together with that of the living Apis." The country's pagans — Greek and native Egyptians alike — rejoiced at the arrival of two gods on earth the same day, except for Cleopatra (II). For her, Ptolemy Soter's birth was the worst day of her life. Physcon was the father, but she was the grandmother!

Physcon had married his stepdaughter, Cleopatra (III), the preceding year — she was the mother of Ptolemy Soter. Although the ancient historians claim that Physcon raped her and forced her into this union, the evidence suggests otherwise. Cleopatra (III) was a cunning young woman with an insatiable lust for power. Physcon loved her and gave her unprecedented honors; he elevated her to equal status with her mother. A document written the next year mentions "the priestesses of queen Cleopatra (II) and of queen Cleopatra (III) the daughter." For the next eight years, until 132 B.C.E. when this unusual alliance ended, Egypt had two queens. The problem was that both were mothers of potential heirs to Physcon's throne.

Cleopatra (III) and Physcon had another son and three daughters: Cleopatra (IV), Cleopatra (V) Tryphaena, and Cleopatra Selene (the latter will later play an important role in Salome Alexandra's life). She was clearly Physcon's favorite wife. Her relationship with her mother, however, worsened. Cleopatra (II) feared that her daughter and brother-husband would remove her from power, and name their son, Ptolemy Soter, as co-ruler instead of her own son. She sent her son, Ptolemy Memphites, to Cyrene in North Africa for his protection, and prepared to remove her brother-husband and daughter from power.

In 132/1 B.C.E. Egypt's political situation changed dramatically when a mob loyal to Cleopatra (II) ravaged Alexandria and burned the royal palace. Physcon fled to Cyprus with Cleopatra (III) and their children. Cleopatra (II) stripped them of their royal titles and proclaimed herself Egypt's sole ruler. To sever any link with the past, she created a new calendar that began with her reign, and bestowed upon herself the rather pretentious title "Queen Cleopatra Thea Philometor Soteria" ("Cleopatra the mother loving goddess, the savior").[18] Just over sixty years after "the Syrian" had left her homeland for Egypt to marry its future king, her daughter had become its first Ptolemaic queen regnant.

Physcon was unwilling to relinquish power. Once again we turn to the historian Justin for the gruesome details of what he did to punish Cleopatra (II):

> He [Ptolemy Physcon] summoned his eldest son [Ptolemy Memphites] from Cyrene and murdered him so that the Alexandrians could not make him king in opposition to himself.... He dismembered the body, put it in a basket and had it presented to his mother [Cleopatra II] at a banquet on her birthday.... The attention of the leading citizens was thus turned from a feast to a funeral. They displayed the mangled limbs to the people and made them see what they could expect in the future from a king who had murdered his own son [Justin, *History*, 38.8.12–14].

The royal family reconciled shortly after this horrible event. As an act of contrition to restore harmony in Egypt, Physcon deified Ptolemy Memphites under name Ptolemy Neos Philopator (Ptolemy, New, Father Loving).[19]

A Ptolemaic Messiah?

The same year Cleopatra (II) expelled her husband and daughter from Egypt, a new threat emerged from the south. An Egyptian named Harsiese (reigned 132–30 B.C.E.) proclaimed himself Pharaoh. He seized the sacred city of Thebes (located across the Nile River from the famed Valley of Kings where Tutankhamen and other Egyptians kings were secretly buried). He is the only native Egyptian to have claimed the position of Pharaoh during the Ptolemaic period.[20] His movement lasted less than one year. It ironically had had no chance of success because most Egyptians remained steadfast supports of Physcon.

An anonymous text known as the *Potter's Oracle* provides us with a rare glimpse of native Egyptian opposition to the Ptolemies. Likely written by an Egyptian priest of the god Khnum (he is often depicted as a potter) in the city of Heliopolis, it predicts that a native Egyptian will overthrow the Greek rulers:

> Egypt will grow when the kindly one who originates from Helios [=the sun] has arrived to be king for fifty-five years, a giver of good things, who is appointed by the greatest goddess, Isis.[21]

This oracle suggests that many Egyptians had supported Harsiese. His death in battle did not end speculation that a savior figure would emerge from Egypt.

While some native Egyptians were trying to subvert Hellenism, a follower of Onias (IV) in Leontopolis was encouraging Jews and pagans to embrace it. He wrote a prophetic text under the guise of a pagan luminary known as the Sibyl — a female who delivered oracles at temples throughout the Hellenistic world. Jews, and later Christians, wrote books under her name in which the Sibyl praises monotheism. One of these Jewish false prophecies, known as the *Third Sibylline Oracle,* makes a rather remarkable prediction — the long-anticipated messiah will be a Ptolemaic king.

The author of the *Third Sibylline Oracle* states that during the reign of the "seventh king of Egypt" the country will be torn by strife and then,

> God will send a King from the sun who will stop evil wars from taking place on earth, killing some, imposing oaths of loyalty on others; and he will not do all these things as he wishes but in obedience to the noble teachings of the great God [*Sib. Or.* 3:652–56].

Because Physcon is the seventh Ptolemaic ruler, he must be the king of this oracle, whose reign heralds the messianic era.

Physcon is an unlikely candidate to be the harbinger of the messiah since he persecuted Jews. But when we consider the dangerous times when this text was written, the author's improbable choice makes sense. During Egypt's civil wars Onias (IV) and his Jewish followers remained loyal to Cleopatra (II). In 124 B.C.E., with Egypt threatening to fall apart, she reconciled with her brother and her daughter, restored the triple monarchy, and ended the civil wars.

For the author of the *Third Sibylline Oracle*, Physcon's return to power, under the influence of his two pro–Jewish wives, heralded the arrival of the messianic age because it brought peace and prosperity to Egypt's Jews.[22] Several Jews rose to the highest levels in the Egyptian military and later helped Cleopatra (III) keep Salome Alexandra's husband as Judea's ruler. Although Physcon's wives actually brought about this era, God was sexist when it came to messiahs: they, and their harbingers, were always men. However, a messiah needed a mother, which means that the author of the *Third Sibylline Oracle* expected Cleopatra (II) or Cleopatra (III) to give birth to Judaism's savior.

The Rise of Cleopatra (Iii)

The triple monarchy continued for another eight years. It was a time of peace and prosperity for native Egyptians and Jews alike. But it was a sad period for Cleopatra (II). Her husband and daughter continued to undermine her. Although she outlived Physcon, he continued to torment her from beyond the grave. He named Cleopatra (III) his successor in his will, and gave her the right to determine which of her sons would become her co-ruler. She chose the youngest, Ptolemy (X) Alexander (140/39–88/87 B.C.E.). The triple monarchy was over.

Now approaching seventy, and having spent some fifty-fifty years as Egypt's queen, Cleopatra (II) was still beloved by her subjects. She simply fades from history: no one saw fit to record her passing. We do not know how or where she died. She is last mentioned in a document dated October 29, 116 B.C.E.; she presumably succumbed to the effects of old age shortly thereafter. She likely died alone, possibly comforted by a few courtiers, and perhaps some of her loyal Jewish supporters. She was one of Egypt's most remarkable Pharaohs. Yet, few today know that she existed, or that there was a time when warrior queens sat upon the thrones of the greatest countries in the Hellenistic world. With female rule now the norm in Egypt and Syria, it was only a matter of time before a woman took power in Judea.

9

A Man Who Knew His Place
King Alexander Jannaeus

After the death of Aristobulus his wife Salina, who the Greeks called Alexandra, released his brothers — for Aristobulus had imprisoned them, as we have said before — and appointed Jannaeus, also known as Alexander, king, who was best fitted for this office by reason of his age and because he knew his place.— Josephus, *Antiquities* 13.320–1

Salome Alexandra grew up in a region dominated by women. During her childhood, the extraordinary mother-daughter team of Cleopatra (II) and Cleopatra (III) ruled Egypt while Cleopatra Thea governed the Seleucid Empire. After Antiochus Sidetes's ill-fated Parthian expedition, the daughters of Cleopatra (III) — Cleopatra Tryphaena, Cleopatra (IV), and Cleopatra Selene — became masters of Syria. But Salome Alexandra's sister-in-law, Salina Alexandra, realized that her people were not ready for a female monarch. She chose Salome Alexandra's husband, Alexander Jannaeus, as Judea's next king and high priest "because he knew his place."

A Man Who Knew His Place?

Josephus's description of Alexander Jannaeus is shocking. Calling him a man who "knew his place" implies passivity: a feminine quality not typically associated with kings and great warriors.[1] Philo echoes Josephus's sentiments, as well as the feelings of many Judean males, when he writes:

Men cannot compete with women, nor women with men.... If mannish women were to imitate men, or womanish men were to act like women, they would suffer ill repute [*Sacr.*, 100–101].

Although Salina Alexandra apparently thought that Alexander Jannaeus was a "womanish" man, he proved her wrong. He was determined to epitomize

129

all the manly qualities of his namesake, Alexander the Great — leadership, courage, and physical strength. He refused to bow to any woman, even though one had anointed him Judea's monarch and high priest.

After Salina Alexandra crowned Alexander Jannaeus king and high priest, he set out to consolidate his power by eliminating all the royal heirs. Josephus tells us that he had two surviving brothers. One, whose name is unknown, apparently staged an unsuccessful coup: Alexander Jannaeus murdered him. The other, Absalom, eschewed politics. Although Alexander Jannaeus held him "in honor," he mysteriously disappears from Josephus's narrative.[2] He undoubtedly met a tragic end. With both siblings eliminated, Alexander Jannaeus was firmly installed as Judea's monarch. Now he prepared for war.

A Gathering Storm

Kings in antiquity faced many perils when they embarked on foreign campaigns. Travel was slow; sieges often last for years; and communication between the frontline and home was difficult to maintain. All monarchs, moreover, faced the possibly of a coup whenever they left their country for an extended period of time. This was especially true for a new ruler like Alexander Jannaeus, whose skills as a leader and a warrior were untested. He knew that it would be foolish to undertake any military venture without leaving a trusted person behind to govern in his stead, and protect his interests. Josephus writes that he placed the government in hands he could trust. He would not have left anyone other than Salome Alexandra in charge of his kingdom when he set out to attack the great Mediterranean coastal city of Ptolemais.

Alexander Jannaeus's siege of Ptolemais was going well until an unexpected foe appeared from the south. Zoilus, tyrant of the port city of Dora (modern Israel), thought he could save Ptolemais and become master of the coastal territories. He attacked Alexander Jannaeus, but his army proved no match for the skilled Hasmonean legions. With no assistance forthcoming, the beleaguered citizens of Ptolemais sought help from a deposed Egyptian king in nearby Cyprus — Ptolemy Soter.

Soter hated his mother, Cleopatra (III). She had deposed him as her co-ruler, expelled him to Cyprus, and replaced him with his sibling, Ptolemy Alexander. She purportedly did this because she believed that Alexander would be more subservient than his bellicose brother. When envoys from Ptolemais asked for Soter's aide, he realized this was the perfect opportunity to overthrow his mother and brother. He knew that Ptolemais was a major coastal stronghold, and a strategic point from which to launch a sea invasion of Egypt. He could also use it to control all trade in the Mediterranean, as well as protect his land forces during his planned attack. Unfortunately, there was a problem that threatened to prevent his dream of conquering Egypt from coming to fruition.

Soter had no way of knowing that the people of Ptolemais had not been candid when they asked for his aid. They led him to believe he would lead a vast coalition — the armies of the coastal tyrant Zoilus of Gaza (modern Gaza Strip), the Sidonians (modern Lebanon), and others. The rulers of these cities and territories were now unwilling to help him after Zoilus's defeat. But Soter had no way of knowing this. Confident he could easily repulse Alexander Jannaeus with this large contingent, he sailed for Syria.

While Soter was heading towards Ptolemais, the situation on the ground changed dramatically. A man named Demaenetus had convinced his fellow citizens they had acted rashly by asking Ptolemy Soter for help. Cleopatra, he warned, would never allow her wayward son to occupy their strategically located city, which he could use as a base to attack her in Egypt. Ptolemais's citizens now realized they had inadvertently declared war against Cleopatra. They feared her more than the Hasmoneans. When Soter arrived, they refused to let him in their city, hoping that he would leave before his mother decided to intervene.

A Broken Promise

Alexander Jannaeus realized that his siege of Ptolemais had unwittingly thrust him in the middle of Egypt's dynastic war. Now fearing the Egyptians more than the Seleucids, he immediately abandoned his campaign and returned to Jerusalem. He offered Soter four hundred talents and a pact of non-aggression if he would eliminate Zoilus. It is unclear from Josephus's Greek whether Soter killed Zoilus or merely imprisoned him. According to Jewish tradition, Alexander Jannaeus took advantage of Zoilus's removal to expand his territorial holdings by capturing the port cities of Strato's Tower and Dora.[3] He would not have attacked these municipalities without Soter's approval. In exchange, Soter apparently assumed his new ally would support his claim to Egypt's throne. But Judea's high priest had no intention of keeping his word.

While Alexander Jannaeus was feigning peace with Soter, he entered into secret negotiations with Cleopatra. When Soter learned of this treachery, he vowed to destroy Alexander Jannaeus and the citizens of Ptolemais. He besieged the city and, after leaving his generals in charge of the assault, departed with the remainder of his forces for Judea.

Soter embarked on a campaign of wanton destruction throughout the

Galilee. He subdued the town of Asochis on the Sabbath and took ten thousand of its inhabitants prisoners. But his assault against the nearby metropolis of Sepphoris proved unsuccessful. Undeterred at this loss, he crossed the Jordan River to link up with the Hellenistic cities in the region. He may have also intended to unite with the Nabatean Arabs of modern Jordan before proceeding southward towards Jerusalem. Once in control of Judea's capital, Soter apparently planned to invade Egypt. Only one thing stood between him and his goal of capturing his homeland and removing his mother and brother from power — Alexander Jannaeus.

Alexander Jannaeus and Soter met east of the Jordan River at an unknown place called Asophon. Josephus's account of their engagement shows the extent to which Judea had become thoroughly Hellenized. According to his sources, Judea's army consisted of fifty to eighty thousand men; not all of them were Jews. He placed his kingdom's salvation in the hands of an elite battalion of pagan mercenaries dubbed the "hundred-fighters." These men, armed with bronze shields, specialized in the Greek manner of warfare known as the phalanx.

The phalanx was a massive rectangular formation of troops. Soldiers in a phalanx marched in rows, shoulder to shoulder, with their spears projecting between their overlapping bronze-plated shields. As the men in the front line moved towards the enemy, their comrades behind pushed them toward the opposing ranks. Unlike modern conflicts, during which soldiers seldom have physical contact with their enemy, ancient warfare was close and personal. Fighting was largely hand-to-hand. Each soldier thrust his sword deep into the stomach of his adversary; disgorged intestines and internal organs spewed upon all. The screams, stench, and cries of the dying were horrendous. As soldiers fell in battle, others stepped forward — literally walking atop their dying comrades — to take their place, while those in the rear pushed them into the killing frenzy. This pressure made the phalanx a nearly impenetrable wall of death. Few armies could withstand its force. Alexander the Great had brought this type of fighting to the Middle East with devastating results: he annihilated nearly all who stood in his way. Only another phalanx could potentially stop Alexander Jannaeus's "hundred-fighters." Unfortunately, Soter had one.

Soter's battle-hardened soldiers would have flinched at the sight of Alexander Jannaeus's elite warriors. With both sides aware of the carnage awaiting them, neither force was eager to make the first move. A commander in Soter's army named Philostephanus — likely a Greek mercenary — decided to make the initial strike. He ordered his troops to cross the river that separated the two forces. Alexander Jannaeus chose not to impede his advance, thinking he could push his foe back into the water. When the two armies met, the battle proved to be a stalemate; Soter's forces would not retreat; and Alexander Jannaeus's troops refused to cede ground. As the fighting continued, Judea's legions began to prevail. And then the unexpected occurred.

Philostephanus was a first-rate military tactician. Realizing that defeat was at hand, he employed a classic stratagem to turn a certain loss into an overwhelming victory. He held back one contingent of soldiers, which he later sent to aide those who were giving up their ground. The men in Alexander Jannaeus's phalanx, seeing a new body of soldiers approaching, apparently thought they were being outflanked by Egyptian reinforcements. Under the false impression they were vastly outnumbered, self-preservation prevailed over military discipline. The Judeans fled.

The Roman historian Livy describes a similar incident that took place in 168 B.C.E., a year before Salome Alexandra's ancestor Mattathias defied the Seleucid edict banning Judaism, which helps us to understand what happened next.[4] On this occasion the Romans inflicted a crushing defeat on the Hellenistic army of the Macedonians by disrupting the discipline of their phalanx. Livy writes that when the soldiers in the Greek forces rotated their long spears, which were cumbersome due to their length and weight, to confront new men on the battlefield to their rear, they became entangled in a confused mass (a phalanx is designed to move forward). Panic ensued and the once-disciplined Greek line was thrown into disarray. The same thing apparently happened to Alexander Jannaeus's men as they tried to turn around to ward off an assault from behind. Their weapons became entangled; their ranks quickly broke apart; panic ensued; and soldiers fled the battlefield. According to Josephus, Soter's troops pursued them "until their swords were blunt from murder."[5] The Egyptians killed approximately 30,000 to 50,000 of Alexander Jannaeus's men.

Soter decided to follow up his victory with a coordinated campaign of terror and psychological warfare to instill fear throughout Judea. According to Josephus,

> Ptolemy [Soter] overran other territory, and when evening fell, lodged in some villages of Judea, which he found full of women and infants; he commanded his soldiers to strangle them and cut them up in pieces, and then to throw the body parts into boiling cauldrons and to consume them. He ordered his men to do this so that those who had escaped from the battle and had returned to their homes might think their enemy were cannibals, and so might be terrified of them [*Ant.* 13.345–6].

In the meanwhile, his men captured Ptolemais. With much of the Mediterranean, the regions east of the Jordan River, and the lands to Judea's north now under Soter's control, Alexander Jannaeus had little chance of saving the Hasmonean State.

Salome Alexandra was thirty-seven years old at this time; Alexander Jannaeus was either twenty-four or twenty-two. She had experienced much suffering in her lifetime. Having survived Antiochus Sidetes's siege of Jerusalem, and her brother-in-law Judah Aristobulus's tumultuous short reign, she was now the most powerful Hasmonean queen in history. She must have governed Judea well during her husband's numerous absences since Josephus does not record any problems in Jerusalem. But this time Judea's survival was doubtful; Soter's forces were ravaging her nation and preparing to attack Jerusalem. Then she and her people received word that a new danger was at hand — Cleopatra III. The War of Scepters had begun.

"When a War of Scepters Came to Syria"

The "War of Scepters"— the name an Egyptian document gives to this nearly three-year conflict (103–101 B.C.E.) — took place shortly after Alexander Jannaeus became king.[6] Josephus writes that after Alexander Jannaeus had betrayed Soter:

> Cleopatra [III] saw her son [Ptolemy Soter] growing in power, and ravaging Judea with impunity and in control of Gaza, she decided not to be idle while he, having grown more powerful, was almost at her gates and coveted the throne of Egypt; and so she at once set out against him with a sea and land force, appointing as leaders of her entire army the Jews Chelkias and Ananias. At the same time she sent the greater part of her wealth and her grandsons and her will to [the island of] Cos for safekeeping. Then she ordered her son [Ptolemy] Alexander to sail toward Phoenicia with a great fleet, while she herself came to Ptolemais with her entire force, and when the inhabitants refused to admit her, she besieged the city. Thereupon Ptolemy [Soter] left Syria and eventually fled to Cyprus, under the belief that there were no forces there, and he could easily capture it, but he was greatly disappointed to find otherwise. It was at this time that Chelkias, one of Cleopatra's two [Jewish] generals, died in Coele-Syria while in pursuit of Ptolemy [Soter] [*Ant.* 13.348–51].

The War of Scepters abruptly ended after Soter fled to Cyprus.[7]

Salome Alexandra's husband is notably absent from the Egyptian records. This evidence, largely military dispatches written during the actual conflict, presents a vastly different account of this conflict than Josephus's version. It reveals that two Egyptian armies — one led by Soter; the other commanded by his brother Ptolemy Alexander — crossed Judea. Both forces undoubtedly left much devastation in their wake. Alexander Jannaeus had to remain idle as Egypt's royal family fought their dynastic wars in Judea. Never before had a Hasmonean king been so helpless. The War of Scepters was a disaster for Judea.

The War of Scepters left Salome Alexandra's homeland an occupied country. Josephus reports that Alexander Jannaeus approached Cleopatra III as a supplicant to beg for his crown. Some of her men urged her to annex Judea. Then, Josephus tells us, her Jewish general, Ananias, threatened her, saying that this would make all the Jews her enemies.[8] She bowed to his demand and spared Judea.

Although Josephus claims a Jew saved Salome Alexandra's homeland, his story is certainly fictional. Cleopatra III had long favored the Jews; she and her mother had supported Egypt's Jewish temple and Jews had served in their legions. Josephus likely fabricated this story to hide the unpleasant fact that a pagan queen had not only saved the Hasmonean State, but had also forced Alexander Jannaeus to pledge allegiance to her. In return, he became her vassal.

Salome Alexandra was certainly there at this momentous summit to witness her husband — Judea's king and high priest — bow as a supplicant before a pagan queen. Her spouse apparently feared this meeting and wisely brought lavish gifts to appease Cleopatra III. Despite his efforts to make this event look good for the Hasmoneans, Josephus reveals something important that suggests Alexander Jannaeus was quite weak at this time. He mentions that it took place in Scythopolis in Samaria. This location is significant; Cleopatra III must have chosen it because of its large Gentile and Samaritan populations. With potentially hostile Samaritans now allied with her, this city posed a potential military and religious threat to Judea's sovereignty. Alexander Jannaeus had no choice but to leave the safe confines of his capital, travel to Egyptian-held pagan and Samaritan territory, and concede to her demands if he wanted to retain his crown.

A Time for War

Alexander Jannaeus's reign was thus far an unmitigated disaster. His sister-in-law had appointed him king and high priest; foreign armies had despoiled his country; and a pagan queen had ratified his offices. He remained idle for nearly five years after the War of Scepters because he feared Cleopatra III. He waited until she had passed away before he set out to expand the Hasmonean State.

Alexander Jannaeus was confident that Cleopatra's death gave him the freedom to annex neighboring lands without any fear of foreign interference. It was also the perfect time for him to wage war against his neighbors since all the great powers of the day were occupied. Egypt and Seleucia were convulsed by civil wars, and therefore unable to hamper Judea's expansion. Many

Italian cities, moreover, were in revolt, forcing Rome to temporarily suspend its Republic, and appoint Sulla as dictator. Because none of these nations believed the Jews were strong enough to threaten Syria and the Mediterranean coast, they ignored Judea and focused on their own internal problems.

Alexander Jannaeus exploited the Middle East's leadership vacuum to expand the Hasmonean state. He began by attacking the wealthy independent Greek city-states to the east of the Jordan River. He captured Gadara (modern Jordan) after a ten-month siege, and then conquered Amathus (modern Jordan), the region's greatest stronghold. Once again, he was extremely unlikely. A local ruler named Theodorus sacked his baggage train and killed ten thousand of his soldiers.

Undaunted by his recent loss, Alexander Jannaeus returned to Judea to pursue an even more arduous and dangerous campaign — the capture of Gaza. Located near the Egyptian border, this mighty stronghold was a major outlet for the Nabatean Arabs, who used its harbor to move their goods from Arabia to Europe. His siege did not go well. Gaza's general Apollodotus successfully employed some unrecorded nighttime stratagem that fooled him into thinking he was under attack by Soter. The Hasmonean army panicked and fled the battlefield; Gaza's considerably less skilled force of two thousand solders and ten thousand slaves killed many of Alexander Jannaeus's troops. When daybreak exposed the ruse, he pressed his attack, but lost an additional thousand men. The Gazans remained defiant, confident that Aretas, king of the Nabatean Arabs, would come to their aide. The siege continued.

Gaza did not succumb to Alexander Jannaeus's military might: it fell from within. The city was divided between two brothers: Apollodotus and Lysimachus. The latter had managed to convince the Gazans to surrender. At first things went well; Alexander Jannaeus entered the city in peace. Then he unleashed his army against its innocent population. In desperation, many men killed their wives and children to prevent their capture and enslavement; some even burned their homes to deny the Judean soldiers any spoils. During the onslaught, five hundred Gazans, including the town council, took refuge in the Temple of Apollo. Alexander Jannaeus slaughtered them.

A Civil War Comes to Judea

Now forty-four years old, Salome Alexandra had witnessed much violence during her husband's twenty-seven year reign. Her people finally had enough of her spouse and decided to remove him from power. Josephus tells us little about how this insurrection began, except that it took place at the most inopportune time — the Festival of Tabernacles. On this occasion, the pilgrims in the temple pelted him with the citrons (a citrus fruit) they carried during the religious holiday. Some people attending worship further inflamed tensions when they yelled that he was a bastard and therefore unqualified to serve as high priest. Alexander Jannaeus was so angry that he unleashed his soldiers against the protestors; his troops killed six thousand pilgrims in the temple precincts. He then placed a wooden barrier around the temple and its altar through which only the priests could pass to view the sacrifices.

The Mishnah (a second century C.E. religious text that preserves many ancient traditions about the temple at this time) provides some important background information that helps us to understand why the Judeans revolted during this holiday. It describes a water ritual that took place at the altar during the Festival of Tabernacles:

> The pouring out of the water took place thus: They [=priests] filled with water from the pool of Siloam [in Jerusalem] a golden bottle containing three logs [ca. 1½ pints]. When they reached the water gate, they sounded a plain note, a tremolo, and another plain note. The bearer of the bottle ascended the inclined plane where there were two sliver basins.... The basin on the west was used for the water, that on the east for the wine; but if the water was poured into the basin for wine, or the wine into that for water, the requirements of the law were complied with.... On one occasion one [high priest] poured the libation over his feet, and all the people pelted him with their citrons [*m. Sukkah* 4.9].[9]

According to the Talmud, the high priest who committed this sacrilege was a Sadducee. Because this incident took place once, this story can only refer to Alexander Jannaeus. It shows that he started this tragic riot when he publicly mocked the Pharisees during a solemn religious ceremony.[10]

It is impossible to understand the magnitude of the Tabernacles incident without knowing what the Jerusalem temple looked like in Salome Alexandra's day. It underwent several expansions during its long history. Most of its extant remains — the Western Wall (the traditional site of Jewish prayer and pilgrimage) among them — are the work of the first century B.C.E. monarch Herod the Great. Josephus provides an eyewitness description, writing that the temple

> had four surrounding courts, and each of these had its own protection in accordance with the law. Thus, anyone was allowed to enter the outer court, even pagans; only menstruating women were not allowed to enter. To the second court all Jews were admitted, together with their wives if they were free of all impurity; to the third, male Jews if they were clean and purified; to the fourth, priests wearing priestly robes; but to the inner sanctuary, only the high priests dressed in a special vestment [*Ag Ap.* 2.103–4].

This is the temple Josephus and Jesus knew, but not Salome Alexandra. She worshipped alongside men. There was no special court for women in her day.

Model of the Jerusalem Mount as it appeared from the north in the first century B.C.E. The temple was essentially an elevated fortress protected by immense walls (Todd Bolen/BiblePlaces.com).

Even the Egyptian shrine of Leontopolis, which was apparently modeled after the Jerusalem temple, did not segregate on the basis of gender.[11] Alexander Jannaeus became the first person to divide the temple, and restrict access to its sacred altar, when he surrounded the sanctuary with a wall. Only the priests could approach the temple building and watch the sacrifices burn on the sacred altar. Alexander Jannaeus had denied common Judeans access to God.

Alexander Jannaeus renewed his wars of conquest beyond the Jordan River. He began by attacking Theodorus, whose forces had sacked his baggage train during his last foray in the region. This time he was successful and destroyed his stronghold of Amathus. A year or two later Alexander Jannaeus fought another campaign against the Nabatean Arabs of Gaulanitis and Batanaea, east of the Sea of Galilee. But this time disaster struck his expedition; the Nabatean king Obedas I (reigned ca. 93–85 B.C.E.) attacked him while his army was traversing a deep canyon. He barely escaped with his life. His army was decimated, leaving him no option but to return to Jerusalem in disgrace. After this devastating loss, the Pharisees were determined to wrest power from him. In desperation, they turned to the most unlikely person for help — the Seleucid king Demetrius III.

Placed on the throne of Damascus largely through the machinations of Ptolemy Soter, Demetrius never amounted to much. Known by the moniker Eukairos ("Lucky"), Josephus preferred to call him Akairos ("Untimely") since he was a rather undistinguished monarch.[12] Despite the unimpressive size of his realm, Demetrius at this time had a formidable military force of 40,000 soldiers and 3,000 cavalry. Alexander Jannaeus could only muster some 6,200 mercenaries and 20,000 Jewish soldiers: A clear indication that his frequent wars had taken an immense toll on his army. Realizing that he was at a numerical disadvantage, he decided to launch a preemptive strike and catch his foe unprepared.

The two armies met in Samaria, near the city of Shechem, close to the place where John Hyrcanus's sons had defeated the Seleucids. As both men lined up their armies for battle, the Greek soldiers in Demetrius's employ urged the Greek mercenaries in Alexander Jannaeus's forces to desert; the Jews in the Hasmonean legion urged their fellow citizens in Seleucia's force to do likewise. Both lines held firm; there were no defectors. When the battle finally ensued, it was a complete rout for the Hasmonean army: virtually all of Judea's foreign mercenaries perished. Alexander Jannaeus and the survivors fled to the mountains. Judea was defenseless. Then an apparent miracle occurred.

Six thousand Jewish soldiers fighting for Demetrius had a sudden change of heart. They defected. Now uncertain of his army's loyalty, and outnumbered in hostile territory, Demetrius panicked and fled Judea. Shortly afterwards, he and his twin brother, Philip, fought one another for Seleucia's throne. Philip invited the Parthians to help him. They captured Demetrius and took him to Parthia where he died in captivity.

Now that Seleucia was no longer a threat, Alexander Jannaeus was free to eradicate the Pharisees and his political rivals. Over the next six years he killed more than 50,000 of his own citizens. Once, while he publicly feasted with his concubines, he crucified 800 Pharisees and slaughtered their children and wives before their eyes.[13] The remainder of his reign was filled with great bloodshed and nearly constant war.

Alexander Jannaeus's Final Days

Josephus's account of Alexander Jannaeus's final days in his *War* is quite brief. He is remarkably reticent about the location and circumstances of his death. He only mentions his illness and his unfulfilled plans:

> Afflicted by a quartan fever, he hoped to shake off the malady by a return to active life. He, accordingly, plunged into ill-timed campaigns and, exerted himself to tasks beyond his physical strength, which hastened his end. He died amid great stress and turmoil, after a reign of twenty-seven years [*War* 1.106].

Josephus tells us that Alexander Jannaeus's funeral monument was among the most prominent landmarks in Jerusalem on the eve of the great revolt against the Romans.[14] Although no trace of it survives, it must have been an imposing structure. Salome Alexandra undoubtedly presided over its construction, as well her husband's internment. We do not know if she ever loved him since neither Josephus nor the rabbis were interested in matters of the heart. Nevertheless, Josephus and the sages agreed that the Judeans hated Alexander Jannaeus and loved Salome Alexandra.

A Dead Sea Scroll likely preserves a contemporary opinion of Alexander Jannaeus that stands in marked contrast to Josephus's glowing obituary of him. Known by its official inventory number as 4Q448, it reads:

> Rise up, O Holy One against King Jonathan [=Alexander Jannaeus] and all the congregation of Your people Israel who are in the four winds of heaven. Let them all be [at] peace and upon your kingdom may your name be blessed.[15]

The prayer is unusual since its author pleads with God to remove the high priest and king to bring peace to Judea. The story of how this nameless Judean's prayer was answered is perhaps the most unusual of all the extraordinary tales found in Josephus's voluminous writings. God chose a woman to save Judea.

10

Queen Triumphant
The Improbable Rise of Salome Alexandra

> She was a woman who showed none of the weakness of her sex; for being one of those inordinately desirous of the power to rule, she showed by her deeds the ability to carry out her plans, and at the same time she exposed the stupidity of those men who continually fail to maintain sovereign power. — Josephus, *Antiquities* 13.430

Josephus's account of how Salome Alexandra led men in battle, captured an strategic enemy stronghold in a foreign land, returned to Jerusalem as its sole ruler, chose the next high priest, and altered her nation's religion, is an astonishing tale. And she did all this as a senior citizen! Josephus pays her the ultimate compliment when he writes, "She was a woman who showed none of the weakness of her sex." To understand how this sixty-four-year-old female became the manliest of all Judeans, we must begin with the unusual circumstances that brought her to the throne.

A Time of Great Uncertainty

Josephus tells us very little about Salome Alexandra during her husband's calamitous twenty-seven year reign.[1] He writes that her spouse suffered from a quartan fever during the last three years of his life, and that his chronic alcoholism and frequent warfare acerbated his condition. Despite his ill health, he spent much of his time campaigning outside Judea. Salome Alexandra must have acted as regent during his many lengthy absences. On at least one occasion, she accompanied the army in battle to besiege the Nabatean stronghold of Ragaba, across the Jordan River in modern Jordan. Josephus claims her husband summoned her there because he was dying. In his *War* he writes that while the blockade was in progress,

> Alexander [Jannaeus] bequeathed the kingdom to his wife [Salome] Alexandra, being convinced that the Jews would bow to her authority as they would to no other, because by her utter lack of his brutality and by her opposition to his crimes she had won the love of her populace. Nor was he mistaken in these expectations; for this frail woman firmly held the reins of government, thanks to her reputation for piety [*War* 1.107–8].

Salome Alexandra continued the campaign, captured Ragaba, and returned home to Jerusalem as its new monarch. The Judeans willingly accepted her as their ruler even though she had two grown sons.

Josephus clearly admires Salome Alexandra in his *War*. He portrays her as a forceful, dynamic, and powerful ruler. But he apparently changed his mind about her when he wrote his *Antiquities*. In this book he stresses her weaknesses. She is pathetic, submissive, and inconsolable when she learns her husband is dying. She does not think of her nation, but, Josephus writes, "she wept and beat her breast, lamenting the grief that was about to befall her and her children."[2] It is Alexander Jannaeus who summons up the fortitude and courage to save Judea by concocting an ingenious plan to trick the Pharisees into naming her as his successor. He orders her to "conceal his death from the soldiers until she has captured the fortress," and then upon her return to Jerusalem "from a splendid victory, yield a certain amount of power to the Pharisees."[3]

Despite his best efforts to attribute Salome Alexandra's ascension to her husband's ruse, Josephus portrays her as the dominant figure in both his *War* and *Antiquities*. She brings peace to Judea; she stifles the Pharisees' quest for revenge against the Sadducees; and she convinces her husband's enemies to give her spouse the most splendid burial of any Hasmonean king. As her first act, she appoints the high priest and changes Judea's religious practices by removing the Sadducees from power and placing the Pharisees in charge of the temple. Despite his efforts to diminish her achievements, Josephus credits Ragaba's capture to her in both his books. But a close reading of his writings suggests that his account of Salome Alexandra's presence on the battlefield is partly true. To understand what really took place at Ragaba, we must look at an episode in the life of the biblical king David (ca. 1040–970 B.C.E.) to understand how ancient readers would have viewed her military victory.

"It Will Be Named After Me"

The city of Rabbah lies just to the south of Ragaba. In King David's time the Ammonites inhabited it. The Israelites (the name of Salome Alexandra's biblical ancestors) and the Ammonites had a long and adversarial relationship. The two were related by a common ancestor, Abraham's nephew Lot. During the Exodus, when Moses led the Jews from their Egyptian captivity to the Promised Land, God expressly ordered them not to harm their Ammonite kin. The Ammonites did not reciprocate this friendly gesture, but tried to prevent the Israelites from crossing their territory. Subsequent relations between the two nations were tempestuous. One of the most sordid incidents in the entire Bible took place in Ammonite territory. Many Jews would have thought of it when they read Josephus's account of the battle of Ragaba. The similarities between the two stories are not coincidental — Josephus fabricated his account of its capture after David's conquest of Rabbah.

The anonymous author of the Second Book of Samuel begins his story of David's Ammonite war with the following rather unusual passage:

> Then it happened in the spring, at the time when kings go out to battle, that David sent [his general] Joab, and his soldiers with him, and all Israel, and they destroyed the sons of Ammon and besieged Rabbah. But David stayed at Jerusalem [2 Sam. 11:1].

Any reader in antiquity would have recognized that something was wrong — kings belonged with the army on the field of battle and not at home with the women.

According to the anonymous biblical author, while Joab besieges the Ammonite citadel of Rabbah, David loiters about the palace. One day — by means and circumstances the writer prefers to leave to the imagination — David notices a woman bathing atop her house (in antiquity people used their rooftops for a variety of activities such as food preparation and sleeping). Her name is Bathsheba. The two have sex; she becomes pregnant. Her husband knows nothing about their clandestine affair. His name is Uriah. He is a Hittite mercenary serving in David's army at Rabbah.

After learning that his lover is pregnant, David concocts a stratagem to fool Uriah into thinking he is the child's father. David summons him from the battlefield to the palace, expecting him to use his leave to spend the night with his wife. But the plan fails; Uriah sleeps outside the royal residence with the king's servants.

When David learns that Uriah did not have sex with Bathsheba, he summons him to the court and demands an explanation. Uriah is shocked. He defends his behavior by telling David,

> The Ark [of the Covenant] and [the armies of] Israel and Judah are living tents, and my commander Joab and the soldiers of my lord are camping in the open field. Shall I then go to my house to eat and to drink and have sex with my wife? By your life and the life of your soul, I will never do such a thing [2 Sam. 11:11].

Now unable to claim Uriah has fathered his child, David has to find some other means to deal with his scandalous, and potentially life-threatening, affair — the biblical penalty for adultery is death for the man and the woman.[4]

Now desperate to cover his transgression, David decides he has no option but to murder Uriah. David gives Uriah a message to deliver to Joab, commander of his forces. David knows he can trust Uriah not to open the letter before delivering it. But Uriah has no way of knowing that this is no ordinary communiqué— it is his death warrant! The dispatch orders Joab to place Uriah in the thick of battle with no chance of retreat. Joab immediately carries out the command. When the fighting intensifies, he orders all units to retreat, except Uriah's contingent. Uriah and many of David's most faithful troops remain at their posts in compliance with their order to continue to attack Rabbah's walls. All are killed.

When a royal courier arrives in Jerusalem bearing the news that the Israelites have just suffered a great defeat at Rabbah, David feigns shock and anger. He demands to know how Joab could have fallen for the same ruse as the biblical warlord Abimelech:

> Why did you go near the city to fight? Did you not know that they would shoot [arrows] from the wall above? Who killed Abimelech, son of Jerubbaal? Was it not a woman who threw a millstone down on him from the wall above, so that he died in Thebez? Why did you go near the wall? [2 Sam. 11:20–21].

David's anger immediately subsides when the messenger tells him Uriah has died fighting. He orders him to return to Ragaba and tell Joab not to grieve over his recent loss, but to continue with the siege. Shortly afterwards, David marries Bathsheba. All is well; no one suspects their sin; only God knows their crime. But then an unexpected situation occurs that demands his immediate presence — Joab is about to enter Rabbah.

Rabbah's imminent fall places Joab in a terrible predicament. According to the biblical account,

> Joab fought against Rabbah of the sons of Ammon and captured the royal city. Joab sent messengers to David and said, "I have fought against Rabbah and am about to take the City of Waters. Now therefore, gather the rest of the army together and camp against the city and capture it, or I will enter the city myself and it will be named after me" [2 Sam. 12:27–8].

If Joab enters Rabbah, according to the ancient tenets of warfare, he would be declared its victor. In a world in which only the strong were deemed worthy to exercise sovereign power, his capture of this important citadel would have been tantamount to a *coup d'état*. David realizes the gravity of the situation and rushes to Rabbah. He arrives just in time to enter it in his name.

According to Josephus's *Antiquities*, Salome Alexandra captures Ragaba by following her husband's stratagem. She purportedly conceals his death from his soldiers until after the battle. But when read in light of the protocols that governed ancient warfare, this story is improbable. How could she have fooled her husband's battle-hardened troops, especially his officers and advisors, into thinking their king was still alive nearby, but absent from the battlefield? And who was in charge of Judea's army?

Josephus apparently used two different sources to write his narrative of Salome Alexandra's reign: the history of Nicolaus of Damascus and a book that was apparently written by a Pharisee.[5] The former is more critical of Salome Alexandra than the latter, which accounts for Josephus's conflicting statements about her throughout his books. Josephus relied on Nicolaus for much of his account of the Hasmonean period. Nicolaus prefers dramatic, emotional, and entertaining stories about Salome Alexandra's ancestors that often portray them unfavorably. But Josephus did not merely copy material about Salome Alexandra from Nicolaus verbatim. He frequently intersperses it with his own commentary to alter its meaning. Josephus transforms Salome Alexandra's great military victory and political success into a warning against female rule: he blames her for the eventual collapse of the Hasmonean state.

Josephus's practice of cutting and pasting material from his books, mixed with his own opinion, results in a confusing, and oftentimes contradictory, narrative. This is especially true of his *Antiquities*. The reader must look closely at his text to disentangle his sources from his opinions. Fortunately, his Pharisaic account of Salome Alexandra's life is more favorable, and historically reliable, than Nicolaus's history. At times it stands in marked contrast to the surrounding narrative: it frequently presents a completely different chronology. In one passage Josephus undoubtedly took from this book, he tells his readers:

> [Salome] Alexandra, after capturing the fortress [of Ragaba], conferred with the Pharisees as her husband had suggested, and placing in their hands all that concerned his corpse and the royal power, calmed their anger against Alexander [Jannaeus], and made them well disposed to her and her friends [*Ant.* 13.405].

Josephus here unambiguously states that Salome Alexandra dictated military strategy, captured Ragaba, ended the Nabatean wars, appeased her husband's enemies, and prevented a civil war. The annals and songs written to commemorate this campaign would have celebrated the deeds of the mighty Queen Salome Alexandra — conqueror of Ragaba and ruler of Judea.

The account of the battle of Ragaba in Josephus's *Antiquities* is a work of fiction that is partly inspired by the biblical story of David and Bathsheba. Ancient readers would have recognized the allusions to David's time and understood the ramifications of what took place. In Josephus and this biblical tale, a lesser person captures an enemy stronghold in modern Jordan (the two cities are in close proximity to one another). In both stories the victory is credited to the reigning monarch, who was not physically present on the battlefield during combat. A close reading of Josephus's narrative in this instance shows that Salome Alexandra is a dynamic and proactive character. She, not her husband, came up with the plan to capture Ragaba, favor the Pharisees, and transform Judea's political, military, and religious institutions. But unlike David, Salome Alexandra's spouse never made it to the field of battle to enter the enemy stronghold in his name.

But what about Alexander Jannaeus's supposed ruse? Either Josephus or one of his sources made it up to conceal Salome Alexandra's position as her husband's co-ruler and leader of Judea's forces. In an astonishing passage scholars have overlooked, Josephus implies that Salome Alexandra governed alongside her husband long before his death: Ragaba was likely not the first time she commanded troops.

The evidence that Salome Alexandra was her husband's co-ruler is found in Josephus's later account of the Herodian dynasty (the pro–Roman family of Jewish kings who, beginning with Herod the Great, replaced the Hasmoneans). In a passage he likely copied from an earlier source about Herod and his family, Josephus states that Antipas, the grandfather of Herod the Great (ca. 74–4 B.C.E.), came to political power when "king Alexander and his wife [=Salome] made him general of all Idumea."[6] Josephus portrays husband and wife as equals; a clear indication that Salome Alexandra was Judea's co-ruler. If the misogynistic Josephus maintains this was so, who are we to dispute his remarkable claim?

We can estimate when Alexander Jannaeus appointed Salome Alexandra as his co-ruler by looking closely at Josephus's account. In his *Antiquities*, he inserts a list of areas firmly under Alexander Jannaeus's control at the time of his death. Josephus writes that he was ill during his last three years (79–76 B.C.E.), yet he undertook a series of campaigns to subdue rebellious territories. Presumably, several of the regions in Josephus's list had tried to break away from Hasmonean rule on hearing of Alexander Jannaeus's quartan fever and his rapid physical decline. He likely appointed Antipas at this time to reduce the danger of further insurrection to the south.[7] This would mean that Salome Alexandra must have been her husband's co-ruler before his illness. She undoubtedly helped her husband subdue many rebellious territories at this time.

Josephus provides another clue that Salome Alexandra was Judea's co-ruler at the time of her husband's death. In his account of her assumption to power, he states that the Judeans accepted her because she had long opposed her husband's crimes. The Slavonic translation of Josephus's *War*, which occasionally preserves a more ancient text of this book than our surviving Greek manuscripts, states that Salome Alexandra had publicly opposed her husband's "impieties." It also claims that she had "pleaded with him on behalf of the people" to observe Jewish law.[8] She could not have taken such a dangerous public stance unless she already wielded considerable power, and had actually assumed many administrative functions long before this time.

Salome Alexandra clearly assumed at least some royal powers before she became Judea's sole monarch. Although Josephus prefers to write nothing about her co-regency, we can calculate the likely year when she became his husband's co-ruler. The most probable time is sometime before 79 B.C.E., the year her husband apparently became bedridden and fatally ill. He must have been more incapacitated than Josephus reveals for him to have appointed her to this position: she was likely Judea's de facto monarch for much of this time. Salome Alexandra undoubtedly governed Judea during her husband's absence, but also made military decisions as well as helped run the temple. When she commanded legions at Ragaba, she had already ruled alongside her spouse and exercised many royal powers for a considerable time. Men were accustomed to obeying her orders before she took command of Judea's legions at Ragaba.

During Alexander Jannaeus's last three years in power, when he suffered from quartan fever and other infirmities, Salome Alexandra likely governed Judea alone. Josephus certainly knew this, but skillfully weaves a clever narrative to diminish her great victory, and overlook her political authority and military command. But he also conceals an even greater falsehood — Alexander Jannaeus was never at Ragaba! Like David, he was at home while his troops were in the field attacking an enemy stronghold. To learn what really happened there, we must turn to the writing of an obscure Christian cleric from Constantinople.

A Byzantine Chronographer

In 313 B.C.E. the Roman emperor Constantine, having emerged victorious from the latest round of civil wars between various claimants for the throne, declared Christianity a protected religion. To commemorate his political and military successes, he moved the capital from Rome to the ancient city of Byzantium, which he renamed Constantinople ("The City of Constantine"). It soon eclipsed Rome as the cultural center of the fledgling Roman Empire, which effectively ended in 476 C.E. when the Germanic chieftain Odoacer deposed the emperor Romulus Augustulus. Afterwards, Constantinople became the seat of the Christian Byzantine Empire, which lasted until 1453 C.E. when Mehmet II ("the Conqueror") captured it for the Turks. It remains a Muslim city; it is now called Istanbul and is the capital of modern Turkey.

George Syncellus was a Christian who lived in Constantinople when it was the cultural seat and capital of the Byzantine Empire. Promoted to the important clerical office of Syncellus (a type of bishop's assistant), he took a rather unusual career path for one holding such an exalted position. He abandoned the tumultuous world of Byzantine ecclesiastical politics for the solitary life of a scholar. From 808 C.E. until his death two years later, he worked on a chronicle of world history. He died before completing it: the book ends with the Emperor Diocletian's reign in the late third century C.E. George's friend Theophanes finished the work.[9] Although few read George Syncellus's chronicle today, it is an important work. It tells us much about Salome Alexandra's life and times. George Syncellus had good reason for documenting the tumultuous events of her age; he was formerly a monk in her homeland, where he likely first learned about her and her amazing family.

George Syncellus's narrative of the Hasmonean period is rather short since his book is merely a chronicle of world history that preserves only brief accounts of the most significant persons and events. For this reason, what he chose to place in his book tells us much about how his generation viewed the Hasmoneans. George Syncellus completely omits Judah Aristobulus; he presumably did not consider his one-year reign worth recording. But he does mention Salome Alexandra and Alexander Jannaeus. Like Josephus, he portrays her husband as a brutal man who killed many innocent people, including women and children. But George Syncellus's account is particularly important for what it tells us about the Hasmonean State at the time of Alexander Jannaeus's death — it reveals that Salome Alexandra was a great warrior.

Salome Alexandra took power at a pivotal moment in the history of the Middle East. The Seleucid Empire was breaking down. Some of its neighboring city-states were taking advantage of its decline to assert their independence, and annex portions of Syria. The rulers across the Jordan River were active in this land grab to control the region's vital ports and trade routes. Salome Alexandra's husband had tired to take advantage of Seleucia's troubles by annexing some of its strategic coastal territories. He was unable to retain them. His territorial greed only brought continual war to Judea.

George Syncellus's account reveals that Alexander Jannaeus almost lost his kingdom. Many of his cities had revolted during the War of Scepters. He tells us that Cleopatra III helped him regain control of them: a clear sign that he was unable to put down this rebellion. This explains why he readily groveled before her, and why some of her subjects likely wanted her to seize Judea: Alexander Jannaeus was so weak and unpopular that Cleopatra III could have annexed his entire nation with minimal effort. George Syncellus also mentions that Alexander Jannaeus became an Egyptian ally, suggesting that he paid Cleopatra III considerable tribute in exchange for her help in subduing Jewish rebels. Without her, the Hasmonean State would not have survived. Salome Alexandra likely played some role in these negotiations, and helped convince Cleopatra III to allow her husband to remain in power. As a pro–Jewish ruler, Cleopatra III would have listened to her female Judean counterpart, and allowed Salome Alexandra's family to continue as Judea's rulers in exchange for their promise not to meddle in Egypt's dynastic affairs.

Cleopatra III's treaty with the Judeans gave Alexander Jannaeus a secure western border with Egypt. This allowed him to campaign unopposed beyond the Jordan River, without fear that she would take advantage of his absence and invade Judea. Josephus's omission of how Cleopatra III saved Alexander Jannaeus's kingdom gives the false impression that he was a successful warrior. In reality, he and the Hasmoneans owed their survival to Cleopatra III: she essentially dictated the early course of his reign. Unfortunately Josephus did not want us to know Salome Alexandra's role in this affair, and her relationship with Cleopatra III. Our queen undoubtedly played some part in keeping her husband on the throne, and convincing Cleopatra III and her Jewish subjects to leave Judea in peace and allow the Hasmoneans to continue to rule.

George Syncellus's rather brief account of the reign of Salome Alexandra's husband supports Josephus's portrayal of his cruelty. He writes of his character:

> Jannaeus was quick to anger, arrogant, and extremely savage.... When the Jews began to revolt, he slaughtered his own people without mercy, even women and children [*Chronicle* 555.8–17].

However, he had access to a very different account of Alexander Jannaeus's death. According to his source,

> Jannaeus, also known as Alexander, was victorious in his war against Antiochus's son Grypus, who was also known as Dionysus. He made war against the Tyrians and besieged their island. When the Nabateans and Itureans led an insurrection against him, he sent the Galilean general Diagos against the Nabateans. But while he was preparing for war against the Itureans, Jannaeus died after a reign of thirty years. He had entrusted his wife Salome [Alexandra] with the administration of his kingdom, even though she had two sons by him, Hyrcanus and Aristobulus. [*Chronicle* 559.5–12].

George Syncellus mentions two military campaigns that Josephus omits from his narrative. The first is Alexander Jannaeus's invasion of the Seleucid Empire, during which he defeated its king, Antiochus Dionysus (reigned 87–84 B.C.E.), in battle. Josephus does not mention this incident. He only records Antiochus Dionysus's later invasion of Judea when he burnt Alexander Jannaeus's great wall. A series of rectangular and hexagonal-shaped stone foundations, commonly known as the "Jannaeus Line," uncovered between the

Iraq El-Amir Palace south façade, built by Hyrcanus of Jerusalem during the 2nd century B.C.E. A member of the powerful Jewish family known as the Tobiads, Hyrcanus and his ancestors moved to this site near the present-day Jordanian city of Amman during the fighting among the Jewish high priests that preceded the Maccabean Revolt. Alexander Jannaeus and Salome Alexandra later ruled over their territories (Todd Bolen/BiblePlaces.com).

ancient port city of Aphek and modern Tel Aviv, are the likely remnants of this fortification.[10] However, such a complex and lengthy defensive wall would have taken considerable time to construct. Alexander Jannaeus, having attacked Antiochus Dionysius earlier, likely expected a Seleucid invasion and began construction of this wall to protect his coastal holdings.

Josephus's account suggests that Antiochus Dionysus delayed his Nabatean campaign to make a foolish diversion to seize Judea's ports. This unnecessary detour gave the Nabateans time to amass additional forces that they used to decimate the Seleucid army and kill Antiochus Dionysus. But George Syncellus tells a different story.

George Syncellus makes it clear that the Antiochus Dionysus's invasion of Judea was not merely a reckless act of aggression. He was actually seeking revenge against Alexander Jannaeus for his earlier unprovoked attack against Syria. The Seleucids and the Nabateans were about to go to war. Antiochus Dionysus had no choice but to subdue Alexander Jannaeus to prevent the Judeans from invading his homeland again while he was fighting the

Architectural detail of the leopard water fountain at the Jewish palace of Hyrcanus the Tobiad at Iraq El-Amir. The style of this fortress and its animal decorations are typical of Hellenistic palaces, showing the extent to which Judea's Jewish elite had adopted Hellenistic culture before Salome Alexandra's birth. Josephus (*Ant.* 12.230) mentions these animals and the site's fountains (Todd Bolen/Bible Places.com).

Nabateans. George Syncellus shows that Alexander Jannaeus was overly aggressive during his reign. He had repeatedly failed in his bids to conquer the Seleucid Empire and neighboring lands.

The second campaign George Syncellus records, Alexander Jannaeus's siege of Tyre, sheds new light on the circumstances surrounding Salome Alexandra's assumption to power. This expedition apparently threatened to deprive the Nabateans and the Itureans use of this strategic port to move their goods overseas. They formed a military alliance, surprised Alexander Jannaeus at Tyre, and forced him to abandon his siege and sign a humiliating peace treaty. Josephus omits this embarrassing episode from his books; however, he mentions that Alexander Jannaeus, for reasons he prefers to leave unspecified, surrendered many cities, including the valuable lands of Moab and Galaaditis beyond the Jordan River, to the Nabatean monarch Aretas at this time.[11] Only the threatened destruction of his army could have forced him to make such humiliating concessions.

When Salome Alexandra took power, her husband had been waging a three-year series of wars to win back this territory. Josephus inserts an ancient list of Alexander Jannaeus's conquests at the time of his death to make it appear that Salome Alexandra inherited a kingdom that spanned both banks of the Jordan River. However, George Syncellus preserves a very different list of lands he supposedly held, but did not conquer.[12] A close reading of this catalog of Alexander Jannaeus's supposed victories reveals that Salome Alexandra took possession of a rapidly dwindling state that was threatened by several of its enemies. Her late husband's warmongering had made the Hasmonean State's survival more uncertain than any time since its creation. Salome Alexandra, moreover, actually captured some of the cities in Josephus's list. But George Syncellus also reveals something even more startling about her husband that completely changes our understanding of how she came to power — Alexander Jannaeus was not at the siege of Ragaba.

According to George Syncellus's ancient source, Alexander Jannaeus passed away while preparing to take the field against the Itureans in the Galilee: a clear indication that he was in Jerusalem with the troops and not on the battlefield when he died. The Nabatean campaign had already commenced and Salome Alexandra was with the legions at Ragaba, leading men in battle with her general Diagos. Her spouse likely expired in a warm bed in the palace, possibly surrounded by a few partisans and concubines, and perhaps his sons.

Although Josephus does not want to portray Salome Alexandra as a warrior, a close reading of his accounts suggest that she was a formidable military figure. In a rather remarkable passage he must have copied from an ancient source he writes:

> She proved to be a wonderful administrator in matters of state, and, by a continual recruiting doubled her army. She amassed a considerable body of foreign troops that she used to strengthen her nation. She also struck fear in the surrounding nations and became their master [*War* 1.112].

Josephus implies that her military buildup was not merely defensive, but that she undertook a series of wars to regain lost Hasmonean territory. His reference to her taking hostages from neighboring rulers indicates that she must have fought and won numerous battles, especially in Nabatea, since the region's monarchs would not have submitted to such undignified treatment unless she had forcibly subdued them.

Salome Alexandra's military campaigns were apparently successful since her reign was peaceful. She controlled many of the neighboring lands. She was not only a skilled military strategist, but a political realist as well. She knew that any further expansion of Judea would weaken its military and economy and therefore did not engage in endless wars of conquests to expand her territorial holdings. Judea likely reached its greatest extent during her reign: her state nearly rivaled the legendary empire of King David.[13]

George Syncellus is not the only source of new information about Salome Alexandra; Scripture likely attests to her deeds. The Bible was in its infancy when she was born; its content was still being collected and debated during her lifetime. Several of its books were likely written, or altered, to support her reign. It is to these remarkable works that we now turn to learn more about her, and the startling changes in gender perceptions that accompanied her rise to power.

Scripture and Salome Alexandra

The Book of Judith was quite popular in antiquity. It recounts the heroic deeds of a beautiful and pious widow named Judith, who uses deceit and seduction to deliver the Jews from foreign occupation. It is included in the Septuagint; a clear sign that many Hellenistic Jews deemed it canonical. But Jews later had second thoughts and removed it from the Bible. Although Christians too debated its canonicity, they tended to favor its inclusion. The Catholic and Orthodox Churches place Judith in a heterogeneous collection of writings deemed sacred, but of lesser spiritual value, known as the Apocrypha. But most Protestants later followed the lead of the Jewish community and rejected Judith, along with the entire Apocrypha.[14]

The Book of Judith is a religious novel that mixes historical fact and fiction. It opens with the campaign of the Assyrian king Nebuchadnezzar (he was actually ruler of the Babylonians) against the city of Arphaxad. Nebuchadnezzar (ca. 634–562 B.C.E.) then appoints his general Holofernes to launch a series of punitive expeditions against rebellious nations. Holofernes destroys many cities and their religious sites before reaching Scythopolis (modern Israel), where Alexander Jannaeus had groveled before Cleopatra III to save his kingdom. From there, he makes preparations for a full-scale invasion of Salome Alexandra's homeland. After learning of this impending attack, the high priest, Joakim, urges Bethulia's citizens to flee to the mountains.

While Bethulia's population cowers in fear, dissent breaks out in the enemy camp. Achior, the leader of the Ammonite contingent in Nebuchadnezzar's army, warns Holofernes not to attack the Jews. Holofernes banishes him for his insolence and cowardice. The Jews bring him to Bethulia, where he informs them of the impending invasion.

Judith appears during this time of distress to save Bethulia. Her name is the feminine form of the word "Jew" or "Judean." The narrator introduces her midway in the book with the longest genealogy of any woman in the Bible — a clear indication of her importance. She is a pious, beautiful, and chaste widow who is renowned for her strict regime of fasting and Sabbath observance. She urges the town's magistrates to recognize that their present circumstance is not a sign of God's abandonment, but a test of their faith. The city's leaders bow to her wisdom, and plead with her to intercede with God on their behalf. She promises to deliver the city on one condition — they must place their complete trust in her and do whatever she orders.

Judith strips off her sackcloth and, at the same time the high priest is performing the incense offering in the Jerusalem temple, prays to God for strength and vengeance. She puts on her finest apparel and, accompanied by her favorite servant, prepares to leave Bethulia. Judith then orders the sentinels to let her pass; the soldiers dutifully obey her command. She allows an Assyrian patrol to intercept her, and demands an audience with Holofernes.

Judith's beauty mesmerizes Holofernes. She agrees to betray her people in exchange for sanctuary. Judith vows to pray to her God each evening to learn the opportune moment for the Assyrians to attack Bethulia. Holofernes accepts her plan, but plots to seduce her. While living in the enemy camp, Judith strictly observes the Jewish dietary laws and eats only the kosher food her maid prepares for her.

One evening Holofernes hosts a lavish party as a ploy to seduce Judith. After everyone is inebriated, he dismisses his guests to have sex with her: willing if possible; by force if necessary. But before he can take advantage of her, he collapses on his bed in a drunken stupor. Judith decapitates him with his sword and carries his head to Bethulia where she holds it aloft for all to see, shouting, "The Lord struck him by the hand of a woman."[15] Achior faints at the sight of Holofernes's bloody head, and, after recovering, demands circumcision to become a Jew. Meanwhile, the Assyrians panic and flee. The citizens of Bethulia, joined by many Jews from Jerusalem and other cities, pursue and kill them. Judith then leads her people in songs celebrating her miraculous deliverance of the Jews from certain annihilation. The Judeans honor her bravery and cunning for the remainder of her life.

The story of Judith's heroism has inspired great works of art by such masters as Donatello, Botticelli, Caravaggio, Michelangelo (he included her in the Sistine chapel), and musical scores by Mozart and Vivaldi. The first century C.E. Christian bishop Clement of Rome praises her "many deeds of manly valor," while others extol her virtuous lifestyle, especially her self-imposed celibacy, as an exemplar of faith.[16] Yet, none of these cultural savants realized that this formidable woman was likely modeled after Salome Alexandra.

A few historical clues in the Book of Judith suggest that its author modeled its heroine after Salome Alexandra. The work's description of Judith as a pious virgin warrior closely resembles Josephus's accounts of Salome Alexandra. Although the mysterious city of Bethulia appears to mean "House of God" or "House of Ascent," its consonants are actually the Hebrew word for virgin, *betulah*. Like Judith, Salome Alexandra was a widowed virgin when she led her people to a great military victory. Judith's faithfulness and confidence in God, and her ardent nationalism, are typical of Pharisaic piety. Even Josephus describes Salome Alexandra like Judith when he praises her faithfulness to Jewish law, and her devotion to the Pharisees.

Because of the similarities between the two women, several scholars have proposed that the Book of Judith was written to legitimate Salome Alexandra's reign. According to this theory, it was intended to promote female rule as an emergency measure in the absence of a qualified male leader. The book contains several clues to support this interpretation. Judith's prayer to the "God of my father Simeon" is not merely a reference to the biblical patriarch, but is intended to recall the deeds of Salome Alexandra's ancestor by that name. Although one could argue that this is merely a coincidence, the book's author embedded several clues throughout the narrative that suggest that Judith was modeled after our queen.

Judith's genealogy provides a clue to its likely date of composition. It contains names of persons related to Salome Alexandra, but excludes the territories of the tribes of Dan and Asher that were not part of her kingdom: a clear indication that the book was written after her death. Recent scholarship recognizes that the figure of Nebuchadnezzar in Judith is modeled after the Armenian king Tigranes the Great (142/1–56/55 B.C.E.), who in 69 B.C.E. threatened Salome Alexandra's kingdom.[17] As we will see when we examine this episode in a later chapter, the "miraculous" withdrawal of the Armenian army, due to Roman intervention, likely inspired the author to pay tribute to Salome Alexandra by writing this tale of female heroism.

Perhaps the best clue to help us determine this book's date of composition is Judith's incredible lifespan of one hundred and five years, which is the approximate length of the Hasmonean period (168–63 B.C.E.). This figure places the Book of Judith's composition sometime after the 63 B.C.E. Roman conquest of Salome Alexandra's homeland and their removal of her family from power. Its author undoubtedly knew Salome Alexandra's story quite well, and modeled his female heroine after her. It shows that many Judeans after the destruction of the Hasmonean State longed for the return of Salome Alexandra's Golden Age, and considered her their greatest ruler.[18]

The Book of Judith was not only written to support female rule, but to encourage the observance of Hanukkah — the holiday associated with the Hasmoneans. Its villain, king Nebuchadnezzar, celebrates his defeat of the king of Arphaxad with a great feast that falls almost exactly on the Festival of

Hanukkah; Judith's three-month celebration ends on the same day the following year. Later Hebrew retellings of the book even connect Judith with Hanukkah. This association was apparently so well known that the famed twelfth century C.E. Rabbi Samuel ben Meir (Rashbam) stated that Judith was responsible for the miracle of Hanukkah. These traditions are quite revealing, for they show that latter rabbis honored and praised a female heroine. We do not know whether they realized that the book's author modeled Judith after the only woman to have ruled Judea, chosen the high priest, and captured an enemy stronghold — Salome Alexandra.[19]

Some contemporary readers consider Judith a woman of dubious moral character because she uses her sexuality to murder her enemy. But this interpretation fails to consider the ethical perspectives of the ancients, who prized deception as a virtue. The first century C.E. Roman aristocrat Frontinus even wrote an entire book containing examples of such military stratagems. The Greeks and Romans would have viewed Judith's ability to protect herself from sexual violation in an enemy camp, while assassinating her foe, praiseworthy — even manly — behavior.[20] The ancients considered her a positive role model, and her cunning a strong argument against restricting the monarchy to males. But this remarkable book may not have been the only work written to legitimate female rule. Two other books likely made it into our canon of Scripture because of Salome Alexandra.

The Book of Susanna is a short story in the Apocrypha. Although it is sometimes printed as a separate work, it is actually one several additions to the Book of Daniel. It is about a beautiful and chaste woman named Susanna. After two elders secretly watch her bathe in her garden, they threaten to accuse her of arranging an illicit assignation with a young man unless she has sex with them. Susanna refuses. They arrest her for alleged promiscuity; no man is charged as her partner in her supposed affair. During her trial, God answers her prayer for help by sending the prophet Daniel to save her. He interrupts the court proceedings, examines the elders separately, and, with the assistance of an angel, exposes their lies. The false accusers are executed and Susanna is vindicated.

Some feminists consider Susanna a disappointing figure because, unlike Judith, she does not take matters into her own hands, but passively allows a man to come to her rescue. But this interpretation fails to consider that the biblical prophet Daniel gains renown for delivering her. She is clearly a blessed woman, which makes her a unique figure in ancient Jewish literature.

Many scholars date the Book of Susanna to the Hasmonean period, sometime between 120 and 35 B.C.E. One early theory proposed that it was written as a Pharisaic response to the problem of witnesses and false verdicts during Salome Alexandra's reign. Although this was a major issue in her day, the evidence suggests that it was actually completed during the time of John

Hyrcanus. It may have been written to legitimate female rule, and to prepare the Judeans for his wife to succeed him as queen regnant. Although Susanna was likely written before Salome Alexandra's reign, it was a popular book during her lifetime. Many Judeans undoubtedly used it to justify her rule since it espouses female piety and virtue.[21] There is one other book whose contents support this interpretation. Fortunately, its date is more certain. It forms part of a work all Jews and Christians accept as sacred scripture — the Book of Esther.

The Book of Esther takes place at the Persian court of King Ahasuerus (ca. 369 B.C.E.). It begins with a marital spat between Ahasuerus and his queen, the beautiful Vashti. After a night of heavy drinking, Ahasuerus decides to display her before his inebriated guests. She refuses to appear. Ahasuerus angrily banishes her, and issues an edict ordering all wives to obey their husbands. He immediately searches for a new spouse. Esther comes to the attention of the court officials and is brought to Ahasuerus. He immediately falls in love with her and selects her as his new queen. She moves to the palace but, at the urging of her cousin Mordecai, does not tell anyone she is a Jew.

Esther does not realize that she and the Jews have an enemy. His name is Haman. He is Ahasuerus's prime minister. The Jews' trouble begins when the king learns from the royal records that Mordeci had informed the palace of an intended coup, but had never been rewarded for his fealty. Ahasuerus publicly honors him. Haman becomes jealous and vows to kill him. He eventually gains his sovereign's permission to exterminate all the Jews. The decree is signed and sealed; the Jews nervously wait the appointed day of their slaughter.

It is at this point in the story where Esther takes charge. Mordecai urges her to intervene to save her people. She appears before her husband unannounced — a severe breach of Persian protocol and a life-threatening offense — and reveals she is a Jew. She convinces him to hang Haman on the gallows he has prepared for Mordecai. But there is a problem. According to the laws of the Persians, a royal decree cannot be annulled — the Jews must die. Unable to help because of his own country's law, Ahasuerus withdraws from the situation and places the Jews' fate entirely in Esther's hands.

Ahasuerus effectively makes Esther Persia's ruler by giving her his royal seal. She has the authority to issue any order she wishes; her edicts cannot be revoked. She writes letters in the king's name and sends them by royal courier throughout the Persian Empire. These dispatches give the Jews permission to gather weapons for their protection. When the day of their extermination arrives, the Jews easily defeat their attackers. Esther then issues a letter authorizing a yearly celebration of their deliverance known as Purim. It is the sole Jewish holiday created by a woman, and the only one that honors female heroism.

Esther's remarkable story was quite controversial in antiquity since it is the only book of the Bible that does not mention God. The Jewish community did not accept it in their canon until the third century C.E. Nevertheless, it became so popular that Jews still recite it in its entirety each Purim to ensure that each generation hears the remarkable story of its heroine.

The version of Esther contained in the Septuagint is very different than the Hebrew original. The Greek translator adds numerous references to God, which suggests that many Jews found the Hebrew text too secular. The Greek edition also highlights Esther's concern with Jewish law. She professes her hatred of mixed marriages, and her strict adherence to the ritual food laws. But the translator surprisingly portrays her as fearful and highly respectful of her husband. The scribe responsible for this version likely made these unexpected additions to the book on the eve of Salome Alexandra's ascension to the throne to make her reign more palatable to men.[22] Although this interpretation may appear to be reading too much into the narrative, the Greek version supports it.

The Greek translator of the Book of Esther appends the following colophon (a note at the end of a manuscript) to the book:

> In the fourth year of the reign of Ptolemy and Cleopatra, Dositheos, who said that he was a priest and a Levite, and his son Ptolemy brought to Egypt the preceding letter about Purim, which they said was authentic and had been translated by Lysimachus son of Ptolemy, a resident of Jerusalem [Esther 10:31].

Because this colophon contains the singular form of the Greek word "reign," and mentions Ptolemy first, it must refer to a period when there was no female co-ruler. This queen cannot be Cleopatra (II) or Cleopatra (III) since both were actual monarchs. The only possible candidate is Cleopatra (V), who is listed after her husband, Ptolemy (XII) Auletos, in all private and public documents. This places the Greek version of Esther around 78–77 B.C.E., approximately one year before Salome Alexander took the throne. It was likely revised and translated at this time to celebrate her elevation to co-ruler, and to prepare her people for her impending reign as Judea's first Hasmonean queen regnant.[23]

The colophon to the Greek version of Esther is rather unusual because it claims that a male translated the book. Because several passages in the Greek edition reflect a women's perspective, we cannot exclude the possibility it is a ruse to hide the female identity of its translator. But Esther may not be the only biblical book to have been revised during Salome Alexandra's lifetime. The Greek translation of the biblical Book of Joshua was even altered to support the Hasmoneans, which shows that her family had an impact on contemporary Jewish and Christian Scripture.[24]

Salome Alexandra shaped our Bible. Several of its texts likely reflect the events of her reign, or were used to support female rule during her lifetime. The books of Judith, Esther, and Susannah depict pious and exemplary females. Esther, in particular, is an important work because it celebrates a holiday in honor of a woman. When the high priest presided over Purim during Salome Alexandra's reign, the Judeans would have immediately thought of her, for she used her might, political acumen, and piety to save her people. The Festival of Tabernacles would have reinforced her right to hold power since it commemorates her family's fight to save the Jews, and their creation of an independent Jewish state. The heroine Judith would have reminded them of Salome Alexandra's deeds of valor on the battlefield, and her piety. Recently, a biblical scholar has suggested that Salome Alexandra is alluded to twice in the biblical Book of Psalms (Psalms 2; 148:12). According to this theory, Psalm 2 even contains an acrostic — a poem in which the first letter of each line spells out a word — that reads, "for Yannai (=Alexander Jannaeus) on one side and his wife (=Salome Alexandra) on the other (by) a lowly/Pharisee."[25] Although this may sound improbable, because our Bible was reshaped after her reign it is possible that a scribe tampered with the text to insert an allusion to our queen. Now let us continue with the story of this remarkable woman whose reign literally changed the Bible, beginning with the strange incident of her husband's corpse.

The Strange Tale of Alexander Jannaeus's Corpse

According to Josephus, Alexander Jannaeus's dying wish was for Salome Alexandra to allow the Pharisees to abuse his corpse. This is an inconceivable request for a high priest to make since Scripture outlaws any mutilation or abuse of a dead body.[26] This story makes sense only if Alexander Jannaeus had violated this biblical commandment, and had allowed the bodies of the Pharisees he had crucified to rot upon their crosses.

Alexander Jannaeus's mass crucifixion of 800 Pharisees was not a rash act, but part of his coordinated policy of using state-sponsored torture to eliminate his political and religious foes. The Pharisees never defeated him, despite their many attempts to remove him from power. He killed many of them, and forced a large number of them to flee Judea. Now that he was dead, many Pharisees were so bent on revenge that they wanted to mutilate his body in clear defiance of Scripture. Salome Alexandra prevented them from doing this because it was a clear violation of God's law.

Josephus made up this story to exonerate Alexander Jannaeus for his sacrilegious treatment of the corpses of the Pharisees he had crucified. But he had another reason for fabricating it, namely to conceal the undignified manner of his passing. Alexander Jannaeus died at home while his wife was on the field of battle. When Salome Alexandra returned from Ragaba as its victorious conqueror, Josephus tells us, the Pharisees gave him the most splendid burial of any Hasmonean king. He writes that the Judeans made many speeches extolling his deeds and justice, all of which moved the common people to tears. However, it is doubtful that Salome Alexandra was there or any such speeches were made: she was fighting her defensive wars to subdue the neighboring states; he was likely interred with little ceremony.

Salome Alexandra would have presided over the construction of her husband's monumental tomb. By Josephus's estimation, it was the most splendid ever built in Jerusalem.[27] But she did not construct it merely as his final resting place, but as a monumental burial complex for her and her entire family. Because Salome Alexandra was likely interred in it, she likely constructed it primarily as a monument to her reign and not her husband's. This tomb was apparently among the largest structures in Jerusalem — perhaps only dwarfed by the temple — and remained so for over a century. It reminded Josephus and countless generations of Judeans that a woman had been their greatest ruler.

Salome Alexandra is the only Hasmonean ruler whose reign begins with a great military victory. During a time of chaos, men chose her to lead their nation and fight their battles. Never before, or since, has a woman commanded such respect, or wielded such power, in her homeland. Her later successes were in no small measure due to her actions at Ragaba. At the time when kings went to war, she was not at home with the women, but in the thick of the slaughter urging men to kill their foes. Later rabbis reflected back on her time in power and concluded that she was the not only the greatest Hasmonean ruler, but the founder of Judea's Golden Age. Their accounts of her are reminiscent of the biblical descriptions of the long-awaited messianic era.

11

Judea's Golden Age
The Blessings of Salome Alexandra

In the time of rabbi Simeon ben Shetach and in the time of Queen Salome Alexandra, the rain would fall on Friday nights, from one week to the next, until the wheat grew to the size of kidneys, the barley the size of olive pits, and the lentils the size of golden denars. — Leviticus Rabbah 35:10

She was the worst ruler in Judean history. Josephus was convinced her unnatural desire for power had destroyed the Hasmonean state. He regretted her reign. However, the rabbis strongly disagreed with his assessment. They considered her Judea's greatest monarch: they were convinced she had presided over Judaism's Golden Age. Which of these two portraits reflects the historical Salome Alexandra? Was she a cunning woman who lusted for power or a devout savior? Although Josephus is our major source for her life and times, few are aware that the rabbis preserved several stories about her. We now turn to their writings to see how they remembered Salome Alexandra in our quest to reconstruct her life and times.

The Traditions of the Sages

The Judaism of the rabbis (a term literally meaning "my master") was a vastly different religion than the faith Salome Alexandra and Josephus practiced. After the Romans destroyed the Jerusalem temple in 70 C.E., Jews could no longer observe the Bible's sacrificial laws. The rabbis emerged from this chaos to unite the Jewish people, and become their religious leaders, by equating scriptural interpretation with temple worship.

The rabbis spiritualized sacrifice. They taught that studying the Bible's laws effectively transported the worshipper back to the time of the temple. Reading Scripture's often arcane rules and procedures about animal sacrifice,

161

Aerial view of the Temple Mount from the south. This elevated square platform once housed the Jewish temple of Salome Alexandra's time. The site of the actual temple is beneath the 7th century C.E. golden-domed Islamic shrine known as the Dome of the Rock. Portions of the walls, and some of the visible stonework, date to Salome Alexandra's time (Todd Bolen/BiblePlaces.com).

and other offerings, was spiritually equivalent to having performed them in the temple: there was no longer any need for a physical sanctuary. Study became the paramount religious duty; it defined the Jews as God's chosen people. Judaism became a religion of the book. But the rabbis faced a problem in their quest to unify the Jews under their leadership — God prefers ambiguity.

The Jewish Bible, which Christians call the Old Testament, is an immensely complex book. It is a compendium of various writings that were produced and compiled by many authors over several centuries. Modern scholars believe that at least four major authors, or possibly communities, contributed to the first part of the Bible, the five books of the Torah (Law) that are traditionally attributed to Moses.[1] The Jewish Scripture is, therefore, not a unified work, but an amalgam of voices. Passages reflecting different historical periods are often juxtaposed, and frequently impossible to understand. Many biblical laws, moreover, are unclear or of no relevance to contemporary Jewish life, making their study either difficult or seemingly useless. Because

the rabbis were convinced that God's laws had to make sense for all generations, they had to find a way to resolve the many problems, and discrepancies,
in their holy book. They found a solution in an ancient concept from Salome
Alexandra's time — the two Torahs.

To modernize the Bible's ancient and often archaic laws, the rabbis cham-
pioned the doctrine of the two Torahs: the Written and the Oral. The Written
Torah, the Bible, contains the text of God's laws that formed the basis of
Salome Alexandra's faith. The rabbis also claimed that God had revealed
another set of laws to Moses that had been passed down orally from him to
successive sages for over a millennium — the Oral Torah. This extensive repos-
itory of tradition clarifies difficult, or contradictory, biblical passages. It also
gives divine sanction to many long-standing customs not found in the Bible
that most Judeans considered sacred, many of which were quite popular during
Salome Alexandra's lifetime.

The religious group known as the Sadducees rejected the doctrine of the
Oral Torah. A large number of priests and aristocrats belonged to this religious
party, which meant that it was inextricably tied to the administration of the
temple and its rituals. Because the Sadducees were so closely associated with
the sanctuary, they had little to offer ordinary Judeans following its destruction. But the Pharisees were different. They were destined to survive the
trauma of the temple's loss because they had long used the Oral Torah to
emphasize that Judaism is simply a religion of pious living. They used the
Oral Law to argue that religion should change and adapt to modern times.
Their scriptural interpretation and understanding of the Oral Law quickly
became normative to such an extent that the rabbis effectively became latter-
day Pharisees.[2]

In the centuries after the temple's destruction, the rabbis began to com-
pile, organize, and assemble the vast body of oral tradition — much of it from
Salome Alexandra's lifetime — in a book known as the Talmud. It is a massive
compendium of Jewish lore, wisdom, religious instruction, philosophy, history, and much more. The Mishnah — a second century C.E. religious text
that preserves much of the Oral law — is its first volume. The remaining books,
collectively known as the Gemara, are an extensive collection of rabbinical
commentaries on the Mishnah, interspersed with Jewish wisdom and cultural
traditions. The rabbis of Tiberius, Israel, produced the earliest version, which
is known as the Palestinian Talmud, in approximately 400 C.E. But Babylon's
rabbis, from approximately 500 C.E. to the seventh century C.E., compiled an
even more detailed, and substantially larger, edition known as the Babylonian
Talmud. This version eclipsed its predecessor and became the authoritative
version of the Talmud. It remains a major source of law and doctrine for many
contemporary Jews.

The Talmud does not include all the rabbinic literature. The rabbis wrote many other books, such as commentaries and legendary expansions of biblical texts that convey moral lessons. Jews still read them for their exegetical insights and spiritual edification; however, none attained the Babylonian Talmud's authoritative status. Nevertheless, these works are important in our quest to uncover Salome Alexandra's lost years and accomplishments since the rabbis who produced them, after combing through the written and oral records of their past, came to the remarkable conclusion that she had presided over Judaism's Golden Age.

The Golden Age of the Pharisees

The rabbis were fascinated with Salome Alexandra. Like Josephus, they acknowledge that she was a devoted Pharisee. One rabbi, in a passage that was widely copied, wrote that her piety not only brought great blessings to her people, but to the land as well:

> In the time of rabbi Simeon ben Shetach and in the time of Queen Salome Alexandra, the rain would fall on Friday nights, from one week to the next, until the wheat grew to the size of kidneys, the barley the size of olive pits, and the lentils the size of golden denars [Lev. Rab. 35:10].[3]

Other stories in the Talmud extol Salome Alexandra's devotion to Jewish law. According to one rabbinic account, when she held a banquet, she discovered that all the dishes were ritually polluted. She refused to use them and had them melted to make new vessels. Salome Alexandra, the rabbis tell us, did this to comply with their teaching that the refining process would restore their ritual purity.[4]

Despite their admiration of Salome Alexandra, the rabbis were misogynists. They devoted an entire tractate (book) of the Talmud, called *Nashim* (women), largely to female impurity: it often places restrictions on their participation in Jewish life. Talmudic law prohibits women from reciting certain prayers, constructing the sukkah (booth) for the Festival of Tabernacles, being counted in a minyan (the quorum of ten persons needed for worship), and making religious pilgrimages. It even exempts them from studying the Torah, which comprises the basis of much Jewish cultural and spiritual life.[5] Given the overt sexism of the rabbinic literature, which is evident from a cursory reading of the Talmud's many sections devoted to women, it is remarkable that the rabbis lavishly praised Salome Alexandra. To understand why, we must look at the group Josephus blamed for her downfall — the Pharisees.

The Talmud contains a story about Alexander Jannaeus that is reminiscent of Josephus's account of his deathbed instructions to Salome Alexandra. According to the rabbis:

> King Yanni [=Alexander Jannaeus] said to his wife: "Do not be afraid of the Pharisees and the non–Pharisees but the hypocrites who ape the Pharisees; because their deeds are the deeds of Zimri but they expect a reward like Phineas" [b. Sotah 22b].

In this story Alexander Jannaeus compares the Pharisees to two biblical figures known for their violent deeds — Zimri and Phineas. Zimri is notable for two dubious reasons: he committed suicide and his seven-day reign as Israel's king is the shortest in the Bible.[6] His name subsequently became a byword for betrayal since he murdered his sovereign to seize power. According to this rabbinic story, Alexander Jannaeus accused the Pharisees of acting like this notorious king when they fought against him. Because of their treason, he believed they deserved to die a horrible death like Zimri. However, they were confident they would receive a divine reward like Phineas for their zealous action.

The Bible praises Phineas for his righteousness. But he too was an extremely violent man. He was adamant that Jews should strictly adhere to biblical law and not associate with pagans. During the Exodus from Egypt, he impaled an Israelite man and a Midianite woman with a spear while they were having sexual intercourse. God rewarded his zealous deed by giving him and his descendants an eternal priesthood.[7] According to the Talmud, Alexander Jannaeus claimed that the Pharisees thought they had acted like Phineas when they had taken up arms against him. But their supposed righteous zeal did not earn them Phineas's reward, but crucifixion.

Although it may seem unusual that the rabbis preserved stories about their ancestors' revolt against Alexander Jannaeus, they had a good reason for doing so. The Jews had twice taken up arms after Salome Alexandra's death to regain their independence from Rome to restore the Jewish state she had ruled. The great Jewish Revolt of Josephus's day (66–70 C.E.) was the first; the rebellion of the pseudo-messiah Bar Kochba (132–35 C.E.) was the second. The former war caused the Romans to destroy the temple and the latter led them to banish all Jews from Jerusalem. In the wake of these catastrophes, the rabbis renounced the militarism of the Hasmoneans, and urged accommodation with the Romans and all subsequent authorities. They preserved this story about Alexander Jannaeus to warn against mixing religion, politics, and violence. According to their accounts, Judea was at peace only during Salome Alexandra's reign: the time when a Pharisee ruled the nation and the temple priests followed the Pharisaic interpretation of the Torah. As the spiritual descendants of the Pharisees, the rabbis encouraged their contemporaries to obey them, like the Judeans had submitted to Salome Alexandra, in order to bring about a new Golden Age.

Some scholars are reluctant to use the rabbinic corpus to reconstruct Salome Alexandra's reign because of its late date. However, a close look at its content suggests that the rabbis, like Josephus, had access to ancient written, and possibly oral, traditions from the first century B.C.E. Take the name of her husband for example. The rabbis call him Yanni, which is the Hebrew equivalent of Jannaeus. Josephus prefers to use his Greek name, Alexander, but on one occasion — ironically in a passage about Salina Alexandra — he tells us that Jannaeus was his Semitic name.[8] However, there is a problem: Yannai/Jannaeus was not his official Hebrew name.

Archaeologists have uncovered thousands of Alexander Jannaeus's coins bearing the Greek inscription "King Alexander." This verifies Josephus's claim that this was his Greek name. But his Hebrew coins call him Jonathan (Yehonatan), which consists of the consonants YHWNTN (some coins use the shorter spelling YHNTN or YNTN). Several seal impressions (pieces of clay bearing the imprint of a signet ring that was used to secure official documents; the ancient equivalent of registered mail) and the Dead Sea Scrolls call Salome Alexandra's husband by this name.[9] Yet, despite this firm archaeological evidence that Salome Alexandra's husband was actually named Jonathan, Josephus and the rabbis call him Jannaeus/Yanni.

Josephus certainly knew that Salome Alexandra's husband was actually named Alexander Jonathan because coins bearing his Hebrew name were in wide circulation throughout the first century C.E. Why does Josephus not use his proper name? And why do the rabbis, writing centuries later, likewise call him Yanni? It is unlikely they learned this name from Josephus since they considered him a traitor and avoided citing his works (Christians preserved his books because they mention Jesus and other New Testament persons).

Josephus and the rabbis must have copied the name Yannai/Jannaeus from some ancient source. Jannaeus/Yannai, therefore, must have been a variant of Jonathan; it was likely his nickname, or the name he commonly used in lieu of his given name. If the rabbis knew such accurate information about Salome Alexandra's family centuries after her death, there is a high probability that at least some of the stories they preserve about her are factual. This is especially true of the religious reforms that took place during her reign, for it is improbable that the rabbis would have attributed such positive changes to a woman if they were not true.

The subject of Alexander Jannaeus's name raises the perplexing issue of Salome Alexandra's coins. Did she mint any? There is no evidence she did. Rather, her husband's coins were widely circulated for over a century: Jews apparently preferred them during the Roman period for nationalistic reasons. Although we do not know why she never produced her own currency, we can offer three plausible explanations based on the historical evidence. First, there was likely no need. Her husband minted an overabundance of coins. He likely buttressed his claim to power by publicizing his titles on his currency. He was also likely forced to mint a considerable amount of money as part of an economic stimulus package to alleviate suffering during the sabbatical year of 79/78 B.C.E. Second, she likely avoided using coins as propaganda due to her religious sensibilities — even Hasmonean currency contained representations of inanimate objects such as anchors and stars — to comply with the biblical law against images. Third, she may have realized that some men may not have been comfortable with a female monarch. By not etching her name and titles on Judea's currency, Salome Alexandra avoided portraying herself as a Hellenistic monarch, preferring to let her actions define her office.[10]

A Righteous Brother?

The Talmud includes several stories about Salome Alexandra and rabbi Simeon ben Shetach (ca. 120–40 B.C.E.), perhaps the most prominent Pharisee of the Hasmonean period. Despite his fame, Josephus tells us nothing about him. But the rabbis considered him one of their greatest leaders. Many of his famed judicial rulings occurred during her reign: she even protected him from her husband's wrath. The rabbis were convinced her patronage of him was a major factor that brought about her Golden Age.

Some rabbis mistakenly identify Salome Alexandra and Simeon as siblings. It is possible that some of them were troubled that a woman had presided over Judea's most glorious and prosperous period, and tried to diminish her achievements by associating her with the powerful and highly respected Simeon. But there may be a simpler, and less sexist reason, for this error. Not all the rabbinic stories claim the two were related. The only clear evidence they were is found in a passage in which Alexander Jannaeus "said to his sister, send and fetch him [=Simeon]." The phrase "to his sister," differs from "to his wife" by a single letter that is often confused with another. In Hebrew and Aramaic, both of which use the same alphabet, *tav* ("t") and *het* ("ch") look alike, and are commonly mistaken. A copyist likely confused the two letters and wrote *het* instead of *tav*, unwittingly making her Simeon's sister. Later scribes unknowingly copied this text, thereby preserving the error.[11]

The rabbis consistently portray Salome Alexandra as an opponent of her husband, and a staunch defender of Pharisaic interests. One of their stories about her recounts the time when some prominent Pharisees fled to the cultural metropolis of Alexandria, Egypt, to escape her husband's persecution. They remained there during his entire reign. According to one Talmudic story, Salome Alexandra hid many of them.[12] In the following rabbinic account of this time, she tricks her spouse into taking an oath so she could summon Simeon to the court:

> King Yannai and his queen were dining together, and since he had killed the rabbis, he had nobody to say grace for them. He said to his wife, "Would that we had somebody to say grace for us." She said to him, "Swear to me that if I bring someone you will not harm him." He swore to her; and she brought him Simeon ben Shetach. She sat him between her husband and herself, saying, "See how much honor I pay you." He [=Simeon] replied, "It is not you that honors me, but it is the Torah that brings me honor; for it is written, 'Exalt her, and she will promote you; she will bring you honor when you embrace her'" [Prov. 4:8; b. Berakhot, 48a].[13]

This story shows that Salome Alexandra was so powerful that she did not hesitate to defy royal protocol and seat Simeon in the spot reserved for monarchs — a indication that she was her husband's political equal. Simeon, moreover, was so confident that she would protect him that he rebuked her husband in public while extolling her virtues. The rabbis loved to praise Salome Alexandra. They not only told stories about her piety and bravery, but they also recounted rather unflattering incidents about her husband that often depict him as spiritually inept.

Another Talmudic story about Alexander Jannaeus portrays him as deficient in his knowledge of Jewish law, suggesting that he had not availed himself of his youthful opportunity to study the Torah. It is a tale about three hundred Nazirites who had come to Jerusalem to be released from their biblical pledge to abstain from wine, vinegar, grapes, raisins, and contact with a corpse. These men would have been easily identifiable; they were not permitted to cut their hair until they had fulfilled all the rituals mandated in the biblical Book of Numbers 6:1–21. The problem was that they were poor and lacked sufficient funds to complete the requisite sacrifice to be released from their vows.

Simeon proposed that he and Alexander Jannaeus each pay for half of these men to fulfill their oaths. Because Alexander Jannaeus's ancestor Judas "the hammer" had protected Nazirites when he had fought the Seleucids, he had no choice but to accept Simeon's offer. But Simeon had no intention of paying his share; he correctly ruled that many of these men had made defective pledges, and therefore no payment was required. The entire episode was embarrassing since Alexander Jannaeus, as Judea's high priest, should have known that some of these men were not true Nazirites. He was forced to hand over a considerable sum to fulfill his vow.

Josephus does not record this rather unflattering story; however, his books support the rabbinic portrayals of Alexander Jannaeus as an impious and cruel ruler. He documents only one religious act during his entire tenure as high priest — his people pelted him with citrons to prevent him from completing it. The rabbis and Josephus agreed that the masses loved Salome Alexandra and hated her husband, and that the two disagreed in matters of religion.[14]

Fasting Forbidden?

The ancient Aramaic work known as the *Megillat Ta'anit* (Scroll of Fasting) tells us a great deal about Salome Alexandra. It is an Aramaic chronicle that documents thirty-five momentous days in Jewish history that are to be celebrated — fasting and mourning are forbidden. Likely written around 7 C.E., the rabbis later appended Hebrew commentaries to it known as *Scholia* (sing. *Scholium*). The *Megillat Ta'anit* and its *Scholia* record several stories about Alexander Jannaeus, including his persecutions of the Pharisees and his confrontation with Judaism's chief judicial body, the Sanhedrin. This combined work even contains several favorable references to Salome Alexandra and Simeon.

The *Scholium* to one version of the *Megillat Ta'anit* states that when Alexander Jannaeus tried to kill the rabbis, some fled to Syria. Another records their escape, and mentions his murder of an influential sage named Bukinus and his brother Bukius.[15] The commentary to the *Megillat Ta'anit* portrays Alexander Jannaeus as the most evil Hasmonean king, and even records a rather unusual story about his death.

The *Megillat Ta'anit* tells us that when Alexander Jannaeus became fatally ill, he cast seventy rabbis in prison and ordered their execution upon his death. When he died, Salome Alexandra removed his signet ring and altered his decree to save them. This day subsequently became a holiday in Judea.

This story is certainly apocryphal since Josephus preserves a nearly identical tale about Herod the Great's death. It is, nevertheless, important for the light it sheds on our queen. This ancient story had a remarkably long life. The sixteenth century C.E. Italian-Jewish scholar and physician, Azariah dei Rossi, mentions it. Europe's Jewish community must have considered Salome Alexandra a great woman to preserve and circulated such favorable stories about her over a thousand years after her death.[16]

The *scholia* portray Salome Alexandra and Simeon as ardent supporters of the Pharisees. One story about them takes place during the time when the Sadducees dominated the Sanhedrin, the nation's leading court. It states that she and her husband were sitting in its chambers: a clear indication the rabbis believed she played an active role in her country's judicial affairs long before she became queen regnant. On this occasion, Simeon rebuked the Sadducees, who were judges in the Sanhedrin, for their inadequate knowledge of Jewish law and legal procedures. He declared that only those proficient in the Torah were worthy to sit in its chambers. He then began to purge the Sanhedrin of Sadducees, even though they controlled the government and the temple at this time, and slowly transformed it into a Pharisaic institution.[17] The rabbis suggest he accomplished this through Salome Alexandra's patronage: she undoubtedly worked with him to remove many of her husband's appointees from the court.

The Pharisees enjoyed a renaissance during Salome Alexandra's reign. They dominated the temple cult and the judicial system. Under her protection, the Pharisaic customs were restored and many of the Sadducean interpretations of the Torah were abandoned. One of the most notable changes concerned the abrogation of the Sadducean ruling that the Festival of Weeks must be observed on a Sunday; the Pharisees believed that it could occur on any day. Salome Alexandra changed its celebration to the Pharisaic calendar. The rabbis considered this, and other similar reforms, so unprecedented that they created four holidays to celebrate the Pharisees' triumph over the Sadducees. The rabbis who compiled the Talmud believed the world was desolate until Salome Alexandra's reign when the Pharisees came to power.[18] But the Sadducees were not the only group to have caused problems for Simeon. Itinerant rabbis, healers, and magicians often posed a direct threat to his authority.

Sages Versus Witches

Many Jews in Salome Alexandra's Judea believed that God still worked miracles. Her homeland later produced the most famous of these peripatetic wonder-working sages and healers — Jesus of Nazareth. During the Hasmonean period, many wandering rabbis traveled throughout the countryside performing miracles. Learned men, like Simeon, were often wary of them since they answered only to God. He believed he had the judicial authority to examine them, and determine whether their actions and teachings conflicted with the Torah. His efforts to reign in these itinerants led to a confrontation with the greatest of all miracle workers in Salome Alexandra's day — Honi (a.k.a. "the Circle-Drawer").

Honi was closer to God than any other rabbi, even Simeon. Once when his beleaguered countrymen begged him to intercede with God to end a drought, he drew a circle in the sand and vowed not to leave it until it rained. God sent a tempest in response to his prayer. Although the Judeans were elated, Simeon was not pleased. He warned, "Were you not Honi ha-Me'aggal ("the Circle-Drawer"), I would pronounce a ban against you."[19] As Jesus of

Nazareth discovered a century later, pious religious officials often viewed such popular miracle workers as threats to their authority.

The story of Honi raises the intriguing question of what Salome Alexandra thought of him, and the other inerrant sages and healers who wandered throughout Judea during her lifetime. The following rather shocking story from the Mishnah about an incident that took place during her reign suggests her tolerance of them only went so far:

> A man is hanged facing the people and a woman facing the tree, according to the words of Rabbi Eliezer. The sages, however, say, "A man is hanged, but a woman is not hanged." Rabbi Eliezer said to them, "Did not Simeon ben Shetach hang eighty women in Ashkelon?" They responded to him, "He hanged eighty women even though two should not be judged on the same day" [m. Sanhedrin, 6:4].

According to the Palestinian Talmud these women were witches.[20]

Jewish tradition suggests that witchcraft was quite popular in Judea. The great first century C.E. rabbi Hillel supposedly opined, "The more women, the more witchcraft." Many females likely practiced witchcraft because men barred them from holding positions of authority in politics, religion, and the military. It was one of the few areas of society in which they could serve as leaders, without seeking the approval of men.[21]

When it came to witchcraft, the situation was different for men. The renowned second century C.E. rabbi Simeon bar Yohai, for example, was not only an ardent opponent of it, but he actually practiced sorcery: he purportedly had the power to raise the dead![22] The rabbis were willing to make exceptions to the biblical prohibition against magic as long as its practitioners were men.

The tragic story of the witches of Ashkelon may provide some valuable historical information about Salome Alexandra's religious beliefs. These women were clearly Jewish since the pagans of this city would not have considered witchcraft a crime. But there is no historical evidence the Hasmoneans conquered Ashkelon; it is the only coastal town Alexander Jannaeus never captured. It gained its independence and minted its own coins after his death, and apparently retained its free status until the Roman period. Salome Alexandra must have commanded considerable authority to force its Gentile population to allow Simeon to pursue and execute these women in their city. As a devout Pharisee, she had to order their deaths since the Bible commands, "You shall not permit a female sorcerer to live." The irony of her strict adherence to biblical law is that the only recorded witch-hunt in Jewish history occurred during the reign of its only lawfully recognized female monarch.[23]

This story suggests that Salome Alexandra could be quite cruel. Although it is a terrible episode that may appear to tarnish her Golden Age, we must view her actions in light of the norms of the ancient world. All kings, even the great biblical monarch David, were guilty of numerous acts of wanton violence, even war crimes. However, Salome Alexandra never committed any atrocity; she never undertook any needless war of conquest; and she never executed her political foes or family members. In a world in which death and suffering were commonplace, it is doubtful any tears were shed at the execution of these witches. Salome Alexandra was responsible for their deaths; however, we must remember that she executed them in accordance with God's will.

The rabbis preserved another version of this story in which the relatives of the executed women sought revenge against Simeon. They hired false witnesses to testify in court that his son had committed a deed punishable by death. He was tried and found guilty. When the accusers confessed to their treachery, Simeon requested his son's sentence be reversed. However, this was impossible because, as his own son pointed out, the legal rulings of the Pharisees forbade a witness from testifying twice.[24] Simeon had no choice but to accept the original verdict. As his son mounted the scaffold, he ratified the death sentence. Although we cannot know whether this story is factual, it does not contradict the rabbinic portrayals of him, which emphasize his zealous, and sometimes harsh, enforcement of Jewish law regardless of the potential consequences. We can easily imagine such a man overseeing the execution of eighty witches.

Women and the Law

Life for women and children greatly improved during Salome Alexandra's reign as a result of her patronage and protection of Simeon. Despite his harsh treatment of the witches, the rabbis preserved stories in which he made rulings on behalf of women that were quite progressive for their time. He required children to attend school. Girls were likely included in this edict since the Pharisees, according to the Talmud, insisted that everyone learn the Bible.[25] Simeon prospered during Salome Alexandra's reign only because she protected him and the Pharisees. The two must have been quite close, which may account for his surprisingly favorable, and often remarkable-sounding, rulings pertaining to women. This is especially true of marriage.

Simeon made a major alteration in Jewish tradition during Salome Alexandra's reign when he introduced the *ketubbah* (the wedding document that specified the obligations of the groom toward his bride). Prior to this time the groom had been required to set aside money or property for the bride's family. Simeon required the groom to write in the *ketubbah* that all his property belonged to his bride.[26] This ruling not only prevented a husband from divorcing his spouse in haste, but it also provided the future bride with some measure of financial security should her marriage break up. Although there is some evidence the *ketubbah* existed before Salome Alexandra's reign, it only became normative during her lifetime under her patronage of Simeon ben Shetach.[27]

The rabbis lavishly praised Salome Alexandra. They considered her reign a Golden Age. Although Josephus disagreed, he nevertheless acknowledges her piety, and recognizes that she changed her nation's religion from the Sadducees to the Pharisees. Since the rabbis considered themselves the spiritual descendants of the Pharisees, they had a vested interest in recording stories about her patronage of their ancestors. Because they insist she had been their protector, their stories must be true: it is unlikely that they would have fabricated such tales of heroism and piety about a woman without some factual basis. But there was another group of Jews who, although they recognized that she had transformed Judean society, considered her reign the worst of times. We now turn to their documents to see what they tell us about Salome Alexandra and her female contemporaries — the mysterious women of the Dead Sea Scrolls.

PART FIVE: THE MYSTERIOUS
WOMEN OF THE DESERT

12

"The Fornications of the Prostitute"
Salome Alexandra and the Mysterious Women of the Dead Sea Scrolls

> Because of the countless fornications of the prostitute, the alluring mistress of sorcery, who ensnares nations with her harlotries and people with her sorcery.— Bible, Book of Nahum 3:4

The Dead Sea is one of the most inhospitable, desolate, and sweltering places on the earth's surface. The few people who live or work along its shores either cater to the tourist industry, or harness its salt and potash for commercial and industrial uses. Yet, in this region — where God destroyed the cities of Sodom and Gomorrah for their immorality — a group of Jewish monks built a settlement during Salome Alexandra's day to pray, study, and await the messiah. Their writings, known as the Dead Sea Scrolls, have radically altered our understanding of her world. They are particularly important in our quest to reconstruct Salome Alexandra's life since their authors believed the Bible predicted her rise to power: they identify her as the prostitute denounced by the biblical prophet Nahum.

The Discovery

For centuries the Bedouin of the Taʿamireh tribe have roamed the shores of the Dead Sea in search of food and water for their flocks. During the winter of 1946–47, a young shepherd named Muhammad edh–Dhib went off in search of a stray goat. He located the wayward animal among the craggy rocks near a small cave. When he threw a stone into its opening to discover whether anything was inside, he heard the unexpected sound of shattering pots. He squeezed through the cavern's small entrance and, after his eyes adjusted to

Qumran Caves and Wadi Qumran. Cave 4 adjacent to the archaeological site of Qumran where the Jewish religious group known as the Essenes collected and wrote many of the Dead Sea Scrolls. This cave contained fragments of over 500 scrolls, including several that mention women. Portions of more than 100 copies of Old Testament books have thus far been pieced together from the remains found in this cave. Today the cave contains multiple entrances, including a hole in its roof visible in the photograph (Todd Bolen/BiblePlaces.com).

the darkness, noticed approximately ten large ceramic jars along its walls. When he and his two cousins later returned to retrieve their contents, they were greatly disappointed to find that they contained not gold or precious jewels, but seven scrolls. They eventually sold their supposedly worthless find for a disappointing sum of approximately $63.80. However, scholars consider their discovery priceless. Over sixty years later, the Dead Sea Scrolls are still revealing their secrets.[1]

Muhammad's discovery prompted Bedouin and scholars alike — the former usually more enterprising and successful than the latter — to search the vast Judean desert for additional scrolls. Their combined efforts yielded a total of eleven caves containing the fragmentary remains of over 900 manuscripts. Unfortunately, layers of dust and the urine and fecal matter of bats and animals covered them, making many difficult to read. Centuries of exposure to the elements caused nearly all these texts to disintegrate into tens of thousands of fragments. For this reason, few of the Dead Sea Scrolls are scrolls; most are scraps.[2]

The Middle East's turbulent political situation hindered efforts to study these documents. They were found in British Mandate Palestine. From 1948 to 1967 the Hashemite Kingdom of Jordan took possession of the territory known as the West Bank, where the Dead Sea Scrolls were discovered. The Jordanians appointed a small team of scholars to clean, assemble, translate, and publish them. Successive wars — including the 1967 Israeli capture of the West Bank and the Dead Sea Scrolls — financial shortfalls, and scholarly rivalries delayed their work. Those charged with publishing the Scrolls, moreover, were reluctant to allow other experts to see these priceless texts. As a result of their secrecy, rumors quickly proliferated. Among the most popular was that the Vatican somehow controlled the official team, all of whom closely guarded the secrets of the Dead Sea Scrolls because they somehow undermined Christianity. Others even claimed that that Jesus, or his predecessor John the Baptist, belonged to the community that produced these texts. A protracted battle largely waged in the periodical *Biblical Archaeology Review* finally secured their public release in 1991 and put an end to all these rumors.[3] Despite recent progress in deciphering and piecing together these ancient documents, some things unfortunately remain the same. Scholars are still engaged in an acrimonious debate over the origin and meaning of the Dead Sea Scrolls, while war continues to plague the region in which they were discovered.

Who Wrote the Dead Sea Scrolls?

Jews and Christians throughout the world were excited to learn of Muhammad's discovery. They were especially fascinated with one scroll: the world's oldest copy of the biblical Book of Isaiah. But scholars were more interested in an unusual document he found containing a detailed list of rules and regulations for communal living. Noting the similarities between it and the ancient accounts of a Jewish group known as the Essenes, many experts wondered if Muhammad had accidentally stumbled upon one of their settlements. Experts quickly turned to Josephus for an answer since he is our greatest extant source concerning the beliefs and practices of this unusual sect.

Josephus tells us a great deal about the Essenes because he had been one. In his autobiography, he describes his teenage spiritual quest:

> When I was about sixteen years old, I decided to gain expertise in the philosophical schools among us. There are three of these: the first, Pharisees; the second, Sadducees; and the third, Essenes, as we have often said. I decided to try them all to help me decide which was the best [*Life*, 10–12].

He also tells his readers that he lived for three years in a Judean desert cave with a hermit named Bannus. The two adopted a rather eccentric lifestyle to purify themselves of sin — they engaged in frequent ritual ablutions and wore clothing made of trees. Although Josephus abandoned the Essenes to become a life-long devotee of the Pharisees, he never forgot his time with them. He tells us much about their beliefs and lifestyle in several of his books.

The Roman writer and naturalist Pliny the Elder (23/4–79 C.E.) was as curious about the Essenes as modern academics. His short account of them is important since he provides us with the exact location of one of their settlements in his description of the Dead Sea:

> From the western shore the Essenes flee the banks that harm; a group set apart and in the entire world beyond all others extraordinary — without any women, stifling every urge, without money, with palm trees as their companions....
> Below them, there had been a town Ein Gedi, second to Jerusalem in fertility and the forests of palm-groves, but now another killing-field. Then comes Masada, a cliff fortress, and itself not very far from the Dead Sea [Pliny, *Nat.*, 5.73].[4]

With Pliny's description in hand, archaeologists set out for the Judean Desert to locate this particular Essene settlement. After searching the shores of the Dead Sea, they found only one site matching his description — a remote and unexcavated ruin called Qumran.

Little was known about Qumran, which is near the cave where the first Dead Sea Scrolls were discovered. A few early explorers had stumbled upon it in their quest for the fabled cites of Sodom and Gomorrah.[5] Many in antiquity attributed the region's bareness and forlorn appearance to this event. Intrepid students of the Scripture made their way to Qumran hoping to prove that this remote ruin was one of these biblical cities. But the first modern visitors quickly surmised that God had not destroyed Qumran. Nobody gave the site any further thought until Muhammad's goat stumbled upon the first Dead Sea Scroll cave nearby. Now this small, remote, and desolate ruin is perhaps the world's most studied, and debated, archaeological site.

Between 1951–56 the French Dominican archaeologist Roland de Vaux excavated Qumran. He was surprised to discover that it looked like a Christian monastery: it contains communal dining halls, meeting rooms, inkwells for writing scrolls, and industrial installations for manufacturing pottery and other items necessary for daily life. But the presence of Jewish ritual purification baths, called *mikvaot* in Hebrew, clearly demonstrated that Jews, not Christians, lived there. The discovery of scroll jars and caves containing texts inside the site makes it difficult to argue that Qumran and the Dead Sea Scrolls are not connected. The numerous similarities between these writings and Josephus's descriptions of the Essenes have convinced the majority of scholars that this religious group wrote, collected, and hid these documents in the caves within, and surrounding, Qumran.[6]

Qumran Mikveh stairs cracked by earthquake. One of the ritual purification baths at Qumran used by the Essenes. The great earthquake of 31 B.C.E. destroyed their settlement, and forced its occupants to temporarily abandon the site. The raised divider marked the entrance (right-hand side) from the exit (left-hand side) so that ritually pure Jews leaving the bath would not touch those entering (Todd Bolen/BiblePlaces.com).

Qumran Cave. During the winter of 1946–47, a young shepherd named Muhammad edh-Dhib went off in search of a stray goat and accidentally found this cave containing the first Dead Sea Scrolls. Known as Qumran Cave 1, it included a copy of texts that mention women (Todd Bolen/BiblePlaces.com).

The Mysterious Women of the Dead Sea Scrolls

We know much about the Qumran Essenes because they are still there. Few visitors take the time to traverse the rocky plateau adjacent to the site to visit their final resting place. Some tourists unknowingly walk atop Qumran's former inhabitants, usually with haste, on the way to the air-conditioned restaurant to escape the Judean desert's oppressive heat. This is because Qumran's graves are rather modest and often difficult to detect. They consist of a simple vertical shaft with a horizontal chamber at the bottom to accommodate the corpse. Each is marked by a heap of stones, many of which have been washed away as a result of occasional winter flooding.

Roland de Vaux was eager to excavate Qumran's cemetery to learn more about the Essene men who lived there. He was quite surprised — perhaps even shocked — to find the bones of a few women and children. Scholars cannot agree on how many he uncovered because they disappeared for several decades. De Vaux gave them to anatomical experts for study. Unfortunately, they did not complete their reports, and de Vaux never kept track of where they were taken. Although scholars recently located them in Germany, France, and Jerusalem, they are of limited value for scientific study. This is because de Vaux sometimes neglected to record the exact location where he found them. There are also discrepancies in his records concerning their gender. Because they have been moved many times, it is possible some have become mixed with bones from other sites. But there is a greater problem with them: de Vaux did not realize that local Bedouin tribes also used Qumran's cemetery.[7]

Some of the skeletons de Vaux excavated are clearly modern Bedouin graves. But can we be certain any are Essenes? Archaeologists recently conducted a few probes of Qumran's cemetery to answer this question. They used the latest scientific dating methods unavailable to de Vaux such as carbon-14 testing to determine the date of organic remains. This new expedition uncovered human remains, including women, that definitively date to the period from Salome Alexandra to Josephus.

Archaeologists have recently produced the first map of the Qumran cemetery, which provides us with many new insights into the site's inhabitants. Although modern military activity and construction have destroyed some graves, the best estimate is that Qumran's cemetery contains at least 1,138 burials. Excavations have revealed that thirty-two of these tombs are clearly ancient and contain between thirty-three to thirty-five persons (graves in antiquity were often used for multiple burials). Five skeletons are women.[8] But what are they doing there?

The Dead Sea Scroll known as the *Rule of the Community* is one of the texts Muhammad discovered. It contains a detailed set of rules and regulations for a communal society in which all members are expected to dine together, engage in religious worship, Bible study, and manual labor. This rulebook also describes a rigorous two-year initiation that includes an examination of the spiritual fitness of candidates (we even possess a fragment of one such meeting recording the infractions of several members). Those who pass this probationary period are required to hand over their property to the financial administrator of the group and take an oath to follow the rules of the sect. Because of the numerous similarities between the Dead Sea Scrolls and Josephus's accounts of the Essenes, it is difficult to argue that the authors of these texts were not Essenes. The discovery of Dead Sea Scrolls inside the Qumran settlement, moreover, appears to confirm that this site housed the very community of Essenes that Pliny mentions.[9] But were there female Essenes at Qumran?

The Qumran Essenes must have followed the *Rule of the Community*'s regulations and precepts since they preserved so many copies of it. This document, therefore, provides us with a unique opportunity to learn more about life at Qumran. Since many of the rooms de Vaux excavated must have been used for the meals and worship ceremonies described in this text, we should

Copper inkwell from Qumran used to write some of the Dead Seas Scrolls. Archaeologists discovered several inkwells from Qumran, which shows that many at the site were literate (Todd Bolen/BiblePlaces.com).

The source of considerable controversy, this scroll, known as *The Rule of the Congregation* (1QSa) mentions women and children as members of the Essene community. It provides firm evidence of female religious leadership in Salome Alexandra's day (Todd Bolen/BiblePlaces.com).

be able to identify these meeting rooms in the archaeological remains. But is there any evidence women resided at Qumran, or participated in the ceremonies described in the *Rule of the Community*?

Because the *Rule of the Community* never refers to women, many scholars have assumed that the Qumran community was celibate. While this conclusion is likely correct, it is important to note that no Dead Sea Scroll requires sexual abstinence. Many of the scrolls even describe marriage. One such document is attached to our only complete copy of the *Rule of the Community*.

The *Rule of the Community* is the first of three texts that a scribe copied onto a single scroll. The second document, known as the *Rule of the Congregation*, describes a religious group that includes men, women, and children. The next text, known as the *Rule of the Blessings,* contains three benedictions. All three works refer to a group of leaders known as "the Sons of Zadok," which shows that they are describing the same religious movement. Since one scribe copied all three writings onto a single scroll, he clearly intended them to be read together, suggesting that he considered both celibacy and marriage valid lifestyles. But there is one other factor that suggests this particular scroll was among the most important of all Essene texts. It, and several other writings that regulate life at Qumran, were found in sealed jars in the very first cave, which scholars refer to as Cave 1.

The Dead Sea Scrolls found in sealed jars in Cave 1 are very different than almost all other texts discovered in the caves surrounding the Qumran settlement. They are quite large; the majority of Dead Sea Scrolls are small. Because no other cave yielded such a large number of magnificent, and carefully preserved, scrolls, Cave 1 is clearly unique. It is likely a storage place for master copies of the most important Essene texts, which had been carefully placed there in sealed jars for preservation.[10] Because some of the documents in this particular cave describe marriage, the readers of these scrolls, even if they were celibate, clearly did not object to chastity. Let us take a brief look at one of these texts, the *Rule of the Congregation*, to see what it tells us about women and children Essenes.

The *Rule of the Congregation* contains detailed regulations for Essene meetings. This rather surprising passage is among them:

> She shall be received to bear witness concerning him [about] the commandments of the Law, and to take her place at the hearing of the commandments [1QSa I 11–12].

The original editors translated the Hebrew of this text verbatim. But some scholars, under the belief that a woman could not have given legal testimony against her spouse, change the feminine pronoun "she" to "he."[11] But there is a problem with this unfounded alteration: it does not remove all traces of women from this rulebook. Elsewhere, the author records the following edict:

> On their arrival, they will assemble all those who come, including children and women, and they will read into [their] ea[rs] all the regulations of the covenant and will instruct them in all its commandments, lest they stray in their e[rrors] [1QSa 1.4–5].

This passage is not an anomaly since the *Rule of the Congregation* is among the most important of all the Dead Sea Scrolls. Archaeologists have discovered fragments of eight or nine older versions of it that are written in a mysterious secret code (its purpose is unknown), which date as early as 191 B.C.E. Because Qumran was built around 100 B.C.E., about the time Salome Alexandra celebrated her fortieth birthday, they were already ancient when they were brought there. The Qumran Essenes must have considered this work extremely important to preserve so many copies of it.[12] But this is not their only rulebook that mentions women and children. There is another. The story of its discovery is as mystifying as its contents.

An Egyptian Dead Sea Scroll

Few are aware that Muhammad was not the first person to discover a Dead Sea Scroll. Fifty years earlier, in 1896, Solomon Schechter, a Jewish scholar from England's famed Cambridge University, found two copies of a Dead Sea Scroll in a tenth century C.E. Synagogue in Cairo, Egypt. He named it the *Zadokite Work* after its references to the "sons of Zadok," and proposed that it is a medieval copy of a pre–Christian document. Scholars later confirmed his dating when they found the remains of several copies of it in the Dead Sea Scroll caves. They have renamed it the *Damascus Document* after a passage in it mentioning this city. How a medieval copy of it ended up in Cairo remains a mystery.

The *Damascus Document* is clearly related to the *Rule of the Community*. Both texts describe an identical leadership structure, communal meetings, and use the same distinctive religious terminology. However, the *Damascus Document* is written primarily for married Essenes living in cities. It discusses menstruation, childbirth, marriage, and divorce. The following passage, known as the "oath of the children," even mentions families:

> All who have entered the covenant for all of Israel as an eternal statue shall let their children, who have reached [the age] of accountability, be enrolled among those that are to take the oath of the covenant [*Damascus Document* XV 5–6].

Because Hebrew masculine plural nouns and pronouns can also refer to both genders, translators must use context to decide how to translate them. Although it is possible that the Essenes excluded girls from this initiation ceremony, this text's content suggests otherwise. Both the *Damascus Document* and the *Rule of the Congregation* contain lists of persons banned from the Essene community. The following excerpt from the former mentions some of them:

> No demented fool shall enter. Neither shall any stupid or insane person, nor anyone with dimmed eyes who cannot see, nor a limping or lame or deaf person, nor a youth, none of these shall come into the congregation, because the holy angels [are in their midst] [4Q266 8 i 6–9].

Neither the *Damascus Document* nor the *Rule of the Congregation* excludes women. The *Damascus Document* even includes many rules and regulations to protect them. It requires a bride to undergo a physical examination before her wedding by "reliable" and "knowledgeable" women to verify her virginity. This degrading procedure was actually intended for her benefit: it prevented her husband from annulling their union by claiming that she had not been a virgin on their wedding night. This text holds marriage in high regard, and even quotes from Scripture to show that it is a holy lifestyle like celibacy. Because the *Rule of the Congregation* also considers marriage acceptable, the Qumran Essenes were clearly interested in regulating the lives of married members of their sect, and maintained regular contact with them.

Josephus and Philo lived when the Essene movement flourished. They write that Essenes reside everywhere, and frequently travel. They apparently stood out in a crowd. Josephus tells us that Essenes carried a small shovel for defecation, wore a loincloth, and donned garments at meals. Josephus mentions that every Judean town had an Essene official in charge of supplying the needs of traveling members. The Essenes were not only visible throughout Salome Alexandra's homeland, but their behavior likely aroused considerable suspicion: they refused to worship in the temple because they rejected the Hasmonean high priests.

Some Essenes — possibly accompanied by their wives and children — likely visited Qumran for the special festivals the sect observed in lieu of those held in the temple, such as Hanukkah and Tabernacles. The *Damascus Document* mentions one such gathering when "all [the inhabitants] of the towns shall assemble" for a spiritual survey. Because the *Rule of the Congregation* and the *Rule of the Community* document women and children attending Essene meetings, and contain nearly identical disciplinary rules, they were clearly written for the same religious group.[13] Women were active members of Essene communities, but did they serve as leaders?

The Dead Sea Scrolls show that there was some measure of gender equality among the Essenes. One document, known as 4Q502, may describe a wedding or some unknown Essene festival in which women played major roles. It mentions a number of Essene leaders, such as "mothers," "sisters," and a council of "male and female elders." The parallel uses of masculine and feminine titles in this text suggests that these women were members of the Essene community since the word "elder" elsewhere in the Dead Sea Scrolls is a title of honor.[14] A passage from the *Damascus Document* even lists punishments for insulting them:

> Whoever complains against the Fathers [shall be expelled] from the community and shall not be allowed to return, [but if] he complains against the Mothers, then he shall be punished te[n] days, since the Mothers do not have authority in the community [4Q270 7 I 13–14].

Although these Mothers were leaders, they were not equal to men. They were not required to hand their property over to the sect — a clear indication of their lesser status. They were authoritative figures, but there is no evidence they led males. These women apparently taught female members of the sect and children. However, this does not diminish their importance. These women testified before the entire assembly in matters that affected the community: their word was as valid as a man's.

We can say with confidence that women were members of the Essene movement, and were visible throughout Judea in Salome Alexandra's lifetime. Some were leaders. But it is doubtful any lived at Qumran. With the exception of a few skeletons, there is no clear archaeological evidence for their presence at the site: no jewelry, weaving objects, or clear evidence of other feminine crafts.[15] Because it is improbable that this community would have allowed impure outsiders to be buried in its sacred cemetery, the few female skeletons found there are certainly Essenes. These women either died while visiting Qumran for religious festivals, or were brought there for burial. Although the desert ascetics of Qumran likely avoided regular contact with women, they were obsessed with one — Salome Alexandra.

The Alluring Mistress of Sorcery

The authors of the Dead Sea Scrolls turned to the Bible to explain the tumultuous events of Salome Alexandra's lifetime. The commentaries they wrote looking to Scripture to interpret the present are called *pesharim* (plural of the Hebrew *pesher*, meaning "interpretation"). A *pesher* cites a scriptural verse and then connects the sacred text to a current event. The *pesharim* rarely name individuals, however; they prefer epithets that describe the personalities of the people they denounce. The authors of these texts were convinced that Scripture had predicted the deeds of Salome Alexandra and her husband.

The *Nahum Pesher* is the most important Dead Sea Scroll for understanding the history of this time. It is one of the few documents that contain names. It mentions the Syrian king Demetrius III who, with the support of the Pharisees, had invaded Judea in an ill-fated effort to remove Alexander Jannaeus from power. The *pesher* then quotes the biblical Book of Nahum 2:12: "The lion catches enough for his cubs, and strangles prey for his mates." The ancient reader would know that Nahum continued, "'I am going to deal with you,' declares the Lord of Hosts" (Nahum 2:14). The *pesher* text then refers to the lion in the Nahum text as "the Lion of Wrath" who kills some of his people by "hanging them alive" (i.e. crucifixion). Because Alexander Jannaeus crucified the Pharisees who had invited the Syrian monarch Demetrius III to invade Judea, it is clear that he must be the "Lion of Wrath." The author then quotes from the biblical book of Nahum 3:1–3, which he believes is a prediction of Alexander Jannaeus's persecution of the Pharisees:

> Spoils will not be lacking, nor the sound of the whip nor the rattling of the wheel. Galloping horses, and bounding horsemen charging, swords flashing,

and spears gleaming. Many slain and heaps of corpses. Countless dead bodies, they stumble over their dead bodies!

The author next describes a change in government, and writes, "Its interpretation concerns the dominion of the "Seekers after Smooth Things," which is the Essene's code name for the Pharisees.[16]

The Essenes were convinced the biblical prophet Nahum had predicted Salome Alexandra's rise to power, and the dominance of the Pharisees during her administration, since the next passage of this biblical book amazingly describes a woman. The prophet's language is quite shocking even in its original context:

> Because of the countless fornications of the prostitute, the alluring mistress of sorcery, who ensnares nations with her harlotries and people with her sorcery.

Again the ancient reader of Scripture would know that this passage was followed by "I am going to deal with you, declares the Lord of Hosts; You shall lift up your skirts up to your face and show the nations [your] nudity and kings ... your shame." Because the Dead Sea Scrolls insist that the "Seekers after Smooth Things" (=Pharisees) only became powerful during the reign of a woman, the *Nahum Pesher*'s references to a female can only refer to queen Salome Alexandra.

The Dead Sea Scrolls denounce Salome Alexandra and her husband because they consider the Hasmonean monarchy illegitimate. But their authors hate her because she is a woman. The writer of the *Nahum Pesher* wants to equate the evil "prostitute" the prophet Nahum denounces with Salome Alexandra: no other person is described in such graphic sexual language in any Dead Sea Scroll. Unlike her husband or other important men in the scrolls, she receives no code name. The authors of the *pesharim* preferred to let this salacious biblical verse allude to her, and did not mention her name in their commentaries. They could not have chosen a worse passage to represent her than this image from the Book of Nahum since they want the reader to assume that she is a prostitute. The scrolls never condemn her husband for his sexual transgressions (Josephus tells us that he consorted with concubines). The reference to "sorcery" in this text, moreover, may be an allusion to her execution of eighty witches in Ashkelon: a transgression the author likely mentions because it involved female sinners.

We have another biblical commentary that documents Salome Alexandra's reign. This Dead Sea Scroll, known as the *Hosea Pesher,* also calls her husband the "Lion of Wrath." Its author interprets the unchaste woman of Hosea 2:6–7 as a prophecy about her. He predicts that God will punish the Judeans for her deeds with a terrible famine:

Therefore, I shall take back my grain again in its time, and my wine [in its season]. I will take away my wool and my flax so she cannot cover [her nakedness]. I will expose her private parts in the sight of [her] lo[vers and] no [one] will withdraw her from my hand [Hosea 2:9–10]. Interpreted this means that He [=God] smote them with famine and with nakedness so that they became a disgra[ce] [*Pesher on Hosea A* (4Q166), col. 2, lines 8–12].

This famine occurred two years after Salome Alexandra's death, during the Sabbatical Year of 65 B.C.E. Nevertheless, the community of the Dead Sea Scrolls, like Josephus, blames her for the tragic events that took place during the reigns of her sons. But this *pesher* also mentions a period of unprecedented prosperity before this famine struck, which its author believes was a time when the Judeans had observed God's commandments. This can only refer to Salome Alexandra's Golden Age, which the author of the *pesher* prefers not to comment upon because it took place during the reign of a woman.

The Essenes loathed Salome Alexandra. But they did not hate all women. In an age when few men were literate, the Essenes allowed their female members to become leaders: one Dead Sea Scroll even mentions a woman scribe.[17] But these Essene women were not unique. A similar, and possibly related, group of contemplative Egyptian men and women put pen to papyrus to produce now lost religious books, songs, and works of philosophy. The remarkable story of these dancing female ascetics provides an important clue about worship at Qumran and elsewhere in Salome Alexandra's Judea.

13

The Dancing Women
of the Egyptian Desert
The Mysterious Therapeutae

They rise up together and standing in the middle of the dining hall form
themselves first into two choirs, one composed of men and one composed of
women ... then they sing hymns to God ... sometimes chanting together,
sometimes taking up the harmony antiphonally, hands and feet keeping time
in accompaniment, and filled with enthusiasm they reproduce sometimes the
lyrics of the procession, sometimes of the stopping and the turning and cir-
cling of a choric dance.— Philo, *On the Contemplative Life*, 83–84

A devout Jew; an ardent Hellenist; a pioneer of the symbolic method of
scriptural interpretation known as allegory; and a member of a dysfunctional
family with powerful connections to the highest levels of Roman government— Philo (20 B.C.E.–50 C.E.) was all these and considerably more. He
lived in the greatest Hellenistic center of learning, the Egyptian city of Alexandria, and became one of its most influential and prolific authors; forty of his
sixty books survive. He was a man comfortable in two worlds who tried to
bring Jews and Gentiles together.

Philo embraced allegory—a method of reading a text that focuses on
the symbolic, or hidden, meaning of its words — with great zeal. The scholars
of the Alexandrian library had long used this exegetical method to reinterpret
Homer's writings as parables of moral philosophy. Philo became its greatest
Jewish practitioner; he used it to explain difficult or contradictory biblical
passages by arguing that Scripture has a hidden, spiritual, meaning. Christians
found his writings so compelling that they adopted his allegorical method as
their primary way of reading the Bible for over a millennia.[1]

In addition to his voluminous exegetical works, Philo wrote several books
about his tumultuous times. With the exception of the Dead Sea Scrolls, no
text is more important for understanding the women of Salome Alexandra's

day than his *On the Contemplative Life*. It is about a religious community of Jewish Egyptian ascetic male and female philosophers known as the Therapeutae, who practiced the allegorical method in a monastic compound outside the city of Alexandria.

Philo's On the Contemplative Life

The famed Christian bishop and historian Eusebius (275–339 C.E.) was so struck by the similarities between *On the Contemplative Life* and the Church of his day that he concluded Philo must have known Jesus' followers. It is easy to understand why he thought the Therapeutae were Christians, for Philo's book reads like an account of life in an ancient Christian monastery. Although many scholars object to Roland de Vaux's use of Christian monastic vocabulary, such as "scriptorium," to describe the archaeological site of Qumran, he is not entirely guilty of an anachronism. Philo is the first known writer to use the word monastery; it appears twice in his account of the Therapeutae. Unfortunately, his description is all that we have of this remarkable group's settlement since modern quarrying has destroyed all traces of it.[2]

Philo's *On the Contemplative Life* never made the list of Alexandrian classics. But early Christians regarded it as an important book because they, like Eusebius, thought it was about a Christian community of apostolic times. Because of its presumed importance as an ancient witness to their faith, they made many copies of it. Their decision to preserve it is especially remarkable since Philo's *On the Contemplative Life* describes a religious community that gave women leadership positions Christianity has denied them for nearly all of its two thousand years. Philo's description of this community sounds so modern that one scholar claims it never existed, and that Philo's book is a work of fiction. However, most experts disagree, and believe that Philo is describing a real community that, although it sounds improbable for its time and place, allowed women to live and worship alongside men.[3]

Born Out of Crisis

Philo's *On the Contemplative Life* is an unusual book. It is actually one of two surviving texts of his five-volume work titled *On Virtues*. He wrote this massive compendium of Jewish philosophy and history in Greek to defend his community following the first known pogrom in history that took place in his hometown in 38 C.E. It appears that the Hellenism of Salome Alexandra's day was partly responsible for it. The city's pagans were angry the Jews had long enjoyed the benefits of citizenship, yet denied the existence of their gods. The Alexandrian Jews sent Philo to Rome to defend their ancient rights that the Cleopatras and their successors had granted them. According to tradition, he read his *On Virtues* before the Roman Senate. If true, then the Romans not only learned about these amazing women from Philo, but about the Essenes.[4]

In his introduction to his *On the Contemplative Life*, Philo mentions his earlier now-lost book on the Essenes that formed part of his *On Virtues*:

> I have previously discussed the Essenes, who zealously desired and practiced the active life in every way or — at least to put it more moderately — excelled in it in many ways. I will now write about what is required about those who have embraced a life of contemplation.... The vocation of these philosophers is clear from their name of Therapeutae [=masculine gender] and Therapeutrides [=feminine gender], a name derived from the word "to heal" (*therapeuo*) either in the sense of "heal," or because they practice the healing art better than is found in the cities where only the bodies are cured [*Contempl. Life*, 1–2].

Philo also tells us that the Therapeutae were much like the Judean Essenes: members of both groups wore white robes, practiced celibacy, prayed towards the sun, produced religious literature, and held communal meals. In light of these parallels, a few scholars believe, along with some ancient writers, that the Therapeutae were members of an Egyptian branch of the Judean Essene movement. Some Greek manuscripts and Latin translations even title the work *Concerning the Life of the Therapeutae Essenes*.[5] The Dead Sea Scrolls now reveal that this equation is only partially mistaken: the numerous similarities between both groups strongly suggest that they were somehow related.

Although the connection between the Therapeutae and the Essenes must remain a matter of conjecture, the descriptions of both sects preserved in the classical sources suggest that, even if there was no direct relationship between the two groups, they likely emanated from a common religious movement. Copies of the *Damascus Document,* and other texts found in Cairo similar to the Dead Sea Scrolls, show that Essene writings somehow reached Egypt. Although we cannot say when they arrived there, the similarities between the practices of the Essenes and the Therapeutae suggests that it was quite early, perhaps even during Salome Alexandra's lifetime. Fortunately, the debate over when these texts reached Egypt does not affect our quest to understand the women of Salome Alexandra's world. Because the extant sources show that the Essenes and the Therapeutae had nearly identical worship practices, we can use Philo's detailed account of the Therapeutae to help us reconstruct what took place at Qumran in Salome Alexandra's day.

A Pleasant Solitude

Philo writes that the Therapeutae, like their Essene counterparts at Qumran, lived in a semi-isolated compound near a major population center from which they could secure provisions. Of the two groups, the Therapeutae chose a more hospitable locale than the Qumran Essenes. According to Philo, they

> are located above the shore of the Mareotic lake on a low hill, which is very well situated because of its security and pleasant air. The safety is secured by the neighboring farm buildings and villages and by the pleasantness of the air, and the continual lake breeze, which blows toward the sea, for the open sea is nearby. The sea breezes are rather light, the lake breeze close, and the two combine to produce a very healthy climate [*Contempl. Life*, 22–23].

Philo also tells us that the Therapeutae, like the Essenes, lived elsewhere, and that many pagans knew about, and admired, their unique lifestyle.

Philo's description of the Mareotic compound of the Therapeutae is so detailed that it allows us to imagine what it looked like:

> The houses of the society are close together and very simple in design, they furnish protection against the two greatest dangers, namely, the extreme heat of the sun and the terrible cold. They are neither too close to one another, as in cities, since such close proximity would prove to be troublesome and displeasing to people who desire to satisfy their desire for solitude, nor, on the other hand, are they too far apart from one another, lest they loose a sense of fellowship. In each house there is a sacred room which is called a sanctuary or monastery; isolated in it they celebrate alone the mysteries of the holy life, they bring nothing into it, including drink and food or any other of the things necessary for life; but only the law and the revelations delivered through the mouth of the prophets, and the Book of Psalms and the other books that promote and perfect knowledge and piety [*Contempl. Life*, 24–5].

Although Philo wrote this passage in the first century C.E., his description of the Therapeutae's settlement accurately describes the remains of the late fourth century C.E. monastery at Kellia, located some thirty-four miles south of Alexandria. The best explanation to account for these similarities is that the earliest generation of Christian monks used Philo's *On the Contemplative Life* as an architectural blueprint when they constructed this monastery. If this interpretation is correct, we should not consider the Therapeutae an isolated fringe group that played no major role in history. Rather, it was religious group whose lifestyle, and possibly teachings, influenced the development of Christian monasticism.[6]

Philo's description of worship among the Therapeutae is undoubtedly the most remarkable part of his book. He describes their synagogue building as follows:

Their common sanctuary in which they meet every Sabbath is divided into a separate chamber for the men and another for the women. The women, too, as well as men, as their custom form part of the audience, having the same fervor and following the same way of life [*Contempl. Life*, 32–3].

When it comes to their seating, Philo writes:

The men sit by themselves to the right, and the women by themselves to the left. It may be thought that their dining couches, though not expensive are still very soft, as appropriate for people of good birth and high character, who are trained in the practice of philosophy. Actually, they sit upon plank beds of the common variety of wood, which are covered with very cheap straw of native papyrus, with a small armrest to lean upon [*Contempl. Life*, 69].

Philo wrote a similar account of Essene worship in his now lost book about them, *That Every Good Person Is Free* (the fourth century C.E. Christian scholar Eusebius preserved this passage):

On that day, the Sabbath, they abstain from other work and proceed to the holy places called synagogues, where they sit in rows according to their ages, the younger below the elder, attentive and well behaved. One of them then picks up the books and reads aloud, and another from among the master teachers steps forward and explains whatever is not easy to understand in these books. The majority of their philosophical study takes the form of allegory, and they zealously emulate the worthy men of the past [*Good Person*, 81–82].

Although Philo writes that a dividing wall separated men and women in the sanctuary, this does not mean that the Therapeutae segregated women. All members of this community shared the same dining table like a family. After meals, moreover, men and women met in the same room to worship and praise God in song.

Communal meals were a central feature of life for the Therapeutae and the Essenes. Both Philo and Josephus describe these meeting rooms in such detail that we can easily imagine what they looked like. Fortunately, we do not have to reconstruct them in our minds; Roland de Vaux found two meeting rooms at Qumran: both contain pantries.[7] They are identical to the meeting halls used for dining described in the Dead Sea Scrolls, as well as the writings of Philo and Josephus. One is located in a second story room, and contains a lower storeroom, while the other is entirely at ground level. One of these halls, known as Locus 77 (a locus is a number given to a room or structure during an excavation), is the largest room at Qumran. It contains the remains of a podium in its extreme western portion where an Essene elder likely delivered sermons, or read from Scripture and rulebooks. But what took place in this room?

Pottery is the chief tool archaeologists use to reconstruct life in antiquity. They meticulously collect, clean, photograph, reconstruct, and draw all the

Qumran dining room, known as Locus 77. The Qumran Essenes used this room for meals and religious worship. Members of the Essene community would have sat atop rugs and wooden benches. The Dead Sea Scrolls and Josephus describe meals and ceremonies taking place in this room (Todd Bolen/BiblePlaces.com).

ceramics they uncover. The types of vessels found during an excavation often allow scholars to determine what types of activities took place in particular rooms. The ceramics discovered at Qumran reveal much about life there.

Roland de Vaux found over one thousand dishes scattered upon the floor of the pantry adjacent to locus 77. They had been stacked on shelves that had collapsed during the earthquake of 31 B.C.E. Archaeologists discovered an identical pile of ceramics that had fallen from shelves in a pantry adjacent to the other dining room (locus 114). But what is most revealing is what de Vaux did not find in these storerooms — cooking pots. He only uncovered large numbers of serving dishes: plates, cups, and bowls. This shows that food was prepared elsewhere and merely eaten in these rooms. This archaeological evidence helps us to understand Josephus's unusual description about Essene meals:

> When they quietly sit down, the baker sets out the loaves of bread in order, and the cook places a single bowl before each participant. Then the priest recites a prayer before the meal; and everyone must wait for him to finish his

prayer before eating. The same priest, after he has eaten, recites another prayer, and then all those seated praise God who provides their food [*War*, 2.130–1].

Josephus's statement that the Essenes served their food on individual dishes is quite revealing. He mentions this inconsequential piece of information because Jews no longer practiced this custom in his time, but ate from communal bowls.[8] He includes this information because he liked to highlight unusual lifestyles; he portrays the Essenes much like a contemporary writer would describe the pre-modern lifestyle of many contemporary Amish orders. The hundreds of small plates, cups, and bowls of equal size in the pantries at Qumran support Josephus's observation, and show that the Essenes were an egalitarian community in which all members received the same portion of food and drink.

Josephus also tells us that the Essenes, like the Therapeutae, regarded their dining halls as sacred spaces, and also used them for worship. Members of both sects ritually immersed themselves in water and changed from work cloths to sacred linen loincloths before entering them. But what type of worship took place in Qumran's rooms? Philo's answer is quite surprising.

Qumran study room and library. Members of the Essene community held meetings and worship ceremonies in the room at the bottom of the photograph. The Essenes sat atop cushions placed on the small raised benches visible in the photograph. The rear room contained scrolls for worship and study (Todd Bolen/BiblePlaces.com).

Dancing in the Desert

The assembly halls of the Therapeutae and the Essenes are synagogues, Jewish houses of worship. Synagogues in antiquity were multi-purpose structures. The Theodotus inscription from Jerusalem — the only extant evidence of a first century B.C.E.–first century C.E. synagogue near the temple — states that it was built for worship, scriptural study, strangers' lodgings, and dinning.[9] Because ancient towns and villages had few, if any, large structures, it should not be surprising to find considerable literary evidence that synagogues were used for many secular functions. They are the ancestors of contemporary mega churches, which often contain similar multi-purpose rooms for worship, dining, meetings, and recreation.

Archaeologists have discovered several Judean synagogues from Salome Alexandra's lifetime that provide additional information about worship at Qumran and elsewhere. The best preserved, and most impressive, is located at Gamla in the Golan region, northeast of the Sea of Galilee. Built in the late first century B.C.E., it served as a place of worship until the Romans

The first century B.C.E. Gamla Synagogue is the best surviving example of a synagogue in antiquity. It is similar in design to the study room and dining hall at Qumran, all of which were constructed to focus worshippers' attention to the center of the room where those giving instruction would have stood. Men, women, and children worshipped together and sat on the benches along all four of its walls. The Romans destroyed the synagogue during the great Jewish War against Rome in 67 C.E. (Todd Bolen/BiblePlaces.com)

destroyed it in 68 C.E. (Josephus watched the battle as a Roman prisoner). Gamla's synagogue is similar in appearance to Qumran's great assembly hall (Locus 77). But it was much more extravagant. Unlike Qumran, where worshippers sat upon wooden benches or rugs, Gamla's residents had stone seating in their sanctuary.

Gamla's synagogue also contains a small room that likely served as a school for religious instruction. Many experts believe that a similar room at Qumran (locus 4) is a small synagogue for Essene elders.[10] Gamla's small school — located in a remote village far from Jerusalem — shows that Jews during Salome Alexandra's lifetime stressed education and religion even in the countryside. The cost, size, and amount of care that went into the design of the synagogues at Gamla and Qumran show that nothing was more important to the ancient Judeans than their faith. But who was allowed to worship in these buildings?

No Judean synagogue built during Salome Alexandra's lifetime, or even a century later, contains architectural features designed to separate women from men. Everyone sat together during worship. Inscriptions from later periods even name women as synagogue leaders, which has led some to conclude that these females were equal to male office holders. While this is likely a misreading of the evidence — many of these inscriptions are clearly honorific titles since some were given to children — the extant literary evidence shows that men honored women in their local congregations.[11] Although ancient Judaism did not grant women full equality with men, it did not discriminate against them on the basis of their gender during worship. Women prayed alongside men in the Jerusalem temple and Judean synagogues during Salome Alexandra's lifetime. But the Therapeutae and the Essenes were unique: they allowed women to become religious leaders.

The Dead Sea Scrolls mention female and male leaders known as the "Mothers" and the "Fathers." Because the scrolls levy fines for disrespecting both, they are not honorific titles, but actual positions of authority. The mention of female scribes in the Dead Sea Scrolls raises the intriguing possibility that women wrote or copied some of these texts. However, the monks of Qumran — likely regarded by their sect as the most holy of Essenes — rarely associated with female members. But the situation was different among the Therapeutae: they permitted men and women to live together.[12]

Philo preserves a rather fascinating account of the religious services of the Therapeutae that may provide some insight into synagogue practices in Salome Alexandra's Judea. He writes that the male and female members of this sect met together on the seventh day to hear the teachings a senior member, and to eat a common meal of bread, flavored with salt, hyssop, and water. Like the Essenes described in the *Rule of the Congregation*, the Therapeutae also sat in hierarchical order and wore special robes. But, unlike the Essenes, men and women in this Egyptian sect worshipped alongside one another.

Philo was a sexist who did not believe that women and men are equal. He employed a rather ingenious explanation to account for the gender equality of this Egyptian movement he admired — celibacy had turned their women into honorary men![13]

Philo's *On the Contemplative Life* reveals that men and women worshipped together along the Mareotic Lake in a rather unusual manner. His description of their gatherings following their communal meals sounds like a contemporary Pentecostal service:

> They rise up together and standing in the middle of the dining hall form themselves first into two choirs, one composed of men and one composed of women ... then they sing hymns to God ... sometimes chanting together, sometimes taking up the harmony antiphonally, hands and feet keeping time in accompaniment, and filled with enthusiasm they reproduce sometimes the lyrics of the procession, sometimes of the stopping and the turning and circling of a choric dance [*Contempl. Life*, 83–84].

While this description may appear surprising, dancing was a common way to praise God in antiquity. In the Bible dances commemorate historical events such as the parting of the Red Sea. According to the biblical Book of Exodus, Moses's sister Miriam and the Israelite women sang and danced in celebration of this great miracle. This scriptural text, however, relegates her song to a mere half verse while Moses's hymn occupies a disproportionate share of the chapter.[14]

A Dead Sea Scroll text known as 4Q365, which has been dated to Salome Alexandra's lifetime, suggests that a longer version of Miriam's song once existed. Among its surviving passages are two lines that read: "You are great, a deliverer ... the hope of the enemy has perished...," and "Extol the one who raises up ... [the one who do]es gloriously." It also uses feminine language similar to the biblical Song of Miriam, such as "and he exalted her to the heights," to describe a victory for the lowly.[15]

It is impossible to tell whether this Dead Sea Scroll preserves a portion of Miriam's song that was removed from the Bible, or whether a devout scribe penned it to complete the missing scriptural narrative. Philo suggests that many such songs were used in worship. In one passage about the Therapeutae, he refers to a hymn that is reminiscent of this Dead Sea Scroll:

> This wonderful sight and experience, greater than could be told or conceived, or even hoped for, men and women alike, filled with such ecstasy that, forming a single choir they sang hymns of thanksgiving to God their savior, the men led by the prophet Moses and the women by the prophetess Miriam.... The choir of the Therapeutae of both sexes, note in response to note and

voice to voice, the high-pitched sound of the women blending with the bass of the men, creates an harmonious concert, pure music in the truest sense [*Contempl. Life*, 87–88].

Philo's account suggests that the female Therapeutae reenacted Miriam's song while the men of this sect imitated Moses's hymn. This musical ceremony, in which both genders play equal roles, is a clear demonstration of the sect's high regard for women. There is no reason to doubt that similar songs and dancing took place elsewhere. Perhaps worship at Qumran and in the synagogues throughout Salome Alexandra's Judea's was much noisier than we have been led to believe.[16]

Female Sages in the Desert

Some Judean women from elite families undoubtedly found life among religious groups like the Essenes and the Therapeutae attractive since they provided outlets for leadership that were unavailable elsewhere. Unfortunately, few traces of these learned females have survived the ravages of time, or the editorial pen of the men who wrote history. Philo is one notable exception. Unlike his contemporary Josephus, he had good reason to document their lives — a female sage had been his teacher.

In his book *On Flight and Finding*, Philo writes that he was once troubled by the following biblical passage in Exodus 21:12: "If a man kills another and he dies, let him be put to death by death." Philo writes that he could not understand why there is a superfluous word in this verse since a murderer can only be put to death once, and not "death by death." Rather than seeking one of Alexandria's great male philosophers or religious scholars to help him understand this text, he sought the tutelage of a female:

So I attended the lectures of a wise woman, whose name is Skepsis, and she rid me of my confusion. She taught me that some people living are actually dead, and that some who are dead are still alive. She explained to me that bad people, prolonging their days to extreme old age, are dead because their life is deprived of virtue, while good people, even if cut off from their partnership with the body, live forever, and are granted immortality [*On Flight and Finding*, 55].

Because Skepsis means "consideration" some scholars do not believe she is an actual person. But there is no reason to doubt Philo's claim she existed since Skepsis was a female name in antiquity (it was likely given to a daughter of a philosopher). His brief tribute to his remarkable female teacher offers us a tantalizing glimpse of Alexandrian intellectual life. It shows that educated woman lectured in the greatest center of learning in the Hellenistic world.[17]

Skepsis taught Philo the allegorical method that emphasizes the symbolic reading of Scripture. But her exegetical technique has become synonymous with his name. The Bishop Augustine (354–430 C.E.), whose allegorical school of interpretation dominated Christendom for most of its history, learned much of his art from Philo's writings. Because Skepsis apparently introduced Philo to the allegorical method, we should give her some credit for shaping Christian history.

Philo's enigmatic passage about Skepsis suggests that female literacy among the affluent in antiquity was fairly common. This was also true of the Jews. Women priests served in the Jewish temple of Onias IV in Leontopolis. Archaeologists have actually found the remains of one in its catacombs. Her grave contains the following inscription:

> O Marin, priest, excellent one, friend of all, who caused pain to none, a friend to your neighbors, farewell. About fifty years old. In the third year of Caesar, Payni 13.[18]

Given the participation of women in Egyptian religion, and the worship there of queens such as Cleopatra II and Cleopatra III as gods, it should not be surprising to see a Jewish female priest in this country. But it is the date on Marin's tombstone that is most intriguing; she was born in 77 B.C.E., which is one year before Salome Alexandra became Judea's ruler. Marin was clearly not the first woman to have held this sacred office since the Leontopolis temple by this time had existed for nearly a century. She is undoubtedly one of a long line of educated Jewish female priests who carried out their sacred duties in Egypt while Salome Alexandra ruled over men.

Salome Alexandra's reign was the most prosperous period of Judean history. The textual and archaeological evidence shows that worship during her lifetime was more egalitarian than many contemporary forms of Judaism and Christianity. It was a bit more energetic and nosier than we have been led to believe. Contemporary Jews and Christians who worship through song and dance are the spiritual heirs of the men and women of the Egyptian and Judean deserts who sang together, making a joyful noise in the name of the Lord. While these women and men were rejoicing in Egypt, Salome Alexandra was using her political skills to end decades of conflict, and ward off the greatest threat any Hasmonean ruler ever faced.

14

"A Wonderful Administrator"
Salome Alexandra's Pacification of the Middle East

> She proved to be a wonderful administrator in matters of state, and, by a continual recruiting doubled her army. She amassed a considerable body of foreign troops that she used to strengthen her nation. She struck fear in the surrounding nations and became their master.—Josephus, *War* 1.112

Salome Alexandra became Judea's first Hasmonean queen regnant at a dangerous time. The Nabatean Arabs to the east threatened her nation, and their alliance with the Itureans made them a formidable foe. Syria, her country's longstanding adversary to the north, still possessed a large army that could potentially overrun the Jewish state. Civil war, moreover, was a distinct possibility; many Pharisees wanted to punish the Sadducees for helping Alexander Jannaeus crucify 800 of their members. Salome Alexandra realized that she had to adopt some of her husband's policies and keep a strong military, lest neighboring powers seek to annex Judea now that a woman held the reigns of power. Through a combination of military action and diplomatic overtures, Salome Alexandra made peace with her husband's enemies and stabilized Judea's eastern and northern frontiers. According to Josephus, she was so successful that "she struck fear in the surrounding nations and became their master."

An Unmitigated Disaster?: Josephus's Portrayal of Salome Alexandra

Josephus both praises and reviles Salome Alexandra. But he mainly denigrates her throughout his books. This is especially true of his *Antiquities,* in which he portrays her nine-year reign as an unmitigated disaster. Four successive misfortunes define her period in office: Aristobulus's attempted coup when she succeeded her husband, a failed military campaign to Damascus, a threatened Armenian invasion of Judea, and Aristobulus's second attempt to remove her from power just before her death. In contrast, God miraculously saves her husband on four occasions: each a battle with a neighboring king.[1] But no divine intervention is forthcoming for Salome Alexandra: she faces four tragedies; she handles them poorly. Josephus portrays her as militarily and politically incompetent. Unlike her husband, who saves his nation while dying, her love for her sons prevents her from taking the appropriate action to preserve the Hasmonean sate. She brought about its demise.

According to Josephus, Salome Alexandra was never Judea's actual ruler. Rather, she was merely a puppet: "While she held the title of monarch, the Pharisees had the power."[2] Her blind allegiance to them brought great suffering to her religious foes. Some Pharisees — apparently without her knowledge — persecuted Sadducees. Her youngest son, Aristobulus — a Sadducee — threatened to overthrow her to protect them. This is the first of her four tragedies. Fearful of civil war, she concedes to his demand that she hand over to her Sadducean enemies some of her strategic fortresses, which they later use to stage a coup when she becomes fatally ill.

Josephus tells us that Salome Alexandra inexplicably placed Aristobulus in command of her army and sent him to Damascus to fight an unnecessary war. This is particularly difficult to understand since he had just tried to remove her from power. Josephus implies that she undertook this foolhardy campaign — the second misfortune of her reign — to keep him and his fellow Sadducees busy and away from Jerusalem. She sent him to oust an Iturean usurper named Ptolemy, who, he implies, was about to take the city from the Nabatean Arab monarch Aretas. The expedition accomplishes nothing: it only weakens her forces.

And then a new threat emerges:

> About this time news came that Tigranes, king of Armenia, with an army of three hundred thousand soldiers had invaded Syria and was heading toward Judea. This terrified the queen and her people [*Ant.* 13.419].

Salome Alexandra sends envoys with valuable gifts to beg Tigranes for mercy. He accepts her costly presents, thanks her messengers, and gives them reason to hope for a favorable outcome. However, he makes no promises but, according to Josephus, prepares to invade Judea. But then the unexpected occurs. Tigranes, apparently after capturing the city of Ptolemais, receives word that the Roman General Lucullus (117–57/6 B.C.E.) has invaded Armenia. Tigranes rushes home to defend his country, and abandons his plan to annex Judea. His departure ends the third calamity to have afflicted Judea during Salome

Alexandra's reign: her kingdom owed its survival to sheer luck, and not her diplomatic skills or any military action on her part.

Josephus was convinced that God was angry with Salome Alexandra. He writes that after Tigranes's departure, the fourth and final tragedy of her reign occurred. She became fatally ill. Aristobulus immediately takes advantage of her incapacitation to stage a coup. Because of her calamitous reign, the collapse of the Hasmonean state is inevitable. This is how Josephus defines her legacy. But how much, if any, of his account of her time in power is true?

The Effeminate Pharisees, the Masculine Sadducees

What about Salome Alexandra's children — Hyrcanus and Aristobulus? After all, in the normal course of things, they could expect to succeed their father. Again, we rely on Josephus:

> Of these sons, the one, Hyrcanus, was too weak to govern and in addition much preferred a quiet life, while the younger, Aristobulus, was a man of action and aggressive. As for the queen herself, the masses loved her because they believed she disapproved of the crimes her husband had committed. (Salome) Alexandra appointed Hyrcanus as high priest because of his greater age, but more especially because he refrained from meddling in politics; and she permitted the Pharisees to do as they liked in all matters, and also commanded the people to obey them; and whatever regulations, introduced by the Pharisees in accordance with the tradition of their fathers, had been abolished by her father-in-law Hyrcanus, these she again restored. And so, while she had the title of sovereign, the Pharisees had the power [*Ant.* 13.407–9].

Although Josephus portrays Salome Alexandra as a pawn of the Pharisees, a close reading of his *War* and *Antiquities* shows that she was a strong-willed and independent monarch. She had, after all, remained a Pharisee while her husband persecuted and crucified them!

Josephus realized he could not blame Salome Alexandra alone for the demise of the Hasmonean state — Hyrcanus and the Pharisees had supported her. He writes:

> They themselves were to blame for their misfortunes, in allowing a woman to rule who had a madly and unreasonable love of power, even though her sons were in the prime of their life [*Ant.* 13.417].

Josephus describes Salome Alexandra as "madly" and "unreasonable" to portray her as a woman who embodies the traits of a man. He claims she was aggressive, forcible, and had an insatiable lust for power. Hyrcanus and the Pharisees, in contrast, were weak, cowardly, and ineffectual — they were womanly! For Josephus, this reversal of traditional gender norms hastened the Hasmonean state's demise.[3]

Although Josephus makes it appear that Salome Alexandra created a rift between the Pharisees and the Sadducees, a close reading of his *War* and *Antiquities* suggests otherwise. The Sadducees rarely appear in these books, and he consistently identifies them as a school, not a political party. Although many members of this religious movement undoubtedly opposed her, their power was largely limited to Judea's elites and priests, from whom they recruited many of their members. The two major opponents of the Pharisees that Josephus identifies, Diogenes and Galestes, do not bear Jewish names; they may have been Gentile politicians in her husband's court. There is no reason to assume that all of Salome Alexandra's political or religious opponents were Sadducees.

There was a major difference between Salome Alexandra and her predecessors when it came to religion. While John Hyrcanus and Alexander Jannaeus were Sadducees for political reasons, she joined the Pharisees because of their reputation for piety. Even Josephus stresses that the Pharisees were the most accurate interpreters of the law, and constituted the leading religious movement of his day. Men willingly accepted Salome Alexandra as Judea's monarch, even though she was a woman, because they realized that she and the Pharisees were not hypocrites, but truly devout observers of Jewish law.[4]

Salome Alexandra gave the Pharisees control over the temple and Judea's judicial system. However, she did not neglect the Sadducees. Many served in her military, including her youngest son. But she was cautious, and did not let either group become too powerful. She made it clear to all that the Pharisees were now in charge of religious affairs when she adopted the Hellenistic institution of "Friends" of the ruler: she chose them to be her "Friends."[5] Josephus's anger at the Pharisees for accepting this honored position causes him to distort his accounts of them, even though he counted himself among their numbers. Like the writers of the Dead Sea Scrolls, Josephus denigrates the Pharisees of this time because they willingly conceded religious and political authority to a woman.

Josephus invented many of his disparaging remarks about the Pharisees. He likely took others from his major source, Nicolaus of Damascus. This is clear in Josephus's Greek text. His account of Alexander Jannaeus's deathbed speech to Salome Alexandra is similar to his story of John Hyrcanus's defection from the Pharisees. He deliberately uses many of the same Greek words in both stories. Josephus does this to contrast Salome Alexandra's failure to recognize the corrupt nature of the Pharisees with John Hyrcanus's wise decision to disassociate from them. He also portrays the Pharisees as vicious partisan politicians to convince his readers that they had deceived Salome Alexandra, and actually controlled her administration. However, there is another reason why Josephus, and likely some of his sources, despised the Pharisees of her time, even though they acknowledge that they were observant Jews. Unlike the Sadducees, the Pharisees welcomed the patronage of aristocratic women such as Salome Alexandra. For this reason, Josephus portrays them as wolves in sheep's clothing who took advantage of a genuinely pious, yet politically gullible, woman. He also despises the Pharisees for their femininity because they allowed Salome Alexandra to dominate them.[6]

Josephus's account of Salome Alexandra's contentious meeting with Aristobulus and the Sadducees reveals much about her political authority and her personality. It shows that she was clearly in command of the government, suggesting that she had long exercised many political functions before becoming queen regnant. He sates that Aristobulus and the leading citizens came to her threatening to seize power. Although Josephus attempts to portray this moment as a great crisis, he acknowledges that the Sadducees also sought justice from her. They agreed to accept her as their sovereign, providing that she protect them. But their promise apparently came with an ominous warning:

> It would be disgraceful both for them and for her who ruled as queen, they added, if, being abandoned by her, they should be given shelter by the enemies of her husband; for Aretas the Arab and the other princes would consider it of a great value to enlist such men as mercenaries, whose very name, they might say, had caused these princes to shudder with fear before they had heard their voices [*Ant.* 13.414–5].

Fearful of loosing her throne, she supposedly capitulates to the Sadducees and entrusts them with all her fortresses, except Hyrcania, Alexandrium, and Machaerus, where she had placed her most valuable possessions.

Josephus's report of Salome Alexandra's reign is clearly not in chronological order: it is full of contradictions. But it is even more inaccurate than it appears — it is largely fictional! The Sadducees could not have sought shelter with Aretas at this time because Salome Alexandra had just defeated him at Ragaba and occupied his country.[7] Josephus's account also makes no sense. Salome Alexandra supposedly gave her enemies control over her strategic fortresses and command of her military after they had threatened to remove her from power and ally with Judea's enemy. She then sent them on a foreign campaign to Damascus, trusting they would not use her army against her. Josephus's account, if true, not only suggests that Salome Alexandra was completely incompetent, but that her entire nation was as well: everyone supposedly obeyed her foolish commands.

Josephus's account of Salome Alexandra's relationship with the Sadducees is clearly false. Aristobulus and the Sadducees were clearly her loyal subjects. She never would have given them any power unless she was convinced they were no threat. If they had posed a danger to her, they would have used the military against her. Salome Alexandra, moreover, appears to have trusted the

Sadduccees, and her son Aristobulus, more than Hyrcanus and the Pharisees since she gave the former control over her military and the latter jurisdiction over the temple. Aristobulus and the Sadducees were clearly her loyal subjects throughout her reign. Salome Alexandra remained in control of Judea's legions and its political system: Aristobulus and the Sadducees protected her and her kingdom.

Josephus has taken a story about Aristobulus's revolt against his brother that took place just before Salome Alexandra's death and turned it into two insurrections: one when she became her nation's monarch; the other at the end of her life. Aristobulus never tried to seize power at the beginning of his mother's reign, but only when she was dying; however, he did not try to remove her as monarch, but his brother, Hyrcanus. Aristobulus, the Sadducees, and Salome Alexandra's army followed her commands during the entirety of her nine-year reign.

Josephus has altered his account of Salome Alexandra's reign to make her look weak. But he also inserted material from his sources that tell another story. These works stress that she was an extraordinary administrator, and presided over an unprecedented expansion of Judea's army. Although Josephus claims she undertook only one military campaign during her reign, a passage he likely copied from one of his sources suggests otherwise. He claims that foreign nations sent her hostages and tribute. No monarch would have willingly submitted to such undignified treatment unless forced. She must have engaged in at least several successful campaigns in the early years of her reign — or perhaps during her tenure as co-ruler when her husband was ill and incapacitated — to have struck such "fear in the surrounding nations" and become their "master."

Josephus provides a clue in his *Antiquities* that suggest Salome Alexandra fought several wars shortly after she took power. He includes a list of cities in Syria, Idumaea, and Phoenicia that her husband supposedly had taken three years before his death. The only region excluded from this list, Nabatea, was the site of his last expedition, during which he died. However, a close reading of this inventory reveals that it is not an accurate description of his conquests, or territory under his domain.[8] Salome Alexandra undoubtedly conquered many of these cities Josephus claims her husband captured. Those she did not take through military action wisely sent her tribute and hostages in exchange for a favorable treaty. Even Josephus reluctantly acknowledges that she achieved something her husband unsuccessfully fought much of his life to accomplish: she subdued Judea's enemies and became master of much of the Middle East.

The new revenue from the nations Salome Alexandra conquered likely explains why the economy flourished during her reign. The constant influx of tribute, coupled with new markets for Judean commerce, meant that there was no need for additional taxes or widespread conscription. She recruited a large body of skilled Greek mercenaries, which caused other rulers to make peace with her rather than wage war.[9] The economy prospered during her largely peaceful reign. Although Josephus emphasizes her military expansion, he suggests that it was not merely the size of her army size that struck fear in the surrounding nations, but the way she used it. His accounts reveal that her fortresses were the key to her success. He tells us that Aristobulus and the Sadducees commanded many of them. Without their loyal service to her, there never would have been a Golden Age.

Queen of the Great Fortresses

Of all the strongholds under Salome Alexandra's control, Josephus insists that three were special: Alexandrium, Hyrcania, and Macherus. Because of their impressive fortifications, and strategic locations along the major routes into Judea, they were her major strongholds. Alexandrium (modern Israel) is atop a mountain overlooking the Jordan River while the other two are near

West slope of ruins of Salome Alexandra's fortress of Alexandrium (Sartaba). Located atop a mountain overlooking the Jordan River, this fortress helped her keep control over the border between her nation and her newly-conquered territory of Nabatea in present-day Jordan (Todd Bolen/BiblePlaces.com).

the Dead Sea: Hyrcania (modern Israel) is to the south of Jerusalem in the Judean Desert and Macherus is across the Jordan River in Nabatea (modern Jordan). John Hyrcanus likely fortified Hyrcania; Alexander Jannaeus, or possibly Salome Alexandra, constructed the others (she may have named Alexandrium after him). While her remaining garrisons were part of an interlocking defensive system, these three were designed to operate independently. They were so important that the Romans destroyed them when they conquered the Hasmonean State to prevent her family from using them to regain power.[10]

Josephus does not explain why Salome Alexandra sent her army to Damascus. He implies it was a foolhardy venture. It was too far from Judea for her to control and she could not have connected its trade routes with those that passed through her country. The Nabatean monarch Aretas, moreover, could have potentially attacked her legions far from home with a larger force and decimated them. Seleucia's rulers also could have viewed this campaign as a hostile encroachment on their border, and possibly launched a preemptive invasion of Judea. However, despite Josephus's insistence that this was a stupid military decision, there may have been a reason for Salome Alexandra's apparent madness.

When Salome Alexandra sent Aristobulus to Damascus, her kingdom included many fortified sites and garrisons on both sides of the Jordan River, including the great fortress of Macherus in Nabatea. She used these citadels, towers, and walled cities to defend Judea against potential and actual enemies from outside, as well as from within. Salome Alexandra used these fortresses to control the local non–Jewish population in the regions under her dominion. The troops she stationed in them helped her enforce law in the countryside, and guard the roads.[11] Salome Alexandra at this time had sufficient manpower to deal with any threat, whether from the Seleucids, the Nabateans, or the Itureans. Damascus, however, was not under her control. To understand why she undertook a campaign to take the city, we must first examine the life of her remarkable female pagan contemporary to the north, and a calendar discovered in the Judean desert.

Cleopatra Selene: A Woman Like Salome Alexandra

Salome Alexandra's reign coincided with the final years of another formidable Seleucid ruler — Cleopatra Selene (ca. 135/30–69 B.C.E.). Despite their religious and cultural differences, the two were alike in many ways. Both became mothers at relatively late ages; both had children who proved to be political failures; both took power while senior citizens; and both governed kingdoms that disappeared shortly following their deaths. But unlike Salome

Alexandra, Cleopatra Selene had a rather tumultuous marital history — she wed four kings.

Cleopatra Selene, sometimes called Cleopatra V, was the daughter of the infamous Ptolemy Physcon and his pro–Jewish sister-wife Cleopatra (III). Likely born in 135 B.C.E., her mother forced her to marry her elder brother, Ptolemy Soter (he was the former husband of her sister, Cleopatra IV). She was twenty years old. Twelve years later, her mother made her wed the Seleucid king Antiochus Grypus (a.k.a. the "hook-nose"). This union must have made her feel uncomfortable since her new spouse had been married to her other sister, Cleopatra Tryphaena. After Grypus's murder, Cleopatra Selene proposed marriage to his half-brother and rival, Antiochus Cyzicenus (he had also been married to her sister Cleopatra IV). She was thirty-nine years old when her third husband was killed. She then proposed marriage to his son, Antiochus (X) Eusebes. It was perhaps her most unorthodox union: she was forty and he was barely over twenty. According to the historian Appian, the Syrians mockingly nicknamed him Eusebes ("Pious") because of his filial piety in marrying a woman who had once been wed to both his father (Antiochus Cyzicenus) and his uncle (Antiochus Grypus).[12]

Cleopatra Selene and her new husband fought off a number of rival claimants for the throne. Then, nomadic tribes from the east threatened to overrun Syria. Unable to deal with this danger, Antiochus Eusebes — undoubtedly with Cleopatra Selene's consent — sought the aide of a powerful warrior queen, Laodice (VII) Thea (ca. 122–? B.C.E.).

Queen Laodice was the daughter of Cleopatra Selene's former husband, Antiochus Grypus, and her sister, Cleopatra Tryphaena. Laodice's father had betrothed her to the crown prince Mithridates (I) of the mountainous realm of Commagene (located in southern Turkey just north of Iraq), to cement a diplomatic treaty between their kingdoms. At this time, the Parthians were threatening to overrun her country. Cleopatra Selene's husband offered to join forces with her to repel these invaders; he died in the ensuing battle.

Having been married to four kings, Cleopatra Selene chose to remain single, and rule alone as Syria's warrior queen. After decades of incompetent monarchs, her people willingly accepted her as their ruler even though she had two grown sons and they faced the threat of a foreign invasion.

For the next fourteen years Cleopatra Selene ruled a portion of the Seleucid Empire. She was so powerful that she tried to accomplish the unfulfilled goal of her ancestors: the merger of the Egyptian Ptolemaic and Syrian Seleucid Empires. She tried to replace Egypt's king, Ptolemy (XII), with two of her sons, Antiochus (XIII) Asiaticus (reign 69–64 B.C.E.) and Seleucus Cybiosactes. She claimed that Egypt's current Pharaoh was the son of a concubine and therefore unfit to rule. Recent numismatic discoveries suggest that she named Antiochus and Seleucus her co-rulers to prepare them to become Egypt's monarchs. But she also wanted to make it clear that she was in charge: she placed her portrait in front of theirs on her currency.

The famed Roman orator Cicero (106–43 B.C.E.) tells us that Cleopatra Selene sent Antiochus Asiaticus and Seleucus Cybiosactes to Rome to convince the Senate to recognize them as Egypt's rightful rulers. The Romans publicly recognized their mother's legitimacy to govern Seleucia, but not to appoint Egypt's Pharaoh.[13] Although she did not get what she wanted from Rome, the Senate clearly regarded her as an important monarch. They carefully considered her claim, and openly ratified her title to the Seleucid throne. Cleopatra Selene was clearly a formidable woman. The Roman Republic, the greatest power of the day, wisely appeased her rather than anger her. With this historical background in mind, let us return to Salome Alexandra's Damascus campaign and explore how it helped Cleopatra Selene.

Salome Alexandra's Mysterious Damascus Campaign

Salome Alexandra's mysterious Damascus campaign cannot be understood apart from the military conquests of another ruler who threatened both her's and Cleopatra Selene's kingdoms — Tigranes I, "The Great," king of Armenia (140–55 B.C.E.). Tigranes had a rather inauspicious start for an aspiring world conqueror. He became the ruler of northern Armenia around 96 B.C.E. as a vassal of the Parthian monarch Mithridates Megas. He took advantage of the Parthian dynastic feuds to annex additional territory. After the death of his overlord, Tigranes captured much of Mesopotamia and, in approximately 83 B.C.E., a portion of northern Syria from the Seleucids. He was so powerful and controlled such a vast territory that he proclaimed himself "King of Kings."[14]

Josephus's chronology of Salome Alexandra's reign is deliberately misleading. He places her Damascus campaign just before Tigranes's invasion of Syria. According to his account, when she sent Aristobulus there, Tigranes unexpectedly arrived in Syria. Aristobulus, Josephus implies, was surprised by Tigranes's appearance and forced to return home and abandon his effort to take Damascus. But there is a problem with Josephus's sequence of events. Salome Alexandra sent Aristobulus to Damascus in 72 B.C.E. However; Tigranes invaded and occupied a portion of Syria a decade earlier, in 83 B.C.E. But he did not try to capture Damascus and the Mediterranean coast until a decade later, in 72 B.C.E.: the same year Salome Alexandra tried to take the city. This means that Salome Alexandra knew that Tigranes was in the region of Damascus when she sent Aristobulus there with her army. This raises a number of questions Josephus does not answer. Why did both Salome Alexandra and Tigranes try to capture this city that year? Why did Tigranes wait nearly ten years before he tried to capture Damascus and the Seleucid Empire's coastal territories? And what was Salome Alexandra doing during at this time?

Damascus was a strategic city that dominated the Seleucid Empire's eastern border. Many of the region's vital trade routes passed through it. The death of Antiochus Dionysus — the Seleucid king who destroyed Alexander Jannaeus's great wall — paved the way for the Nabateans to take it. Aretas captured the city in 85 B.C.E. and annexed it to his Nabatean kingdom. He minted coins there in Greek, rather than Nabatean Aramaic, bearing the epithet "philhellene" (lover of Hellenism) to show his support of Hellenism.

Aretas's annexation of Damascus precipitated a power struggle in the Middle East. At this time the Roman Republic was seeking to control Asia Minor and Armenia. The Iturean ruler Ptolemy was attempting to expand his kingdom (in modern Lebanon) in some of the same lands claimed by the Romans. If successful in his effort to capture Damascus, he could potentially form an alliance with the Armenians or the Romans and become the most powerful monarch of the region. Cleopatra Selene and Aretas needed to stop Ptolemy's territorial expansion before either of these great powers recognized his right to rule a portion of her kingdom. It was also essential for Tigranes to take Damascus if he wanted to become the most powerful ruler in the region.

At this time many of Syria's citizens were so tired of the constant civil wars for the throne of the Seleucid Empire that some in its eastern portion invited Tigranes to be their ruler. They believed that he could bring stability to the region since he had no connection with Rome or the Ptolemies, and presumably would not engage in endless wars of conquest. This is why Tigranes began to campaign in eastern Syria a decade before Salome Alexandra sent Aristobulus to Damascus: he was invited into the region. With so many powerful monarchs vying to control Damascus and its vital trade routes, war was certain. But no one knew exactly where it would take place, or which ruler would survive the ensuing Armenian invasion. But Salome Alexandra at this time likely had little to fear: the Judeans were allies with Tigranes's enemy, the dreaded Parthians. Tigranes was reluctant to fight her; he decided to wait until the opportune moment when he thought she was weak and then attack Judea.

We have discussed how Salome Alexandra's father-in-law, John Hyrcanus, betrayed the Seleucid monarch Antiochus Sidetes during his Parthian campaign. The Judeans appear to have made a treaty with the Parthians at this time: it was still in effect when Salome Alexandra took power. The Talmud recounts a visit of some Parthian envoys to Jerusalem during the reign of her husband. They apparently sent this delegation in 85 B.C.E. to seek an alliance with the Jews against Tigranes.[15] This shows that John Hyrcanus's alliance was still in effect when her spouse governed. Because this treaty was valid when she served as his co-ruler, she undoubtedly met with, and knew, several Parthian envoys before she became her nation's sole ruler. This would account for Tigranes's reluctance to move further inland from Antioch directly into Judea, or Syria. If he did, the Parthians could potentially intervene. As their allies, the Judeans would likely attack Tigranes as well.

Although some scholars are not willing to accept historical testimony from the Talmud because of its late date, we have a contemporary text that bears witness to this alliance between the Jews and the Parthians against Tigranes. Earlier, Tigranes had attacked Parthia when its new king, Mithridates III, ascended the throne in July/August 87 B.C.E. The Parthians shortly after this date likely signed their pact with Alexander Jannaeus against Tigranes. They had good reason to form such an alliance with a small nation. If Tigranes conquered Judea, he could use its coasts and territory to overrun the Parthian Empire and dominate the Mediterranean trade routes. A series of Parthian texts suggest that Tigranes defeated the Parthians in several engagements at this time. One partially preserved document, dated 83 B.C.E., mentions a ruler named "Alexander." This man can only be Alexander Jannaeus.[16] It appears to describe some unknown battle during which he attacked Greeks in Syria on behalf of the Parthians. If this reading of the text is correct, it explains why Tigranes had refrained from attacking Judea. He likely feared the Jews at this time, especially Salome Alexandra's strong military. The Jews, moreover, had fought in collaboration with the Parthians once, and would do so again against Tigranes. For this reason, Tigranes wisely stayed away from Judea until Salome Alexandra sent her army to Damascus. Why?

Josephus omits this complicated historical background to make Salome Alexandra look weak. Several rulers were trying to control Damascus before she sent her army there. It was a dangerous move for her to try to occupy it. The Seleucids, the Armenians, the Itureans, or even the Nabateans, could attack her force. Tigranes was also nearby and eager to defeat the Judeans. Although Josephus implies that her expedition was foolish and claims it accomplished nothing, archaeology suggests otherwise.

Coins are an important source of information about the past. Like contemporary currency, ancient coins contain mintmarks identifying the city where they were manufactured. Kings in antiquity placed their name, titles, and often their portraits, on their currency. We can easily learn who ruled and occupied Damascus by looking at the coins minted there. Aretas issued coins in the city from 72/1 to 69 B.C.E., showing that he held it during those years. However, three coins minted in Damascus in 72/71 B.C.E. bear Cleopatra

Selene's portrait. This explains why Josephus, in a passage he likely copied from a source, mentions that she was ruling over all of Syria when, in 72 B.C.E., Salome Alexandra sent her son, Aristobulus, to Damascus.[17] Cleopatra Selene took possession of Damascus just before Salome Alexandra sent her son there. Why was she in possession of this city?

We do not know the exact circumstances by which Cleopatra Selene came in possession of Damascus. It is possible that she captured it from Aretas. But a close reading of the evidence suggests that he willingly handed it over to her. Because Josephus writes that Ptolemy the Iturean was a "troublesome neighbor to the city" when Salome Alexandra sent Aristobulus there, he was clearly not in possession of the city. Rather, Ptolemy was apparently trying to oust Cleopatra Selene from Damascus. Josephus is certainly correct when he implies that Salome Alexandra was trying to prevent the Itureans from occupying Damascus. But what happened to Ptolemy? Once again, archaeology provides the answer, and offers a new explanation for Salome Alexandra's Damascus campaign.[18]

There is strong circumstantial evidence that Aristobulus made an alliance with Ptolemy the Iturean. Josephus records that the two later became quite close. Ptolemy helped Aristobulus try to remove his brother from power while Salome Alexandra was dying. Twenty years later, Ptolemy took in Aristobulus's orphaned children for their protection. He even married Aristobulus's daughter and helped her try to expel the Romans and restore the Hasmonean Sate. Ptolemy clearly had a long relationship with Salome Alexandra and her family after she sent Aristobulus to Damascus. An alliance between her and Ptolemy not only explains Josephus's claim that the two did not fight for this city, but also why the Itureans subsequently became Hasmonean supporters. It also explains why Ptolemy mysteriously disappears from Josephus's story at this time, only to appear later as a close ally of Salome Alexandra's family. By omitting Damascus's complicated political situation at this time from his narrative, Josephus transforms Salome Alexandra's diplomatic triumph into a great military defeat.[19]

Salome Alexandra apparently convinced the region's three most important rulers — Cleopatra Selene, Aretas, and Ptolemy — to form a military alliance to oppose Tigranes. She undoubtedly sent her army to Damascus to convince, or perhaps force, Ptolemy to join her alliance against Tigranes. Judea's treaty with the Parthians against Tigranes had thus far kept peace in the region, and likely convinced her neighbors to join her when it had become apparent that the Armenians were about to move eastwards. This explains why Josephus writes that that neighboring monarchs feared Salome Alexandra.[20] Her military alliance not only saved Judea, but Seleucia, Nabatea, and Ituraea as well. Although Josephus does not want us to know this information, a recently reconstructed calendrical document from the Judean desert likely provides an eyewitness account of these events.

Salome Alexandra's Secret Mission?

A Dead Sea Scroll that scholars have named 4QHistorical Text D is, despite its misleading designation, part of a calendar containing historical events that mentions Salome Alexandra and her family. As we have already discussed, it preserves her actual name, Shelamzion. There is no doubt this is our queen since a subsequent passage mentions her son Hyrcanus's rebellion against his brother that took place after her death. But the important part of this text is contained in the preceding section. It claims that she honored the Arabs. The next line states that she went to some location, whose name has unfortunately rotted away, for a "secret meeting."[21] With whom did she meet?

Although Josephus does not mention a pact between Salome Alexandra and the Nabateans, this calendar — whose entries were possibly written contemporaneously with the events it describes — provides strong evidence that a treaty between them existed. But a close reading of Josephus also corroborates this Dead Sea Scroll. He writes that following Salome Alexandra's death Hyrcanus called upon Aretas for military assistance after his brother, Aristobulus, removed him from power.[22] Aretas helped Hyrcanus besiege Aristobulus in Jerusalem. Salome Alexandra must have made a mutual defense treaty with the Nabateans that obligated them to support her and her legitimate successor. It was clearly still in effect after her death. Because her secret mission took place sometime after her treaty with Aretas, it is unlikely that she had a secret meeting with him since their longstanding relationship was public. If she did not have clandestine meeting with Aretas, them with whom did she secretly meet?

Historians are often forced to work with incomplete data. This is especially true of women's history because men have largely omitted them from the historical record. Because Josephus does not furnish any information about this time, we must use informed conjecture to determine what likely happened. Because Salome Alexandra had already made a treaty with Aretas, the only other possible candidates for her confidential encounter are Cleopatra Selene and Ptolemy the Iturean. Her "secret meeting" could have been with Cleopatra Selene to win her support, or, more perhaps likely, with Ptolemy the Iturean, to convince him to join her coalition. The clandestine gathering proved to be successful, and literally changed history.

Salome Alexandra's expedition to Damascus resulted in a treaty with the Seleucids, the Nabateans, and the Itureans. When Tigranes learned about

Salome Alexandra's diplomatic success, he realized that he needed to capture Damascus and invade Seleucia and Judea. Cleopatra Selene had no choice but to abandon Damascus and seek refuge in her fortified coastal city of Ptolemais. Tigranes wisely decided to go after her first before invading Judea: he planned to use Ptolemais as a base to prevent the Seleucids, the Itureans, or the Nabateans from coming to Salome Alexandra's aide by cutting off all land and sea access to Judea.

Josephus account is confusing since he jumps into the middle of the story at this point, and does not provide us with a description of Salome Alexandra's negotiations. She created a vast coalition that could potentially crush Tigranes's army if it united on the battlefield. He needed to attack its weakest link, Syria, before he could deal with Judea. By omitting this background information about Salome Alexandra's diplomatic efforts to ward off Tigranes, he portrays her and Cleopatra Selene as weak women. However, he does mention that Tigranes planned to attack Salome Alexandra. But a close reading of his account suggests that she proved victorious in this conflict, and expelled him from the region: a feat the Romans never accomplished. The information is embedded in Josephus's account of the downfall of Syria's last Cleopatra.

The Last Cleopatra of Syria

Cleopatra Selene was the last Cleopatra to rule Syria. Josephus — a man who is reluctant to name women — only identifies her to make Salome Alexandra look weak. According to his account, after her Damascus debacle,

> Tigranes, king of Armenia, came with an army of three hundred thousand men and invaded Syria and was about to invade Judea. This naturally frightened the queen [=Salome Alexandra] and her people. And so they sent many valuable gifts and envoys to him as he was besieging Ptolemais. For Queen Selene, also called Cleopatra, at that time was ruling over Syria and she convinced the inhabitants to shut their gates against Tigranes. The envoys therefore met with him and asked him to grant favorable terms to the queen [=Salome Alexandra] and her people. Thereupon he commended them for coming so great a distance to do homage to him, and gave them reason to hope for the best [*Ant.* 13.419–20].

But this passage contradicts Josephus's earlier *War* where he states that Salome Alexandra,

> by means of treaties and presents prevailed over Tigranes, king of Armenia, who had set a blockade around Ptolemais during his siege of Cleopatra [Selene], to leave the region [*War,* 1.116].

Josephus's choice of the verb "prevail" in this passage is quite surprising since the gender norms of his time equate femininity with passivity, and masculinity with assertive behavior.[23] He portrays Salome Alexandra as the most powerful ruler in the region. She successfully used the threat of military action to ward off what was likely the greatest threat to the Hasmonean state in its entire history. He insists that she dominated Tigranes. She forced him to abandon his quest to capture Syria: she expelled him from the region. Salome Alexandra had prevailed over one of the ancient world's most powerful rulers.

We have another version of these events that historians have thus far ignored. It comes from Moses of Khoren's *History of the Armenians*. The father of Armenian history, Moses likely wrote this book in the fifth century C.E., although some place it a century or two later. His neglected work is important since he had access to many lost histories of Armenia and its relationship with neighboring lands. He includes the following new information about Salome Alexandra:

> He [=Tigranes] took many captives from among the Jews and besieged the city of Ptolemais. But the queen of the Jews, Alexandra — also known as Messalina — who was the wife of Alexander, son of John, son of Simon the brother of Judas Maccabaeus, and who at that time held the throne of the Jews, by giving him many presents turned him back.[24]

Moses's source apparently confused Salome with Salina, which has become garbled into Messalina. Although he too claims that Salome Alexandra paid Tigranes to leave, Moses's account suggests Salome Alexandra's kingdom was in even greater peril than Josephus acknowledges.

Moses's claim that Tigranes took Jews captive suggests that he invaded northern Judea, likely the Galilee, and effectively declared war against Salome Alexandra. Moses, like Josephus, also states that Tigranes abruptly ended his campaign when he heard that Lucullus had invaded his homeland. But he never explains why she traveled to Syria to confront Tigranes's army while it was besieging Cleopatra Selene. Salome Alexandra effectively trapped Tigranes between two armies: Judea's and Cleopatra Selene's. It was likely news of these events that encouraged the Romans to attack Tigranes's homeland. Rather than weak, Salome Alexandra was the strongest of the players: she was in a position to annihilate Tigranes, which is why he was so willing to receive her ambassadors. It was Salome Alexandra's effective use of diplomacy, backed by her military might, that saved both Judea and Syria, and forced Tigranes to leave the region for good.

The Romans never subdued Tigranes; they eventually made a peace treaty with him. He is the only Armenian monarch who unified the lands inhabited by the Armenians, and extended Armenian rule into Syria and northwestern Iran. Judea was the only land he failed to conquer. Although he attacked

Salome Alexandra in 69 B.C.E., he had been in Damascus since 72/1 B.C.E. and Antioch two years earlier. Both were perfect cities from which to launch major invasions of Judea and Syria. Tigranes had been reluctant to wage war against Judea, undoubtedly because he feared Salome Alexandra's political alliances and military force.

Salome Alexandra undoubtedly saved Cleopatra Selene's life and the Seleucid kingdom. Tigranes had to abandon his dream of becoming a great world conqueror when Salome Alexandra confronted him at Ptolemais. He never forgave these two women, but he was powerless to seek revenge against Salome Alexandra. He never confronted her on the field of battle.[25]

Cleopatra Selene was apparently unwilling to forgive Tigranes. She pursued him as he fled her kingdom. The two apparently met on the battlefield; the engagement did not go well for her. According to the Greek historian Strabo, Tigranes besieged her in the fortress of Seleucia, deep in Mesopotamia (modern Iraq). Salome Alexandra was unable to come to her rescue; she was too far from Judea to provide any assistance. Tigranes captured and imprisoned her.[26]

Tigranes was proud he had defeated a warrior queen and wanted everyone to know it. He bestowed upon Cleopatra Selene the honors normally accorded to male leaders captured in battle — a public execution. She must have been a great prize to merit such treatment. But his victory parade, celebration, and execution of her could not erase the disgrace that he had never punished Salome Alexandra — the woman who had ended his dream of becoming a great world conqueror.

Tigranes did not fare well after his encounter with Salome Alexandra. A few years later, the Roman General Pompey occupied his kingdom and forced him to become a Roman vassal.[27]

Sons Unlike Their Mothers

Cleopatra Selene's death effectively marked the demise of the Seleucid Empire. Her two sons meet tragic ends after they returned from Rome. Antiochus (XIII) Asiaticus managed to become king of Antioch with the consent of Lucullus. He retained his title for only one year; Pompey deposed him in 64 B.C.E. and had an Arab chieftain murder him. Her other son, Seleucus, moved to Egypt to marry the Egyptian queen Berenice IV (ca. 77–55 B.C.E.). He was so unpopular that the Alexandrians gave him the unflattering moniker Cybiosactes ("seller of salt-fish"), purportedly because of his ill-mannered demeanor. His wife had him strangled. With his death, the dynasty of Syria's warrior queens comes to an end.[28]

Salome Alexandra was never defeated in battle or captured by an enemy. While Syria and Egypt were in decline, Judea prospered. She formed an unprecedented international coalition that saved Judea from one of the greatest rulers of her day: she forced Tigranes to leave her territory. The result was an unprecedented period of peace and prosperity for her people that the rabbis considered a Golden Age. Her life was remarkable by any measure. Unfortunately, her story has a sad ending. Her younger son betrayed her. Yet, she never stopped loving him.

15

Contention and Conflict
Salome Alexandra's Final Struggle

(Salome) Alexandra's accomplishments ended with her early death. Hyrcanus inherited her kingdom, which she had relinquished to him while she was still living, and became the high priest. Aristobulus nevertheless surpassed him in valor and wisdom. The disputes between them led to contention and conflict.— Pseudo-Hegesippus, *History*, 1.13.8–12

Salome Alexandra's only failure was, perhaps, her younger son Aristobulus. She apparently never won his loyalty. He was too much like his father; he was a military man and a Sadducee. Moreover, her two sons hated one another.

Synagogue from the Hasmonean palace of Jericho. Salome Alexandra built two palaces here for her sons, Hyrcanus and Aristobulus (Todd Bolen/BiblePlaces. com).

When archaeologists excavated the magnificent winter palace of the Has-moneans in the warm desert oasis of Jericho (modern West Bank), they uncov-ered two identical adjacent complexes that Salome Alexandra had built: one for her son Hyrcanus, the other for her son Aristobulus. Salome Alexandra must have loved both of her sons, but she apparently realized that she had to keep them apart from one another even in their leisure time!

Although she sought to provide both with the same comforts and ameni-ties, the elder one, Hyrcanus, was clearly her favorite. She had chosen him to be Judea's high priest. According to Josephus, the younger Aristobulus "let it be plainly seen that if only he should get the opportunity, he would not leave his mother any power at all."[1]

Unworthy Heirs

In 69 B.C.E. Salome Alexandra became ill. She was seventy-three years old and had ruled Judea for nine years. In his *War,* Josephus writes that she gave Hyrcanus some royal powers while she was alive. A largely overlooked passage in his *Antiquities* helps us determine the likely year this took place. In one place in this book Josephus correlates the reigns of Hasmonean kings with the tenures of the Roman Consuls, public officials whose periods of office many ancient historians used to date events. His figures for the length of Hyrcanus's reign suggest that Salome Alexandra elevated him to the status of co-ruler in early 69 B.C.E.[2] Because Josephus does not say that Salome Alexandra was sick for several years before her death like her husband, she presumably appointed Hyr-canus as co-ruler to make certain that he would succeed her as her heir. A co-ruler of several years was common among the rulers of Syria and Egypt, and often smoothed the transition of power following a monarch's death. Salome Alexandra's decision to name her eldest son as her political successor also meant that the Pharisees would continue to dominate the temple and the courts.

Hyrcanus apparently caused his mother no problems as her co-ruler. Then the situation changed dramatically just before her death. Without Salome Alexandra's knowledge, he began to persecute Sadducees, an event that prompted, or likely forced, his brother to try to overthrow him when it was clear to all that she was dying. Josephus does not implicate Salome Alexan-dra in these crimes; he insists she was shocked when she heard of them.[3]

Hyrcanus was not the only problem. Aristobulus also took advantage of his mother's physical limitations during her final days to stage a coup. Yet, she still remained in charge, despite her infirmity, until she literally died. She ordered her son Hyrcanus and her officials to use any means necessary to quell the rebellion.

Salome Alexandra spent her final hours leading the nation. Before her death, she likely appointed Hyrcanus king. His reign lasted only three months, however, before he relinquished the throne to his bellicose brother. Unfortunately, at the urging of his friend Antipater (father of Herod the Great) the inept Hyrcanus tried to regain his former titles. The Romans took advantage of this sibling rivalry and, in 63 B.C.E., invaded Judea. Hyrcanus was restored to his position as high priest, but not as king. Judea was now a Roman possession. The Hasmonean age was over.

The anonymous historian known as Pseudo-Hegesippus tells us that Aristobulus stole money from the treasury to purchase the loyalty of some soldiers — likely Salome Alexandra's mercenary contingent — and recruit his own body of armed men.[4] But he was not alone. He had an accomplice, without whose assistance he never would have removed his brother from power and become king — Salome Alexandra's daughter-in-law.

Salome Alexandra's Forgotten Adversary

Aristobulus's wife was instrumental in helping her husband overthrow his brother, Hyrcanus. It is highly probable that she hatched the plot. Aristobulus had served his mother for nine years; he had led her army; and he had accepted her decision to appoint his brother as high priest. Aristobulus had never wavered in his loyalty until Hyrcanus was about to become king. And he only revolted because of his brother's persecution of Sadducees: he had already accepted Salome Alexandra's choice of her eldest son as Judea's ruler for several years.

Although Josephus greatly exaggerates Aristobulus's disloyalty to his mother, he is likely correct that the Pharisees abused their powers when she was dying. Aristobulus likely had no choice but to wage war against his sibling, lest Hyrcanus become like their father and seek to exterminate his religious opponents. But Aristobulus was likely not the mastermind of this coup; he willingly entrusted his fate to his wife's deception. When Salome Alexandra was near death, he fled Jerusalem for Ragaba (the site of her great victory) to prepare to invade Jerusalem.[5] His wife cunningly hid his departure from her — a strong indication that she was the primary actor in this plot to seize power. She must have been a rather convincing actor, for Salome Alexandra and her court had no idea she was surreptitiously plotting with Aristobulus to take control of the government. By the time Salome Alexandra realized her daughter-in-law had betrayed her, it was too late:

> A large number gathered about him [=Aristobulus]. In less than fifteen days he
> seized twenty-two fortresses, and used them as his base of operations to gather

an army from Lebanon, Trachonitis and the local princes. He easily influenced these men, who were drawn to his strong personality, and at the same time believing that if they aided Aristobulus they could exploit his kingdom no less than those who were closely related to him, since they had helped him seize it [*Ant.* 13.427].

Salome Alexandra was reluctant to believe the news since no Hasmonean woman had ever betrayed another. She was likely surprised at the list of conspirators since it apparently included Ptolemy the Iturean, who had by this time become Aristobulus's close friend. After Salome Alexandra realized the magnitude of her daughter-in-law's deception, she confined Aristobulus's entire family in the Baris fortress. Her youngest son's plan would never have succeeded if not for the actions of his wife. She literally changed the course of Hasmonean history. Yet, like many prominent women in Josephus's books, he does not tell us her name.

Salome Alexandra's Unworthy Heirs

Salome Alexandra could not have passed away at a worse time. The rapidly expanding Roman Republic was now obsessed with annexing the entire Middle East. The Romans felt that now that Salome Alexandra was gone they could annex Judea. The Roman Senate sent the charismatic General Pompey there with the ostensible mission of stabilizing the region's political situation. In reality, he planned to conquer all of it. Given the title "Magnus" (the Great) at twenty-five years of age for his military accomplishments, he was an arrogant and violent man. He even issued a coin bearing his epitaph to publicize his exalted title. One scholar has dubbed him the "teenage butcher" for the atrocities he committed against his fellow citizens during the Roman Republic's civil wars. He wanted to emulate the success of his hero, Alexander the Great, by conquering the entire Middle East, including Judea.[6] Pompey was convinced that he could easily accomplish his goal now that Salome Alexandra was dead.

Pompey sent his envoy Marcus Aemilius Scaurus to Judea to investigate its political situation. He arrived while Hyrcanus and his Nabatean supporters were besieging Aristobulus in the temple. Scaurus, after apparently accepting a bribe from Aristobulus, forced Hyrcanus to cease hostilities, and ordered the Arabs to leave Judea. Aristobulus, likely with troops lent by Scaurus, attacked and killed six thousand of Aretas's soldiers, along with Antipater's brother Phallion.[7]

When Pompey finished his Armenian campaign, he came to Syria in 64 B.C.E. to meet with representatives from both brothers. A third faction of more than two hundred Jews, including many leading citizens, showed up to convince him to remove the Hasmoneans from power, and appoint a high priest as their leader. Judea's population was convinced that neither of Salome Alexandra's sons could restore her Golden Age and therefore wanted to place their future in God's hands.

Aristobulus gave Pompey a golden grapevine worth five hundred talents, which the historian Strabo claims to have seen exhibited in the temple of Jupiter Capitolinius in Rome.[8] Pompey decided to keep Aristobulus in power, but eventually arrested him when it appeared he was preparing to wage war against the Romans.

The Romans joined forces with Hyrcanus to attack the partisans of Aristobulus in Jerusalem. Pompey's legions destroyed much of the city during the ensuing battle. After capturing Jerusalem, he entered the Holy of Holies — the most sacred room inside the temple where only the high priest on the Day of Atonement was permitted to go — to satisfy his curiosity as to what was inside. However, the great Roman orator Cicero (106–43 B.C.E.) states that Pompey did not lay his hands on any item in the Jerusalem Temple.[9]

A collection of Jewish poems known as the *Psalms of Solomon* preserves an eyewitness account of this time. Several of these poems allude to the events of Salome Alexandra's lifetime. They rebuke her husband; denounce her sons; but ignore her because she is a woman.[10] However, unlike Josephus and the Essenes, the anonymous authors of these poems do not blame her for the Roman conquest, but her son Aristobulus.

The community of the *Psalms of Solomon* was convinced that God had allowed the Romans to destroy Jerusalem because Aristobulus and the Sadducean priests had polluted the temple after they had usurped power:

> When the sinner [=Pompey] became proud he struck down [Jerusalem's] fortified walls with a battering ram, and you [=God] did not prevent him.
> Foreign nations [=Romans] wnet up to your altar, / In pride they trampled it with their sandals;
> Because the sons of Jerusalem [=priests] had defiled the sanctuary of the Lord, / Had profaned the gifts of God with lawlessness.
> Because of these things he [=God] said, "Cast them far from me, / I take no pleasure in them" [*Ps. Sol.* 2:1–4].

The psalmist is convinced God had sent the Magnus to punish the Jews because they had allowed Aristobulus and the Sadducees to desecrate the temple by undoing Salome Alexandra's religious reforms.[11] However, the author of this poem refuses to forgive Pompey for entering Judaism's most holy space and proclaiming himself greater than God. The poet cries to the Lord for vengeance.

After patiently waiting fifteen years, the psalmist is convinced that God has finally responded to his petition for divine vengeance when he receives word that, on August 9, 48 B.C.E., the Egyptian supporters of Julius Caesar had decapitated Pompey with a sword in Egypt. They abandoned his body on the shore.[12] The poet rejoices at this news and compares Pompey's ignoble death to the slaying of a mythical dragon:

> I did not wait long until God showed me his [=Pompey] insolence,
> Pierced, on the mountains of Egypt,
> more than the least despised on land and sea;
> His body, carried about on the waves in great insolence,
> And there was no one to bury him,
> For he [=God] had rejected in dishonor.[13]

When Julius Caesar arrived in Egypt to pursue Pompey, Pharaoh Ptolemy (XIII) Philopator — brother and rival of his sister Cleopatra VII — presented him with Pompey's pickled head. But the poet was convinced that God was not finished. He writes that the Lord also promised to destroy Salome Alexandra's heirs and show none of them any pity.[14]

Tragic Ends

Salome Alexandra's family met tragic ends as the psalmist had predicted. Pompey took Aristobulus and his two daughters and his sons, Alexander and Antigonus, to Rome as prisoners of war. Many turned out in the city to watch Pompey's 61 B.C.E. triumphal celebration, see the captured wealth, and mock the captives. Pompey forced Salome Alexandra's son, Aristobulus, to walk in front of his chariot during the parade as a public sign of humiliation.[15] However, her grandson Alexander was not there; he escaped his captors during the journey to Italy. He returned to Judea and unsuccessfully fought the Romans. His father, Salome Alexandra's youngest son Aristobulus, later escaped and led a failed effort to regain power in his homeland. The Romans captured him and returned him to Italy, but freed his sons.

Aristobulus's fortune appeared to change for the better when a new civil war erupted in the Roman Republic between Pompey and Julius Caesar. The latter thought Aristobulus would serve as a useful ally and freed him. But a partisan of Pompey poisoned him. Mark Antony preserved Aristobulus's body in honey so he could be interred in a royal sepulcher, likely alongside Salome Alexandra in her great tomb. Alexander suffered a similar fate: the "Magnus" ordered his execution. Pompey's father-in-law beheaded him at Antioch.[16]

Salome Alexandra's eldest son, Hyrcanus, fared slightly better than his brother. Pompey restored him to the high priesthood, but not the kingship.

But he soon faced a new enemy, his nephew Antigonus, who allied with Rome's adversary, the Parthians, to restore the Hasmoneans to power. In 40 B.C.E. Antigonus captured Jerusalem and proclaimed himself king and high priest. He severed Hyrcanus's ears — a ritual disfigurement that disqualified him from holding the high priesthood — and exiled him to Parthia. But Aristobulus's tenure as king and high priest did not go well. The future Jewish king Herod the Great convinced Mark Antony to behead him in Antioch, in 37 B.C.E., to prevent Salome Alexandra's family from restoring the Hasmonean state.[17]

A Past Remembered

The Judeans soon became nostalgic for the Hasmoneans: they longed for the return of Salome Alexandra's Golden Age. Jews from Judea to Babylon looked to her disfigured son — the only person who had served alongside her during Judea's Golden Age — as their rightful high priest and king, even though he was clearly disqualified from resuming the high priesthood. The Judeans compelled Herod the Great — now a puppet king of the Romans — to return Hyrcanus to Jerusalem.

In 40 B.C.E. Herod convinced the Roman Octavian that he was the best person to rule Judea. But many Judeans refused to accept him as their king. He fought with the Roman general Sosius for three years to win his crown.[18]

Judea's political situation abruptly changed in 31 B.C.E. when Octavian (a.k.a. Augustus) defeated Mark Antony and the famed Cleopatra (VII) at the Battle of Actium. Herod had backed the losing side in this epic conflict and feared Octavian's wrath. He ordered Hyrcanus's execution to prevent the Romans from restoring him to power.

Although Salome Alexandra had been dead for three decades, Herod must have thought of her often during his lengthy and violent reign. The Hasmoneans were not extinct. He had to contend with her formidable female descendants — the other Alexandras.

16

The Last Hasmoneans
The Other Alexandras

> Having related the history of Queen [Salome] Alexandra and her death in the preceding book, we shall now speak of the events that occurred immediately afterwards, keeping in mind one thing above all else ... historians should make their chief aim to be accurate.—Josephus, *Antiquities* 14.1–3

Salome Alexandra was not the last queen regnant of an independent Hasmonean state — there was one other. Her granddaughter by her son Aristobulus led men in battle, opposed the army of Herod the Great and his Roman allies, and governed her own kingdom for six years. Salome Alexandra's granddaughter by her son Hyrcanus was an equally formidable woman. She counted the famed Cleopatra (VII) among her friends; the two conspired to frustrate Herod the Great's ambitions. Despite his assertion that he is presenting a full, honest, and accurate account of this time, Josephus is not entirely truthful — he largely omits the stories of these remarkable women from his books. Both inherited their grandmother's spirit and courage, and undoubtedly performed many unrecorded deeds of valor. They were truly exceptional women; they were the last Hasmoneans. They are the other Alexandras.

Alexandra (II), Daughter of Hyrcanus (II)

Alexandra, sometimes referred to as Alexandra II, was the daughter of Salome Alexandra's eldest son, Hyrcanus. She married her cousin, Alexander, the son of Salome Alexandra's youngest child, Aristobulus (II). The couple had two children, Aristobulus (III) and Mariamme. Herod fell in love with Salome Alexandra's granddaughter Mariamme. According to ancient tradition her beauty captivated him.

Herod married Mariamme in 37 B.C.E. after he captured Jerusalem and became king. He hoped her Hasmonean pedigree would make his position

229

as monarch more palatable to his subjects. But his relationship with his mother-in-law, Alexandra, was always tempestuous. She never accepted him as Judea's lawful monarch. When he refused to appoint her sixteen-year-old son, Aristobulus (III), to the high priesthood, she wrote the famous Cleopatra VII of Egypt for help.

Alexandra urged Cleopatra to convince Mark Antony to force Herod to appoint her son, Aristobulus, as high priest. Antony's friend, Dellius, came to Judea to visit Alexandra's children. He found them so alluring that he had pictures made of them and sent to Antony. Their beauty mesmerized Antony; however, if Josephus is truthful, he took a special fancy to the boy. He sent for Aristobulus, but Herod refused to let him leave Judea, fearful that Antony would fall under the youth's influence.

Herod was now scared that Alexandra's son could influence Mark Antony to favor the Hasmoneans. He needed to placate Alexandra to secure his own position as king. He accomplished this by deposing the current high priest and appointing Aristobulus III to this office. But he resented her interference and kept her under constant surveillance. Alexandra once again wrote Cleopatra to complain of Herod's treatment of her. The Egyptian queen urged Alexandra and her son to seek shelter with her in Egypt. The two planned to escape Jerusalem by hiding in coffins and, once outside the city, flee to Cleopatra's ship. Herod learned of their plan; however, he was afraid to punish them because he feared Cleopatra's wrath, and Alexandra's power.

In 35 B.C.E. Aristobulus III presided over the Festival of Tabernacles. His youth, beauty, and charismatic personality mesmerized the crowds. Many Judeans wanted him to take Herod's place as king. Herod feigned friendship with him and his formidable mother until he could figure out a way to murder him in private. When Alexandra invited Herod to the magnificent Hasmonean palace in Jericho — the edifice Salome Alexandra had constructed — he accepted the invitation. During the party some guests urged Aristobulus III to join them in the palace's great swimming pool. It was a trap. Herod's conspirators drowned him. He was eighteen years old; he had been high priest for one year.

Josephus portrays Alexandra as a woman very much like Salome Alexandra. He emphasizes that she displayed the traits of a man: she was assertive, cunning, and had an insatiable lust for power. Her father, Salome Alexandra's eldest son, Hyrcanus, was the complete opposite: he was womanly — timid, weak, and devoid of any leadership qualities. Josephus writes of their contrasting temperaments:

> Hyrcanus was of so mild a temper, both then and at other times, that he desired not to become involved in public affairs, or to seek any rewards, but left all to fortune, and contented himself with that afforded him: but Alexandra [his daughter] was fond of strife, and was exceeding desirous of a change

of the government, and spoke to her father not to bear forever Herod's terrible treatment of their family, but to think of their future [*Ant.* 15.165–6].

Alexandra acerbated an already tense state of affairs when she urged her father to write Malchus, then king of the Nabatean Arabs, for help in removing Herod from power. But fortune quickly turned against her. Herod executed Salome Alexandra's eldest son, Hyrcanus, in 30 B.C.E. because he was the "only one left of royal rank" and qualified for the kingship.[1]

Alexandra's daughter, Mariamme, soon fell out of favor with Herod. Another woman named Salome deceived them. This Salome was Herod's sister. She knew how to manipulate her brother's paranoia. She told him that Mariamme was having an affair. Herod became so enraged that he ordered her death. Josephus and Boccaccio record the sad tale of Mariamme both to portray her virtues and to demonize her mother as a loveless woman. When Herod's men led Mariamme to her execution, Alexandra supposedly denounced her. In the words of Boccaccio,

> she scorned death and refused to give up, as women tend to do, but with dignified expression on her face she listened silently to her mother's accusations.... She walked to her death as if to a joyful triumph [*Famous Women*, 87.9].

This story, which likely originated from Herod's court historian, Nicolaus of Damascus, cannot be trusted.[2] Alexandra had worked tirelessly to restore the Hasmonean state: she constantly put her own life in danger by openly defying Herod. She would not have abandoned her daughter. Rather, she vowed revenge. When Herod became ill, she staged a coup to restore Salome Alexandra's kingdom. According to Josephus,

> now Alexandra lived at this time in Jerusalem; and being informed what condition Herod was in, she became determined to get possession of the fortified places that were about the city, which were two, the one belonging to the city itself, the other belonging to the temple; since anyone who could gain possession of them would have the entire nation under their power, because without the control of them it was impossible to offer the temple sacrifices; and it is impossible for any Jew to even consider not offering the sacrifices; they are willing to give up their lives than abandon the divine worship during which they have been accustomed to pray to God [*Ant.* 15.247–8].

Her plan failed. Herod executed her in 28 B.C.E.

Alexandra (III): The Last Hasmonean Queen

Salome Alexandra's other granddaughter, sometimes referred to as Alexandra III, was the offspring of her youngest son, Aristobulus. Pompey had taken her, her unnamed sister, and her brother Antigonus in chains to Rome. Pompey made her father, Aristobulus, march in his triumph, which was held in September 61 B.C.E. Pompey also took Salome Alexandra's grandchildren by her son Aristobulus, Alexander, Antigonus, and their two sisters, captive. [3]

Josephus tells us little about Aristobulus's wife at this time. He writes that she had somehow gained possession of Salome Alexandra's fortresses: she could have done so only if she commanded the loyalty of many of Judea's legions. She agreed to hand them over to the Roman General Gabinius in exchange for her family's freedom. [4] But Herod feared her power; he exiled her, along with her children, to the Greek city of Ashkelon — the place where Salome Alexandra had executed eighty witches.

The Romans captured and killed Alexandra's father, Aristobulus, in 49 B.C.E. But her brother, Antigonus, continued to fight to reestablish the Hasmonean state until Herod arranged his execution in 37 B.C.E. Mark Antony crucified him. [5] Josephus writes that with his murder,

> the government of the Hasmoneans ceased, a hundred twenty and six years after it was founded. This family was a splendid and an illustrious one, both on account of the nobility of their stock, and of the dignity of the high priesthood, and for the great wars their ancestors had performed for our nation; but these men lost the government by their fighting with one another, and it came to Herod, the son of Antipater, who was a commoner, and of no royal blood, but one that was subject to other kings. And this is what history tells us brought about the end of the Hasmonean family [*Ant.* 14.490–1].

Although Josephus and the history books recognize Antigonus as the last Hasmonean ruler, they are wrong. This honor goes to his sister and Salome Alexandra's granddaughter — Alexandra.

Before Antigonus's death, Philippion, prince of the Iturean kingdom of Chalcis at the foot of Mount Lebanon, took him and his sister, Alexandra, to his homeland for their protection. He presumably did so out of loyalty to Salome Alexandra's son, Aristobulus, with whom he had a long friendship since their meeting in Damascus. But Philippion's father, Ptolemy — the man Salome Alexandra had made a treaty with to ward off Tigranes the Armenian — became infatuated with Alexandra. He murdered his son to marry her.

We do now know whether Alexandra loved Philippion or Ptolemy since Josephus is typically reticent when it comes to matters of the heart. But Alexandra dominated her spouse. She convinced him to betray his pact with the Romans and support her brother Antigonus's revolt. Sometime after his murder, she took possession of Salome Alexandra's southern Judean fortress of Hyrcania. She must have rallied Antigonus's remaining twenty thousand troops, and sizable contingent of armed men from Chalcis, to carve out her own state in Judea's southern desert. Salome Alexandra's former subjects once again willingly followed a woman into battle.[6]

Alexandra's kingdom is the only Jewish state both created and ruled by a woman. But few contemporary scholars are aware it existed. It lasted for nearly six years, from the 37 B.C.E. execution of her brother to the 31 B.C.E. battle of Actium. Josephus was reluctant to acknowledge it ever existed, or was ruled by a granddaughter of Salome Alexandra. He mentions it in passing in a paragraph he certainly copied from one of his sources:

> Now when the Battle of Actium began, Herod prepared to come to the assistance of Antony, since he was freed from his troubles in Judea, but he instead had to capture Hyrcania, which Antigonus's sister held [*War* 1.364].

This passage reveals that Alexandra had kept Herod from participating in this epic battle. If he had been there, the entire course of Western civilization may have turned out differently: his skilled legions could have possibly turned the tide of battle in Mark Antony's and Cleopatra's favor and prevented Augustus (63 B.C.E.–14 C.E., the first Roman Emperor) from founding the Roman Empire. Josephus was apparently so embarrassed by this story that he chose not to tell us the name of this warrior queen, Alexandra.[7]

Spot where the Roman legions breached the walls of Gamla with a battering ram in 67 C.E. Herod the Great would have used similar equipment to attack Salome Alexandra's granddaughter at her fortress of Hyrcania (Todd Bolen/Bible Places.com).

Josephus tells us nothing about Herod's siege of Alexandra at her Salome Alexandra's fortress of Hyrcania. They encircled the fortress with a massive siege wall to prevent her from escaping. An observation tower and camp visible at the site reveals that Herod and his allies launched a major military operation to capture Alexandra.[8] She led a valiant, but undocumented, effort to retain her kingdom; countless men met their deaths defending her.

Alexandra subsequently disappears from history. It is safe to assume that she died in battle. If Herod and his Roman allies captured her, they would have executed her immediately. Neither Herod nor the Romans would have wanted to march Alexandra at the front of their triumphal parade and acknowledge in public that one of Salome Alexandra's granddaughters had defied the might of Rome and carved out her own kingdom in Herod's country. Perhaps one of the anonymous graves at Hyrcania dating to this time contains her remains. If so, then she is the only Hasmonean queen whose body still resides intact and undisturbed in the kingdom she once ruled.

Alexandra's defeat marks the end of the Hasmonean dynasty. She was the last Hasmonean to rule as an independent monarch over a portion of Salome Alexandra's kingdom. Given Josephus's reluctance to write anything about her, it is amazing that he mentions her, or her valiant effort to restore her grandmother's state. He undoubtedly included a brief reference to her revolt to warn other women of the potential consequences of seeking to emulate the deeds of her mighty grandmother. However, over two thousand years later, Salome Alexandra's modern-day descendants recalled her deeds as they struggled to recreate the nation she once ruled.

Conclusion

The queen, Salome-Alexandra, was a person of rigid piety, and sided with the Pharisees.... A love of power was with her a frenzy. She despised men, and believed that in matters of dynasty women make fewer blunders. She cared neither for justice nor for honesty, provided she could gain her ends. Her piety seems to have been an outward orthodoxy, involving neither delicacy of conscience nor purity of heart.—Ernest Renan (1823–92), *History of the People of Israel,* 1895

Celebrated during her lifetime; praised in the Talmud; demonized in the Dead Sea Scrolls; extolled and denounced by Josephus; Salome Alexandra was unlike any other person in Judean history. She was undoubtedly the greatest Hasmonean ruler. Yet few know she existed, or that she shaped the world in which we live. Rather, modern scholars have, as Renan's influential history makes clear, demonized Salome Alexandra as a woman with an insatiable lust for power. But this was not always true.

I opened this book's preface with a passage from the Italian renaissance diplomat Baldessar Castiglione's (1478–1529 C.E.) influential 1528 manual of etiquette and behavior, *The Book of the Courtier.* This largely forgotten work, which was quite influential in its time, provides us with a glimpse of how later generations viewed Salome Alexandra. Castiglione, although considering her a ruler one of the "barbarian nations," nevertheless chose her as a model for courtiers to emulate, suggesting that many in his time knew her accomplishments and her remarkable story. Castiglione was not the only male author to praise women. A few years prior to the publication of his book, Guillaume Roville (16th century C.E.) produced a magnificent work containing short biographies of the most influential historical figures—Salome Alexandra is among them.[1] He even includes a fanciful portrait of her: it is the earliest such depiction of our queen. Although fictional, it shows a rather forceful woman with a determined gaze that undoubtedly captures the spirit of the historical Salome Alexandra.

Castiglione and Roville are heirs to a long Greco-Roman literary tradition of documenting the deeds of great queens. Many ancient texts portray women as equals of men. Herodotus (ca. 484–425 B.C.E.) — considered the father of history — often depicts women in his *History* as full partners with men; they help establish and maintain the social order. He and other Greek writers recount the deeds of other great warrior queens such as Artemisia I of Caria (fifth century B.C.E.), who fought against the Greeks at the Battle of Salamis. There were many other famous warrior queens, whose deeds were likewise celebrated in antiquity. The third century B.C.E. Seleucid Queens Laodice I and Berenice Syra are among them. They both fought to place their sons on the throne. The Egyptian princess Arisone III (ca. 246/5–204 B.C.E.) even rode into battle against the Syrians; men celebrated her deeds long after her death.[2]

The 2001 publication of a discarded Egyptian papyrus scroll, which was reused to wrap a mummy, containing the poems of the Greek poet Posidippus (ca. 310–240 B.C.E.) have revealed that the ancients were intensely interested in celebrating the accomplishments of prominent women. A poet at the Ptolemaic court in its early days, Posidippus wrote many epigrams praising Egypt's warrior queens. One of his poems describes the Ptolemaic queen Arisone II as a warrior holding a spear in one hand and a shield in another. He also extols Bernice II's victories at the Isthmian Games, and eulogizes many women for their virtuous lives.[3]

The Roman Empire that conquered Salome Alexandra's Judea, and annexed the kingdoms of the Ptolemies and the Seleucids, did much to preserve the legacy of Salome Alexandra's Hellenistic female predecessors. Plutarch (ca. 46–120 C.E.) is a notable example. He urges his readers to study the lives of prominent women:

Fanciful portrait of Queen Salome Alexandra from Guillaume Roville's 1553 book of iconography. Roville also includes a brief biography of her deeds in his book. He is one of the few scholars to consider Salome Alexandra among the notable figures of history (Wikimedia Commons)

There is no better way to learn the about the similarity and difference between the virtues of men and women any other way than by comparing their lives with lives, exploits with exploits, like great works of art [*Moralia*, 143.C].

After examining the accomplishments of prominent women throughout the ages, he concludes, "the virtue of a man and women is one and the same."[4]

Strong-willed women like Salome Alexandra played prominent roles in shaping contemporary Judaism and Christianity through their patronage of the Jewish religious movement of the Pharisees. During the time when the Sadducees controlled the temple, the Pharisees sought their support. Some of these women later shaped the new religion of Christianity, which began as a form of Judaism. Jesus counted many prominent female disciples among his patrons, including at least one Salome: she accompanied Mary Magdalene and Mary the mother of James to anoint Jesus' body.[5] Although one of the original witnesses to the empty tomb, we know nothing about this Salome. But she must have been a rather charismatic figure like her famous namesake to risk potential execution by the Romans to anoint the body of her beloved rabbi.

It is a mistake to assume that Jesus liberated women from the bonds of repressive Judaism, especially the so-called legalism of the Pharisees. Although many women formed part of his movement, Jesus never appointed any to positions of leadership. Women financed his movement; women sat silently at his feet; and women served him. As we have seen, Jewish women worshipped alongside men in the Jerusalem temple and countless synagogues throughout Judea, and held positions of authority in several Jewish movements. Despite the sexism of Salome Alexandra's time, Jewish men chose her to lead their nation, determine the form of their religion, and fight their battles. Salome Alexandra's piety calls into question the stereotype of the Pharisees as hypocrites: they were largely devout Jews who tried to transform daily living into worship — they accepted female leadership.[6]

Generations of Jews and Christians sought to commemorate Salome Alexandra's deeds and piety by naming their daughters after her. The largely unknown Salome, who risked arrest to anoint Jesus' body, became an important figure in non-canonical Christian writings. Many Christians apparently regarded her teachings as authoritative. She frequently converses with Jesus in the *Gospel of the Egyptians*, the *Gospel of Thomas*, the *Pistis Sophia*, and the *Syriac Testament of Our Lord*. These works show that women played important roles in Christianity centuries after Salome Alexandra's death. Unfortunately, this was a short-lived period.

Female religious leaders quickly became the subject of an intense debate in early Christianity: men resented their authority. The prominent Christian theologian Clement of Alexandria (150–215 C.E.) preserves one such tradition showing how many in his day regarded them:

> When Salome inquired when the things concerning which she asked should be known, the Lord [=Jesus] said: "When you have trampled on the garment of

shame, and when the two become one and the male with the female is neither male nor female" [*Stromateis*, 3.13.92].

This Salome, the Essene "mothers," and the dancing women of the Egyptian desert all apparently shared one trait in common — celibacy.[7]

Clement's passage suggests that sexual abstinence eventually became the only way for Christian women to serve as religious leaders in antiquity. These females, like the Therapeutae, became honorary men; they were Christian philosophers who had overcome the weakness of their sex.

A fresco (a mural painted on plaster) from the ancient city of Ephesus (modern Turkey) bears physical witness to the resentment many felt towards female Christian leaders. Located inside a grotto once used for Christian worship, it depicts the Apostle Paul — author of much of the New Testament — and two women known from the apocryphal *Acts of Thekla:* Theoklia and her daughter Thekla. Paul is seated alongside a standing Theoklia, whose virgin daughter appears in the distance. The artist portrays Paul and Theoklia as authoritative teachers: both have their right hands raised in the traditional gesture of religious authority. But a later vandal has defaced Theoklia: her eyes and hands have been gouged out, but not Paul's![8] It is a physical sign that the age of powerful women religious leaders was over.

Salome Alexandra's Legacy

For centuries scholars have largely neglected Salome Alexandra, as well and countless other great women of antiquity. Seldom documented in the written record, or debated in academic tomes, the existence of these females who shaped our world has almost been effaced from history. This is especially true when it comes to politics. The leadership achievements of ancient women are largely forgotten; their legacy is often distorted; and their biographies, when preserved, are usually wanting. Most of the extant accounts of ancient women merely record men's perceptions of them. This male reluctance to document their lives in part stems from their fear of prominent women leaders. When successful, female politicians and warriors are typically portrayed as singular exceptions: they are not to be imitated by either sex.[9] Josephus shared this sentiment. He reluctantly includes Salome Alexandra in his history, but only as an example to be avoided.

There was once was a time when men remembered Salome Alexandra. The writers of the Dead Sea Scrolls thought she was so important that they departed from their practice of not identifying persons to mention her by name so there would be no doubt as to her identity. The rabbis preserved stories about her for centuries, and enshrined some of them in the Talmud.

European Jews, such as the sixteenth century C.E. Italian-Jewish scholar and physician, Azariah dei Rossi, recounted her deeds over a millennium after her death. Baldessar Castiglione extolled her as a model of proper courtly behavior, which suggests that she was a familiar name among Europe's elite. Even prominent Christian writers such as Eusebius (263–339 C.E.), Jerome (347–420 C.E.), and George Syncellus (died 810 C.E.) mention her by name in their chronicles of the great events of world history: they were convinced she was worth remembering.[10] The Bible was shaped by her reign: Some books, such as Psalms, may even allude to her.

Following the 1948 creation of the modern State of Israel, Jerusalem's authorities attempted to rewrite history. They erased the memory of their British occupiers by removing their names from all public monuments. Princess Mary Street became Queen Shlomzion Street in honor of the only female to have ruled ancient Judea.[11] Some Israelis undoubtedly thought of Salome Alexandra when, in 1977, Ariel Sharon (1928-present), the former Israeli politician, general, and prime minister, named his now-defunct political party, Shlomtzion ("Peace of Zion").[12]

Unfortunately, few tourists who happen to stroll down Queen Shlomzion Street know anything about Salome Alexandra. Despite the prevalence of

Formerly Princess Mary Street, it was renamed in 1948 to honor Salome Alexandra — the only female to have ruled ancient Judea (Daniel Frese/BiblePlaces.com).

women's and gender studies programs in academia, scholars — ironically female and male alike — largely ignore the lives of such important females as Salome Alexandra to focus on esoteric theory: history has largely become irrelevant.[13] A recently published review of twenty-five years of scholarly research on women in ancient Judaism, written by a female academic, bears this out. It does not acknowledge biography as a legitimate academic pursuit, or mention Salome Alexandra.[14]

The Jewish scholar Tal Ilan is a notable exception among professionals. Her books include several chapters that examine how Josephus, the Dead Sea Scrolls, and the Talmud, have tarnished the legacy of prominent Jewish females, including our queen. She laments that the academic community still continues to silence these women by largely focusing on men's perceptions of them, rather than writing women's history.[15] Long ignored by scholars, Salome Alexandra is slowly getting some attention in popular culture. *The Daring Book for Girls* praises her as a model of diplomacy and leadership.[16] A short entry in the popular *Encyclopedia of Women in the Ancient World* recognizes her achievements.[17] These books, intended for nonacademics, will hopefully expose the young to Salome Alexandra, and other amazing women of the past.

In recent decades several artists have tried to resurrect the spirit of the historical Salome Alexandra and bring her deeds to public light. The Israeli author, playwright, and politician, Moshe Shamir (1921–2004) recreates her era in his novel *The King of Flesh and Blood*. He eloquently captures Alexander Jannaeus's cruelty and deviousness. But his depiction of Salome Alexandra is deficient. Unlike the shrewd, pious, vibrant, and forceful woman we met in our telling of her story, his Salome Alexandra is passive: "She was a woman worthy of a king — talented, devoted, obedient and fertile."[18]

The contemporary playwright Lauri Donahue has perhaps captured the spirit of the historical Salome Alexandra unlike any other. Her play, "Alexandra of Judea," focuses on Salome Alexandra's strengths, as well as the achievements of her female contemporaries. In Donahue's fictional dialogue between our queen and the pro–Jewish Cleopatra (III), the two women lament at the way men portray women. Cleopatra fears that history will only remember Alexander Jannaeus and ignore Salome Alexandra's achievements. She says to our queen:

> Our hist'ry is unkind to women's words —
> Unsaid, unheard, or lost through lack of care.
> Send me your words, and I will keep them safe.
> Perhaps you've heard about my library —
> It is the pride of Alexandria.

Although fictional, this passage reflects a sad reality. Many scholars have demonized Salome Alexandra by blindly repeating Josephus's criticisms of her: one, in what is perhaps the most widely cited article on her reign, even calls her a "vicious" woman.[20]

The fourth C.E. Christian heresy hunter Epiphanius of Salamis provides us with an example of how later writers sought to change history, and undermine Salome Alexandra's accomplishments. In his book, *Panarion* ("Medicine chest"), Epiphanius inverts the rabbinic portrayal of her reign as a Golden Age in a surprising way:

> And then Christ was born in Bethlehem of Judaea and began to preach, after the last of the anointed rulers descended from Judah and Aaron had come to an end — their line had continued until the anointed ruler Alexander [Jannaeus], and Salome, or Alexandra. This was the fulfillment of Jacob's prophecy [Gen. 49:10], "There shall not fail a ruler from Judah and a governor from his loins, till he come for whom it is prepared, and he is the expectation of the nations" — a reference to the birth of the Lord [*Panarion*, 51.21].[21]

Epiphanius mistakenly believes that Salome Alexandra's husband was the last true ruler to hold the offices of king and high priest, and therefore the messiah's harbinger. He ignores Salome Alexandra because she was a woman; he merely mentions her because of her association with her spouse. Ironically, she actually precedes the messiah in his chronology. Epiphanius's pitiful attempt to erase Salome Alexandra from history is particularly appalling since her husband was anything but a herald of the savior. He was undoubtedly Judea's most cruel ruler: there was nothing messianic about his reign.

Salome Alexandra's death marks the end of a unique period of history when women not only ruled over men, but, as indicated by the Dead Sea Scrolls and Philo's writings, held positions of religious authority. Never before or since has her nation enjoyed such peace and prosperity. Even the sexist Josephus pays her the ultimate compliment when he writes that she

> was a woman who showed none of the weakness of her sex; for being one of those inordinately desirous of the power to rule, she showed by her deeds the ability to carry out her plans, and at the same time she exposed the stupidity of those men who continually fail to maintain sovereign power.[22]

Although largely forgotten today, Salome Alexandra was the greatest Hasmonean ever to have sat upon the throne. May her strength, piety, and fortitude serve as a model for men and women today: Especially those of both genders who continue her struggle to successfully navigate the treacherous worlds of religion and politics.

Historical Chronology

Year	Salome Alexandra's Age	Event
2003 C.E.		Release of Lauri Donahue's play, "Alexandra of Judea"
1958		English translation of Moshe Shamir's 1954 Hebrew novel, *The King of Flesh and Blood*
1977 C.E.		Ariel Sharon creates Shlomtzion party
1967 C.E.		Six-Day War; Israel takes possession of Dead Sea Scrolls
1948 C.E.		Creation of the State of Israel; Dead Sea Scrolls under Jordanian jurisdiction
1946–1947 C.E.		Muhammed edh-Dhib discovers the first Dead Sea Scroll Cave in British Mandate Palestine
1573–75 C.E.		Publication of Azariah dei Rossi's *The Light of the Eyes*
1528 C.E.		Publication of Baldessar Castiglione's *The Book of the Courtier*
1453 C.E.		Mehmet II ("The Conqueror) captures Constantinople
808 C.E.		Death of the Byzantine Chronicler George Syncellus
700 C.E.		Approximate date for the completion of the *Babylonian Talmud*
400 C.E.		Approximate date for the completion of the *Palestinian Talmud*
476 C.E.		Romulus Augustulus last Roman Emperor deposed
403 C.E.		Epiphanius of Salamis' *Panarion*
313 C.E.		Constantine defeats opponents; declares Christianity a protected religion
275–339 C.E.		Eusebius, Christian Historian
132–35 C.E.		Simon bar Kochba leads the Second Jewish War against the Romans

Year	Salome Alexandra's Age	Event
37–100 C.E.		Jewish historian Josephus
73 C.E.		Romans defeat last Jewish rebels at Masada
66–70 C.E.		First Jewish War against the Romans
20 B.C.E. 50 C.E.		Philo, Jewish Scholar
28 B.C.E.		Herod the Great murders Alexandra II, daughter of Hyrcanus II
30 B.C.E.		Herod the Great murders Hyrcanus II
31 B.C.E.		Earthquake strikes Judea; Herod the Great besieges and kills Alexandra III, daughter of Aristoublus II
36/5 B.C.E.		Herod the Great murders the High Priest Aristobulus III High Priest
37–31 B.C.E.		Kingdom of Alexandra III, daughter of Hyrcanus II
37 B.C.E.		Mark Antony murders Antigonus; Battle of Actium; Herod the Great captures Jerusalem and weds Mariamme
40 B.C.E.		Antigonus severs Hyrcanus II's ears and exiles him to Parthia; Romans appoint Herod the Great king of Judea
48 B.C.E.		Supporters of Julius Caesar assassinate Pompey the Great in Egypt
49 B.C.E		Romans murder Aristobulus II
61 B.C.E.		Pompey the Great celebrates his triumph in Rome; Aristobulus II forced to walk in the procession as a prisoner
63 B.C.E.		Roman conquest of Jerusalem by Pompey the Great
65 B.C.E.		Hyrcanus II attacks Aristobulus II in the Temple during Passover; Scaurus arrives in Judea.
67–63 B.C.E.		Aristobulus II, Judea's High Priest and King
67 B.C.E.	73	Death of Salome Alexandra; Hyrcanus II High Priest and King for three months
69 B.C.E.	71	Likely date of Salome Alexandra's elevation of Hyrcanus II as her co-ruler with limited powers; Tigranes, king of Armenia, besieges Cleopatra Selene in Ptolemais
72/1 B.C.E.(?)	68–69	Salome sends Aristobulus II to Damascus to confront Ptolemy Mennaeus; Cleopatra Selene takes possession of the city
72/1 to 69 B.C.E.		Nabatean king Aretas III controls Damascus
76 B.C.E.	64	Death of Alexander Jannaeus (51 or 49 years old); Salome Alexandra becomes Judea's ruler
76–73 B.C.E.	67–64	Alexander Jannaeus's three-year war to recapture lost territory; develops quartan fever

Year	Salome Alexandra's Age	Event
83–80 B.C.E.	57–60	Victories of Alexander Jannaeus east of the Jordan and in the north
85 B.C.E.	55	Aretas III captures Damascus.
87–84 B.C.E.(?)	54–56	Alexander Janaeus besieges Tyre; Nabatean and Iturean insurrection
87 B.C.E.	53	Alexander Janaeus defeats Antiochus XII Dionysus; Invasion of Judea by Antiochus XII Dionysus.
88 B.C.E.	52	Invasion of Judea by Demetrius III; Crucifixion of the Pharisees; end of opposition to Alexander Jannaeus
93–88 B.C.E.	47–52	Intermittent opposition to Alexander Jannaeu's reign
90 B.C.E.	47	Alexander Jannaeus defeated by King Obodas I
95 B.C.E.	45	Protest against Alexander Jannaeus during the Festival of Tabernacles
96 B.C.E.	44	Alexander Jannaeus captures Gaza
100 B.C.E.(?)	40	Construction of monastic settlement of Qumran
103–101 B.C.E.	37–39	War of Scepters
103–76 B.C.E.	37–64	Alexander Jannaeus becomes Judea's High Priest and King (Length of reign: 27 years; Age: 22/24–49/51)
104 B.C.E.	36	Judah Aristobulus Judea's High Priest and King; Salina Alexandra becomes Judea's Ruler; death of John Hyrcanus
108–103 B.C.E.(?)	32–37	Salome and Alexander Jannaus move to the Galilee
110 B.C.E.(?)	30	Birth of Hyrcanus II
111 B.C.E.	29	Likely date of Salome Alexandra's marriage to Alexander Jannaeus (His age: 14 or 16)
112/111–107 B.C.	28/29–33	John Hyrcanus' wars of conquest
116–101 B.C.E.	24–39	Reign of Cleopatra III
120–40 B.C.E.	20–67	Simeon ben Shetach
125/127 B.C.E.(?)	16–14	Birth of Alexander Jannaeus
130/129 B.C.E.	11–12	John Hyrcanus participates in Parthian campaign of Antiochus VII Sidetes
134–104 B.C.E.	7–36	John Hyrcanus becomes Judea's High Priest and ruler
136/135 B.C.E.	5–6	Antiochus Sidetes besieges Jerusalem
134 B.C.E.	7	Death of Simon
141 B.C.E.(?)		Likely year of Salome Alexandra's birth
142 B.C.E.		Simon becomes Judea's High Priest and leader; first year of the Hasmonean State
143/2 B.C.E.		Murder of Jonathan, Judea's High Priest and leader

Year	Salome Alexandra's Age	Event
167 B.C.E.		Antiochus VI Epiphanes outlaws Judaism; beginning of Maccabean rebellion
172 B.C.E.		Menelaus Judea's High Priest
175–172 B.C.E.		Jason Judea's High Priest
?–175 B.C.E.		Onias III Judea's High Priest
180 B.C.E.		Cleopatra I rules Egypt
186 B.C.E.		Roman Senate imposes restrictions on the Bacchanalia cult
356–323 B.C.E.		Alexander the Great
587/6 B.C.E.		Babylonians destroy Jerusalem Temple
721 B.C.E.		Assyrians destroy Northern Kingdom of Israel
842–37 B.C.E. to 841–35 B.C.E.		Athaliah Judah's Queen

Chapter Notes

Preface

1. The correct name for the land Salome Alexandra ruled has been, and continues to be, the source of much debate and conflict. The Bible calls it Israel, Judah, and Canaan. The Romans in the second century C.E. named it Palestine ("Land of the Philistines"), which is a cognate of the ancient word Philistine. During Salome Alexandra's lifetime her country was known as Judea. Because historians always try to remain true to their sources, I only use names that were current during Salome Alexandra's lifetime. The terms Judea, Jew, and Arab, moreover, should not be understood as reflecting the modern Israeli-Palestinian conflict. The peoples of the lands described in this book were very different than their contemporary Jewish and Muslim descendants: Judaism had a temple but no Talmud; the Arabs would not have the prophet Muhammad and the *Qur'an* for nearly six centuries after Salome Alexandra's death. Yet, modern followers of these religions, as well as Christians, will find much in this book familiar since the religions Jesus and Muhammad established are built upon the Jewish faith that Salome Alexandra practiced.

2. I take the concept of an "outlier," and the importance of culture, community, and family for understanding an influential person's ostensibly unprecedented achievements, from the insightful study of success by Gladwell. *Outliers: The Story of Success*, esp. 15–68.

3. B.C.E (Before the Common Era) and C.E. (Common Era) are the preferred scholarly designations for B.C. and A.D.

4. An eclectic compendium of legal materials and other narrative writings compiled in Babylon (modern Iraq) around 500 C.E.

5. Kenneth Atkinson, "Gamla," *Dictionary of Early Judaism*, 657–8.

6. Tuchman, *Practicing History*, 13–24.

Introduction

1. [Salome's dance], Matt 14:6–8; Mark 6:17–19. ["fox"], Luke 13:31–32. The first century C.E. Jewish historian Josephus provides us with the name of Herodias's daughter (*Ant.* 18.136). She is not to be confused with the Salome who accompanied Mary Magdalene and Mary, the mother of James, to anoint Jesus' body. Although mentioned in Mark (16:1–8), the other Gospel writers curiously omit this Salome as one of the first witnesses to the resurrection.

2. Abegg. "Concordance of Proper Nouns," 229–84; Atkinson, "Representations of History," 125–51.

3. Exod 20:3.

4. [Antiochus's decrees] 1 Macc 1:16–63; 2 Macc. 5–7; *War* 1.34–35; *Ant.* 12.242–64; Levine 1999, 231–51. ["Hasmonean"], *Ant.* 12.263. [Judas's nickname], 2 Macc 8:1.

5. Her sons Hyrcanus and Aristobulus ruled for short periods of time, but were not widely

accepted and were overthrown. Her granddaughter, Alexandra (III), governed a portion of her kingdom, but few recognized its existence, or her legitimacy.

6. Figures from the Greek text of Sievers, *Synopsis of the Greek Sources for the Hasmonean period*, 2001.

7. See further, Atkinson, "The Historical Chronology of the Hasmonean Period," 7–27.

8. See further, Pagán, *Conspiracy Narratives*, esp. 1–24.

9. *Ant.* 13.432; Lambers-Petry, "Shelomzion ha-malka," 65–77. [Josephus and Rome], Bilde, *Flavius Josephus*, 57–79.

10. [Nicolaus], Bellmore, "Josephus, Pompey and the Jews," 94–118; Wacholder, *Nicolaus of Damascus*, 14–36. [Literary assistants], Rajak, *The Jewish Dialogue*, 233–36. [Josephus's sources], Eshel, *The Dead Sea Scrolls*, 1–12.

11. Aristotle, *Nicomachan Ethics*, 2.2. [ancient historians], Ogilvie, "Introduction." In *Livy The Early History of Rome*, 1–11.

Chapter 1

1. de Vaux., *Ancient Israel Volume 1*, 1.43–46.

2. Ilan, "The Greek Names of the Hasmoneans," 1–20.

3. *Ant.* 14.126, 15.23; *War* 1.186. [Greek names], Ilan, *Silencing the Queen*, 52–5.

4. Neusner, *The Rabbinic Traditions*, 139. [spellings], Derenbourg, *Essai sur l'historie*, 102.

5. Atkinson, Eshel, and Magness, "Do Josephus's Writings Support the 'Essene Hypothesis'?," 56–59; Atkinson and Magness, "Josephus's Essenes and the Qumran Community," 317–42.

6. Clermont-Ganneau, *Archaeological Researches*, 381–92. [Salome Alexandra in the scrolls], Atkinson, "The Salome No One Knows," 63–4; Ilan, *Integrating Women*, 57–68.

7. Atkinson, "Representations of History," 132–33; Ilan, "New Ossuary Inscriptions," 155–57; Ilan, *Lexicon of Jewish Names*, 249–53.

8. Ilan, *Silencing the Queen*, 259.

9. [pronunciation] Ilan, *Silencing the Queen*, 258–75. [frequency of names], Ilan. "Notes on the Distribution," 198–99; Ilan, *Lexicon of Jewish Names*, 249–52. [nicknames], Williams, "The Use of Alternative Names," 307–27.

10. [burial practices], Magness, "Ossuaries and the Burials of Jesus," 121–54; Nagar and Torgee, "Biological Characteristics of Jewish Burial," 164–71.

11. [changes to Simon's tomb], Fine, *Art and Judaism in the Greco-Roman World*, 60–81. [Josephus's description], *Ant.* 13.211–12.

Chapter 2

1. Pseudo-Hecataeus quoted in Josephus *Ag. Ap.* 1.192; *Ant.* 11.339; Gruen, "Fact and Fiction: Jewish Legends," 72–88.

2. y. Yoma 1:1 (XVII.E-N).

3. Harrison, "Hellenization in Syria-Palestine," 98–108.

4. Livy, *History of Rome*, 39.13.8–14. [mystery religions], Martin, *Hellenistic Religions*, 91–98; Kraemer, *Women's Religions in the Greco-Roman World*, esp. 9–42.

5. 2 Macc 6:7; Cousland, *Women's Religions*, 539–548; Hengel, *Judaism and Hellenism*, 1.298–99.

6. [gymnasia], Giovannini, "Greek Cities and Greek Commonwealth," 265–86. [Barbarians], Hengel, "The Interpenetration of Judaism and Hellenism," 1.167–228. [robber nation], Strabo, *Geography*, 16.2.37.

7. Hall, "Epispasm," 71–86; Rubin, "Celsus's Decircumcision Operation," 121–24.

8. Knox, *The Oldest Dead White European Males*, esp. 11–22.

9. van der Toorn, *Scribal Culture*, esp. 233–64.

10. [Letter of Aristeas], Marcos, *The Septuagint in Context*, 35–52, 67–84. The Septuagint

originally included only the first five books of the Bible that are traditionally attributed to Moses; the others were translated later. For the text of the Septuagint, see Pietersma and Wright, *The New English Translation of the Septuagint*.

11. [Jewish apocalyptic literature], Collins, *The Apocalyptic Imagination*, esp. 1–42.

12. [Jewish wisdom literature], Hengel, *Judaism and Hellenism*, 1.153–75; Martin, *Hellenistic Religions*, 107–11.

13. Fraser, *Ptolemaic Alexandria*, 246–76; Hengel, *Judaism and Hellenism*, 1.157–69.

14. [Orphic literature], Collins, *Between Athens and Jerusalem*, 210–260. ["Bacchic rites"], Philo, *Contempl.* 85.

15. Plutarch, *Antony*, 27.23.

16. Pomeroy, *Women in Hellenistic Egypt*, 67; Gutzwiller, *Poetic Garlands*, 5–88.

17. [Hellenistic female philosophers], Diogenes Laertius, *Lives of the Eminent Philosophers*, 3.46, 4.2; Pomeroy, *Women in Hellenistic Egypt*, 41–82; Taylor, *Women in Hellenistic Egypt*, 93–104. Periktione (lines 29–30) translated from the Greek text in Thesleff, *The Pythagorean Texts*, 143.

18. Varro (*On the Life of the Roman People*) as quoted in the 7th century C.E. Isidore of Seville's *Etymologiae* 20.11.9. [attitudes], Roller, "Horizontal Women," 377–422; Balsdon, *Roman Women*, 282; Fanthan, *et al. Women in the Classical World*, 280–93.

Chapter 3

1. Sources for the Maccabean revolt: 1 Macc 2:1–16:24; 2 Macc 8–15; *War*, 1.36–69; *Ant.* 12.265–13.300.

2. The geographical information throughout this chapter is derived from both personal observation and the extensive descriptions in Aharoni, *The Land of the Bible*.

3. Engels, *Alexander the Great*, 57–8.

4. Eshel and Eshel, "Dating the Samaritan Pentateuch's Compilation," 215–40. [Samaritans and Jews], Egger, *Josephus Flavius und die Samaritaner*, 48–59, 176–213; Pummer, *The Samaritans in Flavius Josephus*, 65–80. [Delos], Berlin, "Between Large Forces," 10–11.

5. [Idumeans], Kasher, *Jews, Idumaeans and Ancient Arabs*, 46–78; Richardson, *Herod: King of the Jews*, 54–62. [Herod and Jesus], Matt 2:16–18.

6. Isa 9:1. [Armageddon], Rev. 16:12–16.

7. [travel], Engels, *Alexander the Great*, 17, 122–30; Casson, *Travel in the Ancient World*, 65–94. The Bible commands all Jews to celebrate in Jerusalem the festivals of Passover, Weeks, and Tabernacles. See Exod 23:14–17; Deut 16.

8. [Greek inscriptions], Berlin, "Between Large Forces,"14–22. [Greek in the Dead Sea Scrolls], VanderKam, "Greek at Qumran," 175–81.

9. [Imported wine and luxury goods], Ariel, *Excavations at the City of David*, 25–28.

10. [grave inscriptions], van der Horst, "Greek in Jewish Palestine," 154–74.

11. Liver, "The Half-Shekel Offering," 173–98. See further, Rooke, *Zadok's Heirs*.

12. Dan 9:26. [Onias in Daniel], Collins, *Daniel: A Commentary*, 356–57.

13. [Judaism and the Bacchanalia], Goldstein, *1 Maccabees*, 104–60. [ass worship], Josephus, *Ag. Ap.* 2.79–80; 2.112–14; Diodorus, *Library of History*, 34.1.1–4; Plutarch, *On Isis and Osiris*, 31; Tacitus, *Histories*, 5.4.2.

14. [resurrection], Collins, *Daniel: A Commentary*, 363–404. [Jewish martyrdom], van Henten, *The Maccabean Martyrs*, 270–94.

Chapter 4

1. Lev 12:2–5.

2. Pastor, "Josephus as a Source for Economic History," 334–46.

3. [statistics], Tropper, "Children and Childhood," 299–343; Ilan, *Jewish Women in Greco-Roman Palestine*, 65–9; Amundsen and Diers, "The Age of Menarche," 125–32; Satlow,

Jewish Women in Greco-Roman Palestine, 105–6. Posidippus epigram # 45 in Nisetich, "The Poems of Posidippus," 27, 55.

4. Ariès, *Centirues of Childhood*.

5. [seclusion], Vitruvius, *On Architecture*, 6.7.1–7; Cornelius Nepos, *Praefatio*, 6–7; 2 Macc 3:19; Philo, *Spec.*, 3.169; Pseudo-Phocylides, 215–16; Archer, *Her Price is Beyond Rubies*, 101–22; Walker, "Women and Housing in Classical Greece," 81–9; Swidler, *Women in Judaism*, 118–25.

6. Gen 6:1–7.

7. Bagnall and Frier, *The Demography of Roman Egypt*, 111–18. [age of marriage], Biale, *Women and Jewish Law*, 64–66; de Vaux, *Ancient Israel Volume I*, 24–40. [Agrippa's daughters], *Ant.* 19.354, 277. [inscription], Satlow, *Jewish Marriage in Antiquity*, 207.

8. Mayer, *Die jüdische Frau*, 52; Satlow, *Jewish Marriage in Antiquity*, 105–9; Ilan, *Jewish Women in Greco-Roman Palestine*, 67–8; Hopkins, "The Age of Roman Girls" 309–27.

9. Atkinson, "Body" 588–90.

10. Archer, *Her Price is Beyond Rubies*, 163–89; Himbaza, "Le débat sur le divorce en Malachie 2:16a," 77–8; Jackson, "Problems in the Development of the Ketubah Payment," 199–225.

11. [dowry for poor] Philo, *Fug.* 29; Archer, *Her Price is Beyond Rubies*, 151–71. [defilement and mourning], Lev 21:1–4.

12. Matt 1:18–25; Luke 1:26–38. [penalty for adultery], Lev 20:10; Deut 22:22–23.

13. Deut 23:3.

14. Chilton, Recovering Jesus' *Mamzerut*," 84–110; Ilan, *Integrating Women*, 88–9, 135–41, 235–51; Satlow, *Jewish Marriage in Antiquity*, 68–73, 166–69.

15. *Life*, 1–6; *Ag. Ap.* 1.30–36.

16. [Wedding procession], 1 Macc 9:37, 39; *Ant.* 13.20. [Dress], *Joseph and Asenath*, 21:5; 3 Macc 4:6–7. [Cana], John 2:2–5. [Seven days], *Joseph and Asenath*, 21:2–7. [Jewish marriage], de Vaux, *Ancient Israel Volume*, 224–38; Archer, *Her Price is Beyond Rubies*, 203–04; Ilan, *Jewish Women in Greco-Roman Palestine*, 94–6; Satlow, *Jewish Marriage in Antiquity*, 168–81.

17. Satlow, *Jewish Marriage in Antiquity*, 176–77.

18. Macurdy, *Hellenistic Queens*, 77–223.

19. [incest], Lev. 18:6–18; Ager, "Familarity Breeds," 1–34. [cousin marriage], *Ant.* 15.23; 14.71.

20. Atkinson, "The Salome No One Knows," 62, 65 n. 7.

21. This theory first appears in Müller, *De Alexandra judaeorum*, 12–14. See also, Ilan, "Queen Salamzion Alexandra and Judas Aristobulus I's Widow," 181–90.

22. [levirate marriage], Deut. 25:10; Lev. 18:6–18; Matt 22:23–44; Mark 12:18–27; Luke 20:27–40; Weisberg, "The Widow of Our Discontent," 403–2; *Ant.*, 4.254–56.

23. Atkinson, "The Salome No One Knows," 62, 72.

24. *Ant.* 15.136; 18.136.

25. Ilan, "Queen Salamzion Alexandra and Judas Aristobulus I's Widow," 186–200; Ilan *Jewish Women in Greco-Roman Palestine*, 47–8. Cf. Mayer, *Jewish Women in Greco-Roman Palestine*, 104–27.

26. [burial], *War* 4.5. [positions], *War* 6.11. [6,000 crucified], Appian, *Civil War*, 1.20. [amulets], m., *Sabb.* 6.20; Apuleius, *Metam.* 3.17; Pliny, *Nat.* 28.46.

27. [800 Jews], *Ant.* 13.14. [women crucified], m. *Sabb.* 6.5.

28. Hass, "Anthropological Observations," 38–59; Tzaferis, "Jewish Tombs," 18–32; Zias and Sekeles, "The Crucified Man," 22–27. The latter study corrects several of the errors made in the initial report.

29. John 11:45–53. [Caiaphas's tomb], Zias, "Human Skeletal Remains," 78–80; Zias, "Anthropological Evidence," 233–34.

Chapter 5

1. Sources for John Hyrcanus's life: 1 Macc 16:18–24; *Ant.* 13.228–300; *War*, 1.54–69.

2. Schürer, *The History of the Jewish People*, 1.201–2 n. 2; Houghton, "A Victory Coin and the Parthian Wars," 65.

3. *Life* 5.

4. 1 Macc 16:2, 14. Josephus apparently refers to John Hyrcanus as Simon's third son to distinguish him from his brothers. Cf. *War,* 1.60; *Ant.* 13.235.

5. 1 Macc 2:65.

6. [Jesus], Murphy-O'Connor, *The Holy Land,* 304. [siegeworks], Eshel, *The Dead Sea Scrolls,* 74.

7. [slaves], Jer 34. [Sabbatical Year regulations], Exod 20:8–11; 21:2–4; 23:9–12; Lev 25:8–17, 23–28; Deut 15:12–15; de Vaux, *Ancient Israel Volume 1,* 173–5. [stimulus], Pfann, "Dated Bronze Coinage," 101–13.

8. *Ant.* 13.234.

9. *War* 3.306.

10. *Ant.* 8.101.

11. Deut 16:16. [festivals], Exod 23:14–17; Lev 23; de Vaux, *Ancient Israel Volume 2,* 484–506.

12. [holiday], 1 Macc 4:59. [rejoicing], 2 Macc. 10:6. [family celebration], Rajak *The Jewish Dialogue Between Greece and Rome,* 39–60. [Zechariah's prophecy], Zech 14:16–19; 2 Macc. 10:6–7. [Solomon], 2 Chr 5:3; 7:8–10; 1 Kgs 8. [Nehemiah and Ezra], Neh 8:13–18.

13. *Ant.* 13.241; Plutarch, *Moralia,* 184 F.

14. [decrees], *Ant.* 13.260–64; 14.249–50. [Antiochus's demands], 1 Macc. 15:28. [Roman threat], Schürer, *The History of the Jewish People,* 1:204–6; Sievers, *The Hasmoneans And Their Supporters,* 138–40; Rajak *The Jewish Dialogue,* 81–98. ["pious"], *Ant.* 13.244.

15. Pseudo Hecataeus, preserved in Josephus, *Ag. Ap.* 1:192–204; *Ant.,* 12:119, 125.

16. *War,* 1.63; *Ant.* 13.255, 14.18, 13.254–56.

17. Barag, "New Evidence," 1–12; Hengel, *Judaism and Hellenism,* 1:62, 2:44–5 n. 32; Schwartz, *Imperialism and Jewish Society,* 36–8; Sievers, *The Hasmoneans And Their Supporters,* 141–44; Finkielsztejn, "More Evidence," 33–63.

18. y. Nazir, 5:3 (IV.G); y. Berakhot, 7:2 (III.F-G). (The Talmud refers to the Parthians as the Persians.) I base my reconstruction on the evidence in the following: Pucci, "Jewish-Parthian Relations," 13–25; Efron, *Studies on the Hasmonean Period,* 148–50. [Josippon], Flusser, *Josippon [Josephus Gorionides],* 1.115.

19. *Ant.* 11.329–39; Cohen, "Alexander the Great," 41–68; Mor, "The Persian, Hellenistic and Hasmonean Period," 1–18.

20. *Ant.* 3.214–28.

21. *Ant.* 13.257–8; 15:254; *War,* 1.63; Strabo, *Geography,* 16.2.3; Steiner, "Incomplete Circumcision," 497–505.

22. ["hypocrites"], Matt 12:13. ["vipers"], Matt 23:33.

23. Acts 23:8.

24. *Ant.* 13.292.

25. *Ant.* 13.372–73.

26. *War,* 5.259; 7.304.

Chapter 6

1. [Athaliah's reign], 2 Kgs 11:1–20; 2 Chr 22:10–23:21; *Ant.* 9.140–56. Scholars continue to debate virtually every facet of Athaliah's life, from her parents to the dates of her reign. I adopt, with some slight variations, the reconstructions offered by the following: Miller and Hayes, *A History of Ancient Israel,* 286–352; Theil, Athaliah," 511–12.

2. Begg, "Athaliah's Coup," 189–210.

3. *Sifre Deuteronomy,* 157 on Deut 17:14 in Neusner, *Sifré to Deuteronomy,* 25; Ilan, *Silencing the Queen,* 44–6.

4. Sources for Judah Aristobulus's reign: *War* 1.70–84; *Ant.* 13.301–19.

5. Isa. 9:1.

6. [occupation of Galilee], Aviam, *Jews, Pagans and Christians,* 9–30, 41–50; Barag, "New

Evidence," 8. [Galilee's population], Freyne, *Galilee from Alexander the Great to Hadrian*, 41–50; Reed, *Archaeology and the Galilean Jesus*, 23–61; 1 Macc 5:14–24; *War*, 1.66.

7. Steiner, "On the Dating of Hebrew Sound Changes," 229–67. [Peter's accent], Matt 26:73.

8. Ilan, "The Attraction of Aristocratic Women to Pharisaism," 1–33.

9. *War*, 1.85.

10. I consider the manuscripts containing the name "Salome" to reflect a later scribal mistake. See Niese, *Flavii Iosephi Opera. Vol. III: Antiquitatum Iudaicarum*, 211.

11. Conway, "Gender and Divine Relativity," 471–90; Baer, *Philo's Use of the Categories Male and Female*, 41–46.

12. *Ant.* 13.318; Klausner, "Judah Aristobulus," 224.

13. *Ant.* 13.318. [Itureans], Freyne, "Galileans, Phoenicians and Itureans," 188–99, 205–10; Horsley, "The Expansion of Hasmonean Rule," 153–65.

14. Hegesippus, *History*, 5.18–24.

15. [execution], Deut. 13:1–5; 18:20–22; *Ant.* 13.2; *War* 1.78–80. [location], Schürer, *The History of the Jewish People*, 2.115–18.

16. 2 Sam 25:25.

17. 2 Sam 25:37–38.

18. For Abigail's role in the conspiracy to murder Nabal, see McKenzie, *King David*, 96–101.

Chapter 7

1. Cleopatra Thea had the following children: Antiochus (VI) Dionysus (with king Alexander Balas), Seleucus (V), Antiochus (VIII) Grypus, a daughter named Laodice (with king Demetrius [II]), Antiochus (IX) Cyzicenus, a daughter named Laodice, and possibly a son named Seleucus (with king Antiochus [VIII] Sidetes). See Macurdy, *Hellenistic Queens*, 93–100; Whitehorne, *Cleopatras*, 149–63.

2. Bevan, *House of Ptolemy*, 270; Whitehorne, *Cleopatras*, 1. ["Syrian"], Appian, *Syriaca*, 1.5.

3. [marriage], Polybius, *Histories*, 18.51.10; Livy, *History of Rome*, 33.40; Macurdy, *Hellenistic Queens*, 141–7; Whitehorne 1994, 80–88. [wedding], Livy, *History of Rome*, 35.13.4. [dowry], Polybius, *Histories*, 28.20.9; Appian, *Syriaca*, 1.5; *Ant.* 12.154.

4. Huß, *Ägypten in hellenistischer Zeit*, 654–70; Whitehorne, *Cleopatras*, 86.

5. 1 Macc. 10:51–58; *Ant.* 13.80–83; Bevan, *House of Ptolemy*, 94–5; Gruen, *The Hellenistic World*, 666–7.

6. [Balas's character], Diodorus, *Library of History*, 32.9; Livy, *Periochae*, 52; Bevan *House of Seleucus*, 212–222.

7. 1 Macc 10–11; *Ant.* 13.86–115; Diodorus, *Library of History*, 32.9; Appian, *Syriaca*, 67; Justin, *History*, 35.2.1–4.

8. Mahaffy, *History of Egypt*, 177.

9. Diodorus, *Library of History*, 33.28a.

10. I follow the manuscripts reading "Gazara."

11. 1 Macc 14:12.

12. Justin, *History*, 36.1.4–6.

13. The account of this incident in Athenaeus, *The Deipnosophists* (8.2) makes it clear that Trypon's men drowned.

14. [Thea and Sidetes], Bevan *House of Seleucus*, 2:236–46; Macurdy, *Hellenistic Queens*, 93–100; Whitehorne, *Cleopatras*, 154–57.

15. Frontinus, *Strategemata*, 2.13.2.

16. For this interpretation, see Whitehorne, *Cleopatras*, 155.

17. Grainger, *A Seleukid Prosopography*, 47–8. [Laodice], Justin, *History*, 38.10.

18. Whitehorne, *Cleopatras*, 158 and plates 7–8.

19. Justin, *History*, 39.1; Appian, *Syriaca*, 11.68.

20. Appian, *Syriaca*, 11.68.

21. Grainger, *A Seleukid Prosopography*, 7.

22. Justin, *History*, 39.1.9; Livy, *Periochae.* 60; Appian, *Syrian Wars*, 69.
23. Justin, *History*, 39.2.5.
24. Justin, *History*, 39.2.7–9.
25. Whitehorne, *Cleopatras*, 163.

Chapter 8

1. Binder, *Into the Temple Courts*, 242–45.
2. Macurdy, *Hellenistic Queens*, 161.
3. Whitehorne, *Cleopatras*, 86.
4. [Arsione at Raphia], Polybius, *Histories*, 5.83–86. [Philometor], Macurdy, *Hellenistic Queens*, 168–9; Thompson, "Egypt, 146–31 B.C.," 315. [Ptolemaic incest], Ager, "Familarity Breeds," 1–34.
5. Whitehorne, *Cleopatras*, plate 3; Poole, *Catalogue of Greek Coins*, 1883, lvii–lxi, plate xviii, nos. 1–6.
6. Havelock, "A Portrait of Cleopatra II(?)," 269–76; Whitehorne, *Cleopatras*, plates 1–12.
7. Kokkinos, *The Herodian Dynasty*, 33–50. Kokkinos also includes a photograph of a head that has been identified as a possible third depiction of Salome. I accept the traditional identification of Salome as the wife as Herod of Chalcis (contra Kokkinos) as argued by Gillman, *Herodias*, 103–119. See also Kokkinos, "Which Salome," 33–50.
8. Schubert, "Une attestation de Ptolémée Eupator regnant?," 119; Chauveau, "Un Été 145," 135, 157.
9. [Ptolemy], Polybius, *Histories*, 31.10.6. [Kakergetes] Athenaeus, *The Deipnosophists*, 12.549d-e. [Physcon], *Ant.* 12.234.
10. Athenaeus (550b-c) also notes that Physcon's great-grandfather, Magas of Cyrene, was so obese that he chocked himself to death.
11. Plutarch, *Moralia*, 201a.
12. [portraits], Bevan, *House of Ptolemy*, 289, 321–2; Poole, *Catalogue of Greek Coins*, lxviii–lxxiii, plates xxi, xxii. [intelligence], Bevan, *House of Ptolemy*, 308; Hölbl, *History of Ptolemaic Egypt*, 203 [*Hypomnemata*], Jacoby, *Die Fragmente der griechischen Historiker*, 983–5.
13. Porphyry, *Adversus Christianos*, cited in Jerome's commentary on Daniel 7:9. Cf. Dan. 7:8, 20, 24. [Egyptian relief and Daniel], Blasius, "Antiochus IV Epiphanes and the Ptolemaic Triad," 521–47.
14. Gruen, *The Hellenistic World*, 692–702; Hölbl, *History of Ptolemaic Egypt*, 181–214.
15. Tracy and Habicht, "New and Old Panathenaic Victor Lists," 188–9, 192–3, 216–7.
16. [temple], Collins, *Between Athens and Jerusalem*, 69–72. Formerly identified as a structure uncovered at Tell-El Yehudiyyeh, scholars now believe this was merely one of the settlements occupied by Onias's followers. See Pietre, *Hyksos and Israelite Cities*, 19–27 and plates 22–7; Taylor, "A Second Temple in Egypt," 313–21. [location], *Ant.* 13.62–73; *War*, 7.426–31. [acceptability], Last, "Onias IV," 494–516.
17. Justin, *History*, 33.8; Diodorus, *Library of History*, 33.13; Whitehorne, *Cleopatras*, 109–110; Bevan, *House of Ptolemy*, 308–9; Hölbl, *History of Ptolemaic Egypt*, 195.
18. Hölbl, *History of Ptolemaic Egypt*, 197; Huß, *Ägypten in hellenistischer Zeit*, 606–7.
19. Chauveau, "Un Été 145," 145; *idem*, "Encore Ptolémée 'VII' et le Dieu Néos Philopatôr!," 257–61; Lanciers, "Some Observations," 33–39; Heinen, "Der Sohn des 6. Ptolemäers im Sommer 145," 1. 449–60.
20. Hölbl, *History of Ptolemaic Egypt*, 198–99.
21. Translation, with parenthesis added, from Kerkeslager, "The Apology of the Potter," 77.
22. Zellentin, "The End of Jewish Egypt," 27–73.

Chapter 9

1. Szesnat, "The End of Jewish Egypt," 140–47. Sources for Alexander Jannaeus's life: Josephus, *War* 1.85–106; *Ant.* 13.320–406; George Syncellus, *Chronicle*, 355.

2. [unnamed brother], *Ant.* 13.323; *War* 1.85. [Absalom], *Ant.* 14.71.

3. Kasher, *Jews and Hellenistic Cities in Eretz-Israel*, 139–45.

4. Livy, *History of Rome*, 44.41.

5. *Ant.* 13.342.

6. Line 12 of the Cairo INV. 9205 that reads, "when a war of scepters came to Syria." Text in Van 'T Dack, *et al. The Judean-Syrian-Egyptian Conflict of 103–101 B.C.*, 83–4.

7. Josephus mistakenly says that Ptolemy Soter returned to Egypt, whereas it is clear from a latter passage (*Ant.* 13.358) that he went to Cyprus.

8. *Ant* 13.354.

9. Translation, with parenthetical comments and minor spelling changes from the Hebrew text incorporating some of the insights of Greenup, *Sukkah, Mishna and Tosefta*, 53–54.

10. t. Sukkah 48b; y. Sukkah 4:6 (VII.A-F). See further Rubenstein, *History of Sukkot*, 123–31.

11. Busink, *Der Tempel von Jerusalem*, 2.1073–79; Richardson, *Building Jewish*, 284–91; Yadin, *The Temple Scroll*, 1.194–97.

12. *Ant.* 13.369; *War* 1.92. I follow the traditional reading "Eukairos," although the existence of this title recently has been disputed. Levenson and Martin, "Akairos or Eukairos?," 307–41.

13. *Ant.* 13.380; VanderKam, "Pesher Nahum," 1.299–311.

14. *War* 5.304.

15. Eshel, Eshel, and Yardeni, A Qumran Composition," 421. My translation follows the understanding of the Hebrew verb proposed by Main, "For King Jonathan or Against?," 113.35.

Chapter 10

1. Sources for Salome Alexandra's life: *War*, 1.107–19; *Ant.* 13.407–32; George Syncellus, *Chronicle*, 555.8–17.

2. *Ant.* 13.398.

3. *Ant.* 13.400.

4. Deut 22:22.

5. [sources], Eshel, *The Dead Sea Scrolls*, 6–8; Ilan, "Josephus and Nicolaus on Women," 1.221–62; Klausner, "Queen Salome Alexandra," 243; Stern, *Greek and Latin Authors*, 1.227–32.

6. *Ant.* 14.10. He was also called Antipas. [Co-ruler], Case, *Salome Alexandra*, 64–66; Derenbourg, *Essai sur l'historie*, 96; Zirndorf, *Some Jewish Women*, 43.

7. *Ant.* 13.395–96; Kokkinos, *The Herodian Dynasty*, 94–5; Schürer, *The History of the Jewish People*, 1.226.

8. Text and translation from Leeming and Leeming, *Josephus' Jewish War and its Slavonic Version*, 123 (V.1).

9. [George Syncellus's background], Adler, *Time Immemorial*, 132–58; Adler and Tuffin, *The Chronology of George Synkellos*, lx–lxi.

10. Fischer, *Untersuchungen zum Partherkrieg Antiochos' VII*, 125–6; Berlin, "Between Large Forces," 38–39; Fantalkin and Tal, "The 'Yannai Line,'" 108–23.

11. [Lost territories], *Ant.*, 13.382; Shatzman, *The Armies of the Hasmonaeans*, 89–92; Kasher, *Jews and Hellenistic Cities in Eretz-Israel*, 153–60.

12. *Ant.* 13.393–97; Schwartz, "Georgius Syncellus's Account of Ancient Jewish History," 5; Shatzman, *The Armies of the Hasmonaeans*, 75–6.

13. *Ant.* 13.409. [military action], Margulis, *The Queenship of Alexandra Salome*, 63–4. [David's kingdom], Lemaire, "The Divided Monarchy," 91–120.

14. [Text and canonicity], Enslen, *The Book of Judith*, 21–56.

15. Jdt 13:15b–16.

16. Clement of Rome, *Epistle to the Corinthians*, 55:6–14. [Judith in art and literature], Moore, *Judith*, 64–66, photos 4–9.

17. [Tigranes in Judith], Boccaccini, "Tigranes the Great,"; Rocca, "The *Book of Judith*, 85–98.

18. [Pharisaic piety], Brüll, "Das apokryphische *Susanna*-Buch," 47–69; Moore, *Judith*, 60–71; Otzen, *Tobit and Judith*, 101–6. The manuscripts contain many different spellings for Bethulia, but this does not affect the underlying Semitic root. See, Hanhart, *Iudith*, 68. ["virgin"], Levine, "Sacrifice and Salvation," 18. [Salome Alexandra as Judith], Ilan *Integrating Women*, 127–53; Patterson, "'Honoured In Her Time,'" 212–83; Moore, *Judith*, 46. [genealogy and date], Patterson, "Re-Membering the Past," 111–23. [Simeon], Jdt 9:2. [lifespan], Jdt 16:23. Simeon and Simon are the same name in Hebrew.

19. Rocca, "The *Book of Judith*, 85–98; Bogaert, "Le calendrier du livre de Judith," 67–72; Steiner, "On the Dating of Hebrew Sound Changes," 264–66; Enslen, *The Book of Judith*, 26, 182–90; Moore, *Judith*, 103–7.

20. deSilva "Judith the Heroine?," 55–61.

21. Clanton, "(Re)Dating the Story of Susanna," 121–40; Ilan, *Integrating Women*, 136–53.

22. Clanton, "(Re)Dating the Story of Susanna," 139–40.

23. [colophon], Bickerman, "The Colophon," 339–362; Ilan, *Integrating Women*, 135.

24. de Troyer, *Rewriting the Sacred Text*, 9–58.

25. Knauf, "Salome Alexandra," 1–16.

26. Deut 21:22–23.

27. *Ant.* 13.4067.

Chapter 11

1. Coogan, *The Old Testament*, 21–29.

2. Edrei and Mendels, "A Split Jewish Diaspora," 163–87; Cohen, "The Significance of Yavneh," 27–55.

3. Quotation, with slight changes, from Neusner, *The Components of the Rabbinic Documents: From the Whole to the Parts 10. Leviticus Rabbah*, 246. For other rabbinic variations of this story, see Neusner, *The Rabbinic Traditions*, 89, 106, 117, 130.

4. b. Shabbath, 16b.

5. Steinsaltz, *The Essential Talmud*, esp. 137–44.

6. 1 Kings 16.

7. Num 25.

8. *Ant.* 13.320.

9. Atkinson, "Representations of History," 145; Avigad, "A Bulla of Jonathan the High Priest," 8–12; *idem*, "A Bulla of King Jonathan," 245–46. Meshorer, *Ancient Jewish Coinage*, 1:76–81; Schürer, *The History of the Jewish People*, 602–4.

10. [coins], Meshorer, *A Treasury of Jewish Coins*, 42; Schürer, *The History of the Jewish People*, 1.228 n. 1; Sievers, "The Role of Women in the Hasmonean Dynasty," 134–5. [sabbatical year], Pfann, "Dated Bronze Coinage," 105, 110.

11. [scribal error], Efron, *Studies on the Hasmonean Period*, 152. For a different view that attributes this change to sexism, see Ilan, *Mine and Yours are Hers*, 108–20; *idem*, *Silencing the Queen*, 160–3.

12. b. Sotah 47a.

13. Translation adapted from the Hebrew text in Simon, *Hebrew-English Edition of the Babylonian Talmud*. I have removed the passage that mistakenly identifies Simeon as Salome Alexandra's brother.

14. [protection of Nazarites], 1 Macc. 3:49.

15. Scholia to 17 Adar in Noam, *Megillat Ta'anit*, 122; Lichtenstein, "Die Fastenrolle," 293. I follow the numbering of Noam's edition.

16. Scholia 2 Shevat in Noam, *Megillat Ta'anit*, 109–11. dei Rossi, *The Light of the Eyes*, 349–50. [legend of Herod's death], *War*, 2.659–60, 665–69.

17. Scholia 28 Tevet in Noam, *Megillat Ta'anit*, 107–9. See also Lichtenstein, "Die Fastenrolle," 297–8; Efron, *Studies on the Hasmonean Period*, 211–3.

18. Derenbourg, *Essai sur l'historie*, 444; Klausner, "Queen Salome Alexandra," 243–44, 252–53; VanderKam, *From Joshua to Caiaphas*, 291.

19. m. Taanith, 3.8. (Translation modernized from Danby, *The Mishnah*, 198.

20. The rabbis do not make it clear whether these women were literally crucified, or whether their deaths preceded their hangings. On this issue, with a slightly different dating of this incident, see Chapman, *Ancient Jewish and Christian Perceptions of Crucifixion*, 66–69.

21. [Witches] y. Ḥagigah 2:5 [V.S]. [Hillel], m. Aboth 2:7; Bar-Ilan, *Some Jewish Women*, 117–31.

22. y. Shebiit 9:1 [38d].

23. [Ashkelon], Ilan 2006, 215–6; Schürer 1979, 2.106. [female sorcerer], Exod. 22:18. Ilan, *Silencing the Queen*, 223. For a different version of this story, see Neusner, *The Rabbinic Traditions*, 90, 92–3, 101, 115–6, 131–2; Ilan, *Silencing the Queen*, 214–22.

24. y. Sanhedrin 63 [III.A-E].

25. y. Ketubot, 8:11. b. Ḥagigah 15b.I.

26. b. Ketubot 82b; y. Ketubot 8:11 [IV.A-E]. See also Neusner, *The Rabbinic Traditions*, 93; Levine, "The Age of Hellenism," 249; Klausner, "Queen Salome Alexandra," 250–1; Urbach, *The Sages*, 572.

27. Deutsch, *Die Regierungszeit der judäischen Königin*, 27–35.

Chapter 12

1. [discovery], Atkinson, "Two Dogs, a Goat and a Partridge," 42–43, 74; Fields, *The Dead Sea Scrolls*, 23–113. [payment], Trever, *The Untold Story of Qumran*, 107.

2. [number of scrolls and their contents], Lange with Mittmann-Richert, "Annotated List,: 130–1.

3. [rumors], Betz and Riesner, *Jesus, Qumran, and the Vatican*. [release], Silberman, *The Hidden Scrolls*, 213–66.

4. This fairly literal translation of Pliny's difficult Latin text adopts several of the suggestions and interpretations proposed by Kraft, "Pliny on Essenes," 256–7. Pliny wrote this passage after the Jewish War against the Romans when some of the places he describes had been destroyed and were still unoccupied.

5. Taylor, "Khirbet Qumran," 144–64.

6. Atkinson, Eshel, and Magness, "Do Josephus's Writings Support the 'Essene Hypothesis'?," 56–59; Atkinson and Magness, "Josephus's Essenes and the Qumran Community," 317–42.

7. [cemetery], Donceel, *Synthèse des observations faites en fouillant les tombes*, esp. fig. 2; Röhrer-Ertl, "Facts and Results," 182–93; Sheridan and Ullinger, "A Reconsideration of the Human Remains," 195–212. [Bedouin burials], Zias, "The Cemeteries of Qumran," 220–53.

8. [excavation], Eshel, Broshi, Freund, and Schultz, "New Data on the Cemetery," 135–65; Magen and Peleg, "Back to Qumran," 55–113; *idem, The Qumran Excavations*, 45. [number of graves], Schultz, "The Qumran Cemetery," 143–54.

9. Atkinson and Magness, "Josephus's Essenes and the Qumran Community."; Beall, *Josephus' Description of the Essenes*; Collins, *Beyond the Qumran Community*, 122–65; Lemaire, "L'expérience essénienne," 138–51; Puech, "Khirbet Qumrân et les Esséniens," 63–102.

10. Dimant, "The Composite Character," 619–20.

11. [Scholarly changes to this text], Baumgarten, "On the Testimony of Women," 266–69; Richardson, "Some Notes on 1QSa," 108–22; Wassen, *Women in the Damascus Document*, 141–2.

12. Magness, *The Archaeology of Qumran*, 47–69. [cryptic script], Pfann, "Cryptic Texts," 523, 534–559.

13. [Essene items], Baumgarten, "He Knew that He Knew,: 53–61. [travel], *War* 2.126–7. [similarities], Wassen, *Women in the Damascus Document*, 131–43.

14. Atkinson, "Women in the Dead Sea Scrolls," 37–56; Baumgarten, "4Q502, Marriage,"

125–35; Elder, "The Women Question," 230–32; Schuller, "Evidence for Women," 252–65; Crawford, "Mothers, Sisters, and Elders," 177–91.

15. Magness, *The Archaeology of Qumran*, 163–87

16. Eshel, *The Dead Sea Scrolls*, 29–61.

17. 4Q274 1 i ln. 7. See further Atkinson, "Queen Salome Alexandra," 15–29; *idem*, "Women in the Dead Sea Scrolls," 37–56.

Chapter 13

1. Armstrong, *The Bible*, 32–54.

2. Eusebius, *Hist. eccl.* 2.17.1. [monastery], Philo, *Contempl.*, 25 & 30. [archaeological remains], Taylor, *Jewish Women Philosophers*, 74–104. [criticisms of de Vaux], Davies, "How Not to Do Archaeology," 203–7.

3. [fictional], Engberg-Pedersen, "Philo's *De Vita Contemplativa*," 40–64. [factual], Beavis, "Philo's Therapeutai," 30–42; Taylor, *Jewish Women Philosophers*, 21–53.

4. Taylor, *Jewish Women Philosophers*, 31–53.

5. Schürer, *The History of the Jewish People*, 2.558–61, 591–97.

6. [Kellia], Richardson, "Philo and Eusebius," 334–59; Taylor, *Jewish Women Philosophers,*, 275–6, 281.

7. Humbert and Chambon, *Fouilles de Khirbet Qumrân*, 316–17, fig. XXV, photos 319–29; Magness, *The Archaeology of Qumran*, 59, 116–7, 122–6; Pfann, "A Table in the Wilderness," 159–178.

8. See further, Atkinson and Magness, "Josephus's Essenes and the Qumran Community," 329–33.

9. Atkinson, "On Further Defining," 491–502.

10. [Locus 77], de Vaux, *Archaeology and the Dead Sea Scrolls*, 11–12, 111. [synagogues], Rapuano, "The Hasmonean Period 'Synagogue,'" 48–56 [Qumran synagogue and Gamla], Atkinson, "On Further Defining," 498–501.

11. [women leaders], Brooten, *Women Leaders*. [honorific titles], Rajak, *The Jewish Dialogue*, 349–52, 393–429.

12. Hay, "Things Philo Said," 680. ["mothers"], Crawford, "Mothers, Sisters, and Elders," 177–91.

13. Baer, *Philo's Use of the Categories Male and Female*, 98–101; Kraemer, "Monastic Jewish Women," 342–370; Taylor, *Jewish Women Philosophers*, 265–310.

14. Davies, "Dancing," 1.760–61. [Miriam], Exod 15:21b; Golberg, "The Two Choruses," 459–70. [Moses], Exod 15:1–19.

15. [4Q365], Brooke, "A Long-Lost Song of Miriam," 62–5; Taylor, *Jewish Women Philosophers*, 329–30.

16. Atkinson, "Dancing at Qumran?," 39–54.

17. I accept that Skepsis was a real person based on the insights of the following scholars: Ilan, *Silencing the Queen*, 30–35; Taylor, *Jewish Women Philosophers*, 240. Philo also mentions Skepsis in chapter 58 of this book

18. Tcherikover, *Hellenistic Civilization*, 2.1514. I accept Brooten's (*Women Leaders*, 78–83) translation of the Greek word *hierisa* as priest.

Chapter 14

1. Josephus claims that Alexander Jannaeus was saved from battles with the following four kings: the Egyptian Ptolemy Soter, the Nabatean Obodas (I), and the Seleucids Demeterius (III) and Antiochus (XII) Doionysus. For this pattern, see Atkinson, "The Historical Chronology of the Hasmonean Period," 12–17; Eshel, *The Dead Sea Scrolls*, 106.

2. *Ant.* 13.409.

3. For this theme, see Mason, *Flavius Josephus on the Pharisees*, 111, 252; Mason with Chapman, *Flavius Josephus Translation and Commentary*, 131–33.

4. [rift], Zeitlin, "Queen Salome," 32. [confidence], *Ant.* 13.298; Mason, *Flavius Josephus on the Pharisees*, 97–110. [Diogenes and Galestes], Efron, *Studies on the Hasmonean Period*, 174. [political power], Margulis, *The Queenship of Alexandra Salome*, 103–5. [Law], *War* 2.162; Mason with Chapman, *Flavius Josephus Translation and Commentary*, 131–2.

5. Dabrowa, *The Hasmoneans*, 126–8.

6. *Ant.* 13.399, 288; Mason, *Flavius Josephus on the Pharisees*, 249–50; Schwartz, "Josephus and Nicolaus," 159. [patronage], Ilan, "The Attraction of Aristocratic Women to Pharisaism," 1–33. [wolves], Mason, *Flavius Josephus on the Pharisees*, 110–111.

7. Atkinson, "The Historical Chronology of the Hasmonean Period," 17–22.

8. Shatzman, *The Armies of the Hasmonaeans*, 75–6.

9. For this evidence, see Kasher, "The Changes in Manpower," 349–50

10. [fortifications], Shatzman, *The Armies of the Hasmonaeans*, 96; Strabo, *Geography*, 16.2.40.

11. Shatzman, *The Armies of the Hasmonaeans*, 92–97.

12. Appian, *Syriaca*, 11.69; Macurdy 1932, 171; Whitehorne 1994, 168. I reject the recent proposal that Cleopatra Selene also married her brother, Ptolemy (X) Alexander, and possibly bore him at least one child, because it lacks any historical support. For this theory, see, Bennett, "Cleopatra V Tryphæna," 39, 55

13. Cicero, *In c. Verrem*, 4.27.61. [Antiochus Asiaticus coin], Bellinger, "Notes on some Coins," 53–63. [Seleucus Cybiosactes coin], Kritt, "Numismatic Evidence," 25–28, 36. Cf. Hoover, "Dethroning Seleucus VII Philometor," 95–99. [Cybiosactes], Grainger, *A Seleukid Prosopography*, 66. [contenders to Egypt's throne] Whitehorne, *Cleopatras*, 168.

14. Boettger, *Topographisch-historisches Lexicon*, 39–43; Manandyan, *Tigranes II and Rome*, 12–63; Sherwin-White, "Lucullus, Pompey and the East," 238–9.

15. y. Nazir, 5:3 (IV.G); y. Berakhot, 7:2 (III.F-G). (The Talmud refers to the Parthians as the Persians.) I base my reconstruction on Neusner, *A History of the Jews in Babylonia*, 25; Pucci, "Jewish-Parthian Relations," 13–25; Efron, *Studies on the Hasmonean Period*, 148–50. [Josippon], Flusser, *Josippon [Josephus Gorionides]*, 1.115.

16. Assar, "A Revised Parthian Chronology," 72–4.

17. [Cleopatra Selene's realm and coins], Bellinger, "The End of the Seleucids," 81–2; Hoover, "Dethroning Seleucus VII Philometor," 95–99; Bevan, *House of Ptolemy*, 263; Macrudy, *Hellenistic Queens*, 171. [chronology of Tigranes's campaigns], Sartre, *The Middle East*, 27–30.

18. [Tigranes in Syria], Justin, *History*, 40.1; Chahin, *The Kingdom of Armenia*, 227–29. [Nabateann coins], Bowersock, *Roman Arabia*, 25–6; Schürer, *The History of the Jewish People*, 578–9. [Tigranes coins], Kasher, *Jews, Idumaeans and Ancient Arabs*, 107; Shatzman, *The Armies of the Hasmonaeans*, 123; Sartre, *The Middle East*, 41; Schürer, *The History of the Jewish People*, 2.128–29. ["troublesome"], *Ant.* 13.418

19. Bowersock, *Roman Arabia*, 26; Margulis, *The Queenship of Alexandra Salome*, 66–68. [alliance], Kasher, *Jews, Idumaeans and Ancient Arabs*, 108.

20. *Ant.* 13.419; Shatzman, *The Armies of the Hasmonaeans*, 122–23.

21. The following interpretation is based on Atkinson, "Representations of History," 134–8. This document is also called 4Q332. For support of my dating, and the references to the Nabateans and the Judeans in this text, see Wise, *Thunder in Gemini*, 205–7. See also, Ilan "Shelamzion in Qumran," 57–68.

22. *Ant.*, 14.19; *War*, 1.126.

23. Niehoff, "Mother and Maiden," 413–444.

24. Translation from the English edition of Manandyan, *Tigranes II and Rome*, 71.

25. For partial support of this interpretation, see Chahin, *The Kingdom of Armenia*, 227–9.

26. The majority of works on this period fail to recognize that Cleopatra Selene fought Tigranes twice. See further Bevan, *House of Seleucus*, 266, 268; Kuhn, *Beitrage zur geschichte der Seleukiden*, 21, 42; Whitehorne, *Cleopatras*, 171; Schürer, *The History of the Jewish People*, 1.134.

27. Manandyan, *Tigranes II and Rome*, 144–65; Sartre, *The Middle East*, 31–37; Sherwin-White, "Lucullus, Pompey and the East," 239–44.

28. [Antiochus Asiaticus], Macurdy, *Hellenistic Queens*, 171–2; Schürer, *The History of the Jewish People*, 1.135–6; Hølbl, *History of Ptolemaic Egypt*, 222. [Cybiosactes and Bernice IV], Macurdy, *Hellenistic Queens*, 181–4; Whitehorne, *Cleopatras*, 184–85; Dio Cassius, *Roman History*, 39.57; Strabo, *Geography*, 17.1.11. Grainger, *A Seleukid Prosopography*, 66. Philip (II) Philoromaeus ruled for a short time as Syria's king, but he was merely a puppet of the Romans (his sobriquet means "Rome-lover"), and not an independent monarch like Cleopatra Selene.

Chapter 15

1. [palace], Netzer, *The Palaces of the Hasmoneans*, 30–39. [Not leave...], *Ant.* 13.411. Josephus documents the infighting between Salome Alexandra's sons in the following books: *War*, 1.120–58; *Ant.* 14.4–79.

2. *War* 1.120; *Ant.* 14.4.

3. *Ant.* 13.426.

4. Pseudo-Hegesippus, *History,* 13.

5. The text of this passage is corrupt. The manuscripts suggest that the original reading was "Ragaba," which is where Josephus places Aristobulus's base of operation. See, *Ant.* 14.4; *War*, 1.120; Boettger, *Topographisch-historisches Lexicon*, 15, 209–10; Niese, *Flavii Iosephi Opera. Vol. III: Antiquitatum Iudaicarum*, 231.

6. [title], Greenhalgh, *Pompey*, 12–29. [coins], Grueber, *Coins of the Roman Republic*, 1:464–65. [butcher], Edwards, "Gnaeus Pompeius Magnus," 69–85. [Roman plans for the region], Sartre, *The Middle East*, 37–53.

7. Leach, *Pompey the Great*, 91.

8. Strabo in *Ant.* 14.34–6; Stern, *Greek and Latin Authors*, 1.275. My reconstruction of the confusing events of this time incorporates many of the insights of the following scholars: Baltrusch, *Die Juden und das Römische Reich*, 126–47; Gelzer, *Pompeius*, 107–19; Ooteghem, *Pompée le grand*, 244–53; Smallwood, *The Jews Under Roman Rule*, 16–30.

9. *Ant.,* 14.72; *War*, 1.152. Cicero, *Orations: Pro Flacco*, 28.670.

10. Atkinson, "Toward a Redating," 95–112.

11. *Ps. Sol.* 2:1–4. [punishment], Atkinson, "Theodicy in the Psalms of Solomon," 546–75.

12. See further, Atkinson, *An Intertextual Study*. 35–57; *idem, I Cried to the Lord*, 30–36.

13. *Ps. Sol.* 2:26–7.

14. *Ps. Sol.* 17:1–10.

15. Abel, Le siège de Jérusalem," 253–55; Broughton, *Magistrates*, 181.

16. [Aristobulus], *War*, 1.183–4; *Ant.* 14.123–4. [beheading] *War*, 1.185; *Ant.* 14.125.

17. *Ant.* 15.5–6. For the classical references, see Broughton, *Magistrates*, 181.

18. Atkinson, "Herod the Great," 313–20.

Chapter 16

1. *Ant.* 15.161–4.

2. Macurdy, *Vassal-Queens*, 66–77; Sievers, "The Role of Women in the Hasmonean Dynasty," 143.

3. *Ant.* 14.71, 79; *War* 1.154–157–8; Plutarch, *Pomp.* 39.2; 45.4; Appian, *Mithridatic Wars*, 116–17. [Triumph], Velleius Paterculus, *Compendium of Roman History*, 240.3; Pliny, *Nat.,* 7.97–8; Broughton, *Magistrates*, 2.181.

4. *War* 1.174; *Ant.* 14.97. Cf. *War* 1.168.

5. This is a discrepancy between the accounts of Dio Cassius (*Roman History*, 49.22.3–23) and Josephus (*War* 1.357; *Ant.* 14.490; 15.8) as to whether Antigonus was merely flogged on the cross and then beheaded, or if his body was mutilated after crucifixion. See further Chapman, *Ancient Jewish and Christian Perceptions of Crucifixion* 70 n. 105

6. [murder], *Ant.* 14.126; *War* 1.186. [captivity], *Ant.* 14.79. [Antigonus's death], *Ant.* 15.124. [Alexandra III's marriage], *Ant.* 14.126; 297; Herman, "Certain Iturean Coins," 81–5; Kokkinos, *The Herodian Dynasty*, 114–5; Schürer, *The History of the Jewish People*, 1.564–5.

7. See further, Sievers, "The Role of Women in the Hasmonean Dynasty," 141–2.

8. Meshel, "Questioning Masada," 46–53, 68.

Conclusion

1. Roville, *Promptuarii iconum insigniorum a seculo hominum*, 147.

2. [Artemisia I of Caria], Herodotus, *History*, 7.99. [Laodice I, Berenice Syra, and Arsinoe III], Macurdy, *Hellenistic Queens*, 82–90, 136–41.

3. Nisetich, "The Poems of Posidippus."

4. Plutarch. *Moralia*, 242.

5. Mark 16:1–8.

6. For the mischaracterization of Judaism as an oppressive religion by many Christians, and the role of women in Jesus' movement, see Levine, *The Misunderstood Jew*, esp. 119–66.

7. For this evidence, see, Burris, *Chastity as Autonomy*; Ilan, The Attraction of Aristocratic Women to Pharisaism," 1–33; Davies, *The Revolt of the Widows*.

8. Pillinger, "Neue Entdeckungen in der sogenannten Paulusgrotte von Ephesos," 16–29.

9. For these observations, see further Spongberg, *Writing Women's History*, 15–33; Fraser, *The Warrior Queens*, 3–13.

10. Eusebius, *Chronicle*, in Schoene, *Eusebi Chronicorum*, 130; Jerome, *Chronicle*, in Schoene, *Eusebi Chronicorum*, 134.

11. Israel Ministry of Foreign Affairs Website April 1, 1999 (Accessed October 4, 2011) (http://www.mfa.gov.il/MFA/Israel%20beyond%20the%20conflict/Whats%20in%20a%20Street%20Name)

12. Hefez and Bloom, *Ariel Sharon*, 185–89.

13. [neglect of women], Ilan, *Silencing the Queen*, 1–3; Levine, *The Misunderstood Jew*, 121–25.

14. Marks, "Women in Early Judaism," 290–320.

15. Ilan, *Silencing the Queen*, and comments on pages 276–80.

16. Buchanan, Peskowitz, and Seabrook, *The Daring Book for Girls*, 95–7.

17. Salisbury, *Encyclopedia of Women*, 6–7.

18. Shamir, *The King of Flesh and Blood*, 108.

19. Donahue, "Alexandra of Judea."

20. Zeitlin 1960–61, 23. [scholarly portrayals], Ilan, *Silencing the Queen*, 1–3.

21. I have substituted Salome for Salina.

22. *Ant.* 13.430.

Bibliography

Primary Texts

Aland, Kurt, et al. Editors. *Novum Testamentum*. 27th rev. ed. Stüttgart: Deutsche Bibelge-sellschaft, 1995.

Alexander, Philip and Géza Vermès, *Qumran Cave 4.XIX: Serekh ha-Yahad and Two Related Texts*. Oxford: Clarendon, 1998.

Appian. *Roman History (Civil Wars)*. Translated by Horace While. Loeb Classical Library. New York, NY: The Macmillan Co., 1912.

Appian. *Roman History (Syriaca)*. Translated by Horace While. Loeb Classical Library. New York, NY: The Macmillan Co., 1912.

Apuleius. *The Metamorphoses (The Golden Ass): Books 1–6*. Translated by J. Arthur Hanson. Loeb Classical Library. Cambridge, MA: Harvard University Press, 1990.

Aristophanes, *Lysistrata*. Translated by Jeffry Henderson. Loeb Classical Library. Cambridge, MA: Harvard University Press, 2000.

Aristotle, *The Nicomachan Ethics*. Translated by Robert Williams. 2d ed. London: Longmans, Green, and Co., 1876.

Athenaeus, *The Deipnosophists*. Translated by Charles Burton Gulick. Loeb Classical Library. Cambridge, MA: Harvard University Press, 1927.

Aristophanes, *Lysistrata*. Translated by Benjamin Bickley Rogers. Loeb Classical Library. Cambridge, MA: Harvard University Press, 1967.

Barthélemy, Dominique. *Discoveries in the Judaean Desert 1, Qumran Cave 1*. Oxford: Clarendon, 1955.

Boccaccio, Giovanni. *Famous Women*. Translated and edited by Virginia Brown. Cambridge, NY: Harvard University Press, 2001. (Originally published 1374.)

Broughton, T. Robert S. *The Magistrates of the Roman Republic: Volume II 99 B.C.–31 B.C.* New York, NY: American Philological Association, 1952.

Cassius, Dio. *Roman History*. Translated by Earnest Cary and Herbert B. Foster. Loeb Classical Library. Cambridge, NY: Harvard University Press, 1917.

Castiglione, Baldessar, *The Book of the Courtier*. Translated by Leonard Eckstein Opdycke. NY: Charles Scribner's Sons, 1903. (Originally published 1528).

Charlesworth, James H. *Old Testament Pseudepigrapha*. 2 vols. New York, NY: Doubleday, 1983 & 1985.

Cicero. *Orations: The Verrine Orations*. Translated by L. H. G. Greenwood. Loeb Classical Library. Cambridge, MA: Harvard University Press, 1927.

_____. *Orations: "Pro Flacco."* Loeb Classical Library; Cambridge, MA: Harvard University Press, 1976.

Cohen, A. Translator. *Soṭtah: Translated into English with Notes and Glossary*. London: The Soncino Press, 1936.

Cohen, A. *The Babylonian Talmud: Tractate Berakot: Translated into English for the First Time, with Introduction, Commentary, Glossary and Indices.* Cambridge: Cambridge University Press, 1921.

Danby, Herbert. *The Mishnah: Translated from the Hebrew with Introduction and Brief Explanatory Notes.* Oxford: Oxford University Press, 1933.

dei Rossi, Azariah. *The Light of the Eyes.* Translated by Joanna Weinberg. New Haven, CT: Yale University Press, 2001. (Originally published 1573).

Diodorus Siculus. Translated by Francis R. Walton. Loeb Classical Library. Cambridge, MA: Harvard University Press, 1933.

Diogenes Laertius, *Lives of the Eminent Philosophers.* Translated by R. D. Hicks. Loeb Classical Library. New York, NY: G. P. Putnam's Sons, 1925).

Epiphanius, *The Panarion of Epiphanius of Salamis Books II and III (Sects 47–80, De Fide).* Translated by Frank Williams. Leiden: E. J. Brill, 1994.

Eshel, Esther, Hanan Eshel, et al. Editors. *Qumran Cave 4.VI: Poetical and Liturgical Texts, Part 1.* Oxford: Clarendon, 1997

Eusebius, *Chronicorum canonum quae supersunt,* 3d ed. Edited by Alfred Schöne. Zurich: Weidmann. 1999.

_____. *The Ecclesiastical History.* Vol. 1. Translated by Kirsopp Lake. New York, NY: G. P. Putnam's Sons, 1926.

Flusser, David. *Josippon [Josephus Gorionides].* 2 vols. Jerusalem: Bialik Institute, 1978. (in Hebrew).

Frontinus. *Strategemata.* Translated by C. E. Bennett and Mary B. Mcelwain. Loeb Classical Library. Cambridge, MA: Harvard University Press, 1925.

García Martínez, F. and Eibert J. C. Tigchelaar, Editors. *The Dead Sea Scrolls Study Edition: Volume 1 (1Q1–4Q273).* Leiden: E.J. Brill, 2000.

_____. *The Dead Sea Scrolls Study Edition: Volume 2 (4Q274–11Q31).* Leiden: E. J. Brill, 2000.

Geffcken, Johannes. *Die Oracula Sibylline.* Leipzig: Hinrichs, 1902.

Ginzel, F. K. *Handbuch der mathematischen und technischen Chronologie.* Vol. 1. Leipzig: J. C. Hinrich, 1906.

Greenup, A. W. *Sukkah, Mishna and Tosefta: With Introduction, Translation and Short Notes.* London: Society for Promoting Christian Knowledge, 1925.

Hanhart, Robert. *Iudith.* Göttingen: Vandenhoeck and Ruprecht, 1979.

Hegesippus (Pseudo). Vincenzo Ussani, Editor. *Hegesippi qui dicitur historiae libri V.* New York, NY: Johnson Reprint Corp, 1960.

Herodotus. Translated by A. D. Godley. Loeb Classical Library. New York, NY: G. P. Putnam's Sons, 19121.

Holladay, Carl R. *Fragments from Hellenistic Jewish Authors,* 4 vols. Atlanta, GA: Scholars Press, 1983–96.

Isidore. *Isidori Hispalensis Episcopi Etymologiarvm Sive Originvm Libri XX.* Edited by W. M. Lindsay. Oxford: Clarendon Press, 1962.

Jacoby, Felix. *Die Fragmente der griechischen Historiker (F GR HIST): zweiter teil: Zeitgeschichte. B, Spezialgeschichten, Autobiographien und Memoiren, Zeittafeln — Zweite und vierte Lieferung— Kommentar zu nr. 106–261.* Leiden: E.J. Brill, 1993.

James, Montague Rhode. *The Apocryphal New Testament.* Oxford: Oxford University Press, 1924.

Jerome, Commentary on Daniel. J.-P. Migne, Editor. *Patrologiae Latina.* Vol. 25. Paris: Garnier fraters, 1844.

Josephus. Translated by H. St. J. Thackeray, Ralph Marcus, and Louis H. Feldman. 10 vols. Loeb Classical Library. Cambridge, MA: Harvard University Press, 1926–1964.

Justin. *De Historiis Philippicus.* Edited by Peter Joseph Cantel. Philadelphia, PA: A. Small, 1815.

Kerkeslager Allen. "The Apology of the Potter: A Translation of the Potter's Oracle." In *Jerusalem Studies in Egyptology.* Edited by Irene Shirun-Grumach, 67–79. Wiesbaden: Harrassowitz, in Kommission, 1998.

Kittel, Rudolph, et al. Editors. *Biblia Hebraica Stüttgartensia.* Stüggart: Deutsche Bibelgesellschaft, 1983.

Krauss, Samuel. *The Mishnah Treatise Sanhedrin Edited with an Introduction, Notes and Glossary.* Leiden: E. J. Brill, 1909.

Leeming, H. and K. Leeming. *Josephus' Jewish War and Its Slavonic Version: A Synoptic Comparison of the English Translation by H. St. J. Thackeray with the Critical Edition by N.A. Mescerskij of the Slavonic Version in the Vilna Manuscript Translated into English by H. Leeming and L. Osinkina.* Leiden: Brill, 2003.

Lichtenstein, Hans. "Die Fastenrolle." *Hebrew Union College Annual* 8–9 (1931–32): 257–351.

Lightfoot, J. B. Editor. *The Apostolic Fathers Part I: S. Clement of Rome. A Revised Text with Introductions, Notes, Dissertations, and Translations.* London: Macmillan and Co., 1890.

Livy, *History of Rome.* 14 vols. Translated by B. O. Foster and others. Loeb Classical Library. Cambridge, MA: Harvard University Press, 1922–1959.

Mason, Steve. *Flavius Josephus: Life of Josephus.* Leiden: Brill, 2001.

Nepos, Cornelius. Translated by John C. Rolfe. Loeb Classical Library. Cambridge, MA: Harvard University Press, 1984.

Neusner, Jacob. Translator *The Components of the Rabbinic Documents: From the Whole to the Parts 10. Leviticus Rabbah: Part Three: Topical and Methodical Outline.* Atlanta, GA: Scholars Press, 1997.

_____. Translator. *Genesis Rabbah: The Judaic Commentary to the Book of Genesis: A New American Translation Volume III: Parashiyyot 68 through 100 on Genesis 28:10 to 50:26.* Atlanta, GA: Scholars Press, 1985.

_____. Translator. *Sifré to Deuteronomy: An Analytical Transl. 2 Pisqaot One Hundred Forty-Seven Through Three Hundred Fifty-Seven, Shofetim, Ki Tese, Ki Tabo, Nesabim, Ha'azinu, Zot Habberakkah.* Atlanta, GA: Scholars Press, 1987.

_____. Translator. *The Talmud of the Land of Israel A Preliminary Translation and Explanation: Baba Mesia,* vol. 29. Chicago, IL: University of Chicago Press, 1984.

_____. Translator. *The Talmud of the Land of Israel A Preliminary Translation and Explanation: Berakhot,* vol. 1. Chicago, IL: University of Chicago Press, 1982.

_____. Translator. *The Talmud of the Land of Israel A Preliminary Translation and Explanation: Ḥagigah and Moed Qatan.* vol. 20. Chicago, IL: University of Chicago Press, 1982.

_____. Translator. *The Talmud of the Land of Israel: A Preliminary Translation and Explanation: Ketubot.* vol. 22. Chicago, IL: University of Chicago Press, 1982.

_____. Translator. *The Talmud of the Land of Israel A Preliminary Translation and Explanation: Nazir,* vol. 24. Chicago, IL: University of Chicago Press, 1982.

_____. Translator. *The Talmud of the Land of Israel A Preliminary Translation and Explanation: Sanhedrin and Makkot,* vol. 31. Chicago, IL: University of Chicago Press, 1984.

_____. *The Talmud of the Land of Israel: A Preliminary Translation and Explanation: Shebiit,* vol. 5. Chicago, IL: University of Chicago Press, 1991.

_____. Translator. *The Talmud of the Land of Israel A Preliminary Translation and Explanation: Sukkah,* vol. 17. Chicago, IL: University of Chicago Press, 1982.

_____. Translator. *The Talmud of the Land of Israel A Preliminary Translation and Explanation: Yoma,* vol. 14. Chicago, IL: University of Chicago Press, 1990.

Niese, Benedict. *Flavii Iosephi Opera. Vol. VI: De Bello Iudaico.* Berlin, Weidman, 1894.

_____. *Flavii Iosephi Opera. Vol. III: Antiquitatum Iudaicarum Livri XI–XV.* Berlin, Weidman, 1892.

Nisetich, Frank. "The Poems of Posidippus." Pages 7–66 In *The New Posidippus: A Hellenistic Poetry Book.* Edited by Kathryn Gutzwiller. Oxford: Oxford University Press, 2005.

Noam, Vered. *Megillat Ta'anit: Versions, Interpretation, History with a Critical Edition.* Jerusalem: Yad Ben-Zvi Press, 2003 (in Hebrew).

Orosius, Paulus. Karl Friedrich and Wilhelm Zangemeister, Editors. *Pauli Orosii Historiarum adversum paganos libri VII. Bibliotheca scriptorum Graecorum Romanorum Teubneriana.* Lipsiae: In Aedibus B.G. Teubneri, 1889.

Paterculus, Velleius. *Compendium of Roman History. Res Gestae Divi Augusti.* Translated by

Frederick W. Shipley. Loeb Classical Library. Cambridge, MA: Harvard University Press, 1924.

Pfann, Stephen J. Editor. *Qumran Cave 4.XXVI: Cryptic Texts and Miscellanea, Part 1.* Oxford: Clarendon, 2000.

Philo. *De Fuga et Inventione.* Translated by G. H. Whitaker Loeb Classical Library. Cambridge, MA: Harvard University Press, 1929.

_____. *Every Good Man is Free. On the Contemplative Life. On the Eternity of the World. Against Flaccus. Apology for the Jews. On Providence.* Translated by F. H. Colson, *Philo.* Loeb Classical Library. Cambridge, MA: Harvard University Press, 1941.

_____. *De Specialibus Legibus.* Translated by F. H. Colson *Philo.* Loeb Classical Library Cambridge, MA: Harvard University Press, 1929.

Pietersma, Albert, and Benjamin G. Wright, Editors. *The New English Translation of the Septuagint and the Other Greek Translations Traditionally Included Under That Title.* Oxford, England: Oxford University Press, 2007.

Pliny. *Natural History: Books 28–32.* Translated by W. H. S. Jones. Loeb Classical Library. Cambridge, MA: Harvard University Press, 1963.

Plutarch. *Lives: Life of Marcus Antonius.* Translated by Bernadotte Perrin. Loeb Classical Library. Cambridge, MA: Harvard University Press, 1914.

_____. *Lives: Life of Pompey.* Translated by Bernadotte Perrin. Loeb Classical Library. Cambridge, MA: Harvard University Press, 1917.

_____. *Moralia: Isis and Osiris.* Translated by Frank Cole Babbitt. Loeb Classical Library. Cambridge, MA: Harvard University Press, 1936.

_____. *Moralia: Sayings of Kings and Commanders.* Translated by Frank Cole Babbitt. Loeb Classical Library. Cambridge, MA: Harvard University Press, 1927.

Polybius, *The Histories.* Translated by W. R. Paton. Loeb Classical Library. Cambridge, MA: Harvard University Press, 1922.

Racine, Jean. *Britannicus, Phaedra, and Athaliah.* Translated by C. H. Sisson. Oxford: Oxford University Press, 1987.

Rahlfs, A. *Septuaginta id est Vetus Testamentum graece iuxta LXX interpretes.* Stüggart: Deutsche Bibelgesellschaft, 1935.

Schoene, Alfred, ed., *Eusebi Chronicorum canonum quae supersunt,* 3d ed. Zurich: Weidmann. 1999.

Sievers, Joseph. *Synopsis of the Greek Sources for the Hasmonean Period: 1–2 Maccabees and Josephus, War 1 and Antiquities 12–14.* Rome: Pontificio istituto biblico, 2001.

Simon, Maurice and Isidore Epstein. *Hebrew-English Edition of the Babylonian Talmud: Berakoth.* London: Soncino, 1960.

Slotki, Israel W., Translator. *Sukkah: Translated into English with Notes, Glossary and Indices.* London: The Soncino Press, 1938.

Stern, Menahem. *Greek and Latin Authors on Jews and Judaism.* 3 vols. Jerusalem: Israel Academy of Sciences and Humanities, 1974.

Strabo, *The Geography of Strabo.* Translated by Horace Leonard Jones. Loeb Classical Library. New York, NY: G. P. Putnam's Sons, 1917.

Syncellus, George. *Georgius Syncellus et Nicephorus Cp.* Edited by Wilhelm Dindorf, Bonnae: E. Weber, 1829.

Tacitus. *Histories: Books 4–5. Annals: Books 1–3.* Translated by Clifford H. Moore and John Jackson. Loeb Classical Library. Cambridge, MA: Harvard University Press, 1931.

Tcherikover, Victor. *Corpus Papyrorum Judaicarum.* Vol. 2. Cambridge, MA: Harvard University Press, 1957.

Tertullian. *De Praescriptionibus Adversus Haereticos,* In *Patrologia cursus completes: Series Latina,* 2. Vol. 20b. J. P. Migne, Editor. Paris: Garner, 1879.

Thesleff, Holger. Editor. *The Pythagorean Texts of the Hellenistic Period: Collected and Edited.* Abo: Abo Akademi, 1965.

Tracy, Stephen V. and Christian Habicht, "New and Old Panathenaic Victor Lists," *Hesperia* 60/2. (1991): 187–236.

Vermes, Geza and Martin D. Goodman, Editors, *The Essenes According to the Classical Sources.* Sheffield: JSOT, 1989.

Vitruvius. *On Architecture.* Translated by Frank Granger. Loeb Classical Library. New York, NY: G. P. Putnam's Sons, 1931.

Secondary Works

Abegg, Jr., Martin G. "Concordance of Proper Nouns in the Non-Biblical Texts from Qumran." In *The Texts from the Judaean Desert: Indices and An Introduction to the Discoveries in the Judaean Desert Series,* edited by Emanuel Tov, 229–84. Oxford: Clarendon Press, 2002.

Abel, F. M. "Le siège de Jérusalem par Pompée." *Revue Biblique* 54 (1947): 243–55.

Adler, William. *Time Immemorial: Archaic History and its Sources in Christian Chronography from Julius Africanus to George Syncellus.* Washington DC: Oaks Research Library and Collection, 1989.

Adler, William and Paul Tuffin. *The Chronology of George Synkellos: A Byzantine Chronicle of Universal History from the Creation.* Oxford: Oxford University Press, 2002.

Ager, Sheila L. "Familarity Breeds: Incest and the Ptolemaic Dynasty." *Journal of Hellenic Studies* 125 (2005): 1–34.

Aharoni, Yohanan. *The Land of the Bible: A Historical Geography.* Revised and Enlarged Edition. Philadelphia, PA: Westminster Press, 1979.

Amundsen, D. W. and C. J. Diers. "The Age of Menarche in Classical Greece and Rome." *Human Biology* 41 (1969): 125–32.

Archer, Léonie J. *Her Price is Beyond Rubies: The Jewish Woman in Graeco-Roman Palestine.* Sheffield: Sheffield Academic Press, 1990.

Ariel, Donald T. *Excavations at the City of David 1978–1985 Directed by Yigael Shiloh.* Vol. 2, *Imported Stamped Amphora Handles, Coins, Worked Bone and Ivory, and Glass.* Jerusalem: Hebrew University Institute of Archaeology, 1990.

Ariès, Philippe. 1962, *Centirues of Childhood.* New York: Vintage Books.

Armstrong, Karen. *The Bible: A Biography.* New York: Atlantic Monthly Press, 2007.

Assar, Gholamreza F. "A Revised Parthian Chronology of the Period 91–55 B.C." *Parthica* 8 (2006): 55–104.

Atkinson, Kenneth. "Body." In *Theologisches Wörterbuch zu den Qumrantexten,* edited by Heinz-Josef Fabry and Ulrich Dahmen. 588–90. Stüttgart: Kohlhammer Verlag, 2011.

_____. "Dancing at Qumran?: Women and Worship at the Dead Sea." In *Proceedings of the Central States Regional Meeting of the Society of Biblical Literature and the American Schools of Oriental Research.* vol. 3. Edited by Scott S. Elliott, 39–54. Kansas City, MO: Central States Society of Biblical Literature, 2000.

_____. "Gamla." In *Dictionary of Early Judaism.* Edited by John J. Collins and Daniel C. Harlow. 657–58. Grand Rapids, MI: Wm. B. Eerdmans, 2010.

_____. "The Historical Chronology of the Hasmonean Period in the *War* and *Antiquities* of Flavius Josephus: Separating Fact from Fiction." In *Flavius Josephus: Interpretation and History,* Edited by Menachem Mohr, Pnina Stern, and Jack Pastor, 7–27. Leiden: Brill, 2011.

_____. "Herod the Great, Sosius, and the Siege of Jerusalem (37 B.C.E.) in Psalm of Solomon 17." *Novum Testamentum* 38 (1996): 313–22.

_____. *I Cried to the Lord: A Study of the Psalms of Solomon's Historical Background and Social Setting.* Leiden: Brill, 2004.

_____. *An Intertextual Study of the Psalms of Solomon.* Lewiston, NY: Edwin Mellen Press, 2001.

_____. "On Further Defining the First Century C.E. Synagogue: Fact or Fiction?" *New Testament Studies* 43 (1997): 491–502.

_____. "Queen Salome Alexandra and the Dead Sea Scrolls: A Period of Enlightenment for Women in Ancient Judea During the First Century B.C." In *Proceedings of the Central States Regional Meeting of the Society of Biblical Literature and the American Schools of Ori-*

ental Research. vol. 4. Edited by Scott S. Elliott, 15–29. Kansas City, MO: Central States Society of Biblical Literature, 2001.

_____. "Representations of History in 4Q331 (4QpapHistorical Text C), 4Q332 (4QHistorical Text D), 4Q333 (4QHistorical Text E), and 4Q468e (4QHistorical Text F): An Annalistic Calendar Documenting Portentous Events?" *Dead Sea Discoveries* 14 (2007): 125–51.

_____. "The Salome No One Knows: Long-Time Ruler of a Prosperous and Peaceful Judea Mentioned in Dead Sea Scrolls." *Biblical Archaeology Review* 34 (2008): 60–65, 72–3.

_____. "Theodicy in the Psalms of Solomon." In *Theodicy in the World of the Bible.* edited by Antii Laato and Johannes C. de Moor, 546–75. Leiden: Brill, 2003.

_____. "Toward a Redating of the Psalms of Solomon: Implications for Understanding the *Sitz im Leben* of an Unknown Jewish Sect." *Journal for the Study of the Pseudepigrapha* 17 (1998): 95–112.

_____. "Two Dogs, a Goat and a Partridge: An Archaeologist's Best Friends." *Biblical Archaeology Review* 22 (January/February 1996): 42–43, 74.

_____. "Women in the Dead Sea Scrolls: Evidence for a Qumran Renaissance During the Reign of Queen Salome Alexandra." *The Qumran Chronicle* 11 (2003): 37–56.

Atkinson, Kenneth, Hanan Eshel, and Jodi Magness. "Do Josephus's Writings Support the 'Essene Hypothesis'?" *Biblical Archaeology Review* 35 (2009): 56–59.

Atkinson, Kenneth, and Jodi Magness. "Josephus's Essenes and the Qumran Community." *Journal of Biblical Literature* 129 (2010): 317–42.

Aviam, Mordechai. *Jews, Pagans and Christians in the Galilee.* Rochester, NY: University of Rochester Press, 2004.

Avigad, Nahman. "A Bulla of Jonathan the High Priest." *Israel Exploration Journal* 25 (1975): 8–12.

_____. *idem,* "A Bulla of King Jonathan." *Israel Exploration Journal* 25 (1975): 245–46.

Baer, Richard, *Philo's Use of the Categories Male and Female.* Leiden: E. J. Brill, 1971.

Bagnall, Roger S. and Bruce W. Frier, *The Demography of Roman Egypt.* Cambridge: Cambridge University Press, 1994.

Balsdon, J. P. V. D. *Roman Women: Their History and Habits.* London: Bodley Head, 1962.

Baltrusch, Ernst. *Die Juden und das Römische Reich: Geschichte einer konfliktreichen Beziehung.* Darmstadt: Wissenschaftliche Buchgesellschaft, 2002.

Bar-Ilan, Meir. *Some Jewish Women in Antiquity.* Atlanta, GA: Scholars Press, 1998.

Barag, Dan. "New Evidence on the Foreign Policy of John Hyrcanus I." *Israel Numismatic Journal* 12 (1992–1993): 1–12.

Baumgarten, Albert I. "He Knew that He Knew that He Knew that He was an Essene." *Journal of Jewish Studies* 48 (1997): 53–61.

Baumgarten, Joseph M. "4Q502, Marriage or Golden Age Ritual?" *Journal of Jewish Studies* 34 (1983): 125–35.

_____. "On the Testimony of Women in 1QSa." "*Journal of Biblical Literature* 76 (1957): 266–69.

Beall, Todd S. *Josephus' Description of the Essenes Illustrated by the Dead Sea Scrolls.* Cambridge: Cambridge University Press, 1988.

Beavis, Mary Ann. "Philo's Therapeutai: Philosopher's Dream or Utopian Construction?" *Journal for the Study of the Pseudepigrapha* 14 (2004): 30–42.

Begg, Christopher. "Athaliah's Coup and Overthrow According to Josephus." *Antonianum* 71 (1996): 189–210.

Bellinger, Alfred R. "Notes on some Coins from Antioch in Syria." *American Numismatic Society Museum Notes* 5 (1952), 53–63.

_____. "The End of the Seleucids." *Transactions of the Connecticut Academy of Arts and Sciences* 38 (1949): 51–102.

Bellmore, Jane. "Josephus, Pompey and the Jews." *Zeitschrift für Geschichte* 48 (1999): 94–118.

Bennett, C. "Cleopatra V Tryphæna and the Genealogy of the Later Ptolemies." *Ancient Society* 28 (1997): 39–66.

Berlin, Andrea M. "Between Large Forces: Palestine in the Hellenistic Period." *Biblical Archaeologist* 60 (1997): 2–57.

Betz, Otto, and Rainer Riesner, *Jesus, Qumran, and the Vatican: Clarifications.* New York, NY: Crossroad, 1994.

Bevan, Edwyn R. *House of Ptolemy: A History of Egypt Under the Ptolemaic Dynasty.* Chicago, IL: Argonaut, 1968 (Reprint of 1927 original).

_____. *House of Seleucus.* 2 vols. London: E. Arnold, 1902.

Biale, Rachel. *Women and Jewish Law: An Exploration of Women's Issues in Halakhic Sources.* New York, NY: Shocken, 1984.

Bickerman, Elias J. "The Colophon of the Greek Book of Esther." *Journal of Biblical Literature* 63 (1944): 339–362.

Bilde, Per. *Flavius Josephus Between Jerusalem and Rome.* Sheffield: Sheffield Academic Press, 1988.

Binder, Donald D. *Into the Temple Courts: The Place of the Synagogues in the Second Temple Period.* Atlanta, GA: Society of Biblical Literature, 1999.

Blasius, Andreas. "Antiochus IV Epiphanes and the Ptolemaic Triad: The Three Uprooted Horns in Dan 7:8, 20 and 24 Reconsidered." *Journal for the Study of Judaism* 37 (2006): 521–47.

Boccaccini, Gabriele. "Tigranes the Great as Nebuchadnezzar in the Book of Judith." Speech at the Ninth Congress of the European Association for Jewish Studies: Judaism in the Mediterranean Context. July 27, 2010. Ravenna, Italy.

Boettger, Gustav. *Topographisch-historisches Lexicon zu den Schriften des Flavius Josephus.* Leipzig: L. Fernau, 1879.

Bogaert, Pierre-Maurice. "le calendrier du livre de Judith et la fête de Hanukka." *Revue théologique de Louvain* 15 (1984): 67–72.

Bowersock, G. W. *Roman Arabia.* Cambridge, GA: Harvard University Press, 1983.

Brooke, George J. "A Long-Lost Song of Miriam," *Biblical Archaeology Review* 20 (1994): 62–5.

Brooten, Bernadette. *Women Leaders in the Ancient Synagogue.* Chico, CA: Scholars Press, 1982.

Broughton, T. Robert S. *The Magistrates of the Roman Republic Volume II: 99 B.C.–31 B.C.* New York: American Philological Association, 1952.

Brüll, Nehemiah. "Das apokryphische *Susanna*-Buch." *Jahrbücher für Jüdische Geschichte und Literatur* 3 (1877): 1–69.

Buchanan, Andrea, Miriam Peskowitz, and Alexis Seabrook, *The Daring Book for Girls.* New York, NY: Collins, 2007.

Burris, Virginia. *Chastity as Autonomy: Women in the Stories of Apocryphal Acts.* Lewiston, NY: Edwin Mellen Press, 1987.

Busink, Th. A. *Der Tempel von Jerusalem, von Salomo bis Herodes: eine archäologisch-historische Studie unter Berücksichtigung des westsemitischen Tempelbaus.* Leiden: E. J. Brill, 1980.

Case, Ellen Irene. *Salome Alexandra: A Study in Achievement, Power and Survival.* M. A. Thesis. Ontario: York University, 1997.

Casson, Lionel. *Travel in the Ancient World.* London: George Allen & Unwin Ltd., 1974.

Chahin, M. *The Kingdom of Armenia.* London: Croom Helm, 1987.

Chapman, David W. *Ancient Jewish and Christian Perceptions of Crucifixion.* Tübingen: Mohr Siebeck, 2008.

Chauveau, Michel. "Encore Ptolémée «VII» et le Dieu Néos Philopatôr!," *Revue d'Égyptologie* 51 (2000): 257–61.

_____. "Un Été 145," *Le Bulletin de l'Institut français d'archéologie orientale* 90 (1990): 135–68.

Chilton, Bruce. "Recovering Jesus' *Mamzerut.*" In *Jesus and Archaeology,* edited by James H. Charlesworth, 84–110. Grand Rapids, MI: Eerdmans, 2006.

Clanton, Jr., Dan W. "(Re)Dating the Story of Susanna: A Proposal." *Journal for the Study of Judaism* 34 (2003): 121–40.

Clermont-Ganneau, Charles. *Archaeological Researches in Palestine During the Years 1873–1874.* London, 1899.

Cohen, Shaye J. D. "Alexander the Great and Jaddus the High Priest According to Josephus." *Association for Jewish Studies Review* 7–8 (1982–83): 41–68.

_____. "The Significance of Yavneh: Pharisees, Rabbis, and the End of Jewish Sectarianism." *Hebrew Union College Annual* 55 (1984): 27–55.

Collins, John J. *The Apocalyptic Imagination: An Introduction to the Jewish Apocalyptic Literature.* rev. ed. Grand Rapids, MI: William B. Eerdmans, 1998.

_____. *Between Athens and Jerusalem: Jewish Identity in Hellenistic Diaspora.* 2d ed. Grand Rapids, MI: William B. Eerdmans, 1999.

_____. *Beyond the Qumran Community: The Sectarian Movement of the Dead Sea Scrolls.* Grand Rapids, MI: Eerdmans, 2010.

_____. *Daniel: A Commentary on the Book of Daniel.* Minneapolis, MN: Fortress, 1993.

Conway, Colleen. "Gender and Divine Relativity in Philo of Alexandria." *Journal for the Study of Judaism* 34 (2003): 471–90.

Coogan, Michael D. *The Old Testament: A Historical and Literary Introduction to the Hebrew Scriptures.* Oxford: Oxford University Press, 2006.

Cousland, J. R. C. "Dionysus Theomachos? Echoes of the Bacchae in 3 Maccabees." *Biblica* 82 (2001): 539–548.

Crawford, Sidnie White. "Mothers, Sisters, and Elders: Titles for Women in Second Temple Jewish and Early Christian Communities." In *The Dead Sea Scrolls as Background to Postbiblical Judaism and Early Christianity,* edited by James R. Davila, 177–91. Leiden: Brill, 2003.

Dabrowa, Edward. *The Hasmoneans and Their State: A Study in History, Ideology, and the Institutions.* Kraków: Jagiellonian University Press, 2010.

Davies, G. Henton. "Dancing." In *The Interpreter's Dictionary of the Bible.* Vol. 1. Edited by G. A. Buttrick, 760–61. Nashville, TN: Abingdon Press, 1990.

Davies, Philip R. "How Not to Do Archaeology: The Story of Qumran." *Biblical Archaeologist* 51 (1988): 203–7.

Davies, Stevan L. *The Revolt of the Widows: The Social World of the Apocryphal Acts.* Carbondale, IL: Southern Illinois University Press, 1980.

Derenbourg, Joseph. *Essai sur l'historie et la géographie de la Palestine, d'après les Thalmuds et les autres sources rabbiniques.* Paris: Imprimerie Impériale, 1867.

deSilva, David A. "Judith the Heroine? Lies, Seduction, and Murder in Cultural Perspective." *Biblical Theology Bulletin: A Journal of Bible and Theology* 36 (2006): 55–61.

de Troyer, Kristin. *Rewriting the Sacred Text: What the Old Greek Texts Tell Us About the Literary Growth of the Bible.* Atlanta, GA: Society of Biblical Literature, 2003.

Deutsch, Immanuel. *Die Regierungszeit der judäischen Königin Salome Alexandra und die Wirksamkeit das Rabbi Simon ben Schetach.* Magdeburg: Jüdischen Litteraturblatts, 1901.

de Vaux, Roland. *Ancient Israel Volume 1: Social Institutions.* New York, NY: McGraw Hill, 1961.

_____. *Ancient Israel Volume 2: Religious Institutions.* New York, NY: McGraw-Hill, 1961.

_____. *Archaeology and the Dead Sea Scrolls.* Translated by David Bourke. Oxford: Oxford University press, 1973.

Dimant, Devorah. "The Composite Character of the Qumran Sectarian Literature as an Indication of its Date and Provenance." *Revue de Qumran* 88 (2006): 619–20.

Donahue, Lauri. "Alexandra of Judea." 2003. Play available from Baker's Plays (http://www.bakersplays.com).

Donceel, Robert. *Synthèse des observations faites en fouillant les tombes des necropoles de Khirbet Qumrân et des environs.* Cracow: Enigma Press, 2002.

Edrei, Arye and Doron Mendels. "A Split Jewish Diaspora: Its Dramatic Consequences I." *Journal for the Study of the Pseudepigrapha* 17 (2008): 163–87.

Edwards, M. "M. Gnaeus Pompeius Magnus from Teenage Butcher to Roman Alexander." *The Accordia Research Papers: The Journal of the Accordia Research Centre* 2 (1991): 69–85.

Efron, Joshua. *Studies on the Hasmonean Period.* Leiden: E. J. Brill, 1987.

Egger, Rita,. *Josephus Flavius und die Samaritaner: Eine terminologische Untersuchung zur Identitätsklärung der Samaritaner.* Göttingen: Vandenhoeck & Ruprecht, 1986.

Elder, Linda Bennet. "The Women Question and Female Ascetics Among Essenes." *Biblical Archaeologist* 57 (1994): 220–34.

Engberg-Pedersen, Troels. "Philo's *De Vita Contemplativa* as a Philosopher's Dream." *Journal for the Study of Judaism* 30 (1999): 40–64.

Engels, Donald W. *Alexander the Great and the Logistics of the Macedonian Army.* Berkeley: University of California Press, 1978.

Enslin, Morton S. and Solomon Zeitlin. *The Book of Judith.* Leiden: E. J. Brill, 1972.

Eshel, Esther and Hanan Eshel. "Dating the Samaritan Pentateuch's Compilation in Light of the Qumran Biblical Scrolls." In *Emanuel: Studies in Hebrew Bible, Septuagint, and Dead Sea Scrolls in Honor of Emanuel Tov,* edited by Shalom M. Paul, et al. 215–40. Leiden: Brill, 2003.

Eshel, Esther, Hanan Eshel, and Ada Yardeni. 1992. "A Qumran Composition Containing Part of Ps 154 and a Prayer for the Welfare of King Jonathan and his Kingdom." *Israel Exploration Journal* 32, 199–299.

Eshel, Hanan. *The Dead Sea Scrolls and the Hasmonean State.* Grand Rapids, MI: William B. Eerdmans, 2008.

Eshel, Hanan, Magen Broshi, Richard Freund, and Brian Schultz, "New Data on the Cemetery East of Khirbet Qumran." *Dead Sea Discoveries* 9 (2002): 135–65.

Fantalkin, Alexander and Oren Tal. "The 'Yannai Line' (BJ I, 99–100; AJ XIII, 390–391): Reality or Fiction?" *Palestine Exploration Quarterly* 135 (2003): 108–23.

Fanthan, Elaine, et. al., eds.. *Women in the Classical World: Image and Text.* Oxford: Oxford University Press, 1994.

Fields, Weston W. *The Dead Sea Scrolls: A Full History: Volume One, 1947–1960.* Leiden: Brill, 2009.

Fine, Steve. *Art and Judaism in the Greco-Roman World: Toward a New Jewish Archaeology.* Cambridge: Cambridge University Press, 2005.

Finkielsztejn, Gerald. "More Evidence on John Hyrcanus I's Conquests: Lead Weights and Rhodian Amphora Stamps." *Bulletin of the Anglo-Israel Archaeological Society* 16 (1998): 33–63.

Fischer, Thomas. *Untersuchungen zum Partherkrieg Antiochos' VII. im Rahmen der Seleukidengeschichte.* Munich, privately published, 1970.

Fraser, Antonia. *The Warrior Queens: The Legends and the Lives of the Women Who Have Led Their Nations in War.* New York, NY: Vintage, 1988.

Fraser, P. M. 1972. *Ptolemaic Alexandria.* Oxford: Clarendon Press.

Freyne, Sean. *Galilee from Alexander the Great to Hadrian 323 B.C.E. to 135 C.E.* Wilmington, DE: Michael Glazier, 1980.

_____. "Galileans, Phoenicians and Itureans: A Study of Regional Contrasts in the Hellenistic Age." In *Hellenism in the Land of Israel,* edited by John J. Collins and Gregory E. Sterling, 184–217. Notre Dame, IN: University of Notre Dame Press, 2001.

Gelzer, Matthias. *Pompeius.* Münich: F. Bruckmann, 1959.

Gillman, Florence Morgan. *Herodias: At Home in That Fox's Den.* Collegeville, MN: Liturgical Press, 2003.

Giovannini, Adalberto. "Greek Cities and Greek Commonwealth." In *Images and Ideologies: Self-Definition in the Hellenistic World,* edited by A. Bulloch, E. S. Gruen, A. Long, and A. Stewart, 265–86. Berkeley, CA: University of California Press, 1993.

Gladwell, Malcolm. *Outliers: The Story of Success.* New York, NY: Little, Brown and Company, 2008.

Golberg, Shari. "The Two Choruses Become One: The Absence/Presence of Women in Philo's *On the Contemplative Life.*" *Journal for the Study of Judaism* 39 (2008): 459–70.

Goldstein, Jonathan A. *1 Maccabees: A New Translation, With Introduction and Commentary.* Garden City, N.: Doubleday, 1976.

Grainger, John D. *A Seleukid Prosopography and Gazetteer.* Leiden: Brill, 1997.

Greenhalgh, P. A. L. *Pompey: The Roman Alexander.* Columbia, MO: University of Missouri Press, 1981.

Grueber, H. A. *Coins of the Roman Republic in the British Museum.* Vol. 1. London: Trustees of the British Museum, 1970.

Gruen, Eric S. "Fact and Fiction: Jewish Legends in a Hellenistic Context." In *Hellenistic Constructs: Essays in Culture, History, and Historiography,* edited by Paul Cartledge, Peter Garnsey, and Erich Gruen, 72–88. Berkeley, CA: University of California Press, 1997.

———. *The Hellenistic World and the Coming of Rome,* 2 vols. Berkeley, CA: University of California Press, 1984.

Gutzwiller, Kathryn J. *Poetic Garlands: Hellenistic Epigrams in Context.* Berkeley, CA: University of California Press, 1988.

Hall, R. G. "Epispasm and the Dating of Ancient Jewish Writings." *Journal for the Study of the Pseudepigrapha* 2 (1988): 71–86.

Harrison, Robert. "Hellenization in Syria-Palestine: The Case of Judea in the Third Century B.C.E." *Biblical Archaeologist* 57 (1994): 98–108.

Hass, Nicko. "Anthropological Observations on the Skeletal Remains from Giv'at ha-Mivtar." *Israel Exploration Journal* 20 (1970): 38–59.

Havelock, Mitchell. "A Portrait of Cleopatra II(?) in the Vassar College Art Gallery." *Hesperia* 51 (1982): 269–76.

Hay, David M. "Things Philo Said and Did Not Say About the Therapeutae." In *Society of Biblical Literature Seminar Papers, 1992,* edited by Eugene H. Lovering, 673–83. Atlanta, GA: Scholars Press, 1992.

Hefez, Nir and Gadi Bloom. *Ariel Sharon: A Life.* Translated by Mitch Ginsburg. New York: Random House, 2006.

Heinen Heinz. "Der Sohn des 6. Ptolemäers im Sommer 145. Zur Frage nach Ptolemaios VII. Neos Philopator und zur Zählung der Ptolemuaerkönige." In *Akten des 21. Internationalen Papyrologenkongresses, Berlin 1995,* Vol. 1. Edited by Barbel Kramer, Wolfgang Luppe, Herwig Maehler, and Günter Poethke, 449–60. Stuttgart: B. G. Teubner, 1997.

Hengel, Martin. "The Interpenetration of Judaism and Hellenism in the Pre-Maccabean Period." In *The Cambridge History of Judaism: Volume Two: The Hellenistic Age.* Edited by W. D. Davies and Louis Finkelstein, Pages 167–228. Cambridge: Cambridge University Press, 1989.

———. *Judaism and Hellenism: Studies in their Encounter in Palestine During the Early Hellenistic Period,* 2 vols. Philadelphia, PA: Fortress, 1974.

Herman, Daniel. "Certain Iturean Coins and the Origin of the Heliopolitan Cult." *Israel Numismatic Journal* 14 (200–02): 84–98.

Himbaza, Innocent, "Le débat sur le divorce en Malachie 2:16a et l'ambivalence de la LXX." *Bulletin of the International Organization of Septuagint and Cognate Studies* 42 (2009): 68–79.

Hölbl, Gunther. *History of Ptolemaic Egypt.* Translated by Tina Saavedra. London: Routledge, 2000.

Hoover, O. D. "Dethroning Seleucus VII Philometor (Cybiosactes): Epigraphical Arguments Against a Late Seleucid Monarch." *Zeitschrift für Papyrologie und Epigraphik* 151 (2005): 95–99.

Hopkins, M. K. "The Age of Roman Girls at Marriage." *Population Studies* 18 (1965): 309–27.

Horsley, Richard A. "The Expansion of Hasmonean Rule in Idumea and Galilee: Towards a Historical Sociology." Pages 134–65 In *Second Temple Studies III: Studies in Politics, Class, and Material Culture.* Edited by Philip R. Davies and John M. Halligan. London and New York: Sheffield Academic Press, 2002.

Houghton, Arthur. "A Victory Coin and the Parthian Wars of Antiochus VII." In *Proceedings of the 10th International Congress of Numismatics.* Edited by I. A. Carradice, 65. London: International Association of Professional Numismatists, 1989.

Humbert, Jean-Baptiste and Alain Chambon. *Fouilles de Khirbet Qumrân et de Aïn Feshkha I.* Göttingen: Vandenhoeck & Ruprecht, 1994.

Huß, Werner. *Ägypten in hellenistischer Zeit 332–30 v. Chr.* Munich: C. H. Beck, 2001.

Ilan, Tal. "The Attraction of Aristocratic Women to Pharisaism During the Second Temple Period." *Harvard Theological Review* 88 (1995): 1–33.

_____. "The Greek Names of the Hasmoneans." *Jewish Quarterly Review* 78 (1987): 1–20.

_____. *Integrating Women into Second Temple History.* Peabody, MA: Hendrickson Publishers, 2001.

_____. *Jewish Women in Greco-Roman Palestine.* Peabody, A. Hendrickson Publishers, 1996.

_____. "Josephus and Nicolaus on Women." In *Geschichte—Tradition—Reflexion.* Vol. 1. Edited by Hubert Cancik, Hermann Lichtenberger, and Peter Schäfer, 221–62. Tübingen: J. C. B. Mohr (Paul Seibeck), 1996.

_____. *Lexicon of Jewish Names in Late Antiquity Part I: Palestine 330 B.C.E.–200 C.E.* Tübingen: Mohr Siebeck, 2002.

_____. *Mine and Yours Are Hers: Retrieving Women's History from Rabbinic Literature.* Leiden: Brill, 1997.

_____. "New Ossuary Inscriptions from Jerusalem." *Scripta Classica Israelica* 11 (1991/92): 155–57.

_____. "Notes on the Distribution of Jewish Women's Names in Palestine in the Second Temple and Mishnaic Periods." *Journal of Jewish Studies* 49 (1989): 198–99.

_____. "Queen Salamzion Alexandra and Judas Aristobulus I's Widow: Did Jannaeus Alexander Contract a Levirate Marriage?" *Journal for the Study of Judaism* 24 (1993): 181–90.

_____. "Shelamzion in Qumran." In *Historical Perspectives: From the Hasmoneans to Bar Kokhba In Light of the Dead Sea Scrolls,* edited by David Goodblatt, Avital Pinnick, and Daniel R. Schwartz, 57–68. Leiden: Brill, 2001.

_____. *Silencing the Queen: The Literary Histories of Shelamzion and Other Jewish Women.* Tübingen: Mohr Siebeck, 2006.

Jackson, B. S. "Problems in the Development of the Ketubah Payment: The Shimon ben Shetah Tradition." In *Rabbinic Law in its Roman and Near Context,* edited by C. Hezser, 199–225. Tübingen: Mohr Siebeck, 2003.

Kasher, Aryeh. "The Changes in Manpower and Ethnic Composition of the Hasmonean Army (167–63 B.C.E.)." *Jewish Quarterly Review* (new series) 81 (1991): 325–52.

_____. *Jews and Hellenistic Cities in Eretz-Israel: Relations of the Jews with the Hellenistic Cities During the Second Temple Period (332 B.C.E.–70 C.E.).* Tübingen, 1990 J.C.B. Mohr, 1990.

_____. *Jews, Idumaeans and Ancient Arabs.* Tübingen: J. C. B. Mohr, 1988.

Klausner, Joseph. "Judah Aristobulus and Jannaeus Alexander." *The World History of the Jewish People VI: The Hellenistic Age,* edited by Schalit, 222–41. New Brunswick; Rutgers University Press, 1972.

_____. "Queen Salome Alexandra." In *The World History of the Jewish People VI: The Hellenistic Age,* edited by Abraham Schalit, 222–54. New Brunswick; Rutgers University Press, 1972.

Knauf, Ernst Axel. "Salome Alexandra and the Final Redaction of Psalms." *Lectio difficilor* 2 (2009): 1–16.

Knox, Bernard. *The Oldest Dead White European Males: And Other Reflections on the Classics.* New York, NY: W. W. Norton & Company, 1993.

Kokkinos, Nikos. *The Herodian Dynasty: Origins, Role in Society and Eclipse.* Sheffield: Sheffield Academic Press, 1998.

_____. "Which Salome Did Aristobulus Marry?" *Palestine Exploration Quarterly* 118 (1986): 33–50.

Kraemer, Ross Shepard. "Monastic Jewish Women in Greco-Roman Egypt: Philo Judaeus on the Therapeutrides." *Signs: Journal of Women in Culture and Society* 14 (1989): 342–370.

_____. *Women's Religions in the Greco-Roman World: A Sourcebook.* Oxford: Oxford University Press, 2004.

Kraft, Robert A. "Pliny on Essenes, Pliny on Jews." *Dead Sea Discoveries* 8 (2001): 255–61.

Kritt, Brian. "Numismatic Evidence For A New Seleucid King: Seleucus (VII) Philomator," *The Celator* 16/4 (2002): 25–36.

Kuhn, Adolf. *Beitrage zur geschichte der Seleukiden vom tode Antiochos' VII. Sidetes vom tode Antiochus XIII. Asiatikos (129–64 V.C.).* Altkirch: E. Masson, 1891

Lambers-Petry, Doris. "Shelomzion ha-malka: The Hasmonean Queen and her Enigmatic Portrayal by Josephus." In *Internationales Josephus-Kolloquium Dortmund 2002,* edited by Jürgen U. Kalms and Folker Siegert, 65–77. Münster: Lit, 2002.

Lanciers, Eddy. "Some Observations on the Events in Egypt in 145 B.C." *Simblos* 1 (1995): 33–39.

Lange, Armin with Ulrike Mittmann-Richert, "Annotated List of the Texts From the Judaean Desert Classified." In *The Texts from the Judaean Desert: Indices and An Introduction to the Discoveries in the Judaean Desert Series,* edited by Emanuel Tov, 115–64. Oxford: Clarendon Press, 2002.

Last, Richard. "Onias IV and the δέσποτος ἱερός: Placing *Antiquities* 13.62–73 into the Context of Ptolemaic Land Tenure." *Journal for the Study of Judaism* 41 (2010: 494–516.

Leach, John. *Pompey the Great.* London: Croom Helm, 1978.

Lemaire, André. "The Divided Monarchy: Saul, David and Solomon." In *Ancient Israel: From Abraham to the Roman Destruction of the Temple.* Revised and Expanded Edition. Edited by Hershel Shanks, 91–120. Washington D.C./Upper Saddle River, NJ: Biblical Archaeology Society & Prentice Hall, 1999.

_____. "L'expérience essénienne de Flavius Josèphe." In *Internationales Josephus Kolloquium Paris 2001.* Edited by Folker Siegert and Jürgen Kalms, 138–51. Münster: Lit, 2002.

Levenson, David B. and Thomas R. Martin. "Akairos or Eukairos? The Nickname of the Seleucid King Demetrius III in the Transmission of the Texts of Josephus' *War* and *Antiquities. Journal for the Study of Judaism* 40 (2009): 307–41.

Levine, Amy-Jill. *The Misunderstood Jew: The Church and the Scandal of the Jewish Jesus.* New York, NY: HarperOne, 2006.

_____. "Sacrifice and Salvation: Otherness and Domestication in the Book of Judith." In *"No One Spoke Ill Of Her": Essays on Judith,* edited by James C. VanderKam, 208–23. Atlanta, GA: Scholars Press, 1992.

Levine, Lee I. "The Age of Hellenism: Alexander the Great and the Rise and Fall of the Hasmonean Kingdom." In *Ancient Israel: From Abraham to the Roman Destruction of the Temple.* Revised and Expanded Edition. Edited by Hershel Shanks, 231–51. Washington D.C./Upper Saddle River, NJ: Biblical Archaeology Society & Prentice Hall, 1999.

Liver, Jacob. "The Half-Shekel Offering in Biblical and Post-Biblical Literature." *Harvard Theological Review* 56 (1963): 173–98.

Macurdy, Grace H. *Hellenistic Queens: A Study of Women-Power in Macedonia, Seleucid Syria, and Ptolemaic Egypt.* Baltimore, MD: The John's Hopkins Press, 1932.

_____. *Vassal-Queens and Some Contemporary Women in the Roman Empire.* Baltimore, MD: The John's Hopkins Press, 1937.

Magen, Yizhak and Yuval Peleg. "Back to Qumran: Ten Years of Excavation and Research, 1993–2004." In *Qumran, the Site of the Dead Sea Scrolls: Archaeological Interpretations and Debates: Proceedings of a Conference held at Brown University, November 17–19, 2002,* edited by Katharina Galor, Jean-Baptiste Humbert, and Jürgen Zangenberg, 55–113. Leiden: Brill, 2006.

_____. *The Qumran Excavations 1993–2004: Preliminary Report.* Jerusalem: Israel Antiquities Authority, 2007.

Magness, Jodi. *The Archaeology of Qumran and the Dead Sea Scrolls.* Grand Rapids, MI: Eerdmans, 2002.

_____. "Ossuaries and the Burials of Jesus and James." *Journal of Biblical Literature* 124 (2005): 121–54.

Mahaffy, J. P. *History of Egypt Under the Ptolemaic Dynasty.* New York: Charles Scribner's Sons, 1899.

Main, E. "For King Jonathan or Against? The Use of the Bible in 4Q448." In *Biblical Perspectives: Early Use and Interpretation of the Bible in Light of the Dead Sea Scrolls,* edited by Michael E. Stone and Esther G. Chazon, 113–35. Leiden: Brill, 1998.

Manandyan, H. *Tigranes II and Rome*. Annotated Translation and Introduction by George A. Bournoutian. Costa Mesa, CA: Mazda Publishers, 2007.

Marcos, Natalio Fernendez *The Septuagint in Context: Introduction to the Greek Version of the Bible*. W. G. E. Watson, Translator. Leiden: E. J. Brill, 2000.

Margulis, Bonnie. *The Queenship of Alexandra Salome: Her Role in the Hasmonean Dynasty, Her Achievements and Her Place in History*. Ph.D. Dissertation. Cincinnati, OH: Hebrew Union College-Jewish Institute of Religion. 1992.

Marks, Susan. "Women in Early Judaism: Twenty-five Years of Research and Reenvisioning." *Currents in Biblical Research* 6 (2008): 290–320.

Martin, Luther H. *Hellenistic Religions: An Introduction*. Oxford: Oxford University Press, 1987.

Mason, Steve. *Flavius Josephus on the Pharisees: A Composition-Critical Study*. Leiden: E. J. Brill, 1991.

Mason, Steve, with Honora Chapman, *Flavius Josephus Translation and Commentary: Volume 1B Judean War 2*. Leiden: Brill, 2008.

Mayer, Günter. *Die jüdische Frau in der hellenistisch-römischen Antike*. Stuttgart: W. Kohlhammer, 1987.

McKenzie, Steven L. *King David: A Biography*. Oxford: Oxford University Press, 2000.

Meshel, Ze'ev. "Questioning Masada Governments-in-Exile: The Judean Wilderness as the Last Bastion of Jewish revolts." *Biblical Archaeological Review* 24 (1998): 46–53, 68.

Meshorer Ya'akov. *Ancient Jewish Coinage*, vol. New York, NY: Amphora Books, 1982.

_____. *A Treasury of Jewish Coins*. Nyack, NJ: Amphora, 2001.

Miller, J. Maxwell and John H. Hayes. *A History of Ancient Israel and Judah*, 2d ed. Louisville, KY: Westminster John Knox, 2006.

Moore, Carey A. *Judith: A New Translation with Introduction and Commentary*. Garden City, NY: Doubleday, 1985.

Mor, Menachem. "The Persian, Hellenistic and Hasmonean Period." In *The Samaritans*. Edited by Alan D. Crown, 1–18. Tübingen: J. C. B. Mohr (Paul Siebeck), 1989.

Müller, Johann. *De Alexandra judaeorum regina tanquam specimine sapientis ex hac gente foeminae ad illustrandam historiam factionum judaicarum*. Altdorffi-Noricorum: Kohlesiano, 1711.

Murphy-O'Connor, Jerome. *The Holy Land: An Archaeological Guide From Earliest Times to 1700*. Oxford: Oxford University Press, 1986.

Nagar, Yossi, and Hagit Torgee, "Biological Characteristics of Jewish Burial in the Hellenistic and Early Roman Period." *Israel Exploration Journal* 53 (2003): 164–71.

Neusner, Jacob. *A History of the Jews in Babylonia*, 1, *The Parthian Period*, Leiden: Brill, 1965.

_____. *The Rabbinic Traditions About the Pharisees Before 70: Part I The Masters*. Leiden: E. J. Brill, 1971.

Netzer, Ehud. *The Palaces of the Hasmoneans and Herod the Great*. Jerusalem: Yad-Ben Zvi Press, 2001.

Niehoff, Maren R. "Mother and Maiden, Sister and Spouse: Sarah in Philonic Midrash." *Harvard Theological Review* 97 (2004): 413–444.

Ogilvie, Robert M. "Introduction." In *Livy The Early History of Rome: Books I-V of The History of Rome from Its Foundations*. Translated by Aubrey De Sélincourt. 1–11. New York: Penguin Books, 2002.

Ooteghem, J. van. *Pompée le grand: bâtisseur d'empire*. Brussels: Palais des Académies, 1954.

Otzen, Benedikt. *Tobit and Judith*. New York: Sheffield Academic Press, 2002.

Pagán, Victoria Emma. *Conspiracy Narratives in Roman History*. Austin: University of Texas Press, 2004.

Pastor, Jack. "Josephus as a Source for Economic History: Problems and Approaches." In *Making History: Josephus and Historical Method*, edited by Zuleika Rodgers, 334–46. Leiden: Brill, 2007.

Patterson, Dilys Naomi. "'Honoured In Her Time': Queen Shelamzion and the Book of Judith." Ph.D. Dissertation. Ottawa: University of Ottawa, 2002.

_____. "Re-Membering the Past: The Purpose of Historical Discourse in the Book of Judith." In *The Function of Ancient Historiography in Biblical and Cognate Studies*, edited by Patricia G. Kirkpatrick and Timothy D. Goltz, 111–23. New York: T & T Clark, 2008.

Pfann, Stephen J. "Cryptic Texts," In *Qumrna Cave 4.XXVI: Cryptic Texts and Miscellanea, Part 1*, Edited by Stephen J. Pfann, *et al.*, 515–74. Oxford: Clarendon, 2000.

_____ "Dated Bronze Coinage of the Sabbatical Years of Release and the First Jewish City Coin." *Bulletin of the Anglo-Israel Archaeological Society* 24 (2006): 101–13.

_____. "A Table in the Wilderness: Pantries and Tables, Pure Food and Sacred Space at Qumran." In *Qumran, the Site of the Dead Sea Scrolls: Archaeological Interpretations and Debates*, edited by Katharina Galor, Jean-Baptiste Humbert, and Jürgen Zangenberg, 159–78. Leiden: Brill, 2006.

Pietre, W. M. Flinders. *Hyksos and Israelite Cities*. Cairo: British School of Archaeology in Egypt and Egyptian Research Account, 1906.

Pillinger, Renate. "Neue Entdeckungen in der sogenannten Paulusgrotte von Ephesos." *Mitteilungen zur Christlichen Archäologie* 6 (2000): 16–29.

Pomeroy, Sarah B. *Women in Hellenistic Egypt: From Alexander to Cleopatra*. New York, NY: Shocken, 1984.

Poole, Reginald Stuart. *Catalogue of Greek Coins: The Ptolemies, Kings of Egypt*. London: British Museum Department of Coins and Medals, 1883.

Pucci, Miriam. "Jewish-Parthian Relations in Josephus." *The Jerusalem Cathedra* 3 (1983): 13–25.

Puech, Émile, "Khirbet Qumrân et les Esséniens," *Revue de Qumran* 25 (2011): 127–31.

Pummer, Reinhard. *The Samaritans in Flavius Josephus*. Tübingen: Mohr Siebeck, 2009.

Rabinowitz, L, I. "Names, In the Talmud," *Encyclopedia Judaica*. Vol. 12. New York: Macmillan, 1971–72, 807.

Rajak, Tessa. *The Jewish Dialogue Between Greece and Rome*. Leiden: Brill, 2002.

Rapuano, Yehudah. "The Hasmonean Period 'Synagogue' at Jericho and the 'Council Chamber' Building at Qumran." *Israel Exploration Journal* 52 (2001): 48–56.

Reed, Jonathan L. *Archaeology and the Galilean Jesus: A Re-Examination of the Evidence*. Harrisburg, PA: Trinity Press International, 2000.

Renan, Ernest. *History of the People of Israel: Period of Jewish Independence and Judea Under Roman Rule: Volume 5*. Boston, MA: Roberts Brothers, 1895.

Richardson, H. N. "Some Notes on 1QSa." *Journal of Biblical Literature* 76 (1957): 108–22.

Richardson, Peter. *Building Jewish in the Roman East*. Waco, TX: Baylor University Press, 2004.

_____. *Herod: King of the Jews Friend of the Romans*. Columbia, SC: University of South Carolina Press, 1996.

_____. "Philo and Eusebius on Monasteries and Monasticism: The Therapeutae and Kellia." In *Origins and Method: Towards a New Understanding of Judaism and Christianity*, edited by Bradley H. McLean, 334–59. Sheffield: JSOT Press, 1993.

Rocca, Samuele. "The *Book of Judith*, Queen Sholomzion and King Tigranes of Armenia: A Sadducee Appraisal." *Materia giudaica* 10 (2005): 85–98.

Röhrer-Ertl, Olav. "Facts and Results Based on Skeletal Remains from Qumran Found in the Collectio Kurth — A Study in Methodology." In *Qumran, the Site of the Dead Sea Scrolls: Archaeological Interpretations and Debates*, edited by Katharina Galor, Jean-Baptiste Humbert, and Jürgen Zangenberg, 182–93. Leiden: Brill, 2006.

Roller, Matthew. "Horizontal Women: Posture and Sex in the Roman *Convivium*." *American Journal of Philology* 124 (2003): 377–422.

Rooke, Deborah W. *Zadok's Heirs: The Role and Development of the High Priesthood in Ancient Israel*. Oxford: Oxford University Press, 2000.

Roville, Guillaume. *Promptuarii iconum insigniorum a seculo hominum, subiectis eorum vitis, per compendium ex probatissimis autoribus desumptis*. Lugduni: n.p., 1553.

Rubenstein, Jeffrey L. *History of Sukkot in the Second Temple and Rabbinic Periods*. Atlanta, GA: Scholars Press, 1995.

Rubin, Jody P. "Celsus's Decircumcision Operation: Medical and Historical Implications." *Urology* 16 (1980): 121–24.

Salisbury, Joyce E. *Encyclopedia of Women in the Ancient World.* Santa Barbara, CA: ABC-Clio, 2001.

Sarte, Maurice. *The Middle East Under Rome.* Translated by Catherine Porter and Elizabeth Rawlings with Jeannine Routier-Pucci. Cambridge, MA: Harvard University Press, 2005.

Satlow, Michael L. *Jewish Marriage in Antiquity.* Princeton, NJ: Princeton University Press, 2001.

Schubert, Paul. "Une attestation de Ptolémée Eupator regnant?" *Zeitschrift für Papyrologie und Epigraphik* 94 (1992): 119–22.

Schuller, Eileen M. "Evidence for Women in the Community of the Dead Sea Scrolls." In *Voluntary Associations in the Graeco-Roman World*, edited by J. S. Kloppenborg and S. G. Wilson, 252–65. London: Routledge, 1996.

Schultz, Brian. "The Qumran Cemetery: 150 Years of Research." *Dead Sea Discoveries* 13 (2006): 194–228.

Schürer, Emil. *The History of the Jewish People in the Age of Jesus Christ (175 B.C.-A.D. 135)*, 3 vols. Revised and Edited by G. Vermes, et. al. Edinburgh: T. & T. Clark, 1973–87.

Schwartz, Daniel R. "Josephus and Nicolaus on the Pharisees." *Journal for the Study of Judaism* 14 (1983): 157–71.

Schwartz, Seth. "Georgius Syncellus's Account of Ancient Jewish History." In *Proceedings of the Tenth World Congress of Jewish Studies: Jerusalem, August 16–24, 1989, Division B, Volume II: The History of the Jewish People.* 1–8. Jerusalem: The World Union of Jewish Studies, 1990.

_____. *Imperialism and Jewish Society, 200 B.C.E. to 640 C.E.* Princeton, NJ: Princeton University Press, 2001.

Shamir, Moshe. *The King of Flesh and Blood.* Translated by David Patterson. New York, NY: The Vanguard Press, 1958.

Shatzman, Israel. *The Armies of the Hasmonaeans and Herod: From Hellenistic to Roman Frameworks.* Tübingen: J. C. B. Mohr (Paul Siebeck), 1991.

Sheridan, Susan Guise, and Maime Ullinger, "A Reconsideration of the Human Remains in the French Collection from Qumran." In *Qumran, the Site of the Dead Sea Scrolls: Archaeological Interpretations and Debates.* Edited by Katharina Galor, Jean-Baptiste Humbert, and Jürgen Zangenberg, 195–212. Leiden: Brill, 2006.

Sherwin-White, A. N. "Lucullus, Pompey and the East." In *The Cambridge Ancient History Volume IX: The Last Age of the Roman Republic, 146–43 B.C.E.* 2d ed. Edited by J. A. Crook, Andrew Lintott, and Elizabeth Rawson, 229 – 73. Cambridge: Cambridge University Press, 1994.

Sievers, Joseph. *The Hasmoneans And Their Supporters: From Mattathias to the Death of John Hyrcanus I.* Atlanta, GA: Scholars Press, 1990.

_____. "The Role of Women in the Hasmonean Dynasty." In *Josephus, the Bible, and History*, edited by Louis H. Feldman and Gohei Hata, 132–46. Leiden: E. J. Brill, 1989.

Silberman, Neil Asher. *The Hidden Scrolls: Christianity, Judaism, and the War for the Dead Sea Scrolls.* New York, NY: Grosset/Putnam, 1994.

Smallwood, E. Mary. *The Jews Under Roman Rule: From Pompey to Diocletian.* Leiden: E. J. Brill, 1981.

Spongberg, Mary. *Writing Women's History Since the Renaissance.* New York, NY: Palgrave Macmillan, 2002.

Steiner, Richard C. "Incomplete Circumcision in Egypt and Edom: Jeremiah 9.24–25 in the Light of Josephus and Jonckheere." *Journal of Biblical Literature* 118 (1999): 497–505.

_____. "On the Dating of Hebrew Sound Changes (°H>Hi and °G>') and Greek Translations (2 Esdras and Judith)." *Journal of Biblical Literature* 124 (2005): 229–67.

Steinsaltz, Adin. *The Essential Talmud.* New York, NY: Basic Books, 1976.

Swidler, Leonard. *Women in Judaism: The Status of Women in Formative Judaism.* Metuchen, NJ: The Scarecrow Press, 1976.

Szesnat, Holger. "Philo and Female Homoeroticism: Philo's use of γύναυρος and Recent Work on *tribades*." *Journal for the Study of Judaism* 30 (1999): 140–47.

Taylor, Joan E. *Jewish Women Philosophers of First-Century Alexandria: Philo's "Therapeutae" Reconsidered.* Oxford: Oxford University Press, 2003.

_____. "Khirbet Qumran in the Nineteenth Century and the Name of the Site." *Palestine Exploration Quarterly* 134 (2002): 144–64.

_____. "A Second Temple in Egypt: The Evidence for the Zadokite Temple of Onias." *Journal for the Study of Judaism* 29 (1998): 297–321.

Tcherikover, Victor. *Hellenistic Civilization and the Jews.* Philadelphia, PA: Jewish Publication Society, 1959.

Theil, Winfried. "Athaliah." In *The Anchor Bible Dictionary.* Vol. 1 Edited by David N. Freedman, Gary A. Herion, David F. Graf, and John D. Pleins, 511–12. New York: Doubleday, 1992.

Thompson, Dorthoy J. "Egypt, 146–31 B.C." In *The Cambridge Ancient History 9: The Last Age of the Roman Republic, 146–43 B.C.* Edited by John A. Crook, Andrew Lintott, and Elizabeth Rawson, 310–26. Cambridge: Cambridge University Press, 1994.

Trever, John C. *The Untold Story of Qumran.* Westwood, NJ: F. H. Revell Co., 1965.

Tropper, Amram. "Children and Childhood in Light of the Demographics of the Jewish Family in Late Antiquity." *Journal for the Study of Judaism* 37 (2006): 299–343.

Tuchman, Barbara Wertheim. *Practicing History: Selected Essays.* New York, NY: Knopf, 1981.

Tzaferis, Vassilios. "Jewish Tombs at and Near Giv'at ha-Mivtar." *Israel Exploration Journal* 20 (1970): 18–32.

Urbach, Epharim E. *The Sages: Their Concepts and Beliefs.* Cambridge, MA: Harvard University Press, 1987.

Van der Horst, Pieter. "Greek in Jewish Palestine in Light of Jewish Epigraphy." In *Hellenism in the Land of Israel,* edited by John J. Collins and Gregory E. Sterling, 154–74. Notre Dame: University of Notre Dame Press, 2001.

van der Toorn, Karel. *Scribal Culture and the Making of the Hebrew Bible.* Cambridge, MA: Harvard University Press, 2007.

Van Henten, Jan Willem. *The Maccabean Martyrs as Saviours of the Jewish People: A Study of 2 and 4 Maccabees.* Leiden: E. J. Brill, 1997.

Van 't Dack, E. W. Clarysse, G. Cohen, J. Quaegebeur, and J. K. Winnicki, eds. *The Judean-Syrian-Egyptian Conflict of 103–101 B.C.: A Multingual Dosier Concerning A "War of Sceptres."* Brussels: Publikatie van het Comité Klassieke Studies, Subcomité Hellenisme Koninklijke Academie voor Wetenschappen, Letterèn en Schone Kunsten van België, 1989.

VanderKam, James C. *From Joshua to Caiaphas; High Priests After the Exile.* Minneapolis, MA: Fortress Press, 2004.

_____. "Greek at Qumran." In *Hellenism in the Land of Israel,* edited by John J. Collins and Gregory E. Sterling, 175–81. Notre Dame: University of Notre Dame Press, 2001.

_____. 2001. "Pesher Nahum and Josephus." In *When Judaism and Christianity Began: Essays in Memory of Anthony J. Saldarini.* Edited by Alan Avery-Peck, Daniel Harrington, and Jacob Neusner. 299–311. Boston: Brill.

Wacholder, Ben Zion. *Nicolaus of Damascus.* Berkeley, CA: University of California Press, 1962.

Walker, Susan. "Women and Housing in Classical Greece: The Archaeological Evidence." In *Images of Women in Antiquity,* edited by Averil Cameron and Amélie Kuhrt, 81–91. Detroit: Wayne State University Press, 1985.

Wassen, Cecilia. *Women in the Damascus Document.* Atlanta, GA: Society of Biblical Literature, 2005.

Weisberg, Dvora E. "The Widow of Our Discontent: Levirate Marriage in the Bible and Ancient Israel." *Journal for the Study of the Old Testament* 28 (2004): 403–29.

Whitehorne, John. *Cleopatras.* London: Routledge, 1994.

Williams, Margaret H. "The Use of Alternative Names by Diaspora Jews in Graeco-Roman Antiquity." *Journal for the Study of Judaism* 38 (2007): 307–27.

Wise, Isaac M. "Women as Members of Congregations," In *Selected Writings of Isaac M. Wise with a Biography,* edited by David Philipson and Louis Grossmann. Cincinnati, OH: Robert Clarke Company, 1900.

Wise, Michael Owen. *Thunder in Gemini: And Other Essays on the History, Language and Literature of Second Temple Palestine.* Sheffield: Sheffield Academic Press, 1994.

Yadin, Yigael. *The Temple Scroll.* Jerusalem: Israel Exploration Society, 1983.

Zeitlin, Solomon. "Queen Salome and King Jannaeus Alexander: A Chapter in the History of the Second Jewish Commonwealth." *Jewish Quarterly Review* 51 (1960–61): 1–33.

Zellentin, Holger M. "The End of Jewish Egypt: Artapanus and the Second Exodus." In *Antiquity in Antiquity: Jewish and Christian Pasts in the Greco-Roman World,* edited by Gregg Gardner and Kevin L. Osterloh, 27–73. Tübingen: Mohr Siebeck, 2008.

Zias, Joseph. "Anthropological Evidence of Interpersonal Violence in First Century A.D. Jerusalem." *Current Anthropology* 24 (1983): 233–34.

_____. "The Cemeteries of Qumran and Celibacy: Confusion Laid to Rest?" *Dead Sea Discoveries* 7 (2000): 220–53.

_____. "Human Skeletal Remains from the 'Caiaphas' Tomb." *Atiqot* 21 (1992): 78–80 [English Series].

Zias, Joseph, and Eliezer Sekeles, "The Crucified Man from Giv'at ha-Mivtar: A Reappraisal." *Israel Exploration Journal* 35 (1985): 22–27.

Zirndorf, Henry. *Some Jewish Women.* Philadelphia: The Jewish Publication Society, 1998.

Index